AN ANTITRUST PRIMER

AN ANTITRUST PRIMER

A GUIDE TO
ANTITRUST AND TRADE REGULATION LAWS
FOR BUSINESSMEN

SECOND EDITION

EARL W. KINTNER

THE MACMILLAN COMPANY *New York*
COLLIER-MACMILLAN PUBLISHERS *London*

PRINTED IN THE UNITED STATES OF AMERICA

THE MACMILLAN COMPANY
866 Third Avenue, New York, New York 10022

COLLIER-MACMILLAN CANADA, LTD., Toronto, Ontario

Library of Congress catalog card number: 72–90540

Printing: 3 4 5 6 7 8 Year: 5 6 7 8 9

To the perplexed businessman
— who must always obey the law
without always knowing what the law is.

PREFACE TO SECOND EDITION

In an area of law as dynamic as that of antitrust and trade regulation, it was inevitable that significant substantive and procedural changes would occur in the eight years since this book first was published. It is hoped that this first revised edition will provide the perplexed businessman with an up-to-date primer to aid him in obeying these often hard-to-understand laws. I am grateful to various businessmen, lawyers, law teachers, and students who have made helpful suggestions for updating and improving this book.

Bernie R. Burrus, Professor of Law at the Georgetown Law Center and my colleague in private practice, rendered invaluable research and editorial assistance in making this revision possible.

Finally, I acknowledge with appreciation the fact that leaders of the Japanese business and legal communities chose the first edition of this book for a special edition in their language.

E. W. K.

FOREWORD TO FIRST EDITION

THE philosophy of the antitrust laws is that the freedom of every person to carry on the business of his choice is in the nature of a personal liberty as much as a property right. To preserve its free exercise is fundamental to our society not merely because of its private necessity but for its public consequences as well. And, as Mr. Justice Bradley has so well said: "This right to choose one's calling is an essential part of that liberty which it is the object of government to protect; and a calling, when chosen, is a man's property and right. Liberty and property are not protected where these rights are arbitrarily assailed." *Slaughter-House Cases,* 16 Wall [83 U.S.] 36, 116 (1873).

The enactment of the antitrust and trade regulation laws is the answer of the Congress to this problem. Beginning almost 75 years ago, it sensed the increasing complexity of our society which made the public interest the more omnipresent and the freedom of competition the more urgent. Presently those laws, as has been aptly said, are the guardians of the free enterprise system upon which the philosophy of our free world is based. This is not to say that the intent of these laws is to interfere in any way with the intelligent conduct of legitimate business operations. On the contrary, they protect such enterprises.

Nevertheless, we often hear the antitrust laws themselves assailed and their administration vilified. And this is understandable, because the broad sweep that characterizes them tends to make for a vagueness and uncertainty that businessmen naturally detest. Indeed, astute lawyers after a lifetime of study of antitrust problems often do not know the answers. They come only from our Supreme Court and there only because of its finality in our judicial process. It is therefore little wonder that the businessman experiences considerable difficulty in translating these laws into terms of everyday business practice.

The adaptation of preventive law to this increasingly more serious demand for economic justice is evidenced by the treble damage claims that now plague the electrical industry as an aftermath of the recent Philadelphia prosecutions. That the situation there brought to light could have been prevented by the application of preventive measures is beyond peradventure. It is into this void that Mr. Kintner's work has been projected, with a view not to teach the businessman to be his own lawyer, with the usual dire consequences, but to alert him to the dangers inherent in some business practices. Likewise, this book will aid the businessman's lawyer in securing a ready answer to many of the perplexing problems with which a general practitioner is unaccustomed to deal.

In an engaging style that is readily understandable to both layman and lawyer, and without the usual disrupting footnotes of exceptions and comparisons, the author explains the history and background of these laws, a procedure which alone has saved many of them from the evils of vagueness. From his vast experience as General Counsel to the Federal Trade Commission and thereafter as its Chairman, Mr. Kintner is able to make ready reference to key decisions of that Commission, as well as the courts, as they relate to business reality rather than the hypothetical. It is just such a talent that has been absent in many such works. Likewise, as one who was a star in many of the games, he outlines the interesting interplay between business activity and government regulation that makes up our free enterprise system. But not satisfied with such generalities, Mr. Kintner also goes into an examination of specific practices which may come within the interdiction of the law, such as price fixing, refusals to deal, monopolization, exclusive dealing arrangements, price discrimination, deceptive advertising, etc.

It may be that I read Earl Kintner's book with predilection, since I have watched him with admiration operate in the antitrust field for nearly two decades. Indeed, while General Counsel he appeared before the Supreme Court in several cases, acquitting himself as an effective advocate most favorably. In addition, it was my pleasure to administer the oath to him when he became a Commissioner and later the Chairman of the Federal Trade Commission. Despite these personal reminiscences, I am sure that all will agree with me that Mr. Kintner's volume brings new light to an important field wherein he is knowledgeable and over which he has long been concerned. If he arouses your interest in the folklore of antitrust, makes you more conscious of the breadth of its requirements, and, perhaps, acquaints you with some of its technical applications, he will not only have achieved his goal but will have rendered a real service.

TOM C. CLARK
Associate Justice, Supreme Court of the United States

1964

PROLOGUE

WHY READ THIS BOOK?

In our time businessmen must learn to live with paradox; a complex economy generates demands upon time and energy that often conflict, demands that often seem unanswerable. Not the least of the modern paradoxes is the demand that the senior executive somehow be a generalist in an age of rampant specialization. It is all very well for members of middle management and even upper-middle management in large corporations to be "production men" or "sales men" or "finance men," but a senior manager (or the sole manager of a small business) must be "THE MAN," capable of exercising competent judgment in situations where a host of special considerations intersect.

For example, consider the question of whether a merger should be effected. The senior management of the acquiring firm must consider not only financial feasibility, product compatibility, possible integration of production facilities or sales forces or both, effect on employee relations, and accommodation of management but also the effect of state corporation laws, tax considerations, and antitrust implications.

No reasonable man can expect the business generalist to develop a close, detailed knowledge of all the disciplines that may impinge upon the area of final corporate decision, but the generalist must be able to recognize the special considerations inherent in a given business operation at an early stage, to know which specialists to call upon, to evaluate properly the recommendations of the specialists, and to formulate plans that give due allowance to all applicable special considerations.

Of all the special disciplines affecting business plans, none is more pervasive than the law, and no body of laws is more pervasive than the antitrust and trade regulation laws. These laws reach into every sector of the economy. The local retail dealer or the direct-mail advertiser with a one-man shop is no less insulated against them than are the international giants in the basic industries. The antitrust and trade regulation laws affect virtually every phase of day-to-day business operations. Dealings with suppliers, relationships with competitors, brokerage agreements, sales to consumers, advertising plans, pricing—all, and more, are governed by the laws designed to insure that competition is free and fair.

Violations of the antitrust and trade regulation laws can be punished severely. As we shall see later, violations of various provisions can result in dismemberment of a company, imprisonment of its officers and employees, cumulative fines, liability for treble damages to parties injured by violations, seizure of goods, and a wide variety of decrees or orders narrowly regulating the future conduct of offending firms and individuals. And, as we shall see also, there are heavy indirect penalties for transgressions against these laws. Major antitrust litigation is notoriously long and notoriously costly. What promised to be a relatively uncomplicated deceptive practices matter before the Federal Trade Commission consumed sixteen years from the time of complaint to final disposition by the courts. A major monopoly case may drag on for a generation. Even an unexceptional case in this area may consume two to five years. Large investments in time inevitably result in large outlays of money. Costs alone, not including attorneys' fees, easily can run into six figures in antitrust cases. When attorneys' fees and executive and employee time lost through file searches, preparation for trial, and attendance at hearings are included, even a victory may evoke the old adage that "the operation was a success, but the patient died." To the sum of these costs must be added the frightful indirect costs in reputation and good will that may result from a well-publicized violation. In this age of public relations possible damage to reputation alone compels the prescient businessman to consider the applicability of the antitrust laws to every phase of his operations.

Enlightened self-interest has another aspect as well. The businessman with a basic knowledge of the provisions of these laws and the way in which they are enforced can detect with some precision the transgressions of competitors or suppliers. Early detection often is essential if the honest businessman is to avoid irreparable damage.

Considerations larger than self-interest and concern for the future welfare of a given enterprise also dictate a regard for the antitrust and trade regulation laws. For these laws are principal guardians of the free enterprise system.

An article of faith lies at the very roots of American political and economic philosophy: that undue concentrations of power are inherently destructive of the aims of a free society, whether those concentrations be in private hands, as in a monopoly, or in governmental agencies. This country has never ceased to doubt the myriad claims of those who urge that a multitude of "benefits" flow from cartelization or statism. The American answer to man's age-old problem of how best to distribute power can be summarized in one word: pluralism. The doctrine of pluralism asserts that the needs of men are best served when power is distributed among many; that the goals of the nation are best implemented by a combination of many individual decisions rather than by a single decision imposed and enforced by a single power source. Both our polity and our economy are premised on the belief that the individual citizen should exercise maximum control over his own development.

In our economy pluralism is implemented by competition. Our system is anchored in the belief that the most efficient allocation of resources is made by the free interplay of market forces. One example taken from the body of antitrust decisions illustrates the depth of this commitment. In 1951 the United States Supreme Court decided the case of *Kiefer-Stewart Company* v. *Joseph E. Seagram & Sons.* This case arose when an Indiana wholesale liquor dealer sued the Seagram and Calvert Corporations for treble damages under Section 1 of the Sherman Antitrust Act. The complaint charged that Seagram and Calvert had conspired to sell liquor only to those Indiana dealers who would resell at prices fixed by Seagram and Calvert and that this agreement deprived the petitioner of a continuing supply of liquor. So far this seems like a standard antitrust action. Price fixing has long been held to be illegal *per se.* When this case went to trial, however, the evidence showed that the distiller had fixed *maximum* prices above which the wholesalers could not resell, leaving the wholesalers free to cut prices if they chose to do so. The United States Court of Appeals for the Seventh Circuit held that there was no violation of the Sherman Act because an agreement to fix maximum resale prices was not anticompetitive in effect. Rather, the court said, such prices promoted competition and aided the consumer. To the surprise of many, the United States Supreme Court reversed, holding that agreements fixing maximum resale prices "crippled the freedom of traders" in the same manner as agreements to fix minimum resale prices. It is the restraint upon the ability of traders to sell in accordance with their own judgment that the Sherman Act reaches. Thus we see that price fixing, even when done with a laudable motive—that of securing lower prices to the consumer—is illegal *per se.* At first the result seems anomalous, but if we refer again to the notion of a pluralistic society, all becomes clear. It is the exercise of power by a dominant concern to the detriment of the establishment of market conditions by the aggregate of individual decisions that is condemned. Far from being anomalous, this decision shows that the American people, speaking through its judiciary, are willing to commit themselves to pluralism even where centralism would seem to provide highly desirable short-term goals.

A precious part of our freedom is the freedom to enter a market, the freedom to win a place there through strenuous competitive effort, the freedom to buy and sell without restraints imposed by others. It is these freedoms that the antitrust laws protect.

If the free enterprise system is to survive, competition must be fair as well as free. Honest competitors must be protected from predators and shielded from the temptation to adopt the tactics of tricksters in the battle for business survival. And consumers must be protected against commercial chicanery, not only because fairness requires that they receive an honest product honestly represented, but because consumers are citizens who will ultimately determine the degree of control that government will exercise over business. The antitrust and trade regulation laws were devised to insure that competition will be conducted in a fair manner.

The freedom to engage in fair competition, like all freedoms, is a privilege, not a right. The continued enjoyment of this privilege, as is the case with all privileges, depends upon the assumption of responsibility. American enterprise is free precisely because freedom is checked and channeled by a variety of factors. Foremost among these factors is an attribute of the national character: a decent respect for the needs of others and a willingness to forego unlimited self-assertion at the expense of others. Without this basic factor freedom becomes meaningless; otherwise, the freedom of a few is won only by the subjugation of the many.

The antitrust and trade regulation laws reinforce this basic attribute. They embody a national policy decision to eschew undue restraints upon business freedom, to avoid both the Scylla of private monopoly and the Charybdis of statism. These laws are conservative in the truest sense of that much abused term. They represent an undertaking by government designed to prevent still wider undertakings by government, for if competition is abused and monopolistic practices and business trickery become widespread, the public inevitably will demand more restrictive governmental control of the economy.

Thus, manifold considerations of enlightened self-interest and the public interest require that honest businessmen achieve a close degree of familiarity with this body of law. This book is intended to aid in that critical task.

Succeeding chapters will relate why these laws were enacted, what they provide, who enforces them, and how they are enforced. Special treatment is given to deceptive advertising, because this problem is a well-nigh universal one among businesses of all sizes. Finally, one man's view of the proper role of government in the nation's economy is offered for consideration.

A word about what this book is *not* designed to do is necessary. This book is not a comprehensive treatise of every phase of the antitrust and trade regulation laws. A library of many volumes would be necessary for that task. Neither is this book designed to plumb various positions on what the philosophic bases of these laws are or should be. Rather, this modest effort is designed simply as a primer for the aware business executive. If the busy general practitioner who counsels businessmen likewise finds the primer helpful, as I hope he will, I shall be content with my effort. Every effort has been made to state carefully every major premise of antitrust and trade regulation and to provide meaningful examples of the application of the law to business practices, but many refinements have necessarily been omitted. The scholarly propensity for elaborate footnoting has been ruthlessly suppressed here.

Nor is this book designed to teach the businessman how to be his own antitrust lawyer. The very idea is folly, because these laws are infinitely subtle and may appear in an infinite variety of guises. But the businessman's awareness of these laws can be heightened, and if he is sufficiently aware to consult a specialist *before* the consequences of a contemplated course of action descend upon him, then a precious gain has been won.

In short, this book is not designed to convert generalists into specialists. It *is* designed to improve the generalist's use of the antitrust specialist.

E. W. K.

ACKNOWLEDGMENT

A FEW words may be appropriate to explain the origin and execution of this project and to acknowledge the great debt that I owe to many valued colleagues.

This book has its origins first in my experiences as general counsel and later as chairman of the Federal Trade Commission. During those years I learned that the antitrust and trade regulation laws are violated more often through ignorance than through intent. I learned also that a host of businessmen throughout the nation had a thirst for knowledge concerning those laws but were bewildered by their complexity and by the professional jargon all too often used in interpretive articles and books. I sought to meet this need as best I could. In the span of twenty months as the commission's chairman, I made over 300 speeches explaining the antitrust and trade regulation laws, primarily to business groups.

Toward the end of a hard day shortly before my term expired in March, 1961, I reassessed my efforts to educate American businessmen in this sphere in a long conversation with my legal assistant, Ralph S. Cunningham, Jr., and with my executive assistant, Edwin S. Rockefeller. We concluded that even the best speech is ephemeral. We also concluded that any treatises on the antitrust laws have only limited utility for businesses. We concluded that what was needed was a primer written in lay language, available to businessmen both for reading and reference. Thus this book was born.

Any book of this character is the product of many minds. I must gratefully acknowledge the assistance of Joseph M. Livermore, Jerome Nelson, and Peter J. McGinn, who made substantial research and editorial contributions to this book as a whole. Charles D. Reaves and James M. Whitescarver also contributed valuable research. My associate Jack L. Lahr contributed heavily to the design of Chapters 9 and 10. I must also thank my associate Sidney Harris for his valuable comments on the practice and procedures of the Antitrust Division of the Department of Justice. My associate Mark R. Joelson assisted in the final review of the text.

Ralph S. Cunningham, Jr., my associate in both government and private practice, has rendered invaluable editorial assistance as we laboriously hammered out the shape and substance of this book over the last three years.

Finally, I must thank my wife, Pat, and my son, Christopher, and my law partners for their patience and understanding during the long and trying period of this book's gestation.

E. W. K.

CONTENTS

Chapter 1. The Rise of Free Competition 1

Chapter 2. The Advent of Government Regulation 7

Chapter 3. A Bird's-Eye View of the Antitrust and Trade Regulation Laws 15

Chapter 4. Contracts, Combinations, and Conspiracies 26

Chapter 5. Price Fixing 30

Chapter 6. Boycotts and Refusals to Deal 37

Chapter 7. Limitations on the Resale Market 42

Chapter 8. Exclusive Dealing and Tie-In Arrangements 47

Chapter 9. The Robinson-Patman Act: The Federal Price Discrimination Law 60

Chapter 10. Patents and Antitrust 82

Chapter 11. Mergers and Acquisitions 90

Chapter 12. Monopolization 101

Chapter 13. Interlocking Directorates 110

Chapter 14.	"Unfair methods of competition . . . unfair or deceptive acts"—The FTC Act and Related FTC Statutes	115
Chapter 15.	Exemptions	124
Chapter 16.	Enforcement by the Department of Justice	131
Chapter 17.	The Federal Trade Commission: Practice and Procedure	142
Chapter 18.	Private Enforcement	150
Chapter 19.	State Antitrust Enforcement	159
Chapter 20.	The Wonderful World of Advertising	164
Chapter 21.	Deceptive Schemes and How They Operate	173
Chapter 22.	Toward Ethical Advertising: A Plan	204
Epilogue:	The Proper Role of Government in the Economy	227
Appendix I.	Selected Bibliography	236
Appendix II.	Selected Federal Trade Commission Guides	254
Appendix III.	Summaries and Texts of the Principal Antitrust Statutes	281
	Index	313

AN ANTITRUST PRIMER

CHAPTER 1

THE RISE OF FREE COMPETITION

No human institution has an inevitable form, but the forms of some institutions are so admirably suited to the conditions confronting them that a conclusion of inevitability is very tempting. So it is with the early development of the American economic system.

At the time of the Revolution the philosophical seed of capitalism was ready for planting in American soil. The publication of Adam Smith's *The Wealth of Nations* in the momentous year of 1776 was something more than an historical accident. Dissatisfaction with the mercantilist system and its restrictions upon individual effort was a powerful element in the hostility of the colonists toward England. Documentation of the defects of mercantilism and the advocacy of capitalism by the "worldly philosophers" provided a strong intellectual base for the American experiment with capitalism.

The social climate of eighteenth-century America was admriably suited to the growth of competitive free enterprise. The colonies were largely free of the rigid class stratification, with its attendant artificial ceilings on ambition, that prevailed in Europe. An immigrant people, worldly, activist, independent, and imbued with stern religious concepts of personal responsibility, would be very likely to embrace eagerly economic individualism. The histories of Tawney, the Beards, Nevins, and Commager offer diverse insights into the American character, but in sum they describe a new breed thirsting for economic adventure.

The political and legal atmosphere of newly independent America was no less cordial to capitalism. The architects of the American polity placed the decentralization of political power at the highest point on their scale of values. Both the short-lived Articles of Confederation and the Constitution reflect a supreme fear of centralized power. Our Constitution divides power between a national government and state governments in a federal system, provides for checks and balances in the interdependent operation of the executive, legislative, and judicial branches of the national government, divides the legislature into two bodies, and establishes fixed, limited terms for all officers. The subsequent enactment of the Bill of Rights provided further checks on the autocratic exercise of political power. The constitutions of the states employ these same devices to guard against centralization. A political system designed to insure a permissive, diversified, and decentralized way of life provides a hospitable atmosphere for economic individualism.

Capitalism cannot flourish in the absence of a complex of legal safeguards. The most important of these safeguards are (1) protection against public disorder; (2) protection against arbitrary seizure of private property; (3) freedom of contract (since contract is the major planning device in a free enterprise system); and (4) access to impartial courts for the settlement of disputes. The newly independent United States inherited these safeguards intact from English jurisprudence.

The land itself welcomed the daring entrepreneur. Given the conditions obtaining at the time of independence, a wild, largely unpopulated continent, but one richly endowed with natural resources, could be developed more rapidly (albeit at risk of waste) by a competitive economic system than by a closed system. Indeed, even if there had been a popular philosophical preference for a more centralized economic system, the wilderness likely would have prevented its successful operation. In a land of isolated communities with poor transportation facilities, only development along independent lines would suffice. It can be argued plausibly that poor transportation and poor communications were positive boons at the inception of an individual enterprise system. Community isolation meant that markets were local and narrow in character and therefore could be served by small enterprises. Isolation and local economic autonomy meant relatively easy entry into the market. Primitive industries needed relatively small amounts of initial capital. Isolation also lessened the attractiveness of absentee ownerships. Applying hindsight, America and the capitalist system also could be thankful that the area of the thirteen colonies contained no large known deposits of precious metals or minerals. The presence of an easily transportable export of great value in a primitive area invites state control or, in the alternative, absentee monopolists.

The coincidence of the dawn of the industrial revolution with the birth of the United States provided still another impetus for pluralistic economic development. Technological breakthroughs can reform an economy in undreamed-of ways, ways that shatter all manner of economic customs and relationships. Centralized systems of control are often too cumbersome to adapt rapidly to explosive change; a system of free competition places a high premium upon rapid, imaginative adaptation to changed conditions.

So the competitive race to build a great nation began.

Even the most enthusiastic advocate of economic autocracy (if he is rational) cannot deny that the early operation of the American free enterprise system produced unprecedented benefits. Daring individual effort produced a prodigious economic momentum at the outset, and rapid progress was made despite the normal calamities of war, depression, and recession. Manufacturing enterprises were established, a banking system was organized, and an extensive ocean commerce was developed.

And how they gloried in their individualism! To early Americans free enterprise was no less an article of faith than was political liberty. To be sure, there were some departures, notably in tariff and patent policy, from the pristine doctrine of *laissez faire,* but these exceptions were justified on the ground that they served the general purpose of economic individualism. Tariffs were proposed to protect infant American industries from destruction by their more developed counterparts abroad. Laws granting patentees the exclusive right to make, sell, or use their discoveries for a limited period were deemed necessary to encourage invention.

In the early morning of the nineteenth century it was evident that the path of the American economy clearly lay down the one-way street of industrialization and specialization. Eli Whitney and Simeon North were moving toward the establishment of the indispensable principle of interchangeable parts and precision methods in manufacture. The Evans high-pressure steam engine provided new motive force for American industry. Whitney's cotton gin, the wealth of information that Samuel Slater brought from England by stealth, and a host of other individual efforts provided the nation with a flourishing textile industry. Smelting, metal working, and fabrication proceeded apace. On every economic front, hand methods and unspecialized labor were being subjected to inexorable pressures.

But the most significant developments were taking place in transportation and communication. Water transport was transformed by the introduction of steam propulsion through the efforts of Morey, Fitch, Fulton, and Livingston. Entrepreneurs flocked to the rivers and coastal waters after the Supreme Court decision in *Gibbons* v. *Ogden* established that the regulation of commerce on interstate waterways was a concern of the federal government, thereby terminating the monopolies of steam transportation some states had granted to private interests. Commercial navigation also was materially aided by the rapid spread of canal systems, notably in New York and Pennsylvania.

In the first half of the nineteenth century railroads rapidly progressed from the stage of doubtful experiment and were developed into extensive operational systems. Meanwhile, the telegraph had been devised by Morse, Cornell, Vail, and Henry. Washburn's development of a wire-drawing machine helped to make it practical. By 1861 the telegraph had spanned the continent, ending the colorful reign of the Pony Express, but geometrically reducing the difficulties of communication.

Banking is an important part of any economic picture. A credit system with adequate facilities for transferring funds and marketing securities is needed to marshal funds from investors and lenders to new investment opportunities in distant areas. Although the Bank of the United States died at the hands of the Jacksonians, a private banking system mushroomed. Unfortunately, the American taste for speculation and the absence of any semblance of regulation exacted a heavy toll of bank failures and panic. Nevertheless, the means for channeling capital and credit to new industries and expanding markets was at hand.

The day of the narrow, isolated, unspecialized market was over once these systems were developed.

The Civil War furnished the primary requisite of explosive industrial growth and change—demand, unprecedented demand. This, the first great industrial war, transformed the American economy for all time to come.

The deployment of mass armies over large territories rapidly developed the latent elements of a modern industrial system. Total war demanded speedy production. Total war demanded quantity production—huge amounts of a great variety of material. And total war demanded uniform production as well. The effort to satisfy these demands produced a convincing demonstration of the economies and efficiencies of size. Intensive use of the now extensive transportation and communications networks demonstrated that production of a given commodity could be concentrated in a given location with no loss of speed in distribution. Considerations of efficiency seemed to favor concentration overwhelmingly. Engineering techniques had not developed to the point where individuals and small enterprises in diverse parts of the country could manufacture an article with uniform characteristics. The times seemed to demonstrate that the accumulation of many workers under a single watchful eye was the best way to achieve efficient, uniform production.

The lessons of the Civil War regarding capital formation and investment were less dramatic, but nevertheless very real. One of the great strictures upon the capacity of small enterprises to meet the demands generated by the war was their inability to obtain ready capital. Small businessmen had been particularly hard hit by the virtual discontinuance of long-term credit following the panic of 1857. They entered the new era with a handicap. On the other hand, the war demonstrated that burgeoning enterprises exploiting the economies of size and concentration could attract capital on a heretofore unprecedented scale. The war produced the National Bank Act of 1864, an important landmark in the development of a sophisticated banking system. The commercial and investment banking techniques of the Civil War era may appear crude to modern observers, but they were equal to the demands of the day and prefigured the gargantuan activities that were soon to follow.

The lessons of the Civil War were not lost in the economy's conversion to a peacetime footing. The new era in transportation, in communications, and in technological innovation produced a trend toward industrial concentration that increased geometrically throughout the remaining years of the nineteenth century. Other factors helped to shape this trend. Population, politics, and philosophy favored the bold and ruthless industrialist of the new era. The tide of immigration became a flood after the middle of the century. The population of the United States was 23 million in 1850; it was over 77 million in 1900. Immigration furnished an ever-replenishing pool of cheap labor for the new mills and lofts and railroads. Many of the immigrants were skilled; most were highly mobile—there was no reluctance to migrate wherever industry could utilize their particular skills, thus promoting the localization and concentration of particular industries. The population explosion of the era also provided expanding markets for the new industries—markets well fortified by protective tariff walls.

The new outlook of the federal government lent further impetus to the rapid movement toward industrial concentration. The Civil War smashed the early coalition between Southern cotton and Western grain. Thus, for the first time, plans for a transcontinental railroad line could be made regardless of the opposition of those Southern interests who would agree to such a line only if it passed through the South and to the Pacific by way of Texas. The newly dominant Republic party was committed to the well-being of industrial interests. The tariff, which had remained high since the close of the War of 1812, rose from less than 20 per cent at the outbreak of the Civil War to over 54 per cent at its end.

The moral and philosophical climate of the era was ideal for the proliferation of self-made tycoons. The concept of economic freedom was assumed to extend to and justify the heedless pursuit of unenlightened self-interest. There was a curious divorcement of private morality from public morality. The industrialist who bludgeoned competitors and victimized customers could still be an object of community veneration provided that he was fastidious about alcohol, sex, and blasphemy. The author of *Acres of Diamonds* could exhort audiences of Christian young men to "Get rich! Get rich!" without the slightest fear of moral or intellectual embarrassment.

"Get rich" some of them did. It hardly mattered that many fortunes of the day were founded upon rate wars, predatory price discrimination, industrial espionage and sabotage, "fighting ships," defamation, commercial bribery, and political bribery. Acquisitiveness was applauded, and nearly everyone was acquisitive.

And so a new era began. The new era demanded new forms of doing business. The traditional forms of business organization were the sole proprietorship and the partnership. These forms obviously were not suited for the stewardship of vast amounts of capital or the concentration of vast economic power in a single business entity. Only the corporation would suffice in the new era. Only the corporation offered perpetual succession, limited liability, relatively free transfer of interests, and anonymity.

The corporation was not a popular business instrument in the early days of the republic. Only 335 profit-seeking corporations had been formed in this country by 1800, and most of these were undertakings involving the public interest, such as highways or canals. Only six were engaged in manufacturing. This paucity of corporations was not due entirely to the free choice of entrepreneurs. Prior to 1850 it was the general practice to incorporate business corporations by special acts of Congress or of a state legislature. General acts of incorporation affording an easy means for forming corporations came into vogue only in the latter half of the nineteenth century. The economic conditions of that era permanently established the popularity of the corporate form of business organization.

Use of the corporate form was only the beginning, for forces were at work which were to mold these new corporations into the industrial giants whose rise to power invoked the countervailing power of government.

Opportunities for limitless profits appeared in the new era, and entrepreneurs responded with a search for efficiency and market power. This search produced a trend toward integration of enterprises.

Hunger for industrial power doubtless was a strong motive for integration, but the motivations of efficiency and simplification of the distribution system should not be underestimated. For example, entrepreneurs of the new era were quick to see the enormous economic advantages enjoyed by a company which controlled its sources of supply, means of production, and marketing outlets. Ironically, federal tax policies encouraged incipient monopolies bent upon vertical integration. Legislation enacted in 1862 imposed excise taxes of 6 per cent on manufactured goods at each stage of their transfer from one concern to the next. This tax penalized the separation of successive processes and therefore encouraged the amalgamation of various manufacturing processes into one enterprise. Finally, the vicious competition of the era drove manufacturers to seek control of sources of supply and distribution outlets to obtain a stranglehold position before their competitors did so.

By the late nineteenth century the techniques of capitalism had tamed a wild continent in an astonishingly brief period and had converted a collection of feeble colonies into an industrial nation of unrivaled power and wealth. Events had reposed that power and that wealth, however, in the hands of a few private citizens who recognized too few responsibilities to their fellow citizens. The shocking imbalance of economic power appeared to be producing an equally shocking imbalance of political power. Many believed that the very foundations of a free nation were crumbling. Ominous tides were rising to threaten the doctrine of free enterprise.

CHAPTER 2

THE ADVENT OF GOVERNMENT REGULATION

In tracing the development of government regulation, we must begin at the point where the trend of business concentration itself began—with the railroads. It is generally agreed that intense and vigorous competition, highlighted by bitter rate wars, gave birth to the first form of railroad corporation, known as the pool. This device was instituted in the early 1870's, largely in order to escape the devastating effect of the rate wars. Under the pool procedure a number of railroads would function together and actually divide up the market. The pool would arrange with a group of shippers for the carriage of a certain percentage of goods by each particular road; in return for the agreement the shippers would receive various forms of rebate from the carriers. Other roads would divide geographical territory by agreement; for example, a large state such as Texas might be divided between railroad tycoons Gould and Huntington. Another technique of the railroad pool was simply to divide earnings according to plan; thus the railroads would not be forced into the task of regulating percentages of goods to be carried by the particular lines.

The net result of the pools and the practices of the railroads was to engender extreme public resentment over abuses. Price discrimination was rampant, discrimination against both geographical areas and individual shippers. The practice of varying rates between the so-called short haul and long haul had a significant anticompetitive effect. It is reported that millers in Minneapolis were able to secure carriage of their flour to New York City at considerably cheaper rates than millers in Rochester, New York. In substance, it was alleged by critics—and there is much evidence in support—that the power to discriminate by area could and did actually determine the future economic existence of whole communities.

Discrimination among shippers had the same adverse effect and produced as much bitter criticism. Under the practice of granting rebates, in the form of anything valuable, to certain favored shippers, the railroad often had the power to decide who should live and who should die in terms of business survival. By way of illustration, it has been estimated that this form of discrimination was so grave that the favored shippers benefited by as much as 50 per cent in comparison with announced freight rates.

The pool system had certain definite disadvantages, as was readily discovered by the railroads and by certain of the manufacturing powers that eventually adopted it. The pool depended upon voluntary adherence by the companies involved; there was no way of enforcing or assuring compliance with pool agreements if some business exigency should intervene. To overcome these problems, attorneys for Rockefeller's Standard Oil interests decided to utilize the common law trust in order to create a more effective business organization. In simple terms, the stockholders of a particular corporation would deposit their certificates with a board of trustees that had full management control and power. The trust could then succeed to the control of any number of corporations located throughout the country. These corporations, standing alone, were hamstrung by the state laws of the day, which often prohibited corporations from owning assets in another state, owning stock in other corporations, and doing business in other states. The trust form supplied a means of enforcing an agreement and a means of introducing great flexibility into corporate operations.

The original trust agreement pertaining to Standard Oil of Ohio was signed in 1882. By 1887 other great trusts had made their appearance: the Whiskey Trust, the Sugar Trust, the Lead Trust, and the Cotton-Oil Trust. By means of the trust, individual business leaders could gain control of virtually an entire industry, a control which extended over all aspects of business from raw materials to consumer sale.

In time, holding companies were developed and replaced trusts as the primary means of obtaining and maintaining control over an entire industry. Several factors produced the change. First, the term *trust* became an odious label because of the business abuses engaged in by the early trusts. Then too, the trust ran into legal barriers in several states. Certain state courts held that the trusts were illegal on the ground that the scope of a trust exceeded the limits of power granted to a corporation by charter of the state. Standard Oil of Ohio, for example, was held an unlawful trust under the laws of Ohio in the year 1892. The court found that the purposes of the trust were "to establish a virtual monopoly of the business of producing petroleum . . . and to control . . . the price. . . ."

At the same time that state judges were evincing a hostility toward trusts, certain state legislatures were busily modifying the corporation laws and making changes which facilitated the rise of the holding company. The greatest liberalization occurred in New Jersey. By 1890 a New Jersey corporation could lawfully carry on its business in other states, own assets in other states, and also purchase and own securities of other corporations. In this way the parent corporation (the holding company) would acquire the voting stock of other corporations and control them as subsidiaries. This era saw the birth of such giants as Standard Oil of New Jersey, American Telephone and Telegraph, and the Federal Steel Company, predecessor of United States Steel.

The development of the trusts and holding companies naturally brought about a concurrent growth in economic power. Many of these organizations were able to effect a substantial monopoly in a given field and thereby control markets and prices. This involved not only the actual setting and maintaining of prices but also the cutting of prices where necessary in order either to eliminate competitive firms or to render them powerless and subject to acquisition. Similarly, control of the means or sources of supply could be utilized to stifle independents. The business practices of the giants were often conducted in such a ruthless manner that widespread public indignation resulted. This resentment, emanating from various groups in America, provided the philosophical and political impetus toward government regulation of business.

That American farmers were probably the first economic group to agitate for regulation is easily understandable. It was often the farmer who felt the effects of the hated railroad rebate system, as well as the scheme of price discrimination between the long and short haul. The major farm pressure of this period came from the Grange movement. Founded in 1867, this organization grew to a membership of nearly 1 million by the 1870's. Grange agitation centered around the railroad as a symbol of monopolistic abuse. Much of the economic frustration felt by the farmer as a result of the low prices he received for his goods and the high prices he paid for consumer goods was directed at the railroads.

To end these abuses, the Grangers entered politics, with singular success. Grange agitation was so important in the passage of numerous railroad regulation bills in state legislatures that these measures came to be known as Granger laws. Some form of Granger legislation appeared in such states as Illinois, Ohio, Minnesota, Iowa, and Wisconsin; similar laws were adopted in most Southern states. More limited forms of regulation were embodied in the laws of certain Eastern states as well. In 1877 the Supreme Court upheld the constitutionality of the Illinois Granger law in the famous case of *Munn* v. *Illinois.* Thus the theory of government regulation, with strong enforcement measures, was substantially recognized during this period in American history. As the years went by, objections were heard concerning state regulation of railroads. The Supreme Court settled the matter in 1886 by holding—to the surprise of few—that state regulation which impinged upon interstate commerce was unconstitutional and must fall.

The next step was that of federal regulation, a step which, surprisingly enough, many railroad men themselves were willing to take. Perhaps they hoped that federal regulation would be an empty thing or that they could cause federal regulation to work for their benefit. It has also been suggested that the railroads saw federal regulation as a way to avoid the complexities and confusion of individual regulation by all the states. At any rate, the movement had support from the agrarian element, of course, from the roads themselves, and from numbers of shippers and merchants.

The year 1887 brought the enactment of the Interstate Commerce Act and the emergence of the first real federal regulation of business. The Act included provisions outlawing the familiar pool, the rebate, and the short-haul discrimination. What is also significant for our purposes is that this Act gave birth to the first strong federal regulatory agency—the Interstate Commerce Commission, designed as the enforcing arm of the policy Declarations in the Act. Here we see the emergence of the theme of federal regulation and theme of agency enforcement.

Labor organizations also sought federal regulation of business, though at times they took a curiously ambivalent attitude toward the trend of concentration in American business. On the one hand, the trust was an employer, and where the conditions of employment were satisfactory, regulation seemed unnecessary. Indeed, some labor leaders took the position that the very size of the large combinations would help to assure better wages and working conditions. More frequently, however, employers maintained a resolute antilabor policy. They operated under the tradition that management should have sole control over any and all labor matters. The worker was hired on an individual basis, with the employer making all decisions governing wages and working conditions. Many employers resorted to the use of the blacklist and forms of boycott in order to oppose the unions. Others hired strikebreakers and utilized the hated "Pinkertons" as intelligence operatives. The lockout was also employed. The result of all this was bitter hostility on the part of labor organizations, who came to realize by harsh lessons the possible abuses of corporate power. Although it is probably not accurate to state that the labor movement in the latter part of the nineteenth century was totally "antitrust" in outlook, most historians do agree that labor's attitude and activities did serve to augment the force of public opinion against the trusts and monopolies.

The antimonopoly movement also found support from smaller businessmen, whose operations had been hampered by the trusts and monopolies. Agitation from this source, combined with labor and agrarian support, resulted in the first direct legal attacks on monopoly. Like railroad regulation, the first success with antimonopoly legislation occurred at the state level. But the early state laws had so many defects that it was generally agreed that they were ineffective.

The opponents of monopoly then turned to the federal government, much as the proponents of railroad regulation had done before them. In the campaign of 1888 the platforms of both major American parties included an antitrust plank. Benjamin Harrison, the newly elected president, called for legislation in his first message to Congress; he spoke of the tendency of monopoly to "crush out" competition and referred to such monopolies as "dangerous conspiracies."

The first antitrust bill was introduced by Senator John Sherman of Ohio, and after numerous legislative amendments and modifications the Sherman Antitrust Act was signed by President Harrison on July 2, 1890. So deep was antimonopoly sentiment that the final bill actually passed both houses of Congress with only one dissenting vote! The Act outlawed "every contract, combination in the form of trust or otherwise, or conspiracy, in restraint of trade. . . ." Another section made it a criminal offense to monopolize or attempt to monopolize any part of interstate commerce. The scope and application of these landmark sections will be examined in later chapters.

The early history of the enforcement of the Act, however, revealed a marked reluctance on the part of the government to institute cases. Indeed, the attorney general of the United States wrote in 1895 that he had taken the "responsibility of not prosecuting under a law I believed to be no good. . . ." Consequently, the passage of the Sherman Act did not silence the antimonopoly movement.

In 1892 the Populist party appeared in national elections. This was a reform party composed largely of Western agrarian interests, who had tried unsuccessfully to enlist the additional support of labor. Even without a significant coalition with labor, the Populists still made a significant impact on the American scene. They saw a nation divided into two groups: the trusts and monopolies on one hand, and the farmers and workers—the "people"—on the other. As they said in their party platform:

> The fruits of the toil of millions are boldly stolen to build up colossal fortunes for the few, unprecedented in the history of mankind; and the possessors of these, in turn despise the Republic and endanger liberty. From the same prolific womb of governmental injustice we breed the two great classes—tramps and millionaires.

What is significant about this movement for our purposes is that the antimonopoly sentiment was strong enough to bolster a third party in a national election, and although the party certainly did not do as well as many conservative leaders had feared it would, its very appearance and drawing power were indications of the temper of the times.

The early 1890's also brought a great depression to the country. Unemployment was rampant; stock prices fell; thousands of corporations were in bankruptcy. The conservatives blamed the radical farmer-labor movements, and these movements in turn placed the blame upon the "capitalists" and monopolies. Out of this atmosphere came increased demand for rigid antitrust enforcement.

This clamor continued unabated until it was answered by Theodore Roosevelt. Roosevelt was, of course, known as the "trust buster," and yet, as many historians have pointed out, he was really something of an enigma as far as business was concerned. On the one hand, many of his advisers and confidants were men of business, and Roosevelt himself had an extreme distaste for the reformers. On the other, we find Roosevelt's administration instituting the famous Northern Securities antitrust action. We find him excoriating the "malefactors of great wealth." Roosevelt supported legislation which measurably toughened the Interstate Commerce Commission, particularly in regard to its power to regulate rates. Actually, the evidence seems to show that Roosevelt did not want to "bust" monopolies so much as simply to make them comply with the law. It has been suggested that his reputation was due much more to the force of his personality and its complete domination of the American scene than to his actual antitrust prosecutions.

Notwithstanding the president's scoffing at the reformers, his administration passed the first Pure Food and Drug Act in the year 1906. The revelation of gross abuses in food and drug production had resulted in vast public indignation. Roosevelt shared in the dismay and urged the passage of the Act, which ultimately prohibited the introduction into interstate commerce of food or drug products which had been adulterated or misbranded. The Act defined adulteration and misbranding and provided for government inspection and laboratory tests. Enforcement procedure was also spelled out, in the form of criminal penalties and certain seizure proceedings. Much of the broad outline was filled in by subsequent regulations. Out of this Act in 1906 grew the present legal scheme for the regulation of food and drug products.

William Howard Taft, Roosevelt's picked successor, occupied the White House from 1909 to 1913, and under Taft the government instituted some ninety antitrust proceedings. This was done during four years, as contrasted with some fifty-four cases initiated over a seven-year period under the "trust buster" himself. Most notable among these cases were those resulting in rulings that Standard Oil of New Jersey and the American Tobacco Company were, after all, illegal monopolies under the Sherman Act.

Despite this activity under Taft, much criticism was in the air. The very announcement in the Standard Oil case of 1911 that only "unreasonable" restraints of trade were forbidden lent support to the critics. This application of "reason," it was argued, amounted to an undue delegation of power to the judges. Why should they decide what was reasonable and what was not? Then, too, many critics felt that the rule "of reason" rendered the Sherman Act too vague and general. Business complained that it could draw no guidelines from the law itself; it was difficult, if not impossible, to formulate any accurate forecast of the "reasonableness," and hence legality, of a particular proposal. Another area of dissatisfaction lay in the view that the Sherman Act appeared to deal only with accomplished fact, with the concomitant result that there was no effective legal device for striking at incipient abuse. There was a need for a preventive law as well as the punitive provisions of the Sherman Act. There was also much talk of "unfair practices" and "unfair methods" themselves. It was argued that such methods were often beyond the reach of the Sherman Act if they were not apparently committed as part of an over-all plan to monopolize. Finally, men like Louis Brandeis felt that if the specter of monopoly was to be banished from the American scene, a new technique in the enforcement of the antitrust laws had to be developed. They placed their faith in an administrative agency.

Uneasiness over these aspects of the Sherman Act, as well as the vagaries of administration by the Department of Justice, finally resulted in a call, contained in the political platforms of the two major parties and the "Bull Moose" (Progressive) party in the 1912 election, for remedial legislation to strengthen the antitrust laws. The newly elected President Wilson promptly urged the passage of laws which would restrict holding companies, interlocking directorates, and other practices of monopolies. Significantly, Wilson, an avid admirer of Brandeis, also recommended the creation of a federal agency for administration of antitrust policies. In 1914 came the enactment of the Clayton Act and the Federal Trade Commission Act. In the former, Congress proscribed certain price discriminations and tying and exclusive dealing contracts, and imposed restrictions upon intercorporate mergers and directorates. The meaning of these provisions will be examined in separate chapters to follow. The Federal Trade Commission Act outlawed "unfair methods" of competition. To give meaning to this broad language, Congress created the Federal Trade Commission, which, as an administrative agency, would possess the flexibility necessary to adapt the law to the commercial mores of a particular period. The commission was given sole power to enforce this provision; at the same time, the commission was brought into the antitrust field as a concurrent enforcer, with the Justice Department, of the Clayton Act provisions. The law of unfair practices will be considered in a later chapter.

Thus were forged the basic links in the chain of antitrust laws. Other important additions were to follow. In 1936 came the Robinson-Patman amendments to the Clayton Act, with their effect on the law of price discrimination and their designation of the granting of allowances as a form of discrimination. In a later chapter we shall examine the intricacies —and there are many—of the Robinson-Patman Act. Similarly, we shall trace the development of the role of the Federal Trade Commission in combatting the use of deceptive advertising in commerce. We shall also look briefly at the requirements of the various labeling acts which were to appear in future years.

In summary, then, we may state that the antitrust and trade regulation laws had their origin in American ingenuity—ingenuity in the development of pragmatic solutions to problems. The extremists who called for a complete *laissez-faire* approach, a sort of economic law of the jungle, were wisely defeated. Those, on the other hand, who called for outright federal ownership and control have never succeeded. A balance was struck, resulting in the growth of economic individualism and the fostering of free and fair competition. This means that the American nation can reap the benefits of an expanding technology, unhampered by the extremes of anarchy or of massive government control. We shall now proceed to a consideration of the meaning of the antitrust laws as they affect the businessman.

CHAPTER 3

A BIRD'S-EYE VIEW OF THE ANTITRUST AND TRADE REGULATION LAWS

THE American antitrust laws are essentially conservative in nature. Their purpose is to maintain free competition by insuring that such competition is fair. They seek to prevent giant aggregations of economic power from being built unfairly, because the use of such power necessarily stifles the opportunities competitors will have to compete meaningfully. In summary, the antitrust laws seek to prevent conduct which weakens or destroys competition.

THE SHERMAN ACT

The basic antitrust law is the Sherman Act. As we have seen, its passage resulted largely from fear aroused by the "vast accumulation of wealth in the hands of corporations and individuals, the enormous development of corporate organization, the facility for combination which such organizations afforded, the fact that the facility was being used and that combinations known as trusts were being multiplied, and the widespread impression that their power had been and would be exerted to oppress individuals and injure the public generally."

The wording of the Sherman Act's two substantive sections reflects these broad policies in very general terms. Section 1 declares: "Every contract, combination in the form of trust or otherwise, or conspiracy, in restraint of trade or commerce among the several States, or with foreign nations, is declared to be illegal." Section 2 is scarcely more specific: "Every person who shall monopolize, or attempt to monopolize, or combine or conspire with any other person or persons, to monopolize any part of the trade or commerce among the several States, or with foreign nations, shall be deemed guilty of a misdemeanor. . . ."

Although the language of the Sherman Act well expresses the end which Congress sought to avoid, it in no way indicates the kind of conduct which is prohibited except in the very general phrase *restraint of trade.* The precise meaning of the statute was to be determined by the courts in the process of deciding specific cases.

Initially, the Supreme Court was split on the proper interpretation of the statute. The language of Section 1, the key provision, is sweeping in the extreme. It declares *every* contract, combination, or conspiracy in restraint of trade to be illegal. If read literally, this language would outlaw many useful business arrangements, such as sales contracts extending over a period of time or covenants not to complete incident to the sale of a business. When first faced with the task of interpreting this language, the Supreme Court, by a five-to-four vote, adopted just such a literal interpretation. Every restraint of trade was declared illegal. The phrase *restraint of trade* was given its ordinary English meaning, thereby making every contract a restraint. Since contracts always limit the rights of the contracting parties, necessarily restraining their exercise of full freedom in trading, this early approach carried grave implications for subsequent enforcement.

Almost immediately, however, the courts began to withdraw from this literal and unjustifiable reading of Section 1, a reading that had, fortunately, only been applied in price-fixing cases. In 1898 a circuit court of appeals in *United States* v. *Addyston Pipe & Steel Company* considered the legality of an agreement among manufacturers of cast iron pipe to fix prices in areas where they competed and to divide markets to avoid the rigors of competition. Judge Taft, who became both president of the United States and chief justice of the Supreme Court, wrote the opinion for the court. While recognizing that the case could be disposed of by applying Section 1 literally, he went on to test the legality of the agreements by reference both to common law rules and to what subsequently developed into the "rule of reason."

At common law, Judge Taft stated, "no conventional restraint of trade can be enforced unless the covenant embodying it is merely ancillary to the main purpose of a lawful contract, and necessary to protect the covenantee in the enjoyment of the legitimate fruits of the contract, or to protect him from the dangers of an unjust use of those fruits by the other party." The classic example of the sort of valid ancillary restraint to which Judge Taft was referring is the seller's limited covenant not to compete contained in the contract of sale of a going business. In such a case the valid main purpose of the contract is the sale of the business. But since the seller may possess the good will of the business personally, the value of what the purchaser obtains could be significantly decreased if the seller were to open a competing business. For example, suppose Smith, the owner of Smith's Bakery in Charlottesville, Virginia, sold the business to Allen. If Smith were to open a new bakery next door to the one now owned by Allen, it would be likely that he would get all the old bakery's business. To protect himself from such a fate, Allen might get Smith to promise not to open a bakery in Charlottesville for five years. As this restraint of trade is limited to the legitimate purpose of maintaining the value of the bakery and is ancillary to a valid main contract, it is not illegal.

A corollary to this proposition is that any ancillary restraints must be limited to protection of a legitimate value. If Smith had promised not to open a bakery anywhere for five years, the agreement would have been invalid. Allen's only legitimate fear is that Smith will open a competing bakery in Charlottesville; if Smith opened a bakery in Elizabethtown, Kentucky, it could not hurt Allen. Hence, this broader promise goes further than necessary to protect Allen and is to that extent invalid.

Extending this approach, Taft stated the common law rule with respect to restraints of trade. That rule was that only those restraints which were "unreasonable" were illegal. As stated by an English court:

> We do not see how a better test can be applied to the question whether this is or is not a reasonable restraint of trade than by considering whether the restraint is such only as to afford a fair protection to the interest of the party in favor of whom it is given, and not so large as to interfere with the interest of the public. Whatever restraint is larger than the necessary protection of the party requires can be of no benefit to either. It can only be oppressive. It is, in the eye of the law, unreasonable. Whatever is injurious to the interest of the public is void on grounds of public policy.

This approach has had a lasting effect on the development of antitrust law. Only those restraints of trade which are unreasonable have been held to violate the law. And in judging reasonableness courts have often looked at the relationship between the legitimate value being protected and the breadth of the restraint. Only those restraints designed for and limited to protecting such values have been upheld.

Returning to the facts of the *Addyston* case, the court held that the agreements to fix prices and divide markets were plainly illegal. Far from being ancillary to a valid main contract, the restraints themselves were the main purpose of the contract. The only purpose of the agreements being to suppress competition, a finding of illegality necessarily followed. This was particularly so because there was no redeeming business justification.

In 1911 the Supreme Court itself adopted the rule of reason in the famous *Standard Oil* case. Henceforth only those restraints of trade which were unreasonable would be considered violations of the Sherman Act. At the same time, the Court stated the general meaning and interrelationship of Sections 1 and 2:

> In other words, having by the 1st section forbidden all means of monopolizing trade, that is, unduly restraining it by means of every contract, combination, etc., the 2d section seeks, if possible, to make the prohibitions of the act all the more complete and perfect by embracing all attempts to reach the end prohibited by the 1st section, that is, restraints of trade, by

> any attempt to monopolize, or monopolization thereof, even although the acts by which such results are attempted to be brought about or are brought about be not embraced within the general enumeration of the 1st section.

This language, although hardly memorable in itself, is the real starting point of modern antitrust law. Under both Section 1 and Section 2 only those acts or practices which are found to be unreasonable are to be illegal. Further, the two sections are to be regarded as complementary methods of accomplishing the same goal, that goal being the prevention of monopoly. With this general purpose and this general rule of legality in mind, we can turn to other major problems arising under the Sherman Act.

The Sherman Act was enacted under the power of Congress to regulate interstate and foreign commerce. As courts have held that in enacting this law Congress exercised all the power it possessed, the scope of the act is coterminous with Congressional regulatory power. The determination of just what activities are in interstate commerce and, accordingly, within the regulatory power of Congress has occupied lawyers and courts continually for the past eighty years. An examination of the development of the concept of interstate commerce is therefore necessary.

In the late nineteenth century a very narrow definition of this concept was given. At that time interstate commerce was thought to consist only of the actual movement of goods across state lines. Neither the production of the goods by the manufacturer prior to shipment nor the retail sale of the goods by the local dealer after he had received them were thought to be a part of interstate commerce.

The first change in this approach came in the famous antitrust case against the meat packing industry, *Swift & Company* v. *United States.* That case involved an agreement among meat packers on the prices they would pay when purchasing livestock. The packers contended that the purchase of livestock at a stockyard was not in interstate commerce. Accordingly, they argued that their price fixing conspiracy was beyond the reach of the Sherman Act. The Supreme Court replied:

> Commerce among the states is not a technical legal conception, but a practical one drawn from the course of business. When cattle are sent for sale from a place in one state, with the expectation that they will end their transit, after purchase, in another, and when in effect they do so, with only the interruption necessary to find a purchaser at the stockyards, and when this is a typical, constantly recurring course, the current thus existing is a current of commerce among the states, and the purchase of cattle is a part and incident of such commerce.

The *Swift* case thus gave birth to what has come to be called the flow-of-commerce approach. Briefly, it provides that anything happening in the flow of interstate commerce, though it happens wholly is one state, is in interstate commerce. The first seventy years of this century have witnessed the steady expansion of the number of activities found to be in the flow of interstate commerce. The intrastate sale of goods at retail is often found to be in the flow of commerce, against the contention that the goods have come to rest on the retailer's shelves and have thereby ceased to be in interstate commerce. Today there is no longer any doubt that the manufacture of goods prior to shipment across state lines is in the flow of commerce. Indeed, acts relating to the intrastate procurement of supplies necessary for manufacturing have been held to be within the flow of commerce. At the retail end of the shipment even long storage in one state prior to sale in that state has not served to withdraw the commodities from interstate commerce.

Even more significant than the flow theory in bringing within the reach of the Sherman Act what had long been thought to be purely local activity is the concept that any activity which *affects* interstate commerce is covered by the Sherman Act. In one important case cloth came from outside Massachusetts to jobbers located in Boston. These jobbers, in turn, sent the cloth to stitching contractors, also located in Boston, for the performance of certain work. The cloth was then returned to the jobbers and eventually shipped out of the state. The Supreme Court held that the stitching contractors were in interstate commerce and that their boycott therefore violated the Sherman Act. As the Court put it: "If it is interstate commerce that feels the pinch, it does not matter how local the operation which applies the squeeze."

Another case involved a chain of bakeries established as separate corporations and located in several states. One of these bakeries, located wholly within New Mexico, drastically reduced its prices in order to drive a local competitor out of business. Although recognizing that a wholly intrastate transaction was involved, the Supreme Court nonetheless held the conduct to be covered by the antitrust laws on the ground that the money to support the local bakery in its predatory price campaign was derived in part from its sister corporations in interstate commerce. This use of the opportunities afforded by interstate commerce to injure local trade, the Court held, was within the Congressional power to regulate interstate commerce and was therefore covered by the antitrust laws.

Section 1 of the Sherman Act relates only to contracts, combinations, or conspiracies. Purely individual conduct is beyond the reach of this statute. A whole body of law has been built up in the effort to determine what is a contract, combination, or conspiracy and to establish what will prove the existence of such agreements. A separate chapter will be devoted to this topic. For the moment, it is enough to note the requirement of multiple actors and to remind the reader that individual conduct may be attacked under other statutes, such as the Clayton Act and the Federal Trade Commission Act, as well as Section 2 of the Sherman Act.

The Sherman Act can be enforced both civilly and criminally. The possible infliction of criminal penalties for antitrust violations provides an accurate indicator of the importance with which we in America view the preservation of free competition. It also acts as a special deterrent to those who would willingly engage in restraining trade.

As we noted earlier, the Sherman Act is extremely general. This led to an early attack on its constitutionality as a criminal statute. The defendant argued that the statute was so vague that it provided no meaningful standards by which to judge whether particular conduct was legal or illegal. No businessman, it was argued, could tell what a court would find to be an unreasonable restraint of trade. Mr. Justice Holmes summarily rejected this contention and stated: "The law is full of instances where a man's fate depends on his estimating rightly, that is, as the jury subsequently estimates, some matter of degree."

Notwithstanding this early ruling that the criminal proscriptions of the Sherman Act were not unconstitutionally vague, the fact is that conduct which is today considered legal may tomorrow be illegal. The body of antitrust law is constantly growing and evolving as new practices threaten our competitive structure. Indeed, an impossible dilemma would be posed for businessmen if every action could lead to criminal penalties. Fortunately, the government enforcement agencies have recognized this difficulty, and the criminal provisions of the Sherman Act are usually invoked only against that conduct, such as price fixing, which has been clearly held illegal for a substantial period of time by the courts.

As we have observed, Section 1 prohibits only unreasonable restraints of trade. Theoretically, a defendant should have the opportunity to show that the practices attacked are reasonable in view of business conditions and that they do not in fact substantially and adversely impair existing competitive conditions. But to allow this is to encourage every antitrust case to become a welter of detail in which the statute's purposes are likely to be lost. To avoid this undesirable result, the courts have in the course of time designated certain conduct which is unreasonable in itself. To engage in the types of conduct which have been so labeled is to commit *per se* violations of the antitrust laws.

No better explanation of the concept of *per se* unreasonableness has been made than that voiced in 1958 by Justice Black in the case of *Northern Pacific Railway* v. *United States.* Although recognizing that the Sherman Act was guided generally by the rule of reason, he stated the reasons for making certain exceptions to this rule:

> However, there are certain agreements or practices which because of their pernicious effect on competition and lack of any redeeming virtue are conclusively presumed to be unreasonable and therefore illegal without elaborate inquiry as to the precise harm they have caused or the business excuse for their use. This principle of *per se* unreasonableness not only makes the type of restraints which are proscribed by the Sherman Act more certain to the benefit of everyone concerned, but it also avoids the necessity for an incredibly complicated and prolonged economic investigation into the entire

history of the industry involved, as well as related industries, in an effort to determine at large whether a particular restraint has been unreasonable—an inquiry so often wholly fruitless when undertaken.

Certain conduct is illegal no matter how laudable the motive underlying its use and no matter how beneficial to competition the results may be. Among the types of conduct that have been held to violate the statute *per se* are price-fixing agreements, group boycotts, agreements to divide markets, and tie-in sales. We shall have much more to say about each of these violations in succeeding chapters.

It should be noted, however, as the quotation from Justice Black suggests, *all* inquiry as to business purpose is not precluded by the *per se* rule. Unusual circumstances or "special industry facts" may relieve price fixing or other traditional *per se* restraints from the onus of the *per se* rule. For example, the National Football League's blackout rule (television broadcasts of football games were precluded in areas where a local team was playing at the time) was upheld on the ground that otherwise weak teams and ultimately the whole league would fail. Thus, the court applied the rule of reason even though the blackout rule was a horizontal territorial market allocation—one of the *per se* restraints listed by Justice Black in *Northern Pacific.* The point is that once it is established that a particular restraint is within the *per se* category, the defendant can make a preliminary showing of "special industry facts." If the court is convinced that a valid business purpose exists, the restraint is judged according to the rule of reason. If not, the "elaborate inquiry" as to harm and business excuse dictated by the rule of reason is precluded.

It is important to note that *per se* violations under the Sherman Act are established only after courts have had sufficient experience with the particular conduct in question to say that it is so "pernicious" that it lacks, in almost every case, any trace of "redeeming virtue." In one case, the Supreme Court refused to hold certain conduct to be a *per se* violation because it knew too little of the actual impact of the conduct on competition to determine meaningfully whether there could be any reasonable justification for it.

The Clayton Act

The Clayton Act was passed by Congress because of the feeling that certain defects and omissions in the Sherman Act had to be cured if our competitive system was to retain its resilience. Notwithstanding the sweeping and apparently all-inclusive prohibitions of the Sherman Act, new legislation was thought necessary both because of the judicial refusal to find certain conduct to be violative of the Act and because of the recognition of additional anticompetitive conduct which had not been considered detrimental before. For example, the recognition that the acquisition by one company of the stock of another could lead to dangerous oligopoly led to the prohibition of such an acquisition by Section 7 of the Clayton Act. Similarly, a fear that predatory price discriminations by a company might drive its competitors out of business inspired Section 2 of the Clayton Act, which forbade certain price discriminations. In short, the Clayton Act patched up what were felt to be specific defects in the Sherman Act by proscribing certain conduct which had proved anti-competitive in practice. Its passage was a reflection of that pragmatic approach that has guided all our efforts in this field. We have always felt that it is better to cure specific evils by patchwork repairs than to change the system completely to reach the same end.

The major substantive sections of the Clayton Act, dealing with price discrimination, exclusive dealing, and mergers, were all designed to reach in the incipiency acts or practices which might eventually lead to adverse competitive effects. Except in the area of *per se* violations, the Sherman Act is not violated unless *actual* and substantial adverse competitive effects have been proved. With the Clayton Act, on the other hand, illegality can be found in conduct which has the *probable* result of substantially lessening competition. This distinction between actual and potential competitive effects is of the utmost importance. We shall return to it again as we explore the types of conduct which pose antitrust difficulties.

The Federal Trade Commission Act

Section 5 of the Federal Trade Commission Act forbids "unfair methods of competition in commerce, and unfair or deceptive acts or practices in commerce." Initially, therefore, reference must be made to interstate commerce.

In contrast to its interpretation of the Sherman Act, the Supreme Court has held that Congress did not seek to exercise its full regulatory power over interstate commerce when it passed the Federal Trade Commission Act. The Court indicated that while Congress could constitutionally regulate matters merely affecting commerce, by its choice of the phrase *in commerce* in the Federal Trade Commission Act the legislature meant only to regulate those acts and practices in the flow of interstate commerce. Purely local intrastate activities, no matter how great their effect on interstate commerce, were put beyond the reach of the newly created administrative agency.

This 1941 ruling by the Supreme Court appears at first blush to be of tremendous significance. In fact, however, the importance of the decision has steadily declined over the ensuing years. Indeed, the decline of the doctrine dates from the very year of its formulation. In that year the commission attacked as misleading an advertisement by the Ford Motor Company. Ford defended by saying that the advertisement related solely to the intrastate sale of Ford cars by local dealers. The court of appeals rejected this and stated that any part of the commerce involved in distributing Ford cars, even though intrastate, was so closely related to the interstate commerce in Ford cars that it was covered by the Federal Trade Commission Act. In effect, this ruling amounts to the conferral of regulatory power upon the commission for acts and practices directly affecting interstate commerce.

Court and commission rulings since 1941 have made it clear that the commission has regulatory power over practically anything substantially affecting interstate commerce. Practices of a local board regulating local tobacco auctions were held to be in commerce because they were an "integral and indispensable part of interstate commerce in tobacco." Similarly, practices relating to the intrastate retail sale of goods were held to be within the jurisdiction of the commission because such sale was in the flow of commerce even though the goods had been warehoused prior to sale. Wholly intrastate sellers of cement have been held to be in commerce because of their act of joining an interstate conspiracy to fix cement prices. Finally, misleading or deceptive advertising is within the reach of the commission if it is conveyed across state lines, on the theory that the unfair or deceptive act or practice is itself in commerce, though the sale to which it relates may be wholly intrastate.

The one area of intrastate commerce which is still not subject to the regulatory power of the commission, no matter what its effect on interstate commerce, is the intrastate sale of goods which have never been in interstate commerce. Thus, if an Illinois candy manufacturer were to utilize deceptive practices only with respect to his sales in Illinois, his conduct might be safe from attack by the commission. This protection is limited, however, and as time passes it is likely to become more so. The safest course of action remains to avoid the substantive prohibitions of the act rather than to violate them in the hope that the conduct will be beyond the reach of the commission.

Although the subject will be discussed more fully in a later chapter, a brief definition of "unfair methods of competition" will be useful here. Unfair methods of competition include acts or practices which violate the Clayton or Sherman Acts. Additionally, acts or practices which are for technical reasons beyond the scope of these acts may be reached by the Commission under Section 5 if they have or are likely to have a substantial anticompetitive effect. But the same standards of proof required in actions under the Clayton and Sherman Acts may not be required under Section 5. Many practices forbidden by the Sherman Act are illegal only if they have an actual deleterious effect on competitive conditions. Section 5, though, would be violated if such an effect was the probable result of continued use of the practice. To use the phrase of the courts, the commission under Section 5 was authorized "to stop in their incipiency acts and practices which, when full blown, would violate" the Sherman and Clayton Acts.

At the same time that it laid down standards of conduct, the Federal Trade Commission Act created the agency to enforce those standards. The commission was created by Congress in the desire to establish an administrative agency "specially competent to deal with" the problems of unfair and competitively dangerous business practices "by reason of information, experience and careful study of the business and economic conditions of the industry affected." What was envisaged then was an expert federal agency to protect the competitive structure from the inroads of monopoly and to protect business from other unfair acts by competitors. By an amendment in 1938 the commission's purpose was broadened to include protection of the public from deceptive business acts.

Enforcement of the Laws

The federal antitrust laws are enforced in three ways: by the Antitrust Division of the Department of Justice, by the Federal Trade Commission, and by private parties asserting damage and/or injunction claims. Each type of enforcing action has contributed to the growth of antitrust law. This overlapping enforcement, however, complicates understanding of the role of each enforcer. There follows a brief summary of the relationships of the enforcement agencies to each other and of each of them to the laws. All matters of enforcement policy and procedure will be covered in greater detail in Chapters 16–18.

The Antitrust Division of the Department of Justice is charged with the enforcement of both the Sherman and Clayton Acts. As we observed earlier, liability under the Sherman Act may be either criminal or civil. Under the Clayton Act (with the exception of a few relatively obscure sections) only civil suits may be brought. Except for *per se* violations of the Sherman Act, the Antitrust Division normally enforces the antitrust laws through civil suits, the aim of which is to have a court declare the practices in question unlawful and forbid the defendant company to engage in such practices in the future.

The Federal Trade Commission is the only agency entitled to enforce the provisions of the Federal Trade Commission Act. That Act, of course, is wholly civil in nature. In addition, the commission has the right to enforce the Clayton Act. In recent years the commission has been most active in enforcing Section 2 of the Clayton Act, as amended by the Robinson-Patman Act—the section relating to price and service discrimination. Several related acts are also enforced by the commission. The Sherman Act, however, is not one of the laws with which the commission expressly deals, though in effect the Sherman Act prohibitions have been incorporated into Section 5 of the Federal Trade Commission Act.

Formal commission enforcement usually takes the following form. The commission first files a complaint charging failure to comply with one of the relevant laws. After necessary preparation, hearings on this charge are held before an administrative judge appointed by the commission. An initial decision is then prepared by the judge. Appeal of such decisions to the full commission is allowed as a matter of right, and it is common procedure for either the counsel supporting the complaint or the counsel for the respondent to make such an appeal. The ruling by the commission may be appealed to a court of appeals, although the presumed *expertise* of the commission as well as the relative finality of its findings of fact provide the losing party with a hard row to hoe.

Finally, the antitrust laws are enforced by private parties. A provision of the Clayton Act permits a suit in federal courts for three times the actual damages *caused* by anything forbidden in the antitrust laws. Court costs and attorneys fees are also allowed. Generally speaking, antitrust laws in this context refer to the substantive provisions of the Sherman and Clayton Acts. Because treble damages are awarded, private suits have become increasingly popular and important in recent years. Further, under the Clayton Act any nonconsent judgments in antitrust actions brought by the United States (that is, government actions contested by the defendants) are *prima facie* evidence of antitrust violations. In addition, the statute of limitations regarding the bringing of private actions is tolled while the government suit is being litigated. This provision makes private suits an almost automatic aftermath of any successful government action. Private injunction actions are also authorized by the Clayton Act.

CHAPTER 4

CONTRACTS, COMBINATIONS, AND CONSPIRACIES

ONE person acting alone cannot violate Section 1 of the Sherman Act. That prohibition applies to *contracts, combinations,* or *conspiracies* in restraint of trade. An agreement between two or more persons is necessary before a violation of Section 1 can be found. The courts have generally used the three terms interchangeably. *Combination* merely describes a union of two or more persons, the underlying connection being the contract or agreement. *Conspiracy* has long defied ready definition. The sinister meaning ascribed to conspiracy in bygone days certainly has no place in the antitrust meaning of the term. Conspiracy has been defined as a combination designed to accomplish an illegal purpose or to carry out a legal purpose by illegal means. All three terms refer to concerted activity in restraint of trade or commerce.

The meaning of these terms may best be grasped by reviewing some situations where the courts have found a contract, a combination, or a conspiracy in restraint of trade. In an early case the Supreme Court found an illegal combination where an association of retail lumber dealers circulated among their members a list of wholesale dealers who were selling directly to customers. When the possible purposes of the list were considered, together with the fact that many of the retail dealers stopped purchasing from the listed wholesalers, the Court concluded that a combination to boycott such wholesalers had been established. The Court reasoned that the circulation of the list served no purpose except to blacklist uncooperative wholesalers. When an association's activities have indicated that individual members have abandoned independent decision in favor of concerted pressure or an implied understanding to restrain trade, the courts have not hesitated to strike down such activities as an illegal combination.

In the 1939 case of *Interstate Circuit* v. *United States* the defendants were distributors and exhibitors of motion picture films. Interstate, a powerful exhibitor, sent a letter to a number of film distributors asking compliance with certain demands as a condition of Interstate's continued exhibition of the distributors' films at its first-run theaters. Interstate demanded that stated minimum admission prices be charged for "A" pictures and that such pictures might not be shown as part of a double feature. Significantly, each letter sent by Interstate to the distributors contained, at the top of the letter, the names of all distributors concerned. Conferences between Interstate and each of the distributors followed the sending of the letters, and the demands were met, at least in certain cities. The Supreme Court held that the evidence warranted a finding that Interstate and the distributors had combined and conspired in violation of the Sherman Act. Such a ruling was justified, the Court indicated, when the nature of the demands was considered, together with the manner in which they were made, the unanimity of action by the distributors, and the fact that the defendant exhibitors at trial did not call as witnesses the superior officials who would, in the normal course of business, know of the existence or nonexistence of agreements with the distributors. The Court noted: "It was enough that, knowing that concerted action was contemplated and invited, the distributors gave their adherence to the scheme and participated in it." Conspiracy is often formed, the Court concluded, without simultaneous action or agreement; acceptance, without previous agreement, of an invitation to participate in a monopolistic plan establishes an unlawful conspiracy. This doctrine of conscious adherence was reiterated by the Supreme Court in 1948 in *Federal Trade Commission* v. *Cement Institute,* in which the Court stated: "It is enough to warrant the finding of a 'combination' within the meaning of the Sherman Act if there is evidence that persons with knowledge that concerted action was contemplated and invited give adherence to and then participate in a scheme."

These decisions form the basis for a number of doctrines labeled "conscious parallelism." One school of legal thought has espoused the theory that the proof of consciously parallel action obviates the need for proving the existence of a conspiracy. The European Economic Community seems to have adopted this approach. Another school asserts that consciously parallel action is merely evidence which tends to establish the ultimate fact that a conspiracy exists, but that in every case the ultimate fact must be found. The second school has clearly had the better of recent decisions. In fact, the notion that conscious parallelism was in itself sufficient proof of an illegal combination or conspiracy was probably, and properly, laid to rest by a 1954 Supreme Court decision. Uniform conduct or identical prices may indicate a violation of Section 1 of the Sherman Act, but their existence does not obviate the necessity of determining whether or not a conspiracy exists. The true test remains whether the conduct in question culminated in illegal agreement and amounted to an abandonment of independent decision. In the language of the Supreme Court, conscious parallelism is not equated to conspiracy. It is merely another evidentiary circumstance to be considered in determining whether or not a conspiracy exists. It can be readily seen that in many circumstances conscious uniformity can in no way be elevated to agreement. Meeting the price of a competitor may result in a conscious uniformity of price, but if such conduct is the result of the individual decision of the businessman, such uniformity establishes no illegal activity. Certainly the antitrust laws do not require that business prudence be cast to the wind. Uniformity, in and of itself, is not prohibited. Only when uniformity is the result of collective agreement, tacit or express, to suppress competition do the antitrust laws condemn the conduct leading to such uniformity.

It is elementary law that direct evidence is not necessary to establish the existence of a conspiracy. As long ago as 1914 the Supreme Court held that the existence of a conspiracy violative of the Sherman Act may be inferred from the actions of the persons charged. In fact, the more sophisticated the businessman, the less likely the possibility that there will exist direct evidence of illegal combination; for example, a written agreement to fix prices. As the preceding cases indicate, agreement may be express or implied. The "gentlemen's agreement" is a familiar term in antitrust law. Such an agreement, or the unwritten understanding, or the unspoken understanding, or even a "knowing wink," if designed and used to restrain competition, is just as vulnerable as a signed and sealed written contract to restrain trade.

The United States Supreme Court in its recent *Container* decision went so far as to hold that the occasional exchange of price information by manufacturers of corrugated boxes violated Section 1 of the Sherman Act. There was "no agreement to adhere to a price schedule," but implicit in a manufacturer's request for price information of a competitor was the understanding that the requesting manufacturer would supply his price data to others on request. Such, in the Court's view, was all that was necessary to supply evidence of agreement. Finally, the combination requirement of Section 1 is not confined to agreements among competitors. In a footnote in its recent *Albrecht* decision, the Supreme Court noted that a dealer's lowering of his prices on threat of termination by his supplier constituted an illegal combination for Section 1 purposes.

As we have seen, a contract, combination, or conspiracy under Section 1 of the Sherman Act requires the concerted activity of two or more persons. Independent activity by a single trader may result in an illegal monopoly under Section 2 of the Act, but the trader cannot contract, combine, or conspire with himself in violation of Section 1. On the other hand, in 1964, the Supreme Court held that officers or directors of a corporation could conspire among themselves for Section 1 purposes. Similarly, shareholders can conspire with their corporation, because a basic tenet of corporate law is that a corporation is an entity separate and apart from its shareholders. A corporation cannot, however, conspire with its officers and directors. A corporation can only act through its officers and employees. To hold that the corporation can conspire with its own officers would distort the meaning of conspiracy under Section 1.

This same reasoning, however, has not been applied to business activity between a parent and a wholly owned subsidiary. In several cases the Supreme Court has found the existence of a conspiracy to restrain trade in such a situation. Thus, conspiracies have been found through mergers under common ownership of previously independent competitors, through the fixing of liquor prices by affiliated corporations, and through the division of international markets by corporations under substantially unified ownership or control. The Supreme Court has concluded that "common ownership and control does not liberate corporations from the impact of the antitrust laws." The extent to which this rule will be applied in the future is not wholly clear, except that a corporation cannot conspire with its unincorporated divisions, nor they with each other. Certainly an inflexible approach requiring competition within a single business unit, although composed of legally separate entities, would introduce chaos, not promote competition. The existence of multicorporate structures is often dictated by sound business reasons quite apart from antitrust considerations. Significantly enough, very few cases have resulted in a finding of conspiracy in the parent–subsidiary context where a wholly owned subsidiary is involved. Often the parent will own less than a majority of the shares of the subsidiary. Furthermore, the courts have been more prone to find an illegal combination where the affiliated corporations hold themselves out as competitors. In such circumstances any agreements designed to suppress competition properly appear to be within the ambit of proscribed activities. Concerted activities between a parent and a subsidiary should not be subject to the same *per se* approach that is taken in certain areas in regard to the activities of true competitors. For example, the division of markets among competitors has long been held *per se* illegal, but the same division between a parent and a wholly owned subsidiary might be reasonable and justifiable by the dictates of business efficiency within the economic unit. In this regard the Attorney General's National Committee to Study the Antitrust Laws (1955) concluded:

> Nothing in these [Supreme Court] opinions should be interpreted as justifying the conclusion that concerted action solely between a parent and subsidiary or subsidiaries, the purpose and effect of which is not coercive restraint of the trade of strangers to the corporate family, violates Section 1. Where such concerted action restrains no trade and is designed to restrain no trade other than that of the parent and its subsidiaries, Section 1 is not violated.

In sum, the proscription in Section 1 of the Sherman Act against contracts, combinations, and conspiracies in restraint of trade looks to concerted activity and agreement. When such combination is found and independent action thus disappears, the antitrust laws have been violated.

CHAPTER 5

PRICE FIXING

PRICE fixing is the prime example and the best-known *per se* violation of the Sherman Antitrust Act. The government enforcement agencies have always regarded price fixing as the most serious of the various antitrust violations. In a long line of cases the courts have zealously extended the prohibitions against price fixing to a host of business activities long thought by many to be both proper and legal. The vast majority of criminal convictions for violations of the antitrust laws have been upon charges of price fixing. And the possibility of a jail sentence for violation of the antitrust laws increases geometrically if the charge is price fixing. Consequently, it will be helpful to review the leading cases establishing price fixing, including resale price maintenance, as a *per se* violation of Section 1 of the Sherman Act.

As early as 1898, in the *Addyston Pipe & Steel Company* case, Judge Taft held that a price-fixing agreement was illegal under the Sherman Act. In response to a contention that the prices fixed by the combination were reasonable, the court answered: "We do not think the issue an important one, because . . . we do not think that at common law there is any question of reasonableness open to the courts with reference to such a contract [i.e., one fixing prices]." Because the reasonable price of today can be the unreasonable price of tomorrow, the reasonableness of a price at a given time is irrelevant under the Sherman Act.

In *United States* v. *Trenton Potteries Company* the Supreme Court unequivocally held price fixing to be a *per se* violation of the Sherman Act. Trenton Potteries and numerous other corporations had formed a combination which agreed, among other things, to fix and maintain prices for the sale of sanitary pottery. The trial judge had refused to allow into evidence and submit to the jury the reasonableness of the price agreement. The trial judge concluded that the "law is clear that an agreement on the part of the members of a combination controlling a substantial part of an industry, upon the prices which the members are to charge for their commodity, is in itself an undue and unreasonable restraint of trade and commerce." The trial judge's conclusion was fully supported by the Supreme Court. The Court noted that the aim and result of all effective price-fixing agreements is the elimination of one form of competition. The very power to fix prices, whether exercised in a reasonable manner or not, involves the power to control the market and fix arbitrary and unreasonable prices.

By 1940 the Supreme Court could say, though not without critics, that "for over forty years this Court has consistently and without deviation adhered to the principle that price fixing agreements are unlawful '*per se*' under the Sherman Act. . . ." This observation was made in the case of *United States* v. *Socony-Vacuum Oil Company*, perhaps the leading case in the price-fixing field. In *Socony-Vacuum* the Supreme Court established that an agreement designed to stabilize prices indirectly is illegal *per se*, even if no actual price is fixed. The defendants in this case were gasoline refiners who had attempted to stem the flow of "distress" gasoline into their markets during the Depression. These refiners made no attempt to fix prices directly; neither did they agree to raise prices by any definite amount. Rather, they reached an implied agreement to establish quotas for the purchase of distress gasoline at a "fair, going market price." The Court held such agreements illegal because they were designed for the sole purpose of stabilizing prices. The Court also said that lack of power to fix a price in a particular market is no defense to a charge of price fixing. Thus, it does not matter whether or not the arrangement in question is aimed at complete elimination of price competition, nor does it matter whether the parties concerned "have power to control the market." The Court concluded: "Whatever economic justification particular price-fixing agreements may be thought to have the law does not permit an inquiry into their reasonableness. They are all banned because of their actual or potential threat to the central nervous system of the economy."

It is apparent that Section 1 of the Sherman Act, the most important law prohibiting price fixing, takes only limited account of competitive abuses or evils whose cure is sought by price-fixing agreements. In *Socony-Vacuum* the Court was careful to point out that an earlier case, *Appalachian Coals, Inc.* v. *United States*, had not reached a different conclusion. The agreements in that case, designed to control "distress" coal and eliminate certain abuses, had not contemplated the fixing of market prices. Significantly, the Supreme Court in *Appalachian Coals* directed the district court to reserve jurisdiction to see if the actual operation of the coal plan proved to be a violation of the antitrust laws.

Trade association activity is an area where price-fixing violations often occur; the individual members of the association must be ever conscious of the antitrust laws, especially in regard to prices. Statistical reporting by a trade association of prices charged in an industry in the past is not an illegal activity in and of itself. In 1925 the Supreme Court held in effect that such a program may be beneficial where it is designed only to inform individual members of an industry and aid them in forming intelligent individual decisions. The Supreme Court indicated that trade associations may openly gather and distribute information in regard to the cost of their product, the volume of production, the price which the product has commanded in the past, the amount of merchandise on hand, and the transportation costs involved. Moreover, such information may be discussed among competing businessmen. The ever-present prohibition remains that in such discussions and exchanges of information no agreement or concerted action with respect to prices or production or restraint of competition be negotiated. Unquestionably, this open dissemination of pertinent information in regard to business operations tends to stabilize a trade or business and produce some uniformity of price and practice within the trade. The Supreme Court has specifically recognized this fact. The effect of this acquisition of a broader scientific knowledge of business conditions, the Court has concluded, "can hardly be deemed a restraint of commerce." Or, if it should be so considered, the restraint is reasonable and lawful. The rationale behind this position was best expressed in the *Maple Flooring* case in 1925, when the Court stated:

> "Free competition" means a free and open market among both buyers and sellers for the sale and distribution of commodities. Competition does not become less free merely because the conduct of commercial operations becomes more intelligent through the free distribution of knowledge of all the essential factors entering into the commercial transaction. General knowledge that there is an accumulation of surplus of any market commodity would undoubtedly tend to diminish production, but the dissemination of that information cannot in itself be said to be restraint upon commerce in any legal sense. The manufacturer is free to produce, but prudence and business foresight based on that knowledge influence free choice in favor of more limited production. Restraint upon free competition begins when improper use is made of that information through any concerted action which operates to restrain the freedom of action of those who buy and sell.

The precise point of departure, therefore, from legal dissemination of trade statistics occurs when such statistics are used as part of a combination or plan to impose unwarranted restrictions such as curtailment of production or the raising and maintaining of prices.

Today statistical reporting of prices charged in the past is a very common trade association program. But programs of this character do present grave antitrust dangers. When the reporting has gone beyond a mere informative function, aspects of such a program have been construed as evidence of the existence of an illegal price-fixing conspiracy. The Supreme Court struck down a trade association agreement which included a reporting system requiring absolute adherence to prices and terms announced by any particular member. Recently the Court went so far as to hold illegal the occasional exchange of price information by manufacturers of corrugated boxes. The price information consisted not of averages, but of specific sales, and it stabilized prices, though notably on a downward trend. This constituted a tampering with the price structure condemned in *Socony* and was consequently illegal. Nor does the professional status of the members of an association exempt them from the price-fixing proscriptions of the Sherman Act. In one case a federal district court in Utah held that fee schedules for prescription drugs set by the Utah Pharmaceutical Association constituted a *per se* violation of the Sherman Act. Consequently, the reasonableness of the association's activity was not open to question. Even on a reasonableness plane, the Utah association would not have prevailed. The district judge recognized the professional capacity of pharmacists yet noted that the regulation of prices concerned drugs, not services. The association's analogy to the fixing of doctors' and lawyers' fees was for this reason held inapplicable by the trial judge. The court strongly hinted that price-fixing violations would be committed if doctors and lawyers drew up fee schedules concerned with the sale of commodities.

A lower court, in *United States* v. *American Medical Association*, specifically held that the Sherman Antitrust Act was applicable to the practice of medicine. The fact that certain restrictive practices of learned professions have not been subjected to attack is the result of forbearance by the federal antitrust enforcement authorities and the interstate commerce jurisdictional requirement, not any recognized exemption to the antitrust laws.

Resale price maintenance is another form of price fixing. The McGuire Act and state fair trade laws provide limited exemptions for such price fixing where the individual state chooses to approve such practice. But cases brought prior to the enactment of such exemptions and cases involving resale price fixing which do not fall within such exemptions unequivocally indicate that resale price maintenance is a *per se* violation of the antitrust laws. As early as 1911 the Supreme Court struck down such price-fixing agreements. The Dr. Miles Medical Company was a manufacturer of proprietary medicines which were prepared in accordance with a secret formula. The company entered into a series of agreements whereby it sought to maintain certain minimum prices for the sale and resale of its product at wholesale and retail levels. The company sued to enforce these limitations on a wholesale druggist who was selling at cut prices. The Supreme Court held that the agreements violated the Sherman Act, as well as constituting unreasonable restraints on alienation, and were invalid. The fact that the proprietary medicines were manufactured by a secret process did not permit the price-fixing agreements. The Court concluded that the manufacturer was not entitled to control the prices on all sales of its own product.

By 1919 the Supreme Court had recognized a very limited exception to this proscription. Colgate, a manufacturer and seller of soap and toilet articles, procured the adherence of wholesale and retail dealers to its resale prices by refusing to deal with those who did not conform with such prices. Yet no agreement obligated the dealer to sell at fixed prices. The Court referred to the "long-recognized right of trader or manufacturer engaged in an entirely private business, freely to exercise his own independent discretion as to parties with whom he will deal." No antitrust violation occurred when such a refusal to deal was exercised.

This refusal-to-deal principle (the "Colgate doctrine") was severely limited, if not totally discarded, in subsequent Supreme Court cases. Whenever the fixed-price condition of sale is made known to wholesalers and retailers and the selling company undertakes an extensive program to secure information on those who do not adhere to its program, the Supreme Court will find a price-fixing agreement in violation of the Sherman Act. By 1942 a federal district court, in referring to the *Colgate* decision and subsequent cases, concluded that a trader may simply refuse to sell to others who do not sell at prices which he fixes, but he may not go beyond the exercise of this right. The Supreme Court has also indicated that even the smallest step beyond a mere refusal to sell may result in a finding of illegal price maintenance. In 1956 a manufacturer and distributor of pharmaceutical products in the Washington and Richmond areas announced its resale price maintenance policy in its catalogues. The company indicated that it would deal only with those who observed its price schedule. To insure maintenance of its price schedules, the company's representatives visited the various wholesalers. The latter were told that they could not buy the pharmaceutical products if they sold them to retailers who did not observe the schedules. In 1960 the majority of the Supreme Court held that the company's program went beyond a mere refusal to deal, even if there was no express or implied agreement concerning price maintenance. A dissenting minority of the Court concluded that the majority's opinion "has done no less than send to its demise the Colgate doctrine. . . ."

By the Miller-Tydings Act and the McGuire Act, Congress provided a limited exception to the antitrust proscription against all agreements fixing resale prices. If state law permits, no antitrust liability will attach to a resale price maintenance contract involving a trademarked or brand name product in competition with other similar commodities. This exception is commonly referred to as the "fair trade exception," and it proceeds on the rationale that certain resale price maintenance contracts should be allowed to protect the manufacturer's good will attached to his trademark or brand name.

It should be carefully noted that the fair trade exception is available only where a valid state law permits such resale price maintenance. In order for fair trade to be effective at the retail level, state law must provide that all retailers are bound to charge that price established by contract between the manufacturer and any single retailer in the state.

State laws have traditionally contained such "nonsigner" provisions. Although seventeen states have upheld such provisions, twenty-three states have ruled invalid either that state's fair trade act or the nonsigner provision in it. The latter states' principal objection to the nonsigner provisions is that the imposition of a price condition upon the retailer who has absolute title to the goods constitutes a violation of the due process clause of the state constitution. In those states upholding the provisions, the state statute usually contains a contract-by-notice clause. The due process objection is thought to be obviated by the fact that the nonsigning retailers took the goods with notice of the manufacturer's intent to fair trade. Such was, thus, an implied term of his contract of purchase and he could not complain that any constitutional rights had been violated.

The courts require strict adherence to the limitations of the Miller-Tydings and McGuire Acts by those who seek to justify a price maintenance program under state fair trade acts. Illustrative is the case of *United States* v. *McKesson & Robbins, Inc.* McKesson sold its drugs both directly to retailers and to retailers through wholesalers. It also sold the products of other manufacturers through its wholesale division. McKesson entered into fair trade contracts with many of the independent wholesalers dealing in its products. The Supreme Court ruled that these contracts were illegal price-fixing agreements. The fair trade exception was not applicable because the Miller-Tydings Act did not legalize horizontal price maintenance contracts, for example, "between wholesalers." Because McKesson competed with independent wholesalers bound by the price maintenance contracts in the resale of McKesson products, no matter whether McKesson was technically a wholesaler or not, the fair trade exemption did not apply, and once the exemption was lost, the price contracts were *per se* illegal.

There is another area of potential price-fixing difficulty of which the intelligent businessman should be aware. Probably as a result of the famous conspiracy case in the electrical industry, the late President Kennedy issued an Executive Order requiring all government departments to report to the attorney general any instances of identical bids on government purchases or sales which exceed $10,000. The order states that its principal purpose is to insure more effective enforcement of the antitrust laws by placing at the disposal of the attorney general information "which may tend to establish the presence of a conspiracy in restraint of trade and which may warrant further investigation with a view to preferring civil or criminal charges."

The order is not limited to bids which are literally identical. A substantial identity can be determined by giving effect to discounts and "other relevant factors." Moreover, the figure of $10,000 may be raised or lowered according to the discretion of the attorney general; similarly, he may decide to exclude certain categories of property or services.

There is also a growing tendency for state and local authorities to file with the Department of Justice or the Federal Trade Commission, or both, information on identical bids on public purchases or contracts. It would seem that this trend will become increasingly widespread.

The lesson is clear that businessmen must avoid every suspicion of agreement with others over price. Under the philosophy of the law an independent businessman is expected to act independently.

As noted in the introduction to this book, the case of *Kiefer-Stewart Company* v. *Joseph E. Seagram & Sons,* decided by the Supreme Court in 1951, illustrates the American commitment to the decentralized exercise of economic power. The precise area upon which that case fixed its disapproval was price fixing. Yet the prices fixed there were *maximum* prices; that is, the wholesale liquor dealers could not charge the public a price in excess of that fixed by the distiller. Such was thought by the lower court not to constitute an antitrust violation because the consumer was not injured, but, in fact, benefitted from the price fixing. The Supreme Court reversed on the ground that price fixing in any guise is impermissible under the antitrust laws. Even an agreement upon a maximum resale price cripples the freedom of traders. The unequivocal hostility of the courts toward price fixing for more than eighty years represents the American rejection of an economy planned by the concerted action of a small minority of the American people.

CHAPTER 6

BOYCOTTS AND REFUSALS TO DEAL

PRICE fixing is not the only type of *per se* violation under Section 1 of the Sherman Antitrust Act. Most, if not all, concerted refusals to deal—more commonly known as group boycotts—are antitrust violations no matter what their purpose or effect. Although earlier notions that boycotts were not *per se* illegal persisted until very recently, it is now clear that nothing will save a concerted refusal to deal from the taint of illegality except in the most unusual situations.

Initially, we must distinguish group boycotts from individual refusals to deal. As we have seen in the resale price maintenance area, the Supreme Court has long recognized the right of an individual trader to deal or refuse to deal for any reason at all in the absence of a purpose to create or maintain a monopoly. It must again be stressed, however, that it takes only a little additional action to make the refusal to deal part of a "contract, combination . . . or conspiracy" in violation of Section 1 of the Sherman Act. A good illustration of this distinction between individual and group refusal to deal is provided by the following hypothetical situation. A manufacturer wishes to establish a set price on the resale of his product by wholesalers and retailers. He may proceed to set his price and indicate to the wholesalers that he will refuse to deal with those who do not abide by the terms he has set. On its face, such an individual refusal to deal seems to be a legitimate exercise of the manufacturer's freedom and no violation of the antitrust laws. Suppose, however, that the manufacturer, in order to insure that his price will be observed, induces wholesalers not to sell to retailers who do not follow his price schedule. Here we find a concerted refusal to deal, the combination of the manufacturer and the wholesaler refusing to deal with nonconforming retailers. Such a boycott violates the antitrust laws. Indeed, illegal concerted refusals to deal may be found in this situation even though no *express* agreement existed between the manufacturer and the wholesalers. The court may find the existence of an agreement as *implied* from the conduct and actions of parties.

The 1966 Supreme Court decision of *United States* v. *General Motors Corp.* is particularly instructive in this regard. This case involved the relationship between General Motors and its Chevrolet dealers, a relationship governed by a franchise agreement containing a "location clause" which prohibited a dealer from moving to or establishing a "new or different location, branch sales office, branch service station, or place of business including any used car lot or location without the prior written approval of Chevrolet." In the Los Angeles market a practice developed whereby Chevrolet cars were being sold through discount houses under various arrangements including referral sales from discount houses to dealers. In 1960 approximately a dozen of the eighty-five Chevrolet dealers in the area were furnishing cars to discounters. To eliminate this practice General Motors and three dealer associations took various steps with the dealers to bring about discontinuance of such sales through discounters. The government attacked the action taken to halt the discounters on the ground that such action violated the antitrust laws.

Justice Fortas, in the majority opinion, stated: "We have here a classic conspiracy in restraint of trade: joint, collaborative action by dealers, the appellee associations, and General Motors to eliminate a class of competitors by terminating business dealings between them and a minority of Chevrolet dealers and to deprive franchised dealers of their freedom to deal through discounters if they so choose." Further, it has long been "settled that explicit agreement is not a necessary part of a Sherman Act conspiracy—certainly not where, as here, joint and collaborative action was pervasive in the initiation, execution, and fulfillment of the plan."

The opinion went on to point out that General Motors' conduct was not unilateral in that it sought "to elicit from all the dealers agreements, substantially interrelated and interdependent, that none of them would do business with the discounters." Continuing, Justice Fortas stated:

> And once the agreements were secured, General Motors both solicited and employed the assistance of its alleged co-conspirators in helping to police them. What resulted was a fabric interwoven by many strands of joint action to eliminate the discounters from participation in the market, to inhibit the free choice of franchised dealers to select their own methods of trade and to provide multilateral surveillance and enforcement. This process for achieving and enforcing the desired objective can by no stretch of the imagination be described as "unilateral" or merely "parallel."

Thus, the Court applied the *per se* rule applicable to group boycotts. The economic motives of the dealers in preserving profit margins were irrelevant.

A corollary of the refusal-to-deal doctrine is the well-established principle that it is illegal for a manufacturer to stop selling to a price-cutting retailer and then to resume doing business with him upon the retailer's assurance that in the future he will adhere to the manufacturer's suggested price. In such a case, the retailer who has promised to abide by the manufacturer's suggested prices if the manufacturer will resume selling to him has entered into an illegal price-fixing conspiracy with the manufacturer. It is thus clear that once a manufacturer refuses to deal with a retailer who has failed to follow suggested prices, the manufacturer cannot later resume doing business with that retailer after teaching the offender "a lesson."

An interesting case illustrates the dangers incurred by a retailer who enters into a program of price scheduling with his manufacturer. A retailer with whom a manufacturer had refused to deal because the retailer sold below suggested prices sued a competing retailer who adhered to the suggested price. The suit was for treble damages under the Sherman Act. The court, in deciding in favor of the price-cutting retailer, found that the manufacturer had explained to each of its retailers its code of suggested prices. The defendant had not only followed the manufacturer's suggested list prices but had agreed with the manufacturer to sell at such prices in violation of the Sherman Act. This retailer had to pay damages to his price-cutting competitor as a result of the manufacturer's refusal to deal, which was part and parcel of the illegal price-fixing scheme in which the defendant was so deeply involved.

The nature of the antitrust laws relating to group boycotts can best be understood by describing some of the situations where the courts have found such illegal activity. A retail lumber dealers' association determined to prevent wholesale dealers from selling directly to consumers. To this end the association prepared and circulated among its members a list of the names of those wholesalers who sold directly to consumers. The circular also asked members for information concerning any other wholesalers selling directly to consumers. The Supreme Court found that the association's activity constituted a combination and conspiracy in violation of the antitrust laws. The Court concluded that there could be but one purpose for the association's activity, namely, to blacklist the wholesalers listed on the circular. The association obviously hoped that retailers would refuse to buy from these wholesalers and thus force the wholesalers to cease competing with retailers. At the same time, the Court was careful to point out that a retail dealer had an individual right to refuse to deal with a wholesaler. But once such refusals became the subject of concerted action, they fell within the ban of the Sherman Act.

As in the area of price fixing, laudable motives will not allow the formation of boycotts to restrain trade. This conclusion was unequivocally demonstrated in the famous "style piracy" case. The Fashion Originators' Guild was an association of manufacturers of original-design dresses. These manufacturers sold medium and high-priced dresses to retailers, who selected the dress designs they wanted from displays in New York City showrooms. The members of the guild agreed to refuse to sell such dresses to retailers who also handled dresses copied or "pirated" from these original designs. The Federal Trade Commission refused to hear evidence on the demoralizing effect of "style piracy" on the guild and its members or the necessity of protection against such practices, on the ground that the combination was *per se* illegal under the Sherman Act. Both the court of appeals and the United States Supreme Court upheld the commission's decision. The fact that the exclusion benefited the customers and producers of the original designs did not excuse the boycott. In regard to the unfairness of "style piracy," the Supreme Court concluded that even if such copying were an acknowledged wrong under the law of every state, that situation would still not justify a combination in violation of federal law.

Many boycotts result from the desire to enforce stable prices. Such cases grow out of pressure by groups of retailers on manufacturers to establish or enforce fair trade pricing. For example, a group of liquor retailers and wholesalers agreed to persuade the manufacturers from whom they purchased to establish fair trade contracts. To accomplish this objective, the retailers agreed to refuse to buy from manufacturers who did not establish fair trade pricing. Moreover, the manufacturers who agreed to establish fair trading also agreed with wholesalers and retailers not to sell to retailers who would not sign fair trade agreements. The United States Supreme Court, without qualification, held that these activities to stabilize prices were in violation of the Sherman Act.

Clearly, then, a concerted refusal either to buy or to sell is a violation of the antitrust law, no matter what its purpose, if that purpose is to be achieved by restricting competition. Equally clear is the proposition that concerted restraints of the previously discussed type are illegal even if designed to meet or overcome an admittedly invidious trade practice.

The United States Supreme Court has even indicated that the fact that an antitrust violator's actions have no appreciable effect on competition will not protect his illegal activity. A small retailer brought an action for treble damages, alleging that a chain of department stores had illegally conspired with brand name appliance manufacturers to prevent him from obtaining such appliances for retail sale or to allow him to obtain them only at discriminatory and unfavorable prices. The Supreme Court rejected the court of appeal's rationale that the defendant's action must somehow injure competition to the detriment of the public. The defendant's monopolistic tendencies could not be tolerated merely because the victim was just one merchant whose business was so small that its destruction made little difference to the economy.

Another area of illegal activity involves the bottleneck boycott. An example of such a boycott was found in the domination of news media facilities by the Associated Press. The boycott arose from the rules regulating membership in the Associated Press. The bylaws of the Associated Press forbade all its members from selling news to nonmembers and granted each member power to block the membership application of nonmember competitors. Morevover, nonmembers seeking membership in the association were required, in certain cases, to pay enormous "admission fees." The United States Supreme Court found that the association's bylaws, on their face and without regard to their past effect, constituted illegal restraints of trade. The Court indicated that arrangements designed to limit competition cannot be immunized by adopting a membership device to accomplish that purpose. The Associated Press was directed to cease its discriminatory practice in regard to membership.

In May, 1963, the Supreme Court reaffirmed its unequivocal position that group boycotts are *per se* unreasonable under the Sherman Act. In *Silver* v. *New York Stock Exchange,* the exchange had directed two of its member firms to discontinue private wire connections with two nonmember, over-the-counter security broker-dealers. The members were given no reason for this action, nor were they provided with an opportunity to challenge it. The Supreme Court indicated that the exchange's peremptory conduct was not protected by its rule-making power under the Securities Exchange Act of 1934 and consequently constituted a group boycott *per se* violative of the Sherman Act.

In summary, the current status of boycotts or concerted refusals to deal appears quite clear. Recent court decisions have discredited earlier court judgments upholding boycotts actuated by a legitimate business purpose which was not outweighed in social importance by an undue restriction of competition. Only in the most compelling circumstances will courts even consider "special industry facts" in cases involving concerted refusals to deal. And in most of those cases where defendants were successful the decisions were grounded upon the absence of a motivation for group action, that is, that the parallel action was merely conscious parallelism and did not constitute "concert of action" or agreement. In this light, and notwithstanding the action of some lower federal courts in continuing to weigh purpose and effect, the only conclusion is the one recently expressed by a federal district court judge: "Any group boycott or concerted refusal to deal, if in fact not a *per se* violation of the Sherman Act, must, at the very least, be viewed with dark suspicion because of the commercial restraints and tendency toward monopoly inherent in such combinations."

CHAPTER 7

LIMITATIONS ON THE RESALE MARKET

THE means by which firms may attempt to control competition among themselves are many and diverse. One method which has been condemned since the earliest days of the Sherman Act is the horizontal division of markets by geographical restrictions. For example, a group of manufacturers of a product might agree to divide up territories; within each "reserved" territory one manufacturer would be allowed to operate free from competition from other parties to the arrangement. Such an agreement has been held to be a *per se* violation of the Sherman Act. In the example given, the geographical restriction would be a horizontal agreement; that is, an agreement among entrepreneurs in direct competition with each other. These agreements could be found among manufacturers, wholesalers, or retailers. Thus, a wholesaler of pharmaceutical products might agree with another wholesaler that the latter would sell to retail druggists only in state A. The first wholesaler would then agree to sell only in state B. Such a *horizontal* agreement would be clearly *per se* illegal under the antitrust laws.

The reason these agreements are so readily condemned is apparent. The direct result of such an agreement is to stifle competition and restrain trade. Indeed, agreements of this sort rarely have any other purpose than suppression of competition. Within his own "reserved" area a party to such an agreement acquires monopolistic power to manipulate prices and dictate terms of sale. This is especially true if the parties to the illegal agreement control the entire industry or product in question or a substantial portion thereof. In the example of the agreement between the pharmaceutical wholesalers: if they are the only wholesalers in the two-state area, it is apparent that their control over prices and terms of sale will be virtually complete.

A classic example of illegal, horizontal geographical restrictions is found in the early *Addyston Pipe & Steel Company* case. That case, as seen earlier, was also a landmark in the evolution of the rule of reason and the *per se* unreasonableness of price fixing. Addyston Pipe & Steel and other manufacturers of iron pipe formed an association and agreed to divide up the territory in which they operated into "reserved" cities and "pay" territory. "Reserved" cities were alotted to certain members, and within such an area the particular member was allowed to operate free from competition with other members. Provision was made, however, for fictional public bidding by other members at prearranged prices. Within "pay" territories all offers to purchase pipe were submitted to a committee within the association. The committee determined the price and awarded the contract to the member who agreed to pay the largest "bonus," which was divided among the others. In condemning these geographical restrictions, the Supreme Court pointed out that the members of the association entered these "reserved" cities not as competitors but under an agreement whose express purpose was the elimination of competition. The division of markets in this manner was held illegal under both English common law and the Sherman Antitrust Act.

Horizontal division of markets can occur in foreign trade as well as in interstate commerce. It is similarly illegal in this context. Often such market divisions are made under color of arrangements exchanging patent or trademark rights or setting up joint subsidiaries to exploit certain markets. If the real purpose of any arrangement is to divide world markets, however, courts have not been hesitant to hold it illegal. The protective coloration of patent or trademark agreements has offered no defense.

If a manufacturer enters into an agreement with a wholesaler or retailer, such an agreement is *vertical,* not horizontal. The manufacturer and the retailer would normally not be in direct competition with each other, nor would they generally be operating at the same levels in the economy. A manufacturer might agree that he will supply his product to a wholesaler in a certain district and also that he will supply no other in that district. Such an agreement is known as an exclusive franchise. The manufacturer may also require that the wholesaler sell only within a certain territory. The manufacturer would confine other wholesalers with whom he deals to other territories. Such agreements constitute the imposition of *vertical* geographical restrictions. Finally, the manufacturer may require the wholesaler (or retailer) to refrain from selling to certain customers. The latter would normally consist of federal or state agencies to whom the manufacturer sells directly. Such an agreement is known as a customer restriction.

Unlike horizontal geographical restrictions, the status of vertical restrictions of this type has only recently been settled. In March, 1963, the United States Supreme Court was faced with such territorial and customer restrictions in the *White Motor Company* case. The Court noted that the case was the first one it had considered involving a territorial or customer restriction in a *vertical* arrangement and concluded that too little was known of the actual impact of such restrictions to rule that they constituted *per se* violations of the Sherman Act.

Unlike horizontal agreements of this type, the Court said that a vertical agreement may serve a purpose other than the illegitimate one of stifling competition. Manufacturers might argue that by restricting a wholesaler to a certain district, maximum sales are insured within that district, and the wholesaler will not neglect fertile "home" ground for greener pastures elsewhere. Therefore, it was argued, such restrictions would encourage and increase economic output, not restrain trade. Also, these vertical restrictions would stimulate *interband* competition. The wholesaler in a particular district would still be in competition with other wholesalers selling the competitive products of different manufacturers.

Prior to a consideration of the *White Motor Company* case, which gives an excellent illustration of many of the vertical agreements outlined above, a warning is necessary. The courts will not permit form to prevail over substance. For example, a group of powerful wholesalers, desiring to stifle competition among themselves, might force a manufacturer to set up vertical geographical restrictions. Here the manufacturer's principal purpose would not be to achieve optimum sales within each district but simply to placate his wholesaler customers. Such an arrangement is in effect a *horizontal* division of markets among the wholesalers, and is illegal. The wholesalers will not be allowed to do indirectly what they are prohibited from doing directly; that is, agree among themselves to divide up territories. In such circumstances the courts will look through the form of the agreement and strike down the illegal arrangement. This is precisely what the Supreme Court did in its 1967 *Sealy* opinion. The case involved the allocation of territories by the licensor of a trademark to its licensees. Because Sealy, the trademark owner, was managed and controlled by a board of directors composed exclusively of Sealy licensees, the arrangement was as a matter of substance horizontal, not vertical, and thus within the *per se* rule.

In the *White Motor Company* case, decided by a divided Supreme Court, White, a manufacturer and seller of trucks, imposed a territorial restriction upon its distributors and dealers. By this restriction the dealer in question was limited to selling White trucks only in a particular area. If he did sell outside his assigned territory, he would be required to give part or all of his profit to the dealer in whose territory the sale was made. This "profit pass-over" was designed to insure that dealers would assiduously develop their own area; in this way, White maintained, competition with the larger truck manufacturers was preserved and heightened. White also required its dealers to agree not to sell White trucks to certain "national accounts." To these accounts—federal, state, and local governments—White sold directly.

The lower court had ruled that these vertical arrangements between White and its dealers and distributors constituted *per se* violations of the Sherman Act. A majority of the Supreme Court held that White should have been allowed to show the reasonableness and necessity of its program in a full trial on the merits. The majority concluded that not enough was known, without a full presentation of evidence at trial, to justify the conclusion that such vertical agreements were *per se* illegal. Considering the rationale behind *per se* rules, the Court's opinion seems eminently correct. A *per se* rule has been adopted where experience indicates that the tendency or effect of a course of action in restricting competition cannot be offset by any reason advanced in favor of its adoption. Thus, outside of the fair trade exception, any alleged economic or social benefits of price fixing are almost always outweighed by the fact that such a practice severely restricts competition. But this weighing process is necessary *prior* to the adoption of a *per se* condemnation of the practice in question. This is what the Supreme Court had in mind in remanding *White* for a full-fledged rule-of-reason inquiry. Unfortunately, this inquiry was never made in this case, because the case was settled prior to trial.

The next vertical (and customer restriction) case to reach the Supreme Court was the *Schwinn* case, decided in 1967. In that case the government attacked Schwinn's requirement that wholesale distributors sell only in respective territories and only to franchised Schwinn dealers within those territories. Also attacked were requirements that franchised dealers not resell the bicycles to other unfranchised dealers, particularly discount house retailers.

First, the Court said that "special industry facts" were not present which would justify a rule-of-reason approach if vertical restrictions were otherwise held to be within the *per se* category. Schwinn was not a "newcomer seeking to break into or stay in the bicycle business. It was not a failing company." Self-interest, in the sense of maximizing profits, does not invoke the rule of reason so as to immunize otherwise illegal conduct. Next, the Court had no difficulty in invalidating the customer restrictions. Restrictions upon resale are "in the nature of restraints upon alienation," and thus *per se* unreasonable.

Turning to the vertical territorial restrictions, the Court distinguished between such restraints in the sale-for-resale situation and in a consignment or agency distribution system. In the first situation—"where the manufacturer has parted with dominion over the goods—the usual market situation"—the supplier loses all right to "allocate territories for resale and confined access to his product to selected or franchised retailers." Such restrictions are thus within the *per se* category. On the other hand, in the agency situation—where the manufacturer retains "all indicia of ownership, including title, dominion and risk"—the *per se* rule was held inapplicable. In applying a rule of reason to Schwinn's consignment arrangements, the Court found no violation. The Court noted that (1) other competitive bicycles were available to the same retailers and distributors of Schwinn; (2) that in fact Schwinn distributors and retailers had handled other brands of bicycles; (3) that there was yet proved no intermixture of price fixing with the vertical restraints; and (4) that vigorous competition in the industry has required the formation of the challenged program.

The most recent Supreme Court ruling in the area of exclusive territories indicates that even economic survival will not save an otherwise *per se* violation of the antitrust laws. Topco was a cooperative purchasing association through which the twenty-three supermarket chains comprising its membership were able to obtain co-op-labeled goods with which to compete against the private labels of the large national supermarket chains. Each member of the association had an exclusive territory within which to promote and sell the brand products of the association. There is little dispute that the exclusive territories were indispensable to survival of the Topco brands against the private labels of the large supermarket chains. The Supreme Court ruled that the territorial restrictions, as well as limitations on reselling at wholesale, were *per se* violations of Section 1 of the Sherman Act and refused to consider the beneficial effects of the restrictions on competition in facilitating competition by small and medium supermarket chains against the large supermarket chains. The members of the majority recognized the competitive anomalies of their decision, but stated that only Congress could alter the dictates of the antitrust laws, as the Court felt constrained to apply them. Chief Justice Burger dissented, suggesting that the Court had abdicated its role in reviewing antitrust cases, a role which he said is never easy but necessary to fulfill.

In summary, then, horizontal geographical restrictions effecting division of markets have long been considered *per se* unreasonable under the Sherman Act. Since *Schwinn,* both customer restrictions and *vertical* territorial arrangements in the sale for resale situation are also within the *per se* category. *Vertical* arrangements in the agency situation are judged by the rule of reason.

CHAPTER 8

EXCLUSIVE DEALING AND TIE-IN ARRANGEMENTS

ALL manufacturers naturally desire to maximize the sales of their goods, and any aid to this end is willingly embraced. Early in the twentieth century several devices were developed to achieve just this purpose. One of these devices, the tie-in sale, utilized the market power of one product to increase the market power of another product. For example, a manufacturer of salt might develop a machine for the processing of salt which is more desirable than any comparable machine. If the machine is sold or leased only on the condition that the user purchase all his salt from the manufacture, a tie-in sale has taken place. The market strength of the manufacturer's salt, the tied product, is thereby raised to the market strength of the processing machine, the tying product. By another device designed to achieve maximum distribution, the manufacturer tries to insulate his customers from his competitors, thus leaving himself free to devote his sales efforts elsewhere. A common example of such a scheme is a contract by which the manufacturer agrees to sell his product only on the condition that the retailer purchaser not deal in the competitive goods of other manufacturers or that he purchase all his requirements of the particular commodity from that manufacturer.

These restrictive methods of distribution can be attacked under Section 1 of the Sherman Act as unreasonable restraints of trade. Initially, of course, proof would be required that the distribution program had had serious anticompetitive effects. In the case of the tie-in sale such proof would be fairly easy to make. The manufacturer's competitors would be denied customers not on the basis of the competitive merit of their product but simply because of their inability to offer their customers the particular inducement available from the offending manufacturer. In the situation involving the salt-processing machine this inability might lead to a virtual monopoly by the tying manufacturer. In the case of exclusive dealing and requirements contracts adverse competitive effects might be shown by the number of customers to whom competitors could not sell. For example, if 40 per cent of the customers for a certain commodity were bound to deal with only one manufacturer, competition between that manufacturer and others could take place only in the remaining 60 per cent of the market. The existence of such market rigidity could well have the effect of stifling competition. The likelihood of such a result would increase with the duration of the contract. Plainly, a twenty-year requirements contract will have a serious effect on competitors. Not only will it prevent sales by competitors for twenty years, but it will also create a relationship between buyer and seller that will be difficult to sever even at the termination of the contract. Short-term requirements contracts, on the other hand, will have a substantially smaller effect on competitive conditions.

Although these distribution arrangements could be prosecuted under Section 1 of the Sherman Act, as today they often are, earlier courts were reluctant to find them illegal. This judicial reluctance in the face of a showing of deleterious effects on competition caused immediate concern in Congress. This concern was translated in 1914 into Section 3 of the Clayton Act, a statute designed specifically to deal with these distribution devices and the market rigidity resulting from them. Section 5 of the Federal Trade Commission Act, also enacted in 1914, likewise encompasses such restraints, because anything that is a violation of the Sherman or Clayton Acts is also an "unfair method of competition" for purposes of Section 5. Section 3 of Clayton is so brief that it cannot profitably be summarized. It reads:

> That it shall be unlawful for any person engaged in commerce, in the course of such commerce, to lease or make a sale or contract for sale of goods, wares, merchandise, machinery, supplies, or other commodities, whether patented or unpatented, for use, consumption or resale within the United States or any Territory therof or the District of Columbia or any insular possession or other place under the jurisdiction of the United States, or fix a price charged therefor, or discount from, or rebate upon, such price, on the condition, agreement, or understanding that the lessee or purchaser thereof shall not use or deal in the goods, wares, merchandise, machinery, supplies, or other commodities of a competitor or competitors of the lessor or seller, where the effect of such lease, sale, or contract for sale or such condition, agreement, or understanding may be to substantially lessen competition or tend to create a monopoly in any line of commerce.

Unlike the broad proscriptions of Section 1 of the Sherman Act against unreasonable restraints of trade, this statute deals with a particular activity only. Because it is purposely specific, a great many technical problems are raised concerning the kind of conduct prohibited by the statute. Such conduct cannot be identified in terms of anticompetitive effect alone but must be defined by analysis of the statute's wording and purpose. It is to this problem that we now turn.

Initially, of course, reference must be made to interstate commerce. To fall within the ambit of the statute, a seller or lessor must be engaged in interstate commerce. As we noted in Chapter 3, the superficial significance of this requirement is in fact misleading. For example, courts have found a person to be engaged in interstate commerce though he makes no interstate sales but merely purchases in interstate commerce. Additionally, however, the statute requires the forbidden lease or sale to be "in the course of such commerce." This provision would appear to save a wholly intrastate sale from the taint of illegality under Section 3. This appearance is deceptive, however, as the courts have long felt free to invalidate intrastate sales having a substantial effect on interstate commerce.

The statute is also limited to sales, contracts of sale, and leases of goods "for use, consumption or resale" within the United States and places under its jurisdiction. This provision would seem to exclude sales by American enterprises in foreign commerce. A significant portion of United States trade is thereby beyond the reach of Section 3. Such foreign sales may be the subject of an action under Section 1 of the Sherman Act, however.

Section 3 deals only with sales or leases of commodities. Sales of services are outside the prohibitions of the statute. This exclusion has prevented attack under this section on conditions in sales of land, newspaper advertising space, unusual credit arrangements and commercial television time. But such sales can be and have been attacked under Section 1 of the Sherman Act, as well as Section 5 of the FTC Act. Also excluded by the commodity requirement are the loans of money.

Another technical prerequisite to the applicability of Section 3 is that the transaction be one of lease or sale. In an early case the Supreme Court held that a publishing company's requirement that its distributors refrain from dealing in competitors' publications did not violate Section 3 because these distributors were agents of the company who did not purchase the publications. This decision would appear to permit a company to avoid the provisions of Section 3 by use of a consignment method of distribution. Two warnings, however, should be added to this initial conclusion. First, a consignment or agency arrangement must in fact involve consignment or agency and not be merely a label to evade the statutory proscription. For example, if the consignment contract provided that the consignee would bear the risk of loss on the goods, rather than having the consignor bear this burden as is normally the case, a court might find the arrangement to be one of sale and not of consignment. Second, although a consignment contract is insulated from the prohibitions of Section 3, it is still subject to attack under other antitrust provisions. In a leading Supreme Court case the defense of agency was rejected as inapplicable to the finding that certain exclusive dealing contracts were illegal under Section 5 of the Federal Trade Commission Act.

By its terms Section 3 applies only to sales or leases on the condition, agreement, or understanding that the lessee or purchaser will "not use or deal in the goods" of a competitor or competitors of the lessor or seller. In a series of cases brought by the Federal Trade Commission, the Supreme Court held that where various national refiners of gasoline used "economic coercion" to push sales to their distributors of the tires, batteries, and accessories (TBA) of particular manufacturers of those items, a violation of Section 5 had occurred. The refiners received a commission on sales made by their distributors from the TBA manufacturers. Such actions could not have been brought under Section 3 of Clayton because the refiners did not manufacture tires, batteries, and accessories, and therefore were not conditioning their arrangements with distributors upon the latter's not dealing in goods of competitors of the refiners.

The language *will not use or deal in the goods* of a competitor or competitors also raises other problems. Initially, it would appear to require that the agreement absolutely preclude the purchaser from using any of another manufacturer's competing goods. What, then, of the tie-in agreement that the purchaser will use only the manufacturer's salt in the salt-processing machine? On its face, this agrement does not prevent the purchaser from using a competitor's salt except in the processing machine. If Section 3 were read literally, the arrangement would be beyond its reach. But the courts have not given the statute such a literal reading. The tie-in arrangement just mentioned was held illegal under Section 3 because, to the extent that it requires the purchaser to obtain his salt from the manufacturer, it precludes him from using or dealing in the salt of a competitor.

But this interpretation poses just as many problems as it solves. Resting as it does on the recognition that in practice such an agreement will prevent purchases from competitors, it makes every lease, sale, or contract for sale suspect under Section 3. A contract for the sale of 10,000 tons of salt might violate this section because, to the extent that 10,000 tons fulfills the purchaser's needs, its practical effect is to prevent the purchaser from obtaining this salt elsewhere. In short, a purchaser can use only a certain amount of salt. If he buys it from one manufacturer, he will not buy it from another. The effect of any sale, then, is to deprive a competitor of business.

What saves Section 3 from the absurd result of making every sale illegal is its further requirement that the effect of the condition, agreement, or understanding "may be to substantially lessen competition or tend to create a monopoly in any line of commerce." Only those arrangements which in practice may produce serious anticompetitive effects are forbidden. It is important to note the use of the word *may*. A finding of illegality under Section 3 as well as Section 5 of the FTC Act, unlike Section 1 of the Sherman Act, does not require evidence of actual adverse effects on the competitive structure. It requires only that such effects be *probable* if the particular arrangement is allowed to continue.

To test whether any agreement might have the forbidden effects, it is first necessary to determine where that test will be made. Section 3 states that the effects must occur in "any line of commerce." As interpreted by the courts this requirement means that the proscribed result must occur in both a product market and a geographic market. Normally, the product market will be defined as the commodity affected by the arrangement. In the example we have been using the product market is salt. The geographic market is framed in terms of the area in which sellers might compete for sales to the particular purchaser involved in the arrangement.

The 1961 opinion in the landmark case of *Tampa Electric Company* v. *Nashville Coal Company* is an excellent example of the application of these concepts in an involved situation. Tampa decided to erect an electrical generating plant in Florida. This plant was to utilize coal as boiler fuel. In order to insure an adequate coal supply, Tampa contracted to purchase all its coal requirements for twenty years from a company located in the principal coal mining region of the United States. Subsequently, this coal mining company decided not to fulfill the contract. When sued for breach of contract, it defended on the ground that the contract was illegal under Section 3 of the Clayton Act.

At trial Tampa contended that the product market in question was all boiler fuels and not just coal. This argument was based on the fact that all other Florida generating plants used oil as a boiler fuel and on the possibility that the new generating station might use oil in the future. Both the district court and the court of appeals rejected this contention. The future use of oil was rejected as remote, and coal was considered sufficiently distinct to be a separate product market. This finding was not reviewed by the Supreme Court.

The lower courts found peninsular Florida to be the relevant geographic market. Coupled with the ruling on product market, this finding meant that the contract affected over 30 per cent of the coal sold annually in the relevant market. This percentage and its projected continuance for twenty years almost compelled a finding that the contract had the probable effect of substantially lessening competition.

We should note carefully the importance of determining the relevant product and geographic markets. If Tampa had prevailed either on the contention that the product market should be both oil and coal or on the contention that the geographic market should be much larger, the percentage of those broader markets accounted for by the coal involved in the contract would have dropped precipitately. The likelihood of a finding of illegality would have decreased correspondingly. One of the key battlefields in Section 3 litigation is the establishment of the relevant market. The defendant usually seeks to broaden the markets; the government or the plaintiff, to narrow them.

When the *Tampa Electric* case reached the Supreme Court, it generated intense interest among antitrust lawyers, and significant rulings were expected. The antitrust bar was not disappointed when the decision was announced. Observing that the narrower the geographic market, "the greater the comparative effect" the contract would have "on the area's competitors," the Supreme Court held that the lower courts had totally misconceived the process of market definition.

The Supreme Court stated that the geographic market should be framed on the basis of the area in which coal mining companies able to sell to Tampa were located. As the purpose of Section 3 is to enhance competition among sellers by preventing any one seller from tying up a substantial part of the market, definition of the geographic market requires delineation of the "area of effective competition" among these sellers. In the *Tampa* case this was held to be the Appalachian coal district, for this was the area in which were located other sellers who were precluded by the contract from selling to Tampa. In short, when market definition is concerned, the focus is on the area in which are located competitors of the seller for this buyer's business.

The change in the defined market in the *Tampa* case resulted in a decrease in the market share affected by the contract from over 30 per cent to less than 1 per cent. This, the Supreme Court said, was, "conservatively speaking, quite insubstantial." Accordingly, the finding of the lower courts that the contract was illegal was reversed.

In reaching its conclusion, the Supreme Court laid down rules for determining whether an arrangement would have the probable effect of substantially lessening competition or tending to create a monopoly. As stated by Mr. Justice Clark:

> To determine substantiality in a given case, it is necessary to weigh the probable effect of the contract on the relevant area of effective competition, taking into account the relative strength of the parties, the proportionate volume of commerce involved in relation to the total volume of commerce in the relevant market area, and the probable immediate and future effects which pre-emption of that share of the market might have on effective competition therein. It follows that a mere showing that the contract itself involves a substantial number of dollars is ordinarily of little consequence.

In applying these considerations to the facts in the *Tampa* case, the Supreme Court noted that the particular contract under attack was an entirely reasonable method of meeting business needs. Tampa was seeking to insure an adequate supply of coal at a predictable cost to avoid the possibility of having to shut down its generating plant or, alternatively, of having to make frequent changes in its prices as coal prices fluctuated.

This willingness by the Supreme Court to apply the rule of reason to requirements contracts provides an important antitrust lesson. Section 3 itself contains no indication that its proscriptions are to be modified by appeals to business necessity and the reasonableness of certain business practices. Courts, however, have frequently considered these factors, though not in a manner designed to aid predictability. Put briefly, if exclusive dealing arrangements are motivated by a legitimate business goal, and if they go no further than necessary to achieve that goal, a court may find them legal. Such legality is usually found by deciding that the arrangements do not have the probable effect of substantially lessening competition.

This unspoken judicial recognition of the rule of reason is most evident in the way the standards of reason are applied to the business arrangements forbidden by Section 3. As we shall see, a tie-in sale is far more likely to be held illegal than a requirements contract or an exclusive dealing arrangement. The explanation for this is to be found in the general absence of any compelling business justification for a tie-in sale, whereas such justification is sometimes present with respect to the other arrangements. It is to the specific treatment of such arrangements that we now turn.

Exclusive Dealing Arrangements

Exclusive dealing arrangements often arise in connection with franchising. Examples are easy to imagine: the Ford Motor Company might require its dealers to sell only Ford cars; Revlon might permit a drug or department store to carry its cosmetics only on the condition that no competing lines were carried; or the Dairy Queen soft ice cream company might restrict its franchisees to handling only its product. Standing alone, these arrangements would violate Section 3 if they have the probable effect of substantially lessening competition. Any arrangement that requires a dealer to handle the products of only one manufacturer is almost certain to violate Section 3. A reasonable business justification for such a sweeping prohibition can rarely be found. Less extreme restraints on a dealer's freedom to handle competing goods, though equally illegal under the express terms of Section 3, may be upheld when reasonable in light of business conditions.

Despite the theoretical possibility of saving a limited exclusive dealing arrangement by resort to the rule of reason, such salvation is unlikely in practice. Normally, businessmen enter these arrangements only for the unjustified purpose of preventing competitors from reaching the market. However, here is an example of a situation that might survive an attack under Section 3. Imagine a manufacturer of expensive glass products who desired to set up a chain of stores, bearing his name, devoted to selling such merchandise. It is conceivable that he might be able to prohibit these dealers from carrying inexpensive glass products. The business justification for such an arrangement would be that if a manufacturer has devoted his time and money to developing a series of prestige stores, he should not be required to allow his dealers to cheapen the stores, and thereby his product, by carrying a wide assortment of inexpensive merchandise. A court *might* permit an arrangement of this sort if it did not limit the dealer in any way except insofar as necessary to preserve the manufacturer's legitimate interest in maintaining his good will. Another possibility is that a trademark owner in the franchise business may require his francisees to use only his ingredients—that is, to preserve quality control—so as to protect the integrity of the trademark. Once an arrangement goes beyond what is clearly necessary for quality control, however, a finding of illegality is probable, given the proscribed result.

The test of whether an exclusive dealing arrangement is likely to lessen competition substantially is usually made first in terms of the percentage of the relevant geographic and product markets affected by the arrangement. Any exclusive dealing system involving more than 5 per cent of the market, though not necessarily illegal, is immediately suspect. Arrangements affecting a lower percentage of the market may also be attacked. Here, however, business justifications and the other considerations enunciated in the *Tampa* decision may save the contracts from the taint of illegality. The obvious moral remains: no exclusive dealing arrangement involving more than a minimal part of the market can be safely undertaken.

A contract between a manufacturer or distributor and a dealer by which the latter agrees to purchase all of his requirements of a certain commodity from the former is in reality nothing more than an exclusive dealing arrangement and is treated as such. Requirements contracts deserve separate treatment, however, when they are between a manufacturer and one who purchases for use rather than for resale. This distinction is not due to any difference in the application of Section 3. It relates solely to the business justifications for the contract. The Supreme Court has noted:

> Requirements contracts, on the other hand, may well be of economic advantage to buyers as well as to sellers, and thus indirectly of advantage to the consuming public. In the case of the buyer, they may assure supply, afford protection against rises in price, enable long-term planning on the basis of known costs, and obviate the expense and risk of storage in the quantity necessary for a commodity having a fluctuating demand. From the seller's point of view, requirements contracts may make possible the substantial reduction of selling expenses, give protection against price fluctuations, and—of particular advantage to a newcomer to the field to whom it is important to know what capital expenditures are justified—offer the possibility of a predictable market.

In this very case, however, the Court went on to hold that once a probable substantial lessening of competition has been shown, these business justifications will not prevent the contracts from being held illegal. Notwithstanding this declaration, the courts have treated requirements contracts more gently than other forms of exclusive dealing, usually by asking for stronger proof of the proscribed effect. This relatively lenient treatment of such contracts should not be taken, however, as a license to use them. They are still extremely dangerous.

A variant of exclusive arrangements beginning to be litigated in the courts is "reciprocal dealing," that is, one manufacturer says to another, I'll buy item X from you (which item I do not produce) if you'll buy item Y from me (which item you do not produce). Although such an arrangement is not cognizable under Section 3—because of the "not use or deal in the goods of a competitor" language of Section 3 discussed above—it may constitute a conspiracy in restraint of trade under Section 1 of Sherman or an "unfair method of competition" under Section 5 of the Federal Trade Commission Act. Potential reciprocity between acquiring and acquired firms has also been held to constitute evidence of a probability of a lessening of competition and thus grounds for invalidating mergers under Section 7 of Clayton.

At the date of this writing, reciprocal dealing arrangements are not *per se* violations of the antitrust laws. Rather, the rule of reason is employed to test their legality, and in this analysis the same market considerations examined earlier with regard to exclusive dealing arrangements in general—that is, the amount of market foreclosure involved in the arrangement—test the legality of the reciprocity.

Tie-In Sales

By far the most harshly treated method of distribution forbidden by Section 3 is the tie-in sale. Indeed, the Supreme Court has stated that such sales "serve hardly any purpose beyond the suppression of competition." Or, as stated in another case: "They deny competitors free access to the market for the tied product, not because the party imposing the tying requirements has a better product or a lower price but because of his power or leverage in another market."

As we noted earlier, a tie-in sale takes place when a party refuses to sell one item—the tying product—unless the purchaser also agrees to take another distinct item—the tied product. But what of an arrangement whereby two distinct products are sold together for a price lower than their combined individual prices? For example, suppose a manufacturer of a particularly desirable piece of shoe machinery agrees to lease it to anyone for $2,000 a year. Suppose also that another type of shoe machinery, one in which this manufacturer has many competitors, can be leased for $1,000 a year. Then suppose that the manufacturer agrees to lease both machines for $2,500 a year. Will an illegal tie-in sale result? The answer to this question is not entirely clear, but if the manufacturer's tying machine is *required* by purchasers, a grave risk of illegality is created. Whether an alternative, nontying arrangement is offered may be immaterial if practical economies demand that the tie-in sale be accepted. Accordingly, such arrangements should be used sparingly, if at all.

Although as a rule Section 3 of the Clayton Act and Section 1 of the Sherman Act have substantially different tests of legality—the former being based on possible anticompetitive effects, the latter on actual effects —this difference may no longer exist in the field of tie-in sales. As late as 1953 the Supreme Court stated the tests for the two sections in this manner:

> When the seller enjoys a monopolistic position in the market for the "tying" product, *or* if a substantial volume of commerce in the "tied" product is restrained, a tying arrangement violates the narrower standards expressed in §3 of the Clayton Act because from either factor the requisite potential lessening of competition is inferred. And because for even a lawful monopolist it is "unreasonable, per se, to foreclose competitors from any substantial market, a tying arrangement is banned by §1 of the Sherman Act whenever both conditions are met.

The Court went on to rephrase these tests in terms of the dominance of the tying product in the marketplace and the necessity that a not "insignificant or insubstantial" amount of commerce in the tied product be thereby affected. The Supreme Court's recent *Fortner* opinion added that for Section 1 purposes the amount of commerce involved in the tying product market need not be substantial in a qualitative sense—that is, percentage share of the market—but must only be "not insubstantial" in a quantitative sense—that is, dollar amount. This case said that $200,000 per year in the business involved was "not insubstantial."

Vague as the 1953 test appeared to be, it was in fact fairly workable. The dominance of the tying product might be shown by the percentage of the market controlled by that product. Alternatively, dominance was sometimes presumed from the fact that the tying product was patented, copyrighted, or in some other manner shown to be unique. That a not insignificant or insubstantial amount of commerce was involved could be deduced from the dollar amount of commerce affected by the contracts. Though these tests were not precise, they were workable, and it was safe to conclude, at least until *Fortner,* that only fairly substantial tie-ins could be reached under either statute.

A 1958 Supreme Court opinion seemed to change the law in this area and to make the substantive test for legality the same under both Section 3 and Section 1. The Court held that Section 1 was violated if a party had "sufficient economic power with respect to the tying product to appreciably restrain free competition in the market for the tied product and [if] a 'not insubstantial' amount of interstate commerce" was affected. The Court went on to suggest that in the absence of some other explanation, the fact that tying arrangements existed was itself "compelling" evidence of the possession of sufficient economic power to restrain competition appreciably. Carried to its extreme, this rationale would imply that any tie-in sale affecting a not insubstantial amount of commerce would be illegal. And it is this thought that has caused courts and commentators to recognize tie-in sales as a *per se* violation of the antitrust laws.

A subsequent case illustrates these points. In some instances, Loew's, Inc., would license local stations to show old movies on television only on the condition that the stations purchase a whole block of movies. Loew's would reject any requests by a local station to purchase only certain films contained in a package deal. The Supreme Court held these block booking arrangements to be illegal tie-in sales. "Sufficient economic power with respect to the tying product to appreciably restrain free competition in the market for the tied product" was presumed from the uniqueness of each film, a uniqueness attested to both by its copyright and, in the case of popular films, by the high consumer demand for it. The dollar amount of the illegal contracts was held to establish that a not insubstantial amount of commerce was involved. The Court summarily rejected a justification of business necessity offered by one of the defendants. In all aspects of the Court's opinion a *per se* approach was obvious.

This refusal to modify the tests of legality by reference to business justifications is in part the result of listening to a number of poor justifications for tie-in sales. For example, in a famous antitrust case IBM was charged with violating Section 3 by leasing certain of its machines only on the condition that the lessee use IBM punch cards in the operation of the leased machines. IBM attempted to defend this naked tie-in by arguing that such a restriction was necessary to protect its goodwill. The use of other cards, IBM contended, would prevent the leased machine from functioning properly and thus would reflect adversely on IBM. The Supreme Court summarily rejected this purported justification and stated that if IBM cards were indeed better for this purpose, buyers, by the laws of the marketplace, would naturally purchase them. Further, the Court suggested that IBM might legally proclaim the virtues of its own cards, explain the dangers of using other cards, or even condition the lease on using cards that conformed to the necessary specifications. As the Court then said: "For aught that appears such measures would protect its good will, without the creation of monopoly or resort to the suppression of competition."

Several cases have modified to some extent the *per se* approach to tie-in arrangements. In these cases business justifications, such as quality control, have been accepted to protect a tie-in arrangement from being found illegal. These cases have involved unusual situations, however, and their value as precedent is open to question. Although legitimate business needs may justify a tie-in arrangement, careful analysis of the proposed system by antitrust counsel is advisable before any tie-in method of distribution is utilized. For general purposes, the proposition to remember is that tie-in sales are *per se* illegal and should be scrupulously avoided.

A variant of the classic tie-in, one that occurs most frequently in a franchising context, is known as "full-line forcing." An automobile company, for example, might require as a condition to the grant of a dealership that the dealer carry a full line of its cars and parts for its cars. This conduct has rarely been challenged, and the reason for this reluctant enforcement is not hard to find. Sound business reasons often justify such arrangements. A manufacturer who grants a dealership becomes associated with the dealer in the public mind. Maintenance of the manufacturer's goodwill dictates that the dealer carry a full line of parts. The manufacturer has a legitimate interest in seeing that if his product is repaired at his dealer's establishment, those parts best suited to the job are used. Even though certain full-line forcing arrangements have been upheld, however, great care should be taken to insure that the terms of any such arrangement go no further than necessary to protect the legitimate business interests of the manufacturer.

Conduct proscribed under Section 3 of the Clayton Act may also be attacked under Section 1 of the Sherman Act. In the case of tie-in sales, as we noted, virtually the same test of legality now applies under both statutes, that is, power in the tying product and a not insubstantial amount of commerce affected in the tied product. With respect to exclusive dealing arrangements and requirements contracts, however, Section 1 is violated only if substantial anticompetitive effects have resulted. Notwithstanding this higher burden of proof, Section 1 may still be utilized for exclusive dealing arrangements that cannot be reached under Section 3. For example, under Section 1 of the Sherman Act or Section 5 of the Federal Trade Commission Act there is no requirement that the arrangement involve a sale or lease of a commodity. Therefore, sales of services or consignment arrangements can be attacked under these sections. Exclusive dealing systems used in foreign commerce may also be attacked. Finally, exclusive dealing arrangements forced on sellers can be reached under these sections. For example, a group of vending machine operators once forced Hershey Chocolate, by threat of boycott, to sell only to them and not to their competitors. This reverse exclusive dealing arrangement was found to violate Section 1 of the Sherman Act.

Briefly summarizing: several methods of distribution designed to restrict a competitor's opportunity to sell to certain customers are expressly prohibited by Section 3 of the Clayton Act. Although theoretically the tests of legality for every method should be the same, a significant distinction has been made in practice between tie-in sales on the one hand and exclusive dealing arrangements and requirements contracts on the other. The latter are violative of Section 3 only if their probable effect in the relevant market is to lessen competition substantially or to tend to monopoly. Courts have indicated that a detailed economic analysis is necessary to determine if the proscribed result is present. Tie-in sales, however, because of the usual absence of any purpose other than suppression of competition, violate both Section 3 of the Clayton Act and Section 1 of the Sherman Act, as well as Section 5 of the FTC Act, if they affect a not insubstantial amount of commerce in the tied product.

The nature of the rules applicable to arrangements forbidden by Section 3 makes it clear that their utilization is quite risky. Before any company undertakes a distribution program involving their use, the advice of competent antitrust counsel should be obtained. A finding of illegality will subject a company to the risk of many private treble-damage actions. Moreover, the public image of a company found to be operating in violation of the antitrust laws is likely to be seriously impaired. These risks compel the conclusion that tie-in sales and exclusive dealing arrangements should be avoided if at all possible.

CHAPTER 9

THE ROBINSON-PATMAN ACT: THE FEDERAL PRICE DISCRIMINATION LAW

History and Purpose of the Act

Thinking back, we recall that the Depression era gave rise to an abundance of Congressional legislation affecting trade. Security transactions, labor, and banking are but examples of areas in which Congress enacted extensive regulatory legislation. Among the measures passed during this period was the National Industrial Recovery Act, with its Codes of Fair Competition. When this Act was held unconstitutional in 1935, many interest groups thought a void had been left. This void was coupled with a concern in Congress over the power wielded by large buying groups; specifically, the chain grocery stores.

Extensive investigation had shown that chain grocery stores were able to secure favored pricing treatment from suppliers by virtue of their large-volume purchases. Price reductions to chain stores were reflected in a lower retail price to the consumer. The independent grocery stores were thus placed in an unfavorable competitive position. In the marketplace the consumer naturally turned to the lower-priced goods—sold by the chain stores.

The future of the independents was considered to be in grave danger, in view of their inability to compete with the large chain stores. There was broad public support for legislation which would compel suppliers to treat all buyers on a fair and equal basis in order that the small independents would not be prejudiced by their lack of purchasing power. This was the nature of the price discrimination which the Robinson-Patman Act sought to remedy. Paradoxically, the 1936 act ended up as a series of restrictions placed primarily on the seller rather than on the buyer, although it was the buyer's purchasing power which was of paramount concern to Congress. The Act does have provisions preventing a buyer from knowingly receiving an unlawful price discrimination, but the unlawful use of a buyer's purchasing power is generally curbed in a "backdoor" fashion by prohibiting the seller from giving unlawful price discriminations to buyers.

The Robinson-Patman Act is sometimes praised, sometimes abused, much interpreted, little understood, and capable of producing instant arguments of infinite variety. In many business quarters the very name is an anathema. There can be little doubt that the Robinson-Patman Act is controversial and complex. Two justices of the Supreme Court once stated that it was a "singularly opaque and illusive statute." Mr. Justice Frankfurter once said that "precision of expression is not an outstanding characteristic of this Act." These judgments are probably correct. Nevertheless, a clear interpretation of the Act is a necessity in view of the subtle problems arising daily from the multitude of diverse situations present in the business world. If we did not have a Robinson-Patman Act, however, it would be necessary to invent one. The imperviousness of the Act to amendment is a significant indication that it was and is a response to a definite need. Therefore, however much we may decry the law's defects, we must recognize that a broad consensus supports its two primary objects:

1. To prevent unscrupulous suppliers from attempting to gain an unfair advantage over their competitors by discriminating among buyers.
2. To prevent unscrupulous buyers from using their economic power to exact discriminatory prices from suppliers to the disadvantage of less powerful buyers.

Summary of the Act

Section 2 of the Robinson-Patman Act is an amendment to Section 2 of the Clayton Act and is divided into six parts. Section 2 of the Robinson-Patman Act imposes civil prohibitions, whereas Section 3, which is not a part of the Clayton Act, contains criminal prohibitions.

Section 2(a) is the heart of the Act. It prohibits sellers from discriminating in price. The section also provides a defense when an otherwise unlawful price discrimination can be cost-justified by the seller, and other limited defenses and exceptions.

Section 2(b) is related to 2(a) and sets forth burdens of proof in defending a violation. Section 2(b) also provides that a price discrimination is not unlawful if it is made in good faith to meet the equally low price of a competitor. That a lower price was made to meet competition is a complete defense to a Section 2(a) violation.

Section 2(c) is a self-contained section prohibiting the seller from paying any brokerage fee, commission, or an equivalent to a buyer or the buyer's agent. Section 2(c) also prohibits a buyer from accepting any such brokerage fee or commission.

Sections 2(d) and 2(e) are closely related sections which prohibit a seller from granting discriminatory allowances [2(d)] and services and facilities [2(e)] to a buyer unless such assistance is made available to other competing buyers on proportionally equal terms.

Section 2(f) is the section of the Act which deals with buyers who knowingly receive price discriminations declared unlawful in Section 2(a). Remembering again the Congressional concern over the purchasing power wielded by large buyers to exact price discriminations, Section 2(f) is designed to deal directly with such buyers.

Section 3, which is not a part of the Clayton Act, declares it unlawful for a seller to provide certain secret allowances to the buyer. It also forbids territorial price reductions or sales at unreasonably low prices where the seller's purpose is to destroy competition or to eliminate a competitor.

Price Discrimination Practices by the Seller: Section 2(a)

We will first consider what sellers are within the reach of Section 2(a). In lawyerlike language, we will first consider the "jurisdictional elements" —those conditions which will invoke the power of the Federal Trade Commission or the courts to consider the lawfulness of the pricing transactions. Next we will define what is a discrimination in price, and we will then consider the competitive effects necessary to give rise to a completed violation of Section 2(a) by a seller.

What Sellers Can Be Reached Under 2(a)?

Turning first to the *commerce* requirements, Section 2(a) begins: "That it shall be unlawful for any person engaged in commerce, in the course of such commerce . . . ." If a seller, such as a corporation, is engaged in purely local commerce within one state, the prohibitions of the Act do not apply. It should be mentioned, however, that many states have comparable acts which can regulate local pricing activities. Also, by contrast, the scope of control is more limited here than in the Sherman Act, under which intrastate activities affecting interstate commerce can be reached. If a local seller in Illinois unlawfully discriminates between his two Chicago buyers, for example, the Act does not apply. But if this seller discriminates between a Chicago buyer and a competing St. Louis buyer, the commerce requirement of the Act is satisfied: a state line has been crossed in the transaction.

In a famous case involving *Standard Oil* the Supreme Court had to interpret this commerce requirement. Gasoline was shipped from Whiting, Indiana, to bulk storage tanks near Detroit, Michigan. The government charged certain unlawful discriminatory practices which took place in the distribution of the gasoline from these storage tanks to local Detroit buyers. The defendant sellers in this suit said, in effect: "You cannot charge any Section 2(a) violation because these Detroit practices are not in commerce—every act charged as unlawful took place entirely in Michigan." The Supreme Court rejected this argument and concluded that the practices all took place in the flow of commerce from Whiting, Indiana, to the Detroit area buyers. The interstate character of the acts was not lost by storing the gasoline in Detroit.

Price discrimination by a United States seller in foreign commerce is not covered by the Act; thus, if a seller in the United States discriminates unlawfully between foreign buyers, the transaction cannot be reached. The Act is, however, applicable to transactions in the import trade. If a foreign seller discriminates between competing American purchasers, it may be difficult as a practical matter to reach the seller because he cannot be served abroad with service of process. But if he is "found" within the United States through the presence of a domestic agent or controlled subsidiary, service of process and federal jurisdiction may be effected on the foreign seller for purposes of enforcing the statute.

Next, there is the requirement that the *same seller make at least two sales to different purchasers, reasonably close in point of time.* A sale to one buyer and an outright refusal to sell to another cannot come under Section 2(a). Similarly, a sale to one buyer and a consignment to another cannot be reached under Section 2(a).

The requirement for reasonably contemporaneous sales affords protection to the seller and prevents any "freezing" of pricing practices over long periods of time. Of course, individual situations in particular industries will determine what are contemporaneous sales under the law. A two-month difference between two sales might not be reached under Section 2(a) in one industry, whereas an even longer period between sales might be reached in another industry. Inventory turnover, fluctuation of prices in the marketplace, and other factors are considered in determining if this time requirement has been satisfied; no rule of thumb exists.

The requirement that the *same seller* make these sales raises interesting questions when a parent corporation makes one of the sales while a wholly owned subsidiary makes the other. Under these circumstances the courts appraise the degree of control exercised by the parent corporation over its subsidiary to determine if the latter is but a "tool" of the former. If the subsidary acts independently and without direction by its parent, it may be considered a separate seller, and differing prices for the same commodity between parent and subsidiary would not be illegal price discriminations.

Another legal invention—the doctrine of the "indirect purchaser"—has been developed over the years to determine who are the actual purchasers to whom the sales are made. Suppose Manufacture *M* sells to Wholesaler *W*, who in turn sells to Retailers R_1 and R_2. Suppose further that Manufacture *M*, not Wholesaler *W*, really controls sales to R_1 and R_2. Such control might occur by having *M's* salesman call on R_1 and R_2, take the order, and then refer it to *W*. Although it would appear that *M* has made only one sale, that being to W, a court might hold that R_1 and R_2 were indirect purchasers from *M* because of *M*'s activity in obtaining these retailers as customers. If different prices were charged R_1 and R_2, an illegal price discrimination may have taken place.

In its 1968 *Fred Meyer* decision, the Supreme Court found such liability on the basis of a redefinition of "purchaser" rather than the indirect purchaser doctrine. By defining *customer* to include "retailers who purchase through wholesalers and compete with direct buyers in resales," an important loophole in the statute was closed.

Now we turn to the requirement that the sales be of *commodities.* This means goods, not services. For example, the Act would not reach a consulting engineering firm which charged different rates for engineering services to different companies. Such a contract would be for the sale of services, not for the sale of goods. Radio or TV broadcasting time is another example of a service. Only tangible goods in the conventional sense are embraced by the term *commodities.* Service discriminations may, however, be illegal as "unfair methods of competition" under Section 5 of the Federal Trade Commission Act.

And these commodities must be of *like grade and quality.* When identical goods are sold, this requisite is of course satisfied. But how much difference between similar commodities will allow an "escape hatch" from a Section 2(a) charge of price discrimination? It has been held that a price discrimination in the sale of identical goods between those sold under a private brand label and those sold under a prominent trademark is embraced by Section 2(a). On the other hand, minute physical differences, strangely enough, have caused some courts to rule the transaction beyond the reach of Section 2(a). The better view seems to be, however, that such small differences will not prevent goods from being of "like grade and quality." For instance, sales of X hydrometer and Y hydrometer (of identical physical construction) were reached under Section 2(a), as were sales of cans $3\frac{14}{16}$ inches and $3\frac{12}{16}$ inches high. The Attorney General's Committee to Study the Antitrust Laws aptly summarized the current rule in these terms: "Actual or genuine physical differentiations between two different products adapted to the several buyers' uses, and not merely a decorative or fanciful feature, probably remove differential pricing of the two from the reach of the Robinson-Patman Act."

Judicial refusal to recognize brand names and trademark differences in considering like grade and quality is not completely consistent with marketing realities. Marketing executives well appreciate that two identical products standing side by side on a shelf will not sell alike where only one is a widely advertised national brand. Hypothetically, Coca-Cola will sell better than Sparkle Cola in the marketplace, even if they are of identical composition. Following this hypothesis a little further, if Coca-Cola and Sparkle Cola are sold in different bottle designs by the same bottling distributor to different competing purchasers at different prices, it will be understandably difficult to convince a sophisticated businessman that this is an unlawful price discrimination under Section 2(a).

Some relief from the harsh consequences of the judicial rulings on like grade and quality may be provided, however, by a recent decision in which a court of appeals gave recognition to the marketing realities by taking into consideration the higher consumer demand for nationally advertised products over the physically identical private label products in assessing whether the requisite injury to competition under Section 2(a) had been occasioned by the price differential. The court held that if the price differential does no more than reflect the greater consumer demand for a product sold under a popular trademark, then no competitive injury can occur.

What Is Price Discrimination?

The Supreme Court has said that a discrimination in price is just a difference in price; the other parts of the Act determine whether a given price difference is lawful or not. It follows that no violation of Section 2(a) is present if there is no difference in price to competing buyers. If the seller has one sales price and sells f.o.b. factory to all customers, he is shielded from problems under Section 2(a).

A direct price discrimination is obvious on its face: a seller charges different prices to different buyers. An indirect price discrimination, on the other hand, occurs when differing terms or conditions of sale result in a lower price to certain buyers. We shall see that some indirect price discriminations have also been held illegal under Sections 2(d) and 2(e) of the Act, the sections requiring allowances and services to be made available to all competing buyers on proportionally equal terms. A workable distinction is that only those discriminations in the furnishing of services or allowances *incident to an original sale* to a buyer, as opposed to services and allowances *incident to resale of the goods by the buyer,* are cognizable as indirect price discriminations in violation of Section 2(a).

What Are the Competitive Effects Necessary to Show a Completed Section 2(a) Violation?

Section 2(a)'s concluding proviso reads: "That it shall be unlawful . . . to discriminate in price . . . where the effect of such discrimination [1] may be substantially to lessen competition or [2] tend to create a monopoly in any line of commerce, or [3] to injure, destroy, or prevent competition with any person who either [a] grants [b] or knowingly receives the benefit of such discrimination, [c] or to customers of either of them. . . ." Basically, Congress sought to distinguish price discrimination practices having no real competitive effect on commerce from pricing situations which have anticompetitive consequences. Only those discriminations having one of the listed effects on competition are illegal.

The nature of the competitive effect necessary to finding a violation of Section 2(a) varies with the type of competition affected.

It should be noted that there are three distinct tests of illegality under Section 2(a) [(1), (2), or (3) above]. The first two, which are carryovers from the original Section 2 of the Clayton Act, require an adverse competitive impact in the total relevant market, whereas the inquiry under the third test—that portion added by the Robinson-Patman amendments to the original Section 2—focuses more narrowly upon the probability of an adverse impact on the competitive relationship between the discriminating seller and his competitors (primary-line injury), between the favored and disfavored purchasers (secondary-line injury), and between the customers of either of them (third-line injury). The Robinson-Patman amendments had the desired effect of easing the burden of demonstrating the illegality of a price discrimination by eliminating the necessity for an exhaustive market analysis. For this reason the original Section 2 tests of illegality contained in the present Section 2(a) generally have not been relied upon to establish a violation of the Act. Let us now consider the contexts in which competitive injury under the Robinson-Patman amendments [(3) above] can be found.

Primary-Line Injury at the Seller's Level

Consider the following hypothetical marketing situation:

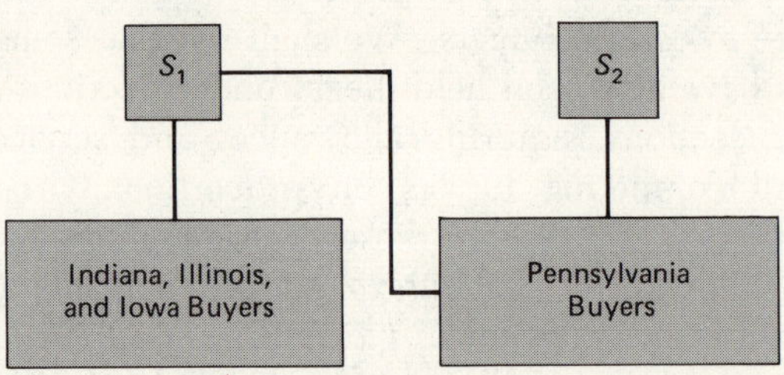

The first seller, S_1, and the second seller, S_2, are competing in the marketplace for the sale of goods. As the diagram illustrates, S_1 and S_2 are competing in Pennsylvania, and S_1 is also selling in other states, but not in competition with S_2. Suppose S_1 ruthlessly sets out to drive S_2 out of business. Suppose further that in order to accomplish this purpose, S_1 slashes his long-established prices by 25 per cent in Pennsylvania. S_1 sells below cost in Pennsylvania but is able to do this because he has raised his prices in the area where S_2 does not compete. Here is a clear case of primary-line or seller's-level injury. The purpose and effect of S_1's price reduction is to destroy S_2 in Pennsylvania. This practice may also amount to an attempt to monopolize, prohibited by Section 2 of the Sherman Act, or to a violation of Section 3 of the Robinson-Patman Act. Of course, if S_1 did not have the economic power to work competitive injury on S_2, no violation would have occurred. It should be noted that even though most primary-line-injury cases involve geographic or territorial price discrimination, this form of discrimination is by no means the only type under which pimary-line injury can arise. Thus, primary-line injury could arise where a supplier cuts his prices to a competitor's customers while selling at higher prices to his own customers in the same market area.

Secondary-Line Injury at the Buyer's Level

Consider the situation in which a hypothetical manufacturer-supplier, M, sells to two buyers, B_1 and B_2, who are in direct competition with each other.

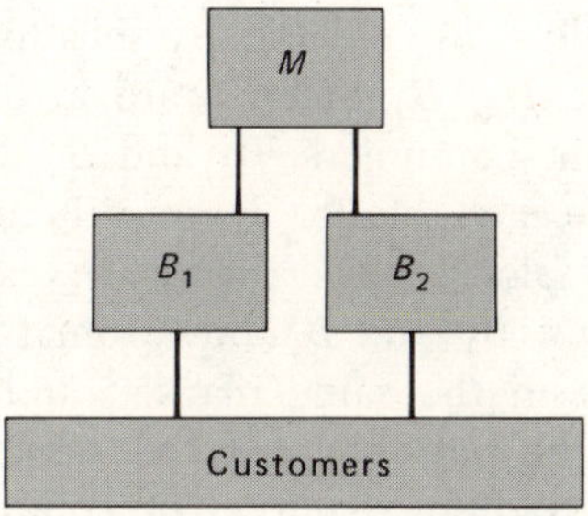

Now, suppose that M lowers his price to B_1 but not to B_2. The requisite effect on competition will be present if B_2 is significantly less able to compete with B_1 because of the price discrimination.

Let us now vary the situation and consider buyer-level injury again.

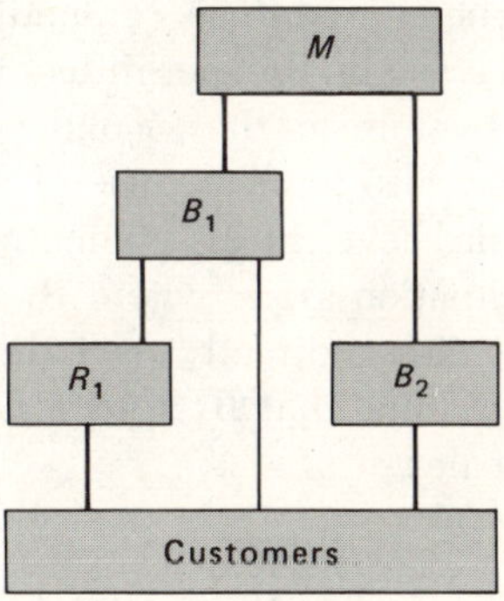

Here B_1 is a split distributor, competing with B_2 for the same customers and also selling to a retailer, R_1, who sells to these customers. The fact that B_1 is not in competition with B_2 on sales to R_1 does not prevent any price differential granted in favor of B_1 from wreaking the necessary competitive injury with respect to the competition that does exist between B_1 and B_2.

A more difficult problem is raised in the following situation:

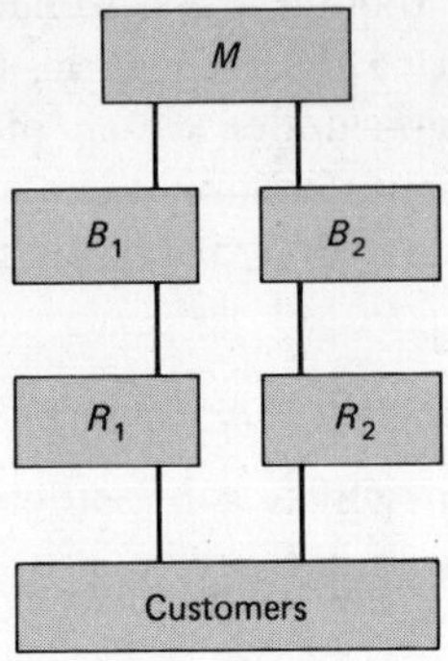

M sells to two wholesalers, B_1 and B_2; B_1 sells to a retailer, R_1; and B_2 sells to another retailer, R_2; R_1 and R_2 are in direct competition with one another for the same consumers; B_1 and B_2 do not directly compete with each other because each retailer, R_1 and R_2, has an exclusive dealing contract with his wholesaler. In other words, B_1 cannot sell to R_2 and B_2 cannot sell to R_1. Thus, B_1 and B_2 buy from the same supplier, each wholesales the product in the same market, and the retailers supplied by each compete for the patronage of the same consumers. Although not falling within the traditional notion of competition, it would seem that B_1 and B_2 are competitors in practical effect because a wholesaler's success will depend in large part upon the success of the retailers to which it sells. If a lower price to one of the wholesalers, B_1, results in a lower price to his customer R_1, enabling R_1 to underprice R_2, and if R_2's business declines as a result, causing a decline in B_2's sales to R_2, then B_2 would appear to be injured in his competition with B_1, the favored wholesaler-purchaser. B_2 should be permitted to sue M for the competitive injury suffered by him at the secondary level. The disfavored retailer R_2, of course, may also have a cause of action against M for the resulting injury at the third level in his competition with R_1.

An entirely different situation arises where B_1 and B_2 do not compete for the same customers, either directly or indirectly. Suppose that M is a refiner-supplier of gasoline, that B_1 runs a fleet of taxicabs, and that B_2 is a retail gasoline dealer.

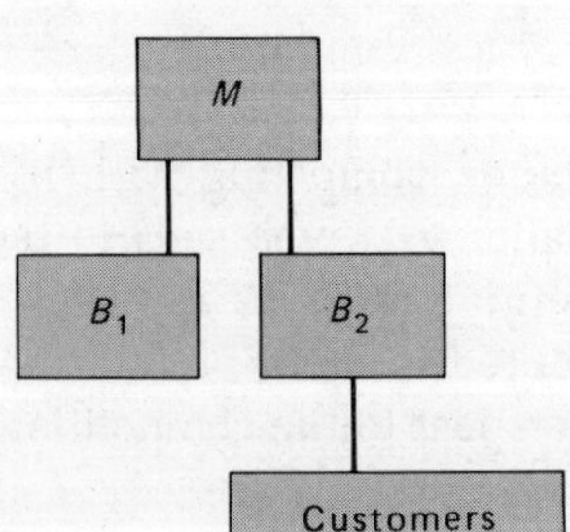

Because B_1 purchases gasoline for use in his taxicabs and not for resale, he is not in competition with B_2. M can, therefore, quote B_1 a lower gasoline price without fear of working any injury to competition.

Another common situation in which no buyer-level injury is present occurs where B_1 and B_2 do not actually compete in a geographic market. Suppose *M*, our gasoline supplier, sells to B_1 in Alaska and to B_2 in Florida.

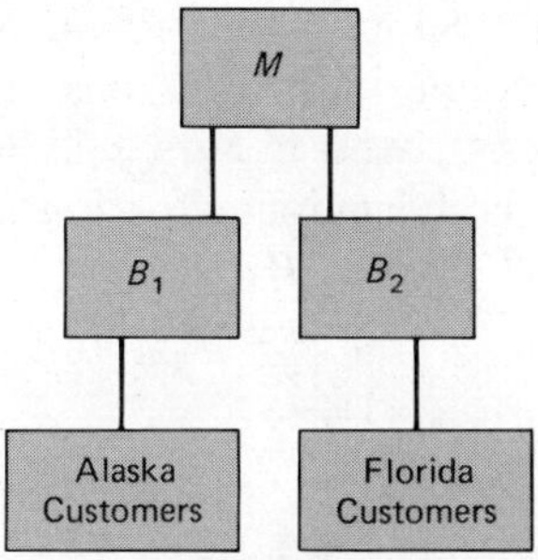

B_1 and B_2 obviously do not compete for the same business, so there is no buyer-level competitive injury if B_2 receives a lower price than B_1. There is a more difficult situation when the geographic areas are close to one another. If B_1 sells to customers in downtown Chicago and B_2 sells to customers in the suburbs of Chicago, it may well be that B_1 and B_2 would be considered as competitors for the same customers. Any price discrimination between B_1 and B_2 could, therefore, have the requisite buyer-level injury.

Third-Line Injury

This type of competitive injury, often referred to as tertiary line, is suffered by a disfavored customer in his competition with customers of the supplier's favored buyer, three steps down the distribution chain. Suppose our gasoline supplier, *M*, who may be a refiner, sells his gasoline both to an integrated jobber-retailer, JR_1, and to an independent jobber, J_2, who in turn sells to a retail gasoline station R_2, who competes with JR_1 for the same retail business.

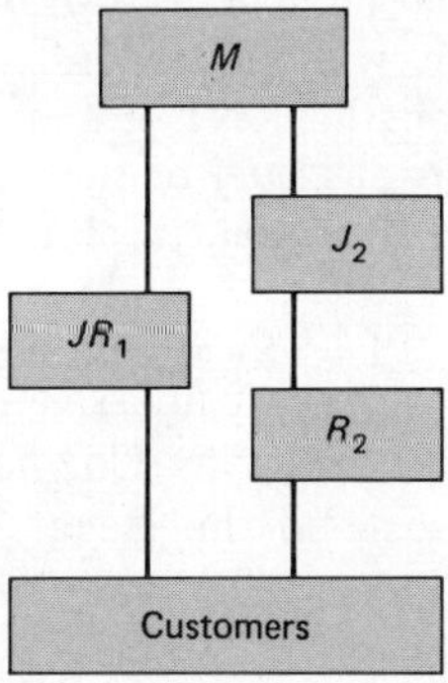

M sells at a lower price to J_2 than JR_1 even though JR_1, in his capacity as a jobber, performs the same functional activities as J_2. If the lower price to J_2 results in a lower price to R_2, enabling R_2 to underprice JR_1 at the retail level, then JR_1 may be injured in his competition with R_2, who, in this instance, operates at the third level in the favored distribution system.

A more controversial example of third-line injury arises out of the following factual context: Suppose our gasoline supplier, *M*, who may be a refiner, sells his gasoline both to a retail gasoline station, R_1, and to an independent jobber, *J*, who in turn sells to another retail gasoline station, R_2. R_1 and R_2 both compete for the same retail business. *M* sells at a lower price to *J* than to R_1.

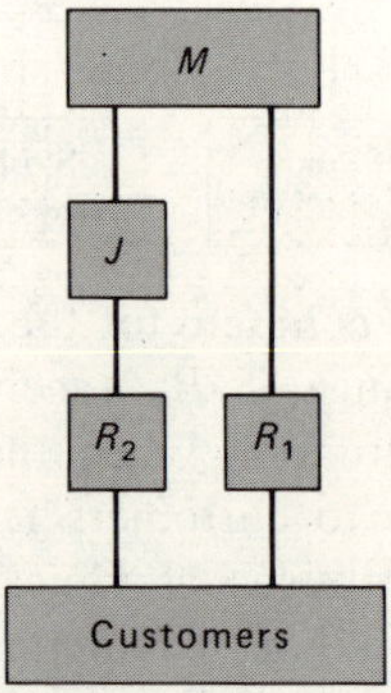

If the lower price to *J* results in a lower price to R_2, enabling R_2 to underprice R_1, the necessary competitive injury may have occurred at the retail level.

Fourth-Line Injury

Fourth-line injury is suffered by a disfavored customer in his competition with a customer of a customer of the supplier's favored customer. The United States Ninth Circuit Court of Appeals held, in *Standard Oil Co.* v. *Perkins,* that competitive injury below the tertiary level is not cognizable under the Robinson-Patman Act. In its opinion:

> Section 2(a) . . . limits the number of distribution levels on which a supplier's price discrimination will be recognized as potentially injurious to competition. These are: on the level of the supplier-seller in competition with his own customer; on the level of the supplier-seller's customers; and on the level of customers of customers of the supplier-seller.

In *Perkins,* the plaintiff-appellee, an independent gasoline dealer who had both a wholesale and retail business, alleged that Standard's price favoritism to the Signal Oil and Gas Co. had impaired and destroyed competition between Perkins and the Regal Stations Company, both of whom sold Standard's products. The evidence showed that Regal, which persistently undercut the prices of other competing retailers, purchased its gasoline from Western Hyway Oil Company, which in turn had purchased it from Signal, which had originally purchased it from Standard. The following diagram best illustrates this system:

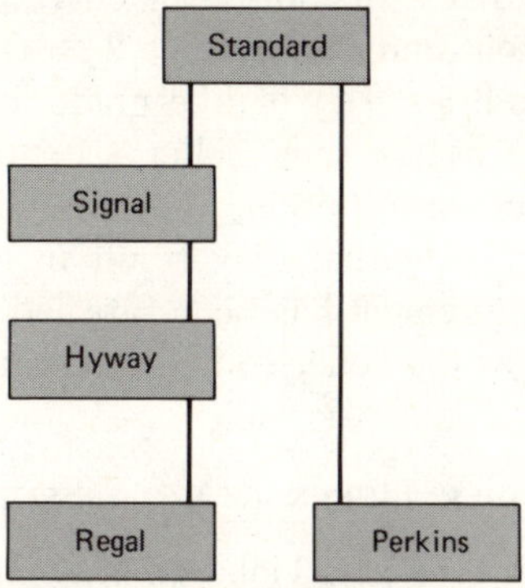

Even granting that the proof demonstrated that Standard uniformly charged Signal substantially less than Perkins, and further granting that Signal similarly passed this price saving on to customers such as Western Hyway, the competition Perkins complained of was not that with Signal or with Signal's customers but rather that with Regal, a customer of a customer of a customer of Standard. Thus, the competition between Regal and Perkins existed at the fourth level, which, according to the Ninth Circuit, was beyond the reach of the Act. According to the court: "Section 2(a) . . . does not recognize a causal connection, essential to liability, between a supplier's price discrimination and the trade practices of a customer as far removed on the distibutive ladder as Regal was from Standard."

The Supreme Court reversed the court of appeals and reinstated the jury verdict for Perkins. Speaking for the Court, Justice Black said that to view Perkins' "fourth-level" injuries as not protected by Section 2(a) is to impose a "wholly . . . artificial" limitation which "is completely unwarranted by the language or purpose of the Act." In reaching its conclusion, the Court relied upon its recent *Fred Meyer* decision in which it was held that any retailer who buys through a wholesaler is a "customer" of the original supplier within the meaning of Section 2(d). It reasoned that to read *customer* more narrowly in Section 2(a) than was done in *Fred Meyer* would allow price discriminators to avoid the sanctions of the Act by the simple expedient of adding an additional link to the distribution chain. Thus, the term *customer* appearing in the competitive injury proviso of Section 2(a) includes all persons in the distribution chain who distribute the supplier's product, regardless of the functional level at which they operate and regardless of whether they are direct purchasers of the discriminating supplier. The Supreme Court has apparently eliminated the third-line limitation heretofore thought to have been contained in Section 2(a). Actionable competitive injury may arise at any level in the distribution scheme, the only limitation being the requirement that there be a causal relationship between the unlawful discrimination and the injury suffered.

Let us now assume that a Section 2(a) charge has been proved; that is, (1) two or more consummated sales, (2) reasonably close in point of time, (3) of commodities, (4) of like grade and quality, (5) with a difference in price, (6) by the same seller, (7) to two or more different purchasers, (8) for use, consumption, or resale within the United States or any territory thereof, (9) that may result in competitive injury, and (10) the commerce requirement has been satisfied. We will now consider the defenses available to the seller to avoid liability under Section 2(a).

The Seller's Possible Defenses to a Section 2(a) Violation

Even if a *prima facie* case of a violation of Section 2(a) is established, a seller may have a complete defense to that charge in the two following situations: (1) the price differentials "make only due allowance for differences in the cost, other than brokerage, of manufacture, sale, or delivery resulting from the differing methods or quantities in which such commodities are to such purchasers sold or delivered"; or (2) the price differentials were "made in good faith to meet an equally low price of a competitor, or the services or facilities furnished by a competitor."

Cost Justification

The cost-justification defense stems from the economic premise that a seller should not be compelled by law to charge an artificially high price to a particular buyer if the seller can show by facts and figures that it costs less to sell to this particular buyer than to other buyers. If the seller were actually to make more money selling to buyer *A* than to buyer *B* when the price is the same to both, the Act allows the seller to reduce the price to *A* to the extent that this reduction in price is based on the actual lower cost of selling to *A*. Such cost savings might result from A's purchasing practices, savings in shipping costs, reduced sales expense, or a host of other factors.

Knowledgeable executives, however, will appreciate that distributive cost accounting is far from an exact science; indeed, in many cases a seller has no precise idea at all of the exact cost of selling a certain quantity of goods to a certain customer. Several accounting distribution techniques are customarily used to determine the approximate cost of different parts of the manufacturing and distribution process. But the inexact nature of these cost figures, together with the traditionally strict requirements of the Federal Trade Commission in proving cost justification, has made this defense a difficult and expensive one to prove. Guidelines for making use of the cost-justification defense are few, and the hazards are many.

There are recent indications that a more reasonable approach will be taken toward this defense in the future. For example, in the *Sylvania Electric Products, Inc.* case Sylvania was charged with a violation of Section 2(a) in granting unlawful price differences in sales of about 600 variously priced types of replacement vacuum tubes. These tubes were sold both through Philco Corporation and through Sylvania's own distributors. Sylvania accounting executives and lawyers doubtlessly appreciated the practical impossibility of cost-justifying *exactly* every price difference in the sales of each of these 600 items. Time and expense militated against such a formidable task, and even if successful on paper, the results would not have had the mathematical certainty of the engineers' calculations that went into the design of these vacuum tubes. Nevertheless, Sylvania was successful in cost-justifying the price difference to the satisfaction of the Federal Trade Commission. Sylvania employed a "weighted-average" method to demonstrate that aggregate price differences in distributing the vacuum tubes through the two outlets justified charging a higher price to Sylvania's own distributors than to Philco. The Federal Trade Commission thus accepted the distribution pricing policy of Sylvania for its entire product line of 600 vacuum tubes, and on this basis the price difference between individual vacuum tubes was not considered to be of competitive significance. One tube was not designed to be competitive against another tube, so the study reflected the realities of electronic tube distribution.

A few generalizations are appropriate in evaluating cost justification. Suppose manufacturer M sells to three buyers—B_1, B_2, and B_3—and discriminates in favor of B_1:

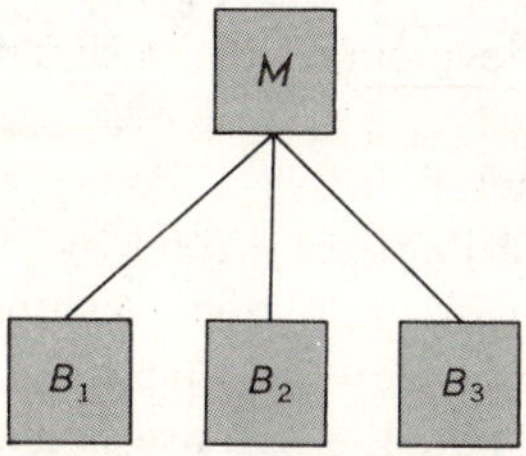

In seeking to cost-justify his price to B_1, M contends that the total purchases by B_1 make M's total volume great enough that certain cost economies are possible in M's over-all production process. This is impermissible. M cannot say that the goods sold to B_1 reflect the entire savings in the unit cost of manufacturing. Because the extra volume necessary to the cost economies would vanish if B_2 and B_3 withdrew their business, B_2 and B_3 have just as much right to a price reduction as B_1 on this basis. On the other hand, if M, as a service to his buyers, maintains warehouse facilities for goods after they are sold and B_1 agrees to take over the warehousing of the goods he buys, or if B_1 accepts less expensive crating, M can pass these cost savings on to B_1 in the form of a price concession.

It is difficult, if not impossible, to cost-justify special treatment to new customers or discounts based on the cumulative volume of business per year which have no relationship to the size of individual shipments. A new customer normally is as expensive to serve as an old customer. Annual volume bears no necessary relationship to shipping costs. Similarly, quantity discount schedules must be developed with care if they are to be protected by the cost-justification defense. Only if these schedules accurately reflect cost differences will the defense be available. In this connection it is important to note that cost justification must be substantially complete. If a seller can only justify part of the price difference, the defense will not prevail.

The seller whose first efforts to cost-justify an otherwise unlawful price discrimination occur *after* a charge under Section 2(a) is made labors under a psychological disadvantage in the ensuing legal proceedings. The prudent businessman should make some realistic cost-justification appraisals to support the price concession *before* the concession is given to a particular buyer. "Good-faith" efforts to comply with Section 2(a) before the pricing practices are challenged put a seller in a much better initial position.

The Defense of Meeting Competition

It is well established that if the seller lowers his price to meet competition, he has a complete defense to a proved violation of Section 2(a). This defense has always been strictly limited by the Federal Trade Commission, however, and Congressional legislation has even been proposed to abolish it entirely. Thus, while the defense is generally available, strict rules have been developed for designating certain situations in which it is not.

One of the recent issues before the courts is whether the defense of meeting competition is available to a seller who uses a Section 2(a) price discrimination agressively to gain new customers by offering such potential customers a price as low as that of a competitor. The Federal Trade Commission ruled that the defense is available only when a lower price was granted in order to retain an old customer and not when motivated by a desire to obtain new customers. But a court of appeals reversed this ruling and held that price discriminations otherwise prohibited by Section 2(a) can be defended by showing that in striving for new business the price discrimination in favor of a new customer was made in good faith to meet the equally low price of a competitor.

There are a number of restrictions on the use of the defense of meeting competition. First, the seller cannot claim this defense if he knows or should have known that the competitor's price he met was itself unlawful under the Robinson-Patman Act. Second, the seller's price discrimination must be a temporary measure to meet competition and not part of a permanent price schedule whereby some customers are systematically charged higher prices than others. Third, an equally low price of a competitor "means an equally low price for a given quantity." Thus, if the competitor sells to a customer in large quantities at a certain price, the seller is not properly "meeting competition" if he meets that price in sales of smaller quantities for which the competitor has a higher price. Fourth, it is the view the Federal Trade Commission that the seller's price discrimination must be limited to meeting a specific individual competitor's price to specific individual customers. Fifth and last, the seller must meet, not beat, his competitor's price to the particular customer.

We can now see that the defense of meeting competition is not an easy "out" for a seller who has violated Section 2(a). This defense is severely limited but still absolute when proven.

Other Defenses and Exemptions

Certain transactions are exempted from the provisions of Section 2(a). For example, price changes made in response to changing conditions affecting the market for or the marketability of the goods concerned may not be illegal. This category embraces actual or imminent deterioration of perishable goods, obsolescence of seasonal goods, distress sales under court process, or sales in good faith in the course of discontinuing business in the goods concerned. Supplementary legislation was passed in 1938 which declares the Act not applicable "to purchases of their supplies for their own use by schools, colleges, universities, public libraries, churches, hospitals, and charitable institutions not operated for profit." Sales to the Federal government are exempt, and state and municipal bodies probably enjoy this exemption as well. The nature and extent of these exemptions is largely unexplored, however.

Prohibitions Against the Buyer: Section 2(f)

Section 2(f) declares it unlawful for a buyer knowingly to induce or receive a price discrimination which is in violation of Section 2(a).

Like Section 2(a), Section 2(f) relates solely to *price* discrimination. As interpreted to date, a buyer cannot be reached for knowing receipt of discriminatory grants of allowances or services and facilities. This apparent legislative omission has been remedied in part by attacking the practice as an unfair method of competition in violation of Section 5 of the Federal Trade Commission Act.

It is a difficult task to prove that a buyer has violated Section 2(f). The Supreme Court has taken the position that there must be some evidence that the buyer knew of the illegality of the price discrimination, and there must also be some evidence of the buyer's knowledge that the concession was not saved from illegality by the defenses of cost justification or meeting competition. It follows that a buyer can avoid a Section 2(f) violation by showing that the seller did not violate Section 2(a) in the first place, that the prices were justified by available defenses, or that the buyer had no knowledge of the seller's violation of Section 2(a).

Unlawful Brokerage Payments: Section 2(c)

Section 2(c) is a self-contained legislative enactment, having no relationship to the other sections of the Robinson-Patman Act. Violation of this section is in the nature of a *per se* wrong, like price fixing under the Sherman Act. By the terms of Section 2(c) it is unlawful:

> [1] to pay or grant,
> [2] or to receive or accept,
> [3] anything of value as a commission, brokerage, or other compensation, or any allowance or discount in lieu thereof, except for services rendered
> [4] in connection with the sale or purchase of goods, wares, or merchandise
> [5] either to the other party to such transaction or to an agent, representative, or other intermediary therein
> [6] where such intermediary is acting in fact for or in behalf, or is subject to the direct or indirect control, of any party to such transaction other than the person by whom such compensation is so granted or paid.

If a seller pays a buyer's broker a sales brokerage commission, Section 2(c) is violated. In effect, it is only the *seller's* broker who can lawfully receive a brokerage fee. And it makes no difference that the buyer's broker is performing some valuable function, such as warehousing or breaking bulk. The "except for services rendered" clause has been emasculated by cases which say that a buyer's broker does not render services to the seller.

This section is aimed at reaching dummy brokerage payments which are in reality "under the table" price concessions eventually falling into the hands of the buyer. Section 2(c), being self-contained, does not permit a defense of meeting competition or cost justification. Also, unlike Section 2(a), only one transaction, one payment by a seller to a buyer's broker, comprises a Section 2(c) violation, and a specific effect on competition need not be shown. For these reasons it is a far simpler task to prove a Section 2(c) violation than a Section 2(a) violation.

In *Federal Trade Commission* v. *Henry Broch & Company*, a seller's broker accepted a lower commission to clinch a sale, the seller passing on the reduction in the broker's commission as a lower price to the buyer. The Supreme Court held that Section 2(c) had been violated by this transaction. The Court perceived no economic difference between such a transaction and one where the seller's broker split his brokerage commission with the buyer. The direct relationship between the brokerage fee and the lower price to the buyer was an important consideration in determining that Section 2(c) had been violated. *Broch* would appear to dictate that any adjustment of a broker's fees should be made with reference to all future sales to avoid the fee-splitting hazard on specific sales that was condemned by the Supreme Court.

Merchandising Allowances and Services: Sections 2(d) and 2(e)

If the Robinson-Patman Act prohibited price discriminations alone, many opportunities for evasion and contravention of the basic purpose of the law would be available. Experienced marketing executives know there are many ways in which a supplier can favor one customer over other customers beyond the grant of a concession in price. Think for a moment of all the various types of merchandising assistance that suppliers customarily offer to retailers: advertising and promotional allowances, handbills and signs, window and floor displays and other point-of-purchase display materials, demonstrators and demonstrations, display and storage cabinets, "push money" for sales clerks, special packaging or package sizes, warehouse facilities, return privileges—the list is virtually endless.

When the Robinson-Patman Act was passed, Congress was well aware of the economic importance of advertising and promotional allowances and of merchandising services and facilities furnished by suppliers to customers. The Act contains provisions to deal with discriminations by suppliers in these critical areas. Section 2(d) of the Act relates to payments or allowances by the seller to the buyer for promotional services and requires such payments to be made available on proportionally equal terms to all competing customers. Section 2(e) deals with services furnished by the seller to the buyer, requiring such services to be made available to all competing customers on proportionally equal terms. Note that these prohibitions are directed only against sellers. The Robinson-Patman Act contains no prohibition against the inducement and receipt of discriminatory advertising and promotional allowances or services and facilities by powerful buyers. As noted, however, the Federal Trade Commission has moved to remedy this omission. The commission has held that the knowing inducement and receipt of discriminatory advertising and promotional allowances by large buyers is an unfair method of competition, prohibited by the Federal Trade Commission Act. The commission's position has been upheld by two United States courts of appeal.

Essentially, Sections 2(d) and 2(e) provide that if a seller offers advertising allowances or merchandising payments or services to one customer, he must make his offer (1) available (2) to all competing customers (3) on proportionally equal terms. Let us examine each of these three requirements.

The requirement of availability imposes an affirmative duty upon a supplier who offers promotional assistance to any of his customers. Suppose that a supplier goes to his largest customer with an offer of an advertising allowance of $1 per case on all goods purchased. In order to comply with the law, the seller must then take action to inform all of his customers who compete with the large customer that the allowance is available to them as well. It is no defense for the seller to say later that the competing customers would have received the allowance had they asked for it if the competing customers were never informed of the availability of the allowance. Preferably, the seller should use the same media to announce the availability of a particular form of merchandising assistance to all competing customers. Thus, if one customer is notified of the availability of an allowance or service by first-class mail, all competing customers should also be notified by first-class mail.

The second requirement is that any promotional plan developed by a supplier must cover all customers who compete with one another. Coverage of all competing customers must be tested in two ways. The first test is essentially geographical: what stores actually compete for the same business? A supplier is required to offer promotional assistance only to those customers who compete in the distribution of the promoted product with any customer who is participating in the promotion. Suppose that a manufacturer sells to ten retail stores in New York City and ten retail stores in San Francisco. The manufacturer can lawfully develop a program of promotional assistance which includes only the New York City retail stores, because they do not compete with the San Francisco retail stores. Caution must be used in defining the area of effective competition, however. Suppose that a manufacturer sells to ten retail stores in Manhattan, ten retail stores in Brooklyn, and ten retail stores in the Bronx. A promotional assistance program limited to the Manhattan customers would be illegal if the Brooklyn and Bronx retail stores compete with the Manhattan retail stores for the same business. The second test of coverage of all competing customers is related to the needs of particular customers. The law prohibits a supplier from so tailoring his promotional assistance plan that it is impossible as a practical matter for some competing customers to participate. It may be that in a particular instance a supplier must even develop alternative promotional assistance plans to insure that each competing customer can participate in some manner. If a seller develops alternative merchandising assistance plans, his customers must be given the opportunity to choose among the plans. In other words, the supplier must offer something that each of his customers, no matter how small, can use effectively.

The law's requirement that promotional allowances or services must be made available to competing customers on "proportionally equal terms" is of cardinal importance. Proportional equality means, basically, to each according to his worth as a retailer. The Robinson-Patman Act does not spell out any single way in which to achieve proportional equality. One method is to compute the amount of payments made or services furnished as a specified percentage of the dollar volume of goods sold or the quantity of goods purchased during a specified time. A seller who offers his customers an advertising allowance of $1 per case on all purchases has made a proportionally equal offer. Offers based upon a sliding scale are suspect. For example, an offer of an advertising allowance of 2 per cent on annual purchases up to $1,000, 3 per cent on purchases up to $5,000, and 5 per cent on purchases over $5,000 is not a proportionally equal offer if only a few large customers are able to purchase in sufficient quantities to receive the maximum allowance.

The supplier has the additional duty of checking to insure that every customer participating in a promotional allowance or service program is using the benefits he receives for the intended purpose. If, for instance, a customer is allowed to pocket an advertising allowance without supplying any advertising, both the supplier and the customer may be in difficulty. The Federal Trade Commission might construe such a payment to be a price concession and proceed against the supplier under Section 2(a) of the Robinson-Patman Act and against the customer under Section 2(f).

A few examples will illustrate the application of the principles just described. Suppose that the National Soap Company markets its toilet soap through supermarket chains, drug chains, and independent drugstores. An executive of National Soap Company proposes a program of television advertising allowances. Under the program National would reimburse its customers for one half the cost of any television spot announcements featuring National Soap up to a maximum of 7½ per cent of the customer's annual purchases. The offer would be announced to all customers by means of a form letter. Superficially, this program appears to meet the requirements of Section 2(d) of the Robinson-Patman Act. The offer would be made available to all competing customers on a proportionally equal formula. As a practical matter, however, this program would fail the test of availability to all competing customers. If National Soap knows that only the large supermarket chains and drug chains can afford television advertising, then the offer would not be available in any meaningful sense to its independent drugstore customers. In order to meet the test of practical availability, National would have to expand its allowance program to include alternative advertising media. Suppose that the program is enlarged to include radio and newspaper advertising on the same basis. The program still may not be available to all competing customers. If some small stores cannot afford television, radio, or newspaper advertising, National Soap should allow its customers to use the advertising allowance for handbills or in-store displays as well. Its customers would then have a meaningful choice, and every customer would be able to use at least one advertising medium.

Suppose that the Association Cosmetics Company distributes its line through the Colossal Department Store and ten independent drugstores in Middletown. The Colossal Department Store is the largest customer by a wide margin. Association Cosmetics employs a traveling demonstrator, and the Colossal Department Store has asked for an all-day demonstration in its store. If Association Cosmetics accedes to the request of the Colossal Department Store, it must make a proportionally equal offer to the independent drugstores in Middletown who distribute its line in competition with the Colossal Department Store. The offer to the drugstores need not be the same as the offer to the Colossal Department Store. Association Cosmetics complies with the Robinson-Patman Act if its offer is proportionally equal. Suppose that Colossal Department Store has an annual volume of $10,000 in Association Cosmetics products and that the value of the all-day demonstration is $100. The Tom Thumb Drugstore across the street has an annual volume of $1,000 in Association Cosmetics products. Association Cosmetics satisfies the requirements of the Robinson-Patman Act if it offers the Tom Thumb Drugstore promotional services worth $10. Here the offer to the independent drugstore might take the form of a short personnel training program or the furnishing of a demonstration kit.

Retail Greeting Cards, Inc., desperately wants the Colossal Department Store to take on its line. The salesman calling upon the store buyer states that if Colossal will take on the line, Retail Greeting Cards will ship to Colossal a complete set of display fixtures and storage cabinets, free. Retail Greeting Cards also sells to a number of small stores who compete with Colossal for the greeting card business. No offer is made to these smaller stores. On these facts, Retail Greeting Cards is clearly guilty of violating Section 2(e) of the Robinson-Patman Act.

The Triple A Cigar Company plans to offer its customers the use of a humidified, self-service display cabinet. The cabinet to be offered will occupy 12 linear feet of store space. Triple A Cigar Company plans to make its offer known to all customers. As a practical matter, however, only very large stores will be able to accommodate a cabinet of this size. On these facts, Triple A Cigar Company is vulnerable to attack under the Robinson-Patman Act, unless it develops alternative offers that can be utilized by smaller stores.

Unlike a Section 2(a) charge, there need be no proof of a competitive injury to show a Section 2(d) or 2(e) violation. Moreover the seller has no defense of cost justification. The defense of meeting competition, however, is available.

Buyers have duties as well as rights with respect to supplier promotional plans. The reader will recall that although the Robinson-Patman Act does not make it illegal for customers knowingly to induce and receive discriminatory promotional payments or services from suppliers, the Federal Trade Commission has held that the knowing inducement and receipt of discriminatory promotional payments by retailers is a violation of the Federal Trade Commission Act. There is every reason to believe that the commission would take the same position with respect to the inducement or receipt of discriminatory services or facilities from suppliers.

Criminal Prohibitions: Section 3

Section 3 of the Robinson-Patman Act is a criminal statute aimed at three specific practices. First, Section 3 declares it a crime for any person who meets the commerce test "to be a party to, or assist in any transaction of sale, or contract to sell, which discriminates against competitors of the purchaser, in that any discount, rebate, allowance or advertising service charge is granted to the purchaser over and above any discount, rebate, allowance, or advertising service charge available at the time of such transaction to said competitors in respect of a sale of goods of like grade, quality, and quantity." This part of Section 3 is designed to reach secret price concessions of a fraudulent nature. It has been little used, both because of the difficulty of proving fraud and because courts have strictly construed its provisions. Where a concession is given on a purchase of 1,000 cases and not on a purchase of 999 cases, some courts have found no violation because a sale of a "like quantity" of goods was not involved.

Second, it is a crime for any person "to sell or contract to sell, goods in any part of the United States at prices lower than those exacted by said person elsewhere in the United States for the purpose of destroying competition, or eliminating a competitor in such part of the United States." Within the reach of this part of Section 3 is a seller who makes a geographic price cut with the predatory purpose of destroying competition or eliminating a competitor. In one case a bakery company with multistate operations cut its bread price substantially in one city in which it operated, thereby destroying the competition afforded by a local baker. This practice was held to be a violation of Section 3.

Finally, it is a crime for any person "to sell, or contract to sell, goods at unreasonably low prices for the purpose of destroying competition or eliminating a competitor." This provision is also aimed at predatory pricing. What is forbidden would appear to be a sudden drop in prices without economic justification and with the intent to eliminate a competitor.

Section 3 of the Robinson-Patman Act is not a popular enactment. Its language has been criticized as being too vague to give any ascertainable standard of prohibited conduct. This argument was used in the *National Dairy Products* case in the hope that the Supreme Court would hold the last part of Section 3 unconstitutionally vague. The argument failed. Moreover, the Supreme Court has held that Section 3 is not an "antitrust statute" and therefore does not provide a cause of action for private litigants seeking treble damages.

CHAPTER 10

PATENTS AND ANTITRUST

The Nature of the Patent Monopoly

Article 1, Section 8, of the United States Constitution provides, in part: "The Congress shall have the power to promote the progress of science and useful arts, by securing for limited times to authors and inventors the exclusive right to their respective writings and discoveries." Long before the Sherman Act was passed, Congress had authorized the granting of patents to inventors. The patent conferred on an inventor is in the nature of a contract with the public. In exchange for a full disclosure of the invention, the public, acting through the United States Patent Office, grants to the inventor the right to exclude others from the manufacture, use, or sale of the claimed invention for a period of seventeen years from the date of issue. Fundamental to the historic rationale for conferring this exclusivity is that the public is deprived of nothing. That is to say, because the public has no previous knowledge of the specific invention which becomes the subject of the patent, nothing is taken from the public in granting this exclusive but limited right to the inventor as his reward for disclosure to the public.

Thus, standing side by side with the prohibitions of the Sherman Act are exclusive patent rights, sometimes characterized as "little monopolies." More aptly phrased, the patent grant is the measure of the scope of the reward accorded to the inventor as determined by the "claims" of the patent. Claims are definitions of the invention, their extent depending upon the contribution to a particular field which the inventor has provided by his invention. If the invention is a substantial contribution, in the nature of a fundamental advance in science or a "giant step" forward, the claims in the patent are broad and give the inventor a liberal scope of patent protection. On the other hand, a relatively narrow contribution in a field which is perhaps already highly developed is rewarded by a correspondingly smaller scope of protection.

The United States Patent Office is the agency which operates to prevent an inventor from obtaining more than his fair share of this contract with the public. The Patent Office, through its examiners, refuses to grant patents where there is no patentable invention and otherwise insures that the claims—the definition of the invention—are no broader than the actual contribution which the inventor has made.

Significant from an antitrust standpoint is a procedure in the Patent Office which serves to resolve the issue of "who gets the patent" when two or more inventors come into the Patent Office at approximately the same time with substantially the same patentable invention. The Patent Office has a procedure called an "interference" for resolving the controversy and for determining the actual inventor at law who is entitled to the patent. Recent legislation provides that any interference settlement agreements must be filed with the Patent Office. Thus, the Department of Justice can review such agreements for possible unlawful provisions under the antitrust laws.

Once the patent is issued, the "right to exclude" starts. The patent, during its seventeen-year lifetime, has the attributes of personal property and as such may be transferred or mortgaged and is subject to state taxes.

A person may acquire a patent in a number of ways. Assignment, of course, is the most common way. When the inventor takes out a patent on an invention, the patent is his. Another "person," commonly a corporation, may acquire the patent by assignment when the patentee conveys his entire (or a partial) right, title, and interest to another party. A person may also acquire patent rights by what is termed a "grant-back" arrangement. In this type of arrangement the patent owner licenses another to "practice" his invention and requires that future inventions relating to the same subject matter be assigned or licensed back to him. The Supreme Court has held that a license agreement with a grant-back provision is not a violation of the antitrust laws. The Court, however, has not spoken definitively on the subject since its 5–4 decision in the *Transparent-Wrap* case in 1947. In view of recent Justice Department studies and attacks on grant-backs or improvement patents, it cannot be said with certainty that the antitrust immunity for such agreements will persist in the future.

The Patent Owner Acting Alone

Rarely, if at all, does the *good-faith* patentee acting alone run into antitrust problems. The reason, of course, is that Section 1 of the Sherman Act requires a concert of action, necessarily involving more than one party. To date there has been no case involving a single patent owner exploiting his invention in good faith where monopolization or attempted monopolization has successfully been charged. This apparent immunity from the Sherman Act has remained intact even where the patent owner has acquired a substantial or dominant share of the market.

Thus the patent owner can, without concern for antitrust violations, freely exploit his patent by manufacturing the patented invention, bringing bona fide actions for patent infringement, and refusing to license others. Indeed, he need not exploit the patent at all during its seventeen-year lifetime. Reasonable nonuse of a patent involves no antitrust dangers. Lack of capital or lack of reasonable market potential are but examples of the many good reasons why a cogent businessman may not use or exploit his patent rights. It is only when there is an unreasonable nonuse—suppression of the patent—that antitrust problems may arise. This area is largely unexplored by the courts, and the future may bring a reappraisal of this entire field of nonuse. Agreements with others not to use patents, however, present an entirely different situation, fraught with antitrust implications.

It is the rare situation when the patentee attempts to monopolize a market by the manufacture of the patented invention. In the case of *United States* v. *Besser Manufacturing Company,* however, such an attempt had been made. Two closely related corporations held 65 per cent of the dollar volume of the concrete block machine market, the balance being divided among fifty other manufacturers. A "purpose and intent" to monopolize was found in the company's practice of acquiring the patent rights of competitors by buying competing corporations and extracting agreements from their executives not to compete. In addition, these formerly competing executives were given jobs, cross-licenses were exchanged with competitors which provided that neither would issue licenses without consent of the other, and sham charges of patent infringement were filed against competitors. The ruthless nature of this removal of competition led the court to find a violation of Section 2 of the Sherman Act.

Recently, the government has taken a more active interest in using the Sherman Act to reach conduct by a patent owner which threatens monopoly. For example, there is the question of whether or not a manufacturer who occupies a dominant market position can lawfully acquire valuable patent rights from a competitor, when a nonexclusive license, short of a complete assignment, would at least have protected this manufacturer from charges of patent infringement. When such a manufacturer receives an assignment, his competitor is removed from competition, and the chances are that the already dominant manufacturer may gain a still greater share of the market. Such acquisitions are also subject to attack as "corporate amalgamations" and may thus violate Section 7 of the Clayton Act.

The Patent Owner Licensing Others

A patent license, in contrast to an assignment, reserves title to the patentee. It is merely an agreement not to sue the licensee for patent infringement. More antitrust problems arise under licensing arrangements because the patent owner often adds terms to the arrangement which are designed to suppress competition. For example, whenever a patentee gives a nonexclusive licensee a veto power in the selection of other licensees, a Sherman Act violation is present.

The traditional test for measuring whether the patent owner is within the scope of his patent rights in specific licensing arrangements was set forth in the *General Electric* case in 1926: "[T]he patentee may grant a license to make, use and vend articles under the specifications of his patent for any royalty, or upon any conditions the performance of which is reasonably within the reward which the patentee by the grant of the patent is entitled to secure." If a provision in a licensing agreement goes beyond what is permitted as a reasonable reward, it is illegal.

The argument has been made that the patentee, when he licenses his invention, should be entitled to control the price at which his licensee will sell the invention, particularly when the licensee competes with the patentee-licensor. The Supreme Court once accepted this argument. Inroads have been made into this position, however, especially where broader, or industrywide, price fixing is accomplished. Even regarding the narrower issue of the right of the patentee to fix the first resale price of his licensee the question of doubt exists. The last Supreme Court decision on the point occurred in the *Huck* case in 1965, which affirmed a lower court holding permitting the practice on a *mere* 4–4 decision.

In the 1948 *Line Material* case, decided by the Supreme Court, two patents which accounted for 40 per cent of the market in electrical circuit cutouts were issued to different corporations after Patent Office interference proceedings. One patent had broad claims, the other had narrow claims. As both patents were necessary to use the invention, the parties entered into an agreement which, among other things, provided for royalty-free cross-licensing. The Supreme Court recognized the need for settling such patent disputes and did not condemn this part of the agreement as unlawful. The Supreme Court did find unlawful an elaborate scheme for fixing the prices at which the electrical circuit cutouts were marketed. Specifically, the Supreme Court condemned an agreement by which one company was given power to license under both patents and the other company agreed to maintain the prices set by the licensing company so long as the licensing company forced its other licensees to maintain such prices. The patents were thus combined to fix prices, a *per se* violation of the Sherman Act.

There are other areas where patent rights confer no antitrust immunity. For example, in its recent *Lear* decision, the Supreme Court reversed the long-standing rule of patent law that a licensee cannot turn around and challenge the validity of the patent if sued by the patentee for royalties. Similarly, where a patent licensor seeks to use patent licenses to control the market for unpatented goods, he may run afoul of the tie-in provisions of the Clayton Act. In one case in which a licensor of a patented punch card machine sought to compel his licensees to purchase his unpatented punch cards for use in the machine, the Supreme Court found a Clayton Act violation.

Imposing Use, Market, Territory, and Quantity Limitations in Patent Licenses

The patent grant confers on the patentee the right to exclude others from the manufacture, use, and sale of the patented invention. To some extent this right to exclude may be "carved up." There is no antitrust problem involved when the patent owner licenses another to manufacture and to sell but not to use, or, conversely, when the patentee licenses another only to use the patented invention.

Few questions arise when the patentee wishes to license parties to practice the invention in different fields. For example, if the patent owner's invention relates to an improved engine component which is useful in the automotive and aircraft industries, he may wish to license one person to practice the invention in the automotive field and another to practice it in the aircraft field, with covenants in the license that neither will practice in the other's field. This "field-of-use" limitation has not been definitely considered by the Supreme Court since the *General Talking Pictures* case in 1938, where the Court said such limitations were not a violation of the antitrust laws. How sound this theory is today is clouded by the subsequent decisions by the Supreme Court on ancillary matters. Consequently, the astute businessman should insure that such agreements receive careful scrutiny to ascertain whether the particular field-of-use agreement involved raises serious antitrust problems.

Territorial limitations on the licensee's practice of the invention are expressly allowed by statute. In situations of this type, however, other factors may be present which have overtones of concert of action or conspiracy. For example, a factor that might be relevant in a division of territory among the patent licensees is the pre-existing competition between the parties. Also, where a trade association holds patents, which trade association consists of the licensees, a violation of the antitrust laws may exist if the effect of the licensing arrangement is a horizontal territorial market allocation.

When the patentee seeks to limit the quantity of patented articles which the licensee produces, the courts have upheld such agreements if the quantity limit is made with reference to the patented article itself. Problems, arise, however, when the patentee seeks to have royalties computed on the basis of nonpatented goods produced by a patented machine. One court has held that if the patentee licenses another to manufacture and use a brickmaking machine, the patentee cannot have his royalties computed on the basis of the number of unpatented bricks manufactured by the machine.

Interchange of Patent Rights: Patent Pools

An interchange of patent rights giving one corporation the right to license others under the pooled patents often raises antitrust implications. As *Line Material* and many other cases have pointed out, bona fide patent conflicts or blocking situations which would prevent independent exploitation of an invention can be resolved by patent cross-licensing agreements. The temptation exists, however, for competitors to use such agreements as a shield for illicit conspiracies or attempts to monopolize. Indeed, entire industries have been unlawfully regimented under the guise of such agreements, with their attendant antitrust violations.

Risking repetition to emphasize the point: such patent interchange agreements cannot be used to fix prices, to suppress the sale of unpatented products, or to engage in other activities which the courts have held to constitute *per se* violations of the Sherman Act. In these situations power in the market place is not a controlling factor, such restraints on competition being considered unlawful regardless of the amount of market power held by the parties to the agreement. In other restraints of trade the purpose and power of the competitors will be a relevant consideration in determining whether an antitrust violation is present.

In the *Gasoline Cracking* case, decided in 1931, the Supreme Court used a rule of reason approach in evaluating the antitrust aspects of certain patent interchange agreements. In that case each of four corporate patent owners had patents on cracking processes useful in producing gasoline. The four companies became involved in patent conflicts concerning the scope, validity, and ownership of the valuable patents. In order to avoid litigation and losses incident to these conflicting patents, the four companies entered into interchange agreements which provided that each of the companies was released from liability for any past infringement and could use all the patents thereafter in its own gasoline cracking process. Each company was empowered to extend to independent concerns licensed under its process a release from claims of patent infringement arising from patents controlled by the other three companies, and each company was to share in the royalties received from all licenses.

The Supreme Court, in dismissing an action brought by the United States for violation of the Sherman Act, rejected the government's contention that such agreements constituted an unlawful pooling of patent royalties, that competition among the four companies in the exercise of their right to issue licenses had been eliminated, and that this practice tended to maintain or increase the royalty charged other parties securing licenses and thus increased the manufacturing cost of gasoline. The Supreme Court observed that there was no provision in any of the agreements which restricted the freedom of any one of the four companies to issue licenses individually under its own patent alone or under the patents of all the others, nor was there any restriction on the quantity or conditions of sale of the gasoline to be produced. The mere division of royalties among the four companies was not considered an unlawful combination under the Sherman Act. In view of the fact that there were legitimate conflicts regarding the patents, the arrangement merely constituted a settlement to avoid patent litigation. That other licensee-manufacturers might have to pay higher competitive royalty rates was not by itself considered to give rise to a violation of the Sherman Act. The Court recognized that the power to fix and maintain royalties was tantamount to the power to fix prices. Accordingly, when domination exists in a market, a pooling of competing process patents or an exchange of licenses for the purpose of curtailing the manufacture and supply of an unpatented product is beyond the privileges conferred by the patents and constitutes a violation of the Sherman Act. The Court found, however, that no monopoly or restriction of competition in the business of licensing patented cracking processes resulted from the execution of these agreements. This conclusion was reached after an extensive consideration, by the classic "rule of reason," of the facts and of the purpose and effect of the agreements.

United States v. *Krasnov* illustrates another situation. Two corporations controlled 62 per cent of the ready-made slip cover market, the remaining market being divided among thirteen manufacturers. As part of a settlement agreement to resolve a patent controversy, they exchanged cross-licenses, one corporation agreeing not to license others without the second corporation's consent. In order to divert business from competitors, false threats of patent infringement were brought against the retailer customers of their competitors. In addition to price fixing, efforts were made to avoid adjudication of the patents' validity. Sherman Act violations were found in all these circumstances.

Patent Misuse Not Involving Antitrust Violations

The doctrine of patent misuse is grounded on a "public policy" and may operate on equitable grounds to deny relief in a private suit for patent infringement. Although patent misuse is technically not an area of antitrust law, there is a close relationship. Use of a patent in violation of the antitrust laws may constitute misuse, and the patent owner may therefore be denied relief against infringement of his patent.

The *Mercoid* cases concerned a patent on a new combination heating system. The combination included a fuel-input thermostat, a mechanical stoker, and a switch which operated to keep the heating system stoked when the thermostat did not signal for an increase in room heat. The patented invention was complete only when this combination was employed, because there was no patent on any of the elements which made up the combination.

The patent owner, in order to promote his patent rights, licensed a company under the patent, giving this company the right to grant sublicenses to others. The licensed company made only the stoker switches. The patent owner's royalties were computed by the number of stoker switches which the licensee company sold when it granted its sublicensees the right to practice the invention with its switches. Mercoid Company, an outsider to this agreement, also made and sold these stoker switches specifically for use in the patented combination and was sued as a contributory infringer. Mercoid said in defense that the patent owner's licensing program involved misuse of patent rights. The Supreme Court agreed and denied relief, even though Mercoid was deliberately seeking to have its switches used in the patent combination. The Court considered this licensing program to go beyond the traditional rights accorded the patentee. The case was viewed as a contest over the unpatented wares which went into the patented product, and the patent owner's misuse led the Court to deny relief for contributory infringement.

In the *Morton Salt* case the owner of a patent on a machine for dispensing salt tablets brought a patent infringement suit. The suit was dismissed in view of the patent owner's requirement that licensees who leased the machines use only unpatented salt tablets sold by the patent owner in the patented machines. Although this case might have been decided on a number of grounds, the Supreme Court decided that such a practice was against public policy. The Supreme Court thus denied relief on equitable grounds.

The doctrine of patent misuse is largely based on the equitable principle of "unclean hands." The prudent businessman should have license agreements carefully reviewed for any possible tie-in provisions like those in *Morton Salt;* licenses of combination patents should likewise be scrutinized for possible patent misuse based on any requirement that the licensee purchase an element of the combination from a particular source.

Trademarks

Trademarks, like patents, may be a vehicle for violation of the antitrust laws when they go beyond the purpose of safeguarding the property interest and the intangible good will of the manufacturer. In the *Timken Roller Bearing* case the Supreme Court said:

> The trademark may become a detrimental weapon if it is used to serve a harmful or injurious purpose. If it becomes a tool to circumvent free enterprise and unbridled competition, public policy dictates that the rights enjoyed by the ownership be kept within their proper bounds. If a trademark may be the legal basis for allocating world markets, fixing prices, restricting competition, the unfailing device has been found to destroy every vestige of inhibition set up by the Sherman Act.

CHAPTER 11

MERGERS AND ACQUISITIONS

A COMPANY contemplating the acquisition of all or part of the stock or assets of another company should carefully consider the possible applicability of the antitrust laws to the proposed acquisition, just as it should consider the applicability of corporate, tax, and securities laws. The antitrust laws do not forbid all mergers or acquisitions, but they do provide an extensive range of drastic penalties against companies which make acquisitions later found to be illegal. These penalties include the divestiture of the stock or assets acquired, the restoration of the acquired company as a going concern, injunctions against future mergers, and, in some instances, criminal sanctions.

Mergers are commonly referred to as "horizontal," "vertical," "conglomerate," "product-extension," or "market-extension." The type of merger determines the likelihood of a finding of illegality, as well as the method by which illegality will be determined. At the outset, then, it is important to understand the business context out of which each sort of merger arises. Then we will proceed to consider the legal tests applicable to any given merger.

A horizontal merger involves the acquisition by one company of all or part of the stock or assets of a competitor which offers the same goods or services in the same market area. For example, if the Recap Tire Company, national manufacturer of tires distributing its products in all states, including Arizona, were to acquire the assets of the Arizona Tire Corporation, a company manufacturing and selling tires only in Arizona, a horizontal merger would have been effected. By virtue of the merger the horizontal competition between the two companies in selling tires in Arizona would end. The extent of the competition between these two companies ended by the merger provides the initial test of legality.

Closely allied to a horizontal merger is a market-extension merger. Such a merger involves the acquisition of a company whose general business is the same as that of the acquiring company but in a geographic area in which the acquiring company does not operate. If a dairy operating only in Washington, D.C., were to acquire a dairy operating only in Richmond, Virginia, the resulting merger would be one of market extension. Because the two companies had not been in direct competition with each other, no horizontal elimination of competition would occur.

A vertical merger is one in which the acquiring company merges with a supplier or a customer. If the merger is with a supplier, it is a backward vertical integration; with a customer, a forward vertical integration. For example, if the Recap Tire Company were to purchase a rubber plantation, a backward vertical integration would have taken place, as the merger would provide this tire manufacturer with a supply of rubber. If, on the other hand, Recap were to purchase a chain of auto supply stores, a forward vertical integration would be involved, for the merger would provide Recap with retail outlets through which to sell its tires.

A product-extension merger involves the acquisition of a company by another which produces related, but not exactly the same products. For example, if a company producing a wide variety of household cleaning products, but not liquid bleach, acquires a manufacturer of such bleach, a product-extension merger would have taken place.

A conglomerate merger involves the acquisition of a company engaged in a business unrelated to that of the acquiring company. The acquisition of an electronics manufacturer by a soap distributor is an example of such a merger.

Each type of merger is subject to attack under a number of antitrust laws. The test of legality varies, depending on the particular statutory provision involved. It is to these statutes and their tests of legality that we must now turn our attention.

By far the most important provision under which the legality of an acquisition must be judged is Section 7 of the Clayton Act. Briefly, Section 7 provides that an acquisition by a corporation engaged in interstate commerce of all or part of the stock or assets of another corporation also engaged in interstate commerce is illegal "where in any line of commerce in any section of the country, the effect of such acquisition may be to substantially lessen competition, or tend to create a monopoly."

Two threshold questions are immediately posed by this section: First, are both the acquiring and acquired firms corporations? Second, are both companies engaged in interstate commerce? The requirement that both firms be corporations eliminates from the taint of illegality under this section any acquisition by or of any individual enterprise or noncorporate entity. Acquisitions of or by individuals and partnerships may be attacked under other antitrust provisions applicable to mergers, however. Such provisions will be discussed later in this chapter. It should also be noted that a corporation cannot avoid the provisions of the Clayton Act simply by effecting an acquisition through a noncorporate dummy. The Federal Trade Commission held in an early case that an acquisition of a corporation by another corporation was illegal even though initially the purchased company was acquired by the president of the acquiring company in his capacity as an individual.

The requirement that both corporations be engaged in interstate commerce appears superficially to be rather restrictive, but the ease with which a company can be found to be so engaged was described in Chapter 3. A few more examples will sharpen this point. A Federal Trade Commission hearing examiner held a company to be engaged in interstate commerce for purposes of Section 7 even though it had made only two or three sales in commerce over a two-year period. In another case the commission held that a company purchasing supplies in commerce was subject to Section 7. Finally, it should be noted that to violate Section 7 it is only necessary that the respective corporations be engaged in commerce, not that deleterious competitive effects be felt in interstate commerce.

Before turning to the substantive application of Section 7, one final procedural point should be made. Although the phrase *acquisition of assets* would appear to require a company to obtain actual title to the assets involved, at least one court has indicated that this is not so. The case involved a company engaged in licensing old movies for television showing. This company contracted for the exclusive right to license the film inventory of a major motion picture studio to local television stations. The acquisition of these licensing rights was attacked as violative of Section 7; although the district court eventually held the acquisition legal for other reasons, it did state that the contract involved an acquisition subject to Section 7.

Let us now turn to a discussion of the test of legality of acquisitions subject to the Clayton Act. Section 7 condemns only those mergers whose probable effect is either a substantial lessening of competition or a tendency to create a monopoly. This emphasis on *probable* effect means that a merger need not in itself *actually* substantially lessen competition or create a monopoly. It is sufficient that the merger *may* produce one of those effects in the future.

The first step in determining the legality of a merger is to determine the market within which to judge the probability of a substantial lessening of competition or a tendency to monopoly. Section 7 indicates that the proscribed effect may occur in any line of commerce in any section of the country. Thus, there will be both a product market and a geographic market. The product market may consist of one or a number of the products or services offered by either the acquired or acquiring company. The geographic market is determined by ascertaining the area in which the acquired company, the acquiring company, or both companies conduct operations.

The definition of the relevant product and geographic markets is normally the major issue in a merger case. Because the character of these markets often determines the extent of the competitive effects by which the merger will be judged, tremendous amounts of time and money have frequently been expended to produce sophisticated economic analysis showing that these markets should be framed in terms favorable to the company attacked.

The importance of market definition to the testing of competitive effect can be demonstrated by a brief example. Suppose that two dairies which produce only fluid milk for sale only within the city limits of San Francisco have merged. Suppose also that together they account for 40 per cent of the sales in that city. If the two dairies were to prevail in their argument that the product market should be defined as all dairy products, including ice cream, butter, and cheese, their market share might drop to 15 per cent, because they are engaged only in the sale of fluid milk. Similarly, if they were also to prevail in their argument that the geographic market should be the Bay area rather than the city of San Francisco, their market share might drop even further to 5 per cent. No economic training is necessary to conclude that a merger affecting only 5 per cent of the market is far less likely to have adverse competitive effects than one affecting 40 per cent of the market. Recent cases, however, have suggested that even relatively small percentage shares of the relevant market may be sufficient for Section 7 purposes if there is a tendency toward concentration in the industry. The Supreme Court held that a combined market share of 7 per cent of grocery sales in the Los Angeles area after the merger was sufficient to violate the Clayton Act in its *Vons* decision. And, 4.5 per cent of the brewery business was held not insubstantial and the Blatz-Pabst merger was invalidated.

Unfortunately, the example regarding the two dairies is deceptive in its definition of the product market. Naturally, the government is interested in framing the market narrowly, and because Section 7 speaks in terms of "*any* line of commerce in *any* section of the country," the government is frequently able to prevail. In the horizontal merger of the two dairies described, the product market would probably be defined as the sale of fluid milk. Of course, a company should always argue for a broader market definition, but it should be recognized that the chance of success is limited.

In a vertical merger the product market is usually defined on the basis of the product which the acquired customer or acquired supplier bought from or sold to the acquiring company. In our Recap Tire Company example, if Recap purchased a rubber plantation, the product market might be defined as raw rubber. But if Recap had acquired a chain of auto supply stores, the product market would probably be the sale of tires to retailers.

The product market of conglomerate mergers is usually framed in terms of one or a number of the products of the acquired company. Similar product market definition is involved in market-extension and product-extension mergers.

A number of factors may lead to a refinement of the product market beyond the definition initially selected on the basis of the analysis suggested. In a leading antitrust case the Supreme Court, in framing a product market under another section of the antitrust laws, looked to the factors of interchangeability of use and cross-elasticity of demand. In that case the government contended that the product market was cellophane. The Court noted, however, that other products, such as Saran-Wrap and polyethylene film, competed with cellophane for the purchaser of flexible packaging material. Although cellophane had some advantages for certain purchasers, these purchasers would use other flexible packaging products if the price of cellophane were to rise. Because of this interchangeability of use, an interchangeability that occurred in practice when price differentials changed, the Supreme Court held the proper product market to be all flexible packaging products, not just cellophane. Merger cases since this decision have applied the same kind of analysis. These factors are not important in all markets, however, and their use will depend on the economic facts of life in the particular market involved in a given case.

The classic statement of product market definition, given in the leading Supreme Court case of *Brown Shoe Company* v. *United States,* is a good summarization of this complex area:

> The outer boundaries of a product market are determined by the reasonable interchangeability of use or the cross-elasticity of demand between the product itself and substitutes for it. However, within this broad market, well-defined submarkets may exist which, in themselves, constitute product markets for antitrust purposes. . . . The boundaries of such a submarket may be determined by examining such practical indicia as industry or public recognition of the submarket as a separate economic entity, the product's peculiar characteristics and uses, unique production facilities, distinct customers, distinct prices, sensitivity to price changes, and specialized vendors. Because §7 of the Clayton Act prohibits any merger which may substantially lessen competition "in *any line of commerce*" [italics added], it is necessary to examine the effects of a merger in each such economically significant submarket to determine if there is a reasonable probability that the merger will substantially lessen competition. If such a probability is found to exist, the merger is proscribed.

The Court then went on, over the strenuous objections of the defendant, to frame separate markets for men's, women's, and children's shoes. The defendant's contention that further refinement of the defined market should be made to create submarkets for lower and higher-priced shoes was rejected by the Court on the basis that shoes of different prices were in effective competition with each other for the purchaser's dollar. This case should illustrate the complex economic analysis involved in defining a product market.

Once product-market definition is accomplished, the geographic market must be framed. Again, the broader this market, the less likely that the merger will have the proscribed effect. In a horizontal or market-extension merger a geographic market may be as small as a town or as broad as the whole nation. The nature of the product may have an important bearing on this determination. For example, if the product were ready-mix concrete, the geographic market would be small because of the impossibility of transporting the concrete economically for any distance prior to sale. Similar limitations on market size might be dictated by the perishable nature of the commodity or the localized nature of the industry involved, such as the retail sale of groceries. On the other hand, a national industry such as the manufacture of automobiles would involve a national geographic market. In summary, careful analysis of the product, the industry, and the nature of competition between the acquired and acquiring company is necessary in defining the geographic market.

Once the relevant product and geographic markets have been established, the legality of the merger can be measured against its probable effect of substantially lessening competition or tending to create a monopoly.

The most important single factor is the proportion of the relevant market held by the acquiring and the acquired companies. Indeed, some commentators seeking ease of judicial administration have contended that this factor should be controlling. They have argued that any horizontal merger in which the companies have a combined market share of over 30 per cent should be held illegal without further proof. In May, 1963, in its *Philadelphia National Bank* decision, the Supreme Court indicated approval of this position. As a consequence, the percentage of the relevant market controlled by the combined companies will be a factor uppermost in the minds of the enforcement agencies. Any merger involving more than 5 per cent of the market is one in which legal repercussions might well arise.

Of almost equal importance is the economic size and strength of the acquiring company, both in absolute terms and with reference to the particular market involved. A merger by General Motors will excite great interest in an enforcement agency simply because of General Motors's size. A fear of such economic giants is strong in this country; as we have seen, it was in part this fear that motivated the passage of the antitrust laws in the first place. Similarly, a merger by a company that has achieved dominance in its industry will be far more suspect than most acquisitions. In short, because Section 7 was passed to prevent any company from becoming big enough to be immune from competition, any merger by a very large company or one dominant in its industry is likely to be attacked.

Another important and similar factor in judging legality is the trend in the industry with respect to concentration. If individual firms within an industry are engaged in a wave of mergers, with the resultant threat of oligopoly, then any given merger within the industry is likely to be attacked. If concentration within an industry is increasing by means other than acquisitions, attack is a distinct possibility. In *Philadelphia National Bank,* the Supreme Court said that the increase in concentration of one third as a result of a merger would render the merger illegal. The courts have frequently stated that the purpose of Section 7 was to prevent the growth of concentration within an industry and thus to preserve small, autonomous, and competitive economic units. Also significant is the merger history of the acquiring company. A company that has been growing steadily through acquisitions is a prime target for a charge of illegality.

The ease with which new companies may enter the market is also important in determining the competitive effect of a given merger. If new entries have occurred and are likely to continue to occur, then the adverse effects of a merger will be lessened. If the merger does have an adverse competitive effect, this effect will be only temporary, for once competition diminishes, new competitors can be expected to enter the market and revitalize competition.

The cumulative effects of a series of mergers may subject an otherwise valid merger to attack. Assume that a company has made ten mergers in recent years, that all ten of these mergers are attacked by the government in a single complaint, and that no one of these mergers is found, of itself, to violate Section 7. Nevertheless, the government may contend that the cumulative effect of all ten mergers is a substantial lessening of competition or tendency toward monopoly. If the court or the Federal Trade Commission agrees with the government's contention, some or all of the acquired companies may have to be divested in order to restore effective competition, notwithstanding the fact that the mergers thus dissolved would be legal if considered in isolation. In one case, a district court ordered a chain store found guilty of violating Section 7 to divest itself of at least one store for every five months that divestiture was delayed. The existence of the cumulative effects theory means that companies which have had an active merger history must be particularly careful in assessing the antitrust dangers of future mergers.

The legality of a horizontal merger is usually tested initially in terms of the amount of competition thus eliminated. If the combined market strength of the two companies is greater than 5 per cent of the relevant market, the merger immediately becomes suspicious. As this combined market percentage increases, the risk of illegality becomes greater. Other significant factors include the merger history of the acquiring company, the trend toward oligopolistic concentration in the industry, the ease of entry into the industry, and the cumulative effects of prior mergers by the acquiring company. To the extent that these additional factors appear in aggravated form, a finding of illegality is likely even though only a small percentage of the total relevant market is controlled by the merged company.

Vertical mergers are tested in much the same way. In a backward vertical integration, when a company is acquiring a supplier, the critical question is whether the merger will deprive the acquiring company's competitors of a source of supply necessary to their effective competition with the acquiring company. That percentage of the market for the supply in question controlled by the acquired company is especially significant in testing the legality of the merger. But even a higher percentage can be defended by proof that adequate quantities of the supply are readily available to the competitors of the acquiring company. In a forward vertical integration, when a company acquires a customer, illegality is usually found if competitors of the acquiring company have been deprived of a substantial customer necessary to the maintenance of their effective competition. Again, the percentage of the market represented by the customer's purchases is the major criterion of legality.

Although experience would indicate that both types of vertical merger are somewhat less vulnerable than horizontal mergers because of the greater difficulty of market analysis, a recent Supreme Court case indicated that the trend toward integration in the industry is particularly significant. A forward vertical integration involving only 2 per cent of the market was found to be illegal because of the threat of industry-wide integration. The FTC has been particularly vigilant in stemming the tide of vertical integration in the cement industry.

Conglomerate mergers have only recently been attacked by the enforcement agencies, and the guidelines of illegality are only beginning to emerge. The significant factor is the economic or marketing strength of the acquiring company and the probable effect of that strength on the market in which the acquired company operated. For example, if a financial giant acquires a company in an industry composed of small competitors of roughly equal size, a court might infer that competition in the acquired company's market will be detrimentally affected because of that company's heightened economic strength as a result of having a "rich parent." Small competitors would fear to compete vigorously on such matters as price and promotion, and potential competitors would be "scared off." Postacquisition economic data concerning the actual competitive effects of the merger are frequently used in conglomerate merger cases.

A recent development in the law of conglomerate mergers is the finding of illegality from the possible use of reciprocal buying practices by the acquiring company. In one case which involved a product-extension rather than a pure conglomerate merger, a large food distributor acquired a leading company in the dehydrated onion and garlic industry. Because many of the acquiring company's suppliers used such onion and garlic in their food products, the Federal Trade Commission inferred that the acquiring company might buy only from those suppliers who agreed to buy their dehydrated onion and garlic from the acquired company. Post-acquisition data showed that such practices had indeed been utilized by the acquiring company, and the commission held the merger illegal because of the substantial distortion of competitive relationships in the dehydrated onion and garlic industry. The United States Courts of Appeals reversed, but ultimately the Supreme Court upheld the FTC's findings.

Market-extension acquisitions are judged in a manner similar to that which applies to conglomerate mergers. The likely effect of the imposition of the acquiring company's economic strength on the competitive structure of the geographic market in which the acquired company did business will provide the test of legality. Potential competition in the form of the likelihood that one of the company's would enter the other's market on its own is another factor. Of paramount importance, though, is the trend toward concentration in the industry. To date market-extension acquisitions have been attacked mostly in those industries, such as the dairy products industry, in which a wave of mergers has changed a traditional pattern of local competition into one of national oligopoly. More recently, the Supreme Court held illegal a market-extension merger in the pipe-line industry.

Product-extension mergers are judged by similar tests of illegality as exist with respect to conglomerates and market extensions. The economic strength of the acquiring company, the effects on competition in the market of the acquired company, and barriers to entry are all significant factors.

A Federal Trade Commission case involved an acquisition which does not fit into any of the usual situations so far discussed. A large manufacturer of sanitary paper products acquired additional production facilities from companies with which it had not been in competition. The commission held this acquisition illegal because the increase in size in turn increased the manufacturer's dominant position in the industry—with the resultant threat of substantially lessened competition in that industry.

It should be noted that a merger can be attacked years after its occurrence if its anticompetitive effects first become apparent at that time. In one Supreme Court case a merger effected more than thirty years before the suit was brought was successfully attacked under Section 7, and an order requiring divestiture of the acquired stock was entered. Though such attack is a rarity, its possibility should be seriously considered, particularly by large companies contemplating an acquisition.

Some mergers otherwise thought to be illegal may be beyond the reach of Section 7 because of the presence of a special defense. The statute itself provides:

> This section shall not apply to corporations purchasing such stock solely for investment and not using the same by voting or otherwise to bring about, or in attempting to bring about, the substantial lessening of competition. Nor shall anything contained in this section prevent a corporation engaged in commerce from causing the formation of subsidiary corporations for the actual carrying on of their immediate lawful business, or the natural and legitimate branches or extensions thereof, or from owning and holding all or a part of the stock of such subsidiary corporations, when the effect of such formation is not to substantially lessen competition.

Although this provision is not of great practical significance, its application should be carefully considered when any acquisition is attacked.

Other defenses include that asserted by two small companies combining better to compete with established giants, and the failing-company defense. The latter doctrine provides that the merger is not illegal if the acquired company is in imminent danger of business failure. If the failure of the company would have caused a substantial lessening of competition, then the merger itself cannot be held as the cause of any competitive effect forbidden by Section 7. The failing-company defense, however, may not apply if other prospective purchasers of the acquired company were available whose purchase would not have caused the adverse competitive effects which resulted from purchase by the acquiring company, and one recent case emasculated the doctrine by confining its application to the situation where the failing company is practically walking in the doors of the bankruptcy court.

Even over-all procompetitive effects constitute no defense in a Section 7 action. In its recent *Ford* opinion, the Supreme Court struck down the Ford Motor Company's 1961 acquisition of The Electric Autolite Co. (Autolite), one of the three major producers of spark plugs in the country, and ordered Ford's divestiture of the Autolite assets. The Court rejected Ford's contention, in ruling that the acquisition was illegal under Section 7 of the Clayton Act, that the procompetitive effects of the merger offset and outweighed any injuries to competition. Not only was this contention rejected, but the categorical suggestion that anticompetitive effects can be balanced out by procompetitive effects was also thoroughly rejected by the Court. The Court concluded that a merger is not saved from illegality "because, on some ultimate reckoning of social or economic debits and credits, it may be deemed beneficial. Congress . . . proscribed anti-competitive mergers, the benign and the malignant alike, fully aware, we must assume, that some price might have to be paid." In addition to ordering divestiture, the Court also approved relief against Ford, requiring it to purchase one half of its spark plug requirements from the divested company, prohibiting it from manufacturing its own plugs for ten years, and prohibiting it from marketing plugs bearing its trade name for five years. This extensive relief against Ford is novel and without litigated precedent.

Although Section 7 is the usual law under which a merger will be attacked, action may be taken by the government under three other statutory provisions. An acquisition of a partnership or individual proprietorship not subject to Section 7 may be attacked under Section 5 of the Federal Trade Commission Act as an unfair method of competition. The Section 7 tests of legality would probably be applied under Section 5 as well.

Section 1 of the Sherman Act also provides a vehicle by which the Department of Justice could challenge the acquisition of a noncorporate enterprise. With one significant difference, the Section 7 approach to test legality would be used under the Sherman Act as well. Section 7, however, requires proof only that the merger *may* substantially lessen competition or tend to create a monopoly. Section 1 of the Sherman Act, on the other hand, can be satisfied only by showing an *actual* substantial lessening of competition. Given this additional burden, the government clearly prefers to attack a merger under Section 7 of the Clayton Act rather than under Section 1 of the Sherman Act.

Finally, a merger might be found to violate Section 2 of the Sherman Act. That section prohibits monopolizing, attempts to monopolize, and conspiracies to monopolize. A company might be guilty of monopolizing if by a merger it acquired the power to exclude competitors from or to fix the prices in an identifiable market. Because courts have occasionally defined markets in a very narrow fashion under this section, a company occupying a dominant position in its home market must be wary of a charge of monopolizing if it is considering an acquisition in that market.

If a company has the specific intent to acquire monopoly power—that is, the power to fix prices or exclude competitors within a market—a merger might result in liability for attempting to monopolize or entering a conspiracy to monopolize. Liability becomes more likely if a company has engaged in a series of mergers. A company with an active merger history should be very careful to disprove the existence of an intent to acquire monopoly power in its market, particularly if any further acquisitions are contemplated.

Once illegality is found, consideration must be given to the remedies available to the government. A violation of Sections 1 or 2 of the Sherman Act could result in the imposition of criminal penalties. The normal remedy for the violation of any of the sections, however, is an order requiring the divestiture of all the stock or assets acquired. If the illegality inheres in only a part of the business acquired, then partial divestiture might be ordered if that remedy will cure the violation and if it can be carried out practically. In the event that the acquiring company has been involved in a number of mergers, an order preventing any future acquisitions for a given period of time might also be entered. Alternatively, future acquisitions might be conditioned upon prior notification to or prior consent by one of the government enforcement agencies. As these remedies, particularly divestiture, are extremely disruptive to a business, great care should be taken to avoid them by refraining from illegal acquisitions in the first place.

This examination of the substantive prohibitions against mergers has been necessarily brief. While it was not intended to treat all the legal problems which arise, it has, hopefully, covered the principal factors which are important in judging a merger's legality. A businessman aware of such problems is in a position to consult competent antitrust counsel far enough in advance to insure that any proposed merger will have the maximum chance of withstanding a charge of illegality.

CHAPTER 12

MONOPOLIZATION

SECTION 2 of the Sherman Act declares the acts of monopolizing, attempting to monopolize, or conspiring to monopolize illegal and subjects those found guilty of breaching its provisions to fines not exceeding $50,000 or imprisonment not exceeding one year or both. Section 2 is primarily concerned with the situation in which a single firm or corporation achieves or seeks to achieve a position of such size and power that it is capable of restraining trade by its own, unaided efforts. Neither mere size nor the virtual absence of competition is illegal or prohibited in itself, however. Not all monopoly is proscribed. In some instances monopolies or exclusive privileges may be granted by federal, state, or local governments because the geographical area is unable to support more than one firm of a particular type. In others, the monopoly may be "thrust" upon the firm because of its unequalled efficiency in organization or production or the sheer quality and utility of its product. Monopoly may also be "thrust" upon the firm by virtue of the fact that the nature of things dictates that only one firm can effectively operate in the market area. An example would be the one-newspaper town. That which is forbidden, therefore, is not the status of monopoly, but the act or planned or attempted act of "monopolization." Monopolization is the possession of monopoly power coupled with the attainment of that power by unfair means or the use of that power unfairly for the purpose of excluding competition. In ascertaining permissible monopoly and distinguishing it from the forbidden acts of monopolizing, a case-by-case analysis of the intent of the firm in question and the business practices which it employs are essential.

The degree of power necessary to establish monopolization has not been definitely established. *Monopoly,* or *monopoly power,* has been defined as the power or ability to fix or control prices in or exclude competition from a relevant market. If neither of these abilities can be shown directly, they may be presumed if there is an indication that the firm in question controls a massive percentage of its relevant market. No precise percentage has been established, either legislatively or judicially, because the relative effect of a percentage command of a market varies with the type of market. On a case-by-case basis the courts have ruled different percentages to be sufficient indications of a monopoly position. In one case 94 per cent was clearly sufficient. Between 75 and 80 per cent was sufficient in another. Seventy-five per cent, when coupled with attempts to use this power to gain an advantage in other fields, was also sufficient. When two related corporations dominated 65 per cent of the field and their nearest competitor had less than 8 per cent, the two firms together had sufficient power to be held a combination for monopoly purposes. Between 60 and 64 per cent was classified as "doubtful" whereas 50 per cent was insufficient. Percentages less than 50 have been held clearly insufficient. As a result, if a corporation has the power to fix prices or to exclude competition in the market in which it competes, or if it dominates roughly 75 per cent of the market in which it competes, there is a good chance that a court will hold that it possesses the requisite power for monopolization.

The difficult and crucial issue at stake in determining market power is not the percentage of the market that establishes monopoly but the scope of the market to which that figure is applied. Applicable here are many of the factors which were discussed in Chapter 11 with regard to determining the relevant market or line of commerce within which to judge the legality of a merger. In the 1956 *Cellophane* case the Supreme Court was faced with the problem of deciding whether the relevant market should be limited to cellophane or should encompass the entire flexible packaging industry. After deciding that the relevant market extended to the entire flexible packaging industry, the Court quickly reached the conclusion that because Du Pont possessed only about 17 per cent of this broad market, the Sherman Act was not applicable. In the *Alcoa* case, on the other hand, a circuit judge reached the conclusion that the relevant market was only virgin aluminum ingot rather than the entire aluminum industry. Once this question had been resolved, he had no difficulty in deciding that Alcoa's 90 per cent domination of this market constituted monopoly power.

The term *relevant market* involves a resolution of two questions. The first is a determination of the geographic boundaries of the market. A relevant market may include a single city, several large cities, a state, a section of the country, or the entire nation. In one case the geographic market was held to encompass only four large cities. In the *Paramount Pictures* case the Supreme Court indicated the necessity for deciding whether the relevant geographic market was the first-run motion picture field for the entire country, the first-run field in ninety-two large cities, or the first-run field in separate localities. The geographic location of the market is usually determined by an examination of the areas in which the particular firm actually competes or operates. If it concentrates its sales and service in one area, this area will normally be the relevant geographic market. If a firm's activities are nationwide, the relevant geographic market will be the whole nation.

In addition to the geographic factor, the term *relevant market* includes the concept of product differentiation. The product in question must be categorized. The *Cellophane* and *Alcoa* cases mentioned earlier illustrate the difficulty of determining the category of the product. Are cellophane and aluminum categories unto themselves, or is each merely one product in a wider category? For many years the courts considered the uses of the product, its physical qualities, the cost of its production, and the final market price. If the products in question had virtually identical uses, prices, and physical qualities, they were considered to be a part of the same relevant market. A small difference in the uses, physical qualities, or cost of production served at times to isolate a product and to establish a limited relevant market. For example, one court reached the conclusion that starch syrup made from corn was a separate product from starch syrup made otherwise, even though the products were indistinguishable in use. In another case the relevant market was hydraulic pumps, as distinguished from rod and other types of pumps. Reasonable interchangeability or the availability of a substitute for the product in question were not factors generally considered to be important. In fact, the Supreme Court once noted:

> For every product, substitutes exist. But a relevant market cannot meaningfully encompass that infinite range. The circle must be drawn narrowly to exclude any other product to which, within reasonable variations in price, only a limited number of buyers will turn; in technical terms, products whose "cross-elasticities of demand" are small. Useful to that determination is, among other things, the trade's own characterization of the products involved.

In the *Cellophane* case, however, the Supreme Court indicated that the interchangeability of products was of vast importance in delineating the relevant market. If, because of a slight change in price or because of scarcity, consumers switched easily to one product from another, the two products were a part of the same relevant market. By such a test the physical qualities or costs of production are less important. In the *Cellophane* case the Court reached the conclusion that cellophane was a part of a broad market that included all flexible packaging materials having a wide range of uses, qualities, and prices, because they were available as substitutes and were reasonably interchangeable. Here the use of this test resulted in a broad relevant market, and many were of the opinion that in all future cases the application of such a test would result in the finding of a broad market. In *International Boxing Club* v. *United States,* however, the Supreme Court applied this test, and the result was a narrow market. The question was whether championship boxing was separate for relevant market purposes from the entire field of professional boxing. In reaching a conclusion, the Court considered evidence of the average dollar income, the average audience ratings, and the testimony of various representatives of radio, television, and the advertising industry to the existence of a special demand for championship boxing which could not be satisfied by nonchampionship bouts. As a result the Court concluded that there was no substitute for championship boxing and that it therefore comprised a separate relevant market. As a result of these cases the availability of a substitute has been established as an important factor in determining the relevant market. Similarity of physical qualities, the cost of production, and market prices are still considered in conjunction with interchangeability, but they now appear to be less important. If the products are reasonably interchangeable and may be substituted for each other by consumers, great difference in their physical characteristics or the cost of production would be necessary before they would be declared to be part of separate relevant markets. A case in point involved the baseball picture card industry. One company, which had a virtual monopoly of baseball picture cards packaged with bubble gum—because of exclusive contracts with most major league baseball players—was charged by the Federal Trade Commission with monopolization. In rejecting the hearing examiner's finding of a violation of Section 5 of the Federal Trade Commission Act, the commission broadened the relevant market to all picture cards, baseball or not, and to baseball picture cards sold in combination with products other than gum.

As we observed earlier, all monopoly is not illegal. If the monopoly is achieved through sheer efficiency, if it is granted by government, or if it is thrust upon the monopolist in some manner, the status of monopoly is generally not condemned. A determination that a firm or product controls a substantial percentage of its relevant market is not in itself a finding that this firm has transgressed the law. In addition to a finding of monopoly power in the relevant market, there must be an indication that the firm intended to obtain this position of power or that it obtained this position through unfair or forbidden business practices. If the firm obtained its position of power through normal business methods, then, in order to prove a violation, there must be evidence that the firm is seeking to maintain or expand its position by the use of unfair or unconscionable means. These unfair or other-than-normal business methods are generally considered to be those restraints of trade cognizable under Section 1 of the Sherman Act, and include refusals to deal, boycotts, and tying clauses. If no such predatory practices can be shown, there must be an indication of general intent to obtain or expand a position of dominance or power in the relevant market. General intent, however, can be presumed, because as Judge Hand said in *Alcoa,* no one monopolizes without being aware of what he is doing.

Several cases have indicated that mere size or dominance of a relevant market alone is insufficient to establish the forbidden act of monopolization. In the early *United Shoe* case it was found that the defendant clearly dominated the field of manufacturing and marketing machinery used in the production of shoes. The Supreme Court ruled, however, that no predatory or forbidden practices had been used by the defendant in obtaining this position of power. Because there was no indication that the defendant had indulged in prohibited business practices in obtaining or expanding its position of power in the relevant market, and because there was no showing of an intent to monopolize, the Court found no antitrust violation. In *United States* v. *United States Steel Corporation,* there was ample evidence that United States Steel was a gigantic corporation. Figures adduced at the trial indicated that it controlled only slightly less than 50 per cent of its relevant market. Two of the four trial judges decided that the various consolidations which had produced that vast organization had been made for the purpose of integrating and streamlining production rather than for the purpose of controlling the market. Accordingly, these two found no intent to achieve monopoly; in their eyes, the element of achieving size for the purpose of domination was lacking. Two others thought that United States Steel possessed the requisite intent to monopolize, but had failed in the attempt. The government was unable to show predatory practices, such as coercive price leadership, price cutting, or other types of discrimination or unfair competition. There was no indication that United States Steel was maintaining its leadership by unfair practices. The government, therefore, was forced to rely on the argument that mere size was illegal. This argument was not answered, because the Supreme Court concluded simply that control of less than 50 per cent of the relevant market was not the position of power required for a finding of monopolization.

Although monopoly power is not sufficient in and of itself to constitute monopolization under Section 2, it was for some time unclear as to upon whom existed the burden of proof of the "plus" element or "thrust" upon argument necessary to translate monopoly power into monopolization. In the *Grinnell* case, a district judge suggested that once it is established that the defendant has a predominate share of a relevant market a rebuttable presumption arises that the defendant has monopolized in violation of Section 2. The United States Supreme Court, however, repudiated this dictum, holding that the burden is on the plaintiff to establish both elements of a Section 2 offense: "(1) the possession of monopoly power in the relevant market and (2) the willful acquisition or maintenance of that power as distinguished from growth or development as a consequence of a superior product, business acumen, or historic accident."

Although extreme size or a position of monopoly power in the relevant market is insufficient for a finding of monopolization when standing alone, a finding of monopolization will result if such size or position was obtained through the use of practices considered to be in restraint of trade. If the firm in question resorted to means cognizable under Section 1 of the Sherman Act to drive its competitors from the market or to make it difficult or impossible for competitors to enter the market, the firm has clearly been guilty of monopolizing in violation of Section 2. For example, in one case an affiliated group of motion picture exhibitors insisted that the distributors of motion pictures grant them monopoly rights in towns where the exhibitors were in competition with other theater owners. If the distributor refused to cooperate, the exhibitors declined to give the distributors outlets in other towns where the exhibitors controlled the only available theaters. The Supreme Court held that such action was obviously in restraint of trade and resulted in an increase of the exhibitors' monopoly power.

The courts have extended Section 2 to cover those situations in which a firm has lawfully obtained its position of power through normal, competitive means or has had monopoly thrust upon it by circumstances if the firm has sought to maintain or expand its properly obtained power by engaging in acts in restraint of trade. In one such case, for example, an association of railroads lawfully obtained possession of the only feasible railroad entrances into the city of St. Louis. By unjustifiably refusing to allow a competing railroad to utilize these entrances, the defendant association was attempting to maintain, by predatory means, a position of power lawfully obtained. In another case the defendant was a manufacturer of unfinished linen rugs and held a monopoly in this field. The defendant also maintained a small rug-finishing business. When an independent finisher and dealer underbid the defendant on a government contract, the latter, as the only manufacturer of unfinished linen rugs, refused to sell to the independent dealer in an attempt to force him to default on the government contract. This abuse of power constituted a Section 2 violation. In the case of *Lorain Journal Company* v. *United States* a newspaper occupying a monopoly position refused to accept any advertising clients who also advertised through a local radio station. Monopoly power which had been obtained normally and legally was thus unlawfully used to suppress competition. The prudent businessman learns from cases like these that when monopoly power is obtained legally, such power must not be utilized to restrain competition. Because illegal monopolization results when a position of monopoly power is coupled with the use of unfair or other-than-normal methods of competition, a firm in a position of power should avoid exercising this power in any underhanded or unfair attempt to drive a competitor from the market.

A finding of monopolization may occur even without evidence of predatory or unfair acts when there is sufficient size coupled with an intent to monopolize. In the *Northern Securities Company* case the Great Northern Railroad and the Northern Pacific Railroad purchased the capital stock of a competitor, the Chicago, Burlington, and Quincy Railroad. The stock of all three was united in the Northern Securities Company. The government's case charging monopolization was based entirely upon the acquisition of control of the competing railroad and the resulting loss of competition. The court required dissolution of the merger on the basis of the loss of competition. In another case the defendants were affiliated corporations which operated motion picture theaters in eighty-five cities and towns. They employed a common agent to negotiate with distributors for films. Even though there was no evidence that they used unfair methods to restrain trade, the court held that the use of a common agent restrained trade by placing independent competitors at an extreme disadvantage.

Perhaps the best-known finding of illegal monopolization despite an absence of evidence of acts in restraint of trade is the *Alcoa* case. The defendant had not engaged in unfair or forbidden business practices. Its 90 per cent domination of the virgin aluminum ingot field resulted from its practice of embracing each new field as the opportunity opened and thereby expanding to meet the market demand for aluminum. Judge Learned Hand held, however, that such conscious expansion was evidence of an intent to monopolize:

> It was not inevitable that it [Alcoa] should always anticipate increases in the demand for ingot and be prepared to supply them. Nothing compelled it to keep doubling and redoubling its capacity before others entered the field. It insists that it never excluded competitors; but we can think of no more effective exclusion than progressively to embrace each new opportunity as it opened, and to face every newcomer with new capacity already geared into a great organization having the advantage of experience, trade connections and the elite of personnel.

When a corporation increases its power in the market by acquiring the assets of suppliers or consumers, and when such acquisitions reduce competition, there may be a violation of Section 2. Such an acquisition, called vertical integration, occurs when a firm purchases the assets of or gains control of other firms engaged in a segment of the business different from that of the purchasing firm. For example, an automobile manufacturer might gain control of a steel corporation which supplies it, or of a manufacturer of glass, tires, or other automobile accessories. When a manufacturer of almost any material or product acquires control of either a supplier or a consumer, vertical integration has occurred. Although there may be legitimate business reasons for vertical integration, such as greater efficiency and lower cost, the acquisition could be condemned as monopolizing if it evinces an intent to restrain competition or to create a dominant power in the market. On the other hand, when the market control by the integrated company is insignificant, or when there is effective competition, such a finding is unlikely. Even when the market share of the integrated company is substantial, vertical integration will in all probability not be condemned unless there is some evidence of an intent to monopolize. As illustrated in the *Alcoa* case, however, when there is dominant market power and a conscious expansion of facilities, there may be a finding of intent to monopolize. A firm already in a dominant market position would definitely be hard pressed to justify any major vertical integration, even if the acquisition was prompted by legitimate business reasons.

In summary, a firm is clearly guilty of monopolization if it occupies a dominant position of power in the relevant market and if it has obtained this position by predatory practices or is utilizing this position to engage in acts forbidden by Section 1 of the Sherman Act in an attempt to suppress competition. In addition, if the firm occupies a substantial position of power, and if there is also evidence of a general intent to increase and strengthen this position, monopolization has occurred even though the firm's business practices are not unfair, unlawful, or forbidden by Section 1. If a firm in a dominant market position acquires the assets of competing firms or seeks to expand through vertical integration, the acquisitions may result in a finding of monopolizing if a general intent to monopolize is apparent. Such acquisitions, however, are not *per se* violations, even by firms of dominant size. If there is effective competition by other firms or a lack of an intent to monopolize, the acquisitions will not be condemned under Section 2.

Attempts and Conspiracies

Section 2 also prohibits attempts and combinations or conspiracies to monopolize. In attempts and conspiracies there is no requirement that the firm involved occupy a dominant position in the relevant market, as is required when the charge is monopolizing. For corporations to be guilty of attempts or conspiracies to monopolize, there must be an indication that the firms are sufficiently strong to pose the threat of achieving monopoly status. There is no necessity that the firms actually achieve monopoly power before an attempt or a conspiracy to monopolize can be established. The firms may fail in their efforts, yet be guilty of an attempt or conspiracy. In addition to the dangerous possibility of achieving a monopoly, there must be evidence that the firms possess a specific intent to monopolize, obviously a more stringent requirement than the general intent necessary to make out a cause of action for monopolizing. This specific intent may be inferred from acts or business practices which, if performed with complete success, would have resulted in monopoly. In proving the conspiracy, there need not be proof of a formal or particular agreement, but there must be evidence of some common scheme or purpose in which the alleged conspirators knowingly participated. The conspiracy condemned under Section 2 differs from that covered by Section 1. A Section 1 conspiracy involves restraint of trade. Section 2 is concerned with conspiracy of which monopolization is the primary end, whether it specifically restrains trade or not. Combinations in support of monopolization usually involve situations in which several large firms dominate the market and engage in activities which prevent new firms from entering. There must be some evidence indicating a genuine meeting of the minds. If the actions of the various firms result in a demonstrably unreasonable effect on competition, however, the requirement that they be done in combination is satisfied if each firm understands what the others are doing and apparently intends the results.

In summary, therefore, that which is proscribed by Section 2 is the effort to obtain dominance in a relevant market, not the mere status of monopoly. This drive for dominance is called monopolizing. Monopolizing occurs when a firm holds a strong position of power in a defined relevant market, and when this position is coupled with an intent to obtain or maintain a monopoly status or with business practices considered to be in restraint of trade. Attempts, combinations, and conspiracies toward this end are likewise prohibited. Because there is no requirement that a finding of dominance precede a finding of an attempt or a conspiracy, even business occupying less than dominant status must beware of concerted acts which would be interpreted as attempts, combinations, or conspiracies to monopolize if there is a possibility that the firms thus combined could dominate the market or exclude competitors.

CHAPTER 13

INTERLOCKING DIRECTORATES

INTERLOCKING or common directorates between competing corporations are specifically forbidden by Section 8 of the Clayton Act. Interlocking relationships involving officers, agents, and employees may also be illegal under various sections of the Sherman Act if there is evidence that the relationship causes a restraint of trade or results in a propensity toward monopoly.

The enactment of Section 8 of the Clayton Act was prompted by the possibility that a few individuals or groups could effectively control and eliminate vigorous competition between corporations through the use of common directorates and thus circumvent other sections of the antitrust laws. Section 8 contains a general prohibition against interlocking directorates between corporations engaged in commerce and a specific provision regulating interlocking relationships between banks, banking associations, and trust companies. Common carriers are exempted from these provisions.

The general prohibition is applicable only when one of the corporations involved has capital, surplus, and undivided profits aggregating more than $1 million. It states: "No person at the same time shall be a director in any two or more corporations . . . engaged in whole or in part in commerce . . . if such corporations are or shall have been theretofore, by virtue of their business and location of operation, competitors, so that the elimination of competition by agreement between them would constitute a violation of any of the provisions of any of the antitrust laws."

An interlocking directorship is not forbidden by the terms of the general provision of Section 8 unless it exists between corporations engaged in interstate commerce. Any amount of interstate commerce is sufficient to invoke jurisdiction. In addition, it must appear that the two corporations compete with each other in some line of commerce. It is not necessary that the particular field of competition exists in interstate commerce as long as both companies engage in some activity in interstate commerce. Further, there does not have to be a substantial amount of competition between the two corporations before Section 8 is applicable. It must appear, however, that the elimination of such competition by agreement would constitute a violation of any of the provisions of any of the antitrust laws. This requirement has been interpreted to mean that if the two corporations could agree to fix prices, restrict territories, or otherwise restrain trade by common action, and if such action would violate any provision of any of the antitrust laws, a common directorship between the two is forbidden. Because Section 8 is essentially preventive in nature, the government need not prove any actual restraint of trade, that the two corporations are large enough to form a hypothetical monopoly, or that there is any substantial effect upon commerce. Instead, the common directorship is *per se* illegal if an agreement between the two competing corporations to eliminate competition in some manner could violate any of the antitrust laws.

Only interlocking directorships between corporations directly competing with each other are forbidden by Section 8. If two corporations engaged in similar lines of commerce do not compete with each other by virtue of their geographic location, a common directorship would not be forbidden. For example, an East Coast distributor and a West Coast distributor whose businesses are confined to separate geographical areas would not be prohibited from utilizing a common director. In like manner, this section has not been violated if a director serves concurrently on the boards of a vendor and a vendee. For example, if a supplier of raw materials and a manufacturer utilizing these materials possess an interlocking directorship, Section 8 has not been violated because the two are not competing corporations. Even though there is no violation of this section, however, competition with other suppliers might nevertheless be reduced by this arrangement, because part of the competitive market might be pre-empted by the common directorship. Similarly, in times when raw materials or supplies are scarce, competition between manufacturers using these materials may be reduced if the supplier or vendor sells primarily to the manufacturer with which it has the common tie. Of course, if the relationship between the two corporations involves any sort of contractual tying or exclusive dealing arrangement, the possibility of a violation of Section 3 of the Clayton Act must be considered. A third relationship not prohibited occurs if a bank has one of its partners or directors serving as a director in a nonbanking corporation and, simultaneously, a second partner or director of the bank serving as a director in a second nonbanking corporation in competition with the first nonbanking corporation. For example, Mr. Jones and Mr. Smith are directors in a metropolitan bank specializing in service to large corporations. Mr. Jones could serve as a director of X Steel Corporation, and Mr. Smith could serve as a director of Y Steel Corporation, a company in competition with X Steel Corporation, while at the same time both continued to serve as directors of the bank. This type of indirect interlocking arrangement does not violate Section 8, because neither individual is serving simultaneously as a director of competing corporations. Such arrangement could conceivably violate Section 7, however, within the meaning of the "corporate amalgamation" language of *Philadelphia National Bank,* discussed in Chapter 11. Still another common relationship not forbidden by Section 8 is an interlocking directorship between parent corporations that are not in competition with each other when these parent corporations have subsidiary corporations that are in competition with each other. Although this type of interlocking arrangement is not specifically forbidden, there is a possibility of violation if it can be shown that the parents have complete control over the affairs of their subsidiaries. The court would then look through the two parent-subsidiary structures and find a Section 8 violation.

This section does not extend to interlocking or common relationships other than interlocking directorates. An individual does not violate Section 8 by serving as an employee of one corporation and as a director of a competing corporation. Thus, an individual could serve as an officer of one company and a director of a competing one. In addition, this section does not proscribe service by an individual as an officer of one firm while he simultaneously possesses a majority of the stock in a second firm competing with the first. Yet, although Section 8 itself does not extend to interlocking relationships other than directorships, this does not mean that the courts are entirely powerless to forbid other common relationships among competing corporations pursuant to this section. In 1953 a district court found that a director was serving on the boards of Sears, Roebuck & Company and B. F. Goodrich Company, and that such service violated Section 8. The court issued a decree requiring the individual to resign his directorship in one of the corporations and to "withdraw from participation in the direction, control, or conduct of the business of the corporate defendant from which he resigned." The director resigned from the board of Sears. Some five years later this director desired to serve as a trustee of Sears "Savings and Profit-Sharing Pension Fund" while he continued to serve as a director of B. F. Goodrich. Although such an interlocking relationship is not expressly forbidden by Section 8, the court found that the director would be participating in the direction, control, or conduct of the business of Sears. This type of participation violated the original decree, and, therefore, the director was forbidden from serving as a Sears trustee. Had this individual resigned from the board of directors of Sears prior to the issuance of a decree by the court, he could have immediately assumed the position of trustee in the Sears empire concurrently with his directorship in Goodrich without violating Section 8.

Actions requiring the resignation of directors may be brought against the corporations or the individual directors or both. As a practical matter, enforcement of Section 8 is primarily extrajudicial. Letters are sent to individuals and corporations suspected of transcending this section by either the Federal Trade Commission or the Department of Justice. If the interlocking directorship is not eliminated, several remedies may be invoked. A cease and desist order may be obtained from the Federal Trade Commission. In addition, either the Department of Justice or injured individuals may institute actions in a district court. If, subsequent to the filing of such an action, the interlocking directorship is eliminated, the action may be dismissed as moot if it appears that there is no reasonable expectation that the violation will be repeated. An interlocking directorship as defined by the general provision of Section 8 may lawfully exist for a period of one year from its inception before it becomes illegal.

The specific provisions of Section 8 applying to banks, banking associations, and trust companies are even more restrictive. They not only prohibit common directorships but also extend to individuals serving simultaneously as officers and employees in two or more banking institutions. This provision states, in part: "No private banker or director, officer, or employee of any member bank of the Federal Reserve System or any branch thereof shall be at the same time a director, officer, or employee of any other bank, banking association, saving bank, or trust company organized under the National Bank Act or organized under the laws of any State or of the District of Columbia or any branch thereof. . . ." The board of governors of the Federal Reserve System may by regulation permit simultaneous service in not more than one other banking institution. Among the several statutory exceptions are banks owned by the United States, banks engaged principally in international or foreign transactions, banks not in competition with each other, and banks in which more than 50 per cent of the common stock is owned by the same persons. A state bank does not, by joining the Federal Reserve System, become subject to this section. The board of governors of the Federal Reserve System enforces compliance with this section. In addition, relief may be pursued in a district court by the Department of Justice or by injured individuals. Here, as in the general provision, the proscriptions of Section 8 are not applicable until the forbidden interlocking relationship has existed for more than one year.

Interlocking directorates, as well as other interlocking relationships, may also be illegal, even though not specifically forbidden, under Sections 1 or 2 of the Sherman Act. Evidence that an interlocking relationship has restrained trade or tends toward monopoly in violation of these sections might be sufficient for a finding that the relationship is illegal. For example, we have noted some of the interlocking relationships which did not violate Section 8 of the Clayton Act, yet these same relationships might conceivably be prohibited by one of the Sherman Act sections. But the problem of proving that such a relationship restrains trade is infinitely more difficult than proving a violation under Section 8. The case law pertaining to interlocking relationships under the Sherman Act has been limited to uncontested decrees in which all parties consented. All of these decrees encompassed other violations of the antitrust laws in addition to the interlocking relationship. These consent decrees usually prohibited the consenting corporations from having any common officers, directors, or employees and required the various individuals involved to resign at least one of their positions. Not only did these consent decrees forbid interlocking relationships other than the directorships defined by Section 8, but they were also extended to include noncompeting corporations, such as the hypothetical supplier and manufacturer previously discussed. For example, a producer of legitimate theater attractions was prohibited from having on its staff any officers or directors who also exercised managerial or policy-making functions in theaters booking the producer's attractions. In another case a well-known company engaged in the business of licensing studios to teach its dancing methods was prohibited by a consent decree from employing as an officer, director, or agent anyone who at the same time served in one of these capacities at any financial institution. Here the corporations involved in the interlocking relationship were not in competition with each other and, hence, would not have violated Section 8 by their actions. Because these arrangements tended to reduce competition in some manner, however, they were in violation of the Sherman Act, and the negotiated decrees prohibited them.

In summary, it should be emphasized that Section 8 clearly forbids interlocking directorships between competing corporations. The proof of such a violation is simple, so that few cases involving an infraction of this nature are contested. The wise businessman, when confronted with an accusation by either the Federal Trade Commission or the Department of Justice, resigns from one of his directorships without contesting the issue. Where the interlocking relationships are not covered by Section 8, the law is not clearly defined, and the proof of an infraction is much more difficult and complicated. If the interlocking relationship has the effect of restraining trade or tends to establish a monopoly, there is a possibility that its existence is illegal under one of the sections of the Sherman Act. The government has not, in the past, sought to eliminate interlocking relationships by use of the Sherman Act unless the firms involved were also suspected of other violations of the antitrust laws. This is not to say that a flagrant case might not be pursued under the Sherman Act, perhaps even as a criminal matter. The prudent executive will always avoid any interlocking relationship which tends to restrain trade.

CHAPTER 14

"UNFAIR METHODS OF COMPETITION... UNFAIR OR DECEPTIVE ACTS"— THE FTC ACT AND RELATED FTC STATUTES

SECTION 5 of the Federal Trade Commission Act declares unlawful "unfair methods of competition in commerce, and unfair or deceptive acts or practices in commerce. . . ." It is the task of the Federal Trade Commission to prevent such acts, methods, and practices. But what are they? The language of the Supreme Court on various occasions illustrates the impossibility of giving a precise answer to that question:

> It is unnecessary to attempt a comprehensive definition of the unfair methods which are banned, even if it were possible to do so. . . . New or different practices must be considered as they arise in the light of the circumstances in which they are employed.
>
> This general language was deliberately left to the "commission and the courts" because it was thought that "there is no limit to human inventiveness in this field."
>
> The point where a method of competition becomes "unfair" within the meaning of the Act will often turn on the exigencies of a particular situation, trade practices, or the practical requirements of the business in question. . . . Congress advisedly left the concept flexible to be defined with particularity by the myriad of cases from the field of business.

Clearly enough, these "definitions" are of little help to the intelligent businessman who simply wishes to know whether or not a particular proposal or act will incur the wrath of the commission. We shall have to take the Supreme Court's advice and look at the "myriad of cases" in order to get some idea of what is prohibited and what is not.

First of all, it is clear that violations of the Sherman Act are also violative of Section 5 and thus may be proceeded against by the commission. For example, such Sherman Act violations as price fixing, boycotts, and resale price maintenance are cognizable under the FTC Act. Section 5 may also be used by the commission against those acts which would amount to violations of the Clayton Act, such as price discrimination, tie-ins, or mergers. The reader is invited to re-examine the discussion of each of these prohibited practices in preceding chapters.

Moreover, the rule is widely accepted that the broad language of Section 5 may be used to reach incipient Sherman Act violations. The Supreme Court has observed that "[a] major purpose of [the FTC Act], as we have frequently said, was to enable the commission to restrain practices as 'unfair' which, although not yet having grown into Sherman Act dimensions, would most likely do so if left unrestrained."

There are a few cases wherein courts have sustained the use of Section 5 to reach acts or practices which themselves do not precisely violate either the Sherman or Clayton Acts but which are so closely related that they violate the basic policy of the original statutes. In this area the courts talk of Section 5 as "bolstering" or "supplementing" the earlier acts. For example, in one case the commission proceeded against the *inducement* of discriminatory advertising allowances on the part of a large chain store. As we previously noted, the Robinson-Patman Act prohibits the *granting* of advertising allowances under certain discriminatory circumstances. The precise terms of the statute do not relate to the knowing inducement of such allowances by a company. Notwithstanding that the conduct the commission sought to reach was not within the literal terms of the Robinson-Patman Act, the federal court nevertheless upheld the commission. The court reasoned in this case that jurisdiction under Section 5 went slightly beyond the "technical confines" of the Robinson-Patman Act "but only fully to realize the basic policy of the . . . Act, which was to prevent the abuse of *buying* power."

Similarly, in the *S and H* case, the FTC ruled that the nation's oldest and largest trading-stamp company illegally restrained trade by (1) requiring retailer licensees to dispense not more than one stamp for each 10-cent purchase; (2) conspiring with others to enforce this policy; and (3) suppressing trade exchanges and redemption activity. Trading-stamp use goes back some seventy years and itself "provides a form of means of competitive rivalry at the retail level." The commission noted that it could find a violation of Section 5, "without a showing of such anticompetitive effects as would be required under" the Sherman or Clayton Acts. Because the trading-stamp industry is highly concentrated and dominated by the respondent, the commission concluded "that respondent's one-for-ten policy, by limiting retailers' opportunities to compete, has substantially impaired or may substantially impair competition." Such practice was, therefore, a violation of Section 5.

The Fifth Circuit, over the dissent of Judge Wisdom, reversed the commission, stating that "Congress would not have intended to vest the Commission with such broad discretion as to allow it to hold a restraint 'unfair' without applying some judicial guidelines in making their findings." The court concluded: "To be the type of practice that the Commission has the power to declare 'unfair' the act complained of must fall within one of the following types of violations (1) a *per se* violation of antitrust policy, (2) a violation of the letter of either the Sherman,

Clayton or Robinson-Patman Acts, or (3) a violation of the spirit of these acts as recognized by the Supreme Court of the United States." In the view of the court, the contested practices did not fall within any of these three violations.

The Supreme Court affirmed the judgment of the court of appeals setting aside the FTC's order, but it modified that court's judgment and remanded with instructions to return the case to the commission for further proceedings. The basis of the Supreme Court's action was that the court of appeals erred in its construction of Section 5. Citing the *Keppel* case, the Supreme Court held that the reach of Section 5 extends past anticompetitive or antitrust activity and protects "consumers as well as competitors." "Thus, legislative and judicial authorities alike convince us that the Federal Trade Commission does not arrogate excessive power to itself if, in measuring a practice against the elusive, but congressionally mandated standard of fairness, it like a court of equity, considers public values beyond simply those enshrined in the letter or encompassed in the spirit of the antitrust laws." Nevertheless, the Court refused to sustain the FTC's order. The commission did not challenge the Circuit Court's finding of no violation of the antitrust laws, nor did it attempt to rest its order on "considerations of consumer interest independent of possible or actual effects on competition. Nor were any standards for doing so referred to or developed." Thus, although Section 5 extends beyond the antitrust laws, FTC orders must be supported by findings. The Court concluded:

> Arguably, the Commission's findings, in contrast to its opinion, go beyond concern with competition and address themselves to noncompetitive and consumer injury as well. It may also be that such findings would have evidentiary support in the record. But even if the findings were considered to be adequate foundation for an opinion and order resting on unfair consequences to consumer interests, they still fail to sustain the Commission action; for the Commission has not rendered an opinion which by the route suggested, links its findings and its conclusions.

Apart from those cases either directly or closely involving particular antitrust statutes, the commission has also proceeded against deceptive advertising and against practices which do not conform to "good business morals." The line between the deceptive advertising cases and the "bad morals" cases is not clear. For example, the false disparagement of competitors is often a technique of deceptive advertising. Yet this practice may be considered as an unfair act, wholly apart from any advertising aspect.

At this point we must note the significance of the 1938 Wheeler-Lea amendments to the Federal Trade Commission Act. Prior to 1938, Section 5 of the Act dealt only with unfair methods of *competition*. In a deceptive advertising case, for example, this phrase required the commission to prove both that the advertising was deceptive and that it injured competitors. All of that was changed in 1938 with an amendment designed to broaden the emphasis of the statute to protect the consumer as well. As noted in the *S and H* case, the commission can now proceed against unfair or deceptive acts which injure consumers without reference to any competitive effect.

Because the techniques of deceptive advertising will be examined at length in Chapter 21, we shall be concerned here primarily with those practices evincing bad business morals. First among these is commercial bribery, described by the commission as "bribing buyers or other employees of customers and prospective customers, without the employers' knowledge or consent, to obtain or hold patronage." In this category are a number of cases prohibiting the now familiar practice of "payola" whereby disc jockeys, in return for value received, would give undue public exposure to certain phonograph records, representing to the listening audience that the records in question were being played as a result of their popularity. Thus the market would be conditioned for the purchase of certain records, records which were produced, of course, by the firm giving the payola.

Commercial bribery is certainly not limited to disc jockeys and record distributors. In fact, the more standard case involves the payments by a manufacturer to employees of a purchaser or prospective purchaser. Through such payments the manufacturer seeks to obtain additional purchases of his goods. On the other hand, if the payments of what is sometimes called "push money" are made known to the recipient's employer, the cases indicate no violation of Section 5. At the time of this writing, the commission is reconsidering its "push-money" policy with the possibility that further limitations on the lawfulness of push money may be made in future cases or regulations. The real illegality comes in the aspect of secrecy, for therein lies the obvious deception.

Section 5 can also be used to cover "procuring the business or trade secrets of competitors by espionage or by bribing their employees, or by similar means." Illustrations of espionage include the use of paid spies and individuals posing as customers. Merely obtaining information which a company "was willing to furnish to any possible customer" is not an unfair or deceptive act under Section 5. Related to the problem of stealing trade secrets is enticing an employee. If the purpose is to induce a breach of an employment contract, a violation may occur. The commission has also proceeded in a few cases where the inducement was committed by means of false and fraudulent statements to the employees in question. Usually such statements operate to disparage the original employer.

Another category of unfair and deceptive practices in the institution of vexatious lawsuits designed solely to harass a competitor. The commission has acted to prohibit certain unethical operators from even threatening to institute groundless lawsuits against competitors. Several cases have involved false statements to the effect that a certain competitor has infringed a patent. The same prohibition, of course, extends to the practice whereby one company finances or promotes litigation against its competitor by a third party.

Product and name simulation is another area which we will explore more fully in Chapter 21. Suffice it to say here that any semblance of "passing off goods" as the product of a competitor will invoke the strictures of Section 5. More serious is the actual tampering or "lifting" of a competitor's products. Under a lifting scheme a company will acquire a competitor's merchandise and then proceed to flood the market by selling this merchandise at distress prices. Often the price will be below cost. Sometimes the competitor's goods will be taken as part of a trade-in or credit arrangement. The result of these acts is, of course, to damage the competitive standing of the concern whose goods are being lifted. To tamper physically with goods of a competitor in order to present an erroneously disparaging impression is illegal under Section 5.

The illegality of lottery schemes under Section 5 has been determined by the Supreme Court itself. In the famous *Keppel* case of 1934 the commission brought proceedings against the use of so-called break-and-take candy packages in the penny candy trade. Some of the packages would contain a penny as a prize, thus enabling the purchaser to obtain the candy free. Other packages would contain slips recording the price to be paid for the candy, from 1 to 3 cents. Still others would contain authorizations for certain small prizes. The goods were sold primarily to children, and the prize system induced children to buy the manufacturer's candy. It was this factor of exploiting children which contributed to the downfall of the scheme. The Court ruled that the break-and-take prize packages constituted an unfair practice and rested its decision essentially on moral grounds.

Illegal lottery schemes have certainly not been limited to the area of children's candy. They have been used in a wide variety of merchandising plans. One federal court summed up the law in this language: "The practice of selling goods by means which involve a game of chance, gift enterprise or lottery . . . is contrary to the established public policy of the United States. . . ." Anyone using a lottery system should be aware of possible criminal liability involved in using the mails to disseminate lottery matter, in addition to liability under Section 5 of the FTC Act.

One rule of the lottery cases is that "consideration" must be present in order for the scheme to constitute an illegal lottery. If the consumer can truly participate in the lottery, contest, or whatever it be called without the expenditure of any money or personal effort, then the practice is not an illegal lottery. In the ordinary case, where the consumer must purchase some merchandise in order to participate, consideration is clearly present.

Section 5 also has been held to prohibit "using containers ostensibly of the capacity customarily associated by the purchasing public with standard weights or quantities . . . or using standard containers only partially filled to capacity, so as to make it appear to the purchaser that he is receiving the standard weight or quantity." Since the writing of the first edition of this book, Congress has passed the so-called truth-in-packaging bill, standardizing certain packaging requirements. By virtue of this statute, the FTC now has the statutory authority to accomplish what it had previously attempted through trade practice conferences and rules—that is, to establish standards of weights and measures applicable to packaging.

Three types of practice related to filling orders for goods have been held unfair and deceptive under Section 5. First is the scheme of delivering goods which were never ordered or an amount of goods far in excess of the order. Such shipments are often followed by various forms of coercion to induce payment. The supplier may, for example, threaten suit or refuse to cooperate with the overburdened "customer" in any way. A few cases have revealed that certain companies following this scheme so thoroughly garbled the many records of the transaction that it was virtually impossible for a customer to determine either what had been ordered or what had been shipped or both. A second theme is the substitution of goods for those actually ordered. This is, of course, unlawful, and several courts have also held that it is no defense that the substituted goods were substantially equal to those ordered. A final variation is the practice of causing unreasonable delays in the filling of orders. No businessman should undertake to fill an order unless he knows he can do so in a reasonable time.

These, then, are some of the acts which have been held to be unfair or deceptive under Section 5 of the Federal Trade Commission Act. The reader should certainly not assume that because a certain practice has not been discussed, it is therefore lawful. No attempt has been made to exhaust the catalogue of unfair practices. The reader may be assured that when newer and more devious schemes are attempted, the law will still be there to inhibit them. Take the case of payola as an example. The older commercial bribery cases dealt with situations in which a purchaser's agents had been bribed to order from a certain supplier or manufacturer. These cases did not squarely fit the disc jockey payola situation, because records were not ordered from a manufacturer but rather were exposed to the public at large. But the fact of a new variation on the old theme of commercial bribery did not stop the commission from prohibiting payola practices all over the country.

In addition to broadening the emphasis of the original Federal Trade

Commission jurisdiction from competitor to consumer protection, the Wheeler-Lea amendments of 1938 also strengthened the commission's hand in the field of food, drug, cosmetic, and therapeutic advertising. In this area the mere dissemination of interstate advertising—apart from any considerations in regard to the sale of the product in interstate commerce—invests the commission with jurisdiction. Further, in such cases the commission is authorized to obtain temporary injunctions while the cease and desist proceedings are in progress. Finally, when the use of such advertised items—food, drug, or cosmetic—"may be injurious to health," criminal penalties attach. The "use" described in the statute is either the use prescribed in the advertisement itself or the sort of use which might be "customary or usual." It is also a criminal offense to advertise these goods "with intent to defraud or mislead." The maximum sentences which may be imposed for violations of the food and drug portions of the FTC Act extend to a fine of $5,000 and six months' imprisonment for the first offense and a $10,000 fine and one year's imprisonment for each future offense.

The commission also enforces a number of labeling acts. The first such statute is the Wool Products Labeling Act of 1941. The Wool Act provides that every wool product manufactured for introduction into interstate commerce must bear a label which states in terms of percentages the various materials of which the product is composed. The label must also identify the manufacturer or other person or concern which has shipped the product in interstate commerce and must accompany the product until it is sold to the consumer. Examples of violations of this act are misrepresenting reprocessed and reused wool as virgin wool, passing off alpaca fibers as "Baby Llama," and misgrading products by representing that they are wool when they actually contain appreciable amounts of synthetic materials.

Another statute of this type is the Fur Products Labeling Act, passed in 1952. This act extends not only to labeling but also to the advertising of furs. In substance, it requires accurate information concerning the type of animal from which the fur was taken, the country of origin if it is imported, bleaching or dyeing, and the existence of used fur. One of the situations which gave rise to the passage of the Act was the practice of skillfully sewing together hundreds of small pieces of fur and finishing the item so that it appeared to have been made from whole pelts. Prior to the Act there was no way for the buyer to avoid such an item unless he wanted to rip open the lining and look at the back of the fur. Now any such composite piece must be fully and accurately described in all advertising and labeling. Other typical violations of the Fur Act include passing off tip-dyed mink as "natural," passing off furs which have been bleached as "natural," and passing off skunk fur as "Zorilla."

Next is the Textile Fiber Products Identification Act, passed in 1958 but effective as of 1960. This law applies to all household textile products except those under the Wool Act, and it covers both labeling and advertising. Labels and ads must disclose percentages of fibers, manufacturer, and country of origin if the product is imported.

One example of a violation of this Act is the use of the term *pima* or *pima cotton* to describe products containing only small percentages of long-staple, pima cotton. Investigation has indicated that a composition of at least 25 per cent pima is necessary to give a product any of the favorable characteristics of the fiber. Another example is the mislabeling of certain ironing board covers through statements indicating that the covers contained much greater amounts of asbestos than was true. A final example, akin to the pima cases, is that of men's trousers represented to contain large quantities of Dacron polyester fiber, when in fact they contained only small percentages, if any at all. To obtain the particular characteristics desired and promoted for Dacron polyester, at least 65 per cent polyester fiber is mandatory.

All of these labeling acts are enforced by the commission through cease and desist orders. In addition, however, the commission is empowered to seek injunctions against violations. Wool and fur products which are in violation may be seized in condemnation proceedings. Finally, we should note that all the statutes also carry criminal penalties for "willful" violations. These penalties may extend to a fine of $5,000 or imprisonment for one year or both. Facts leading to criminal prosecutions are certified to the Department of Justice by the commission.

The commission also enforces the Flammable Fabrics Act, which became effective in 1954. The need for this statute arose from the commercial use of certain highly flammable fabrics—in children's cowboy suits, for example—that burned and caused serious injuries. The Act prohibits the introduction into commerce of fabrics which do not meet specified standards of noninflammability. The standards are defined in bulletins promulgated by the Secretary of Commerce. To enforce the Act, the commission's normal powers are again bolstered by authorization of the use of injunction and condemnation proceedings. Violators of the Act are also subject to criminal prosecution, which may result in a $5,000 fine or imprisonment for one year or both. A provision of the Act allows one to defend on the ground of having received a guarantee from a manufacturer or supplier stating that the goods meet the required standards of noninflammability. The furnishing of a false guarantee, however, is an unfair practice, and the commission may proceed against it. Further, the furnishing of such a false guarantee can also result in criminal prosecution.

Such is not an exhaustive catalogue of the laws which the commission administers. Indeed, with the current clamor for consumer protection, each year witnesses new statutory authority for the FTC to act in preventing unfair competition and accomplishing truth in advertising. The fair-packaging statute has already been mentioned. Others include the truth-in-lending statute (requiring full disclosure in credit transactions, for example, the exact interest to be charged) and the recent Fair Credit Reporting Act (protecting the subjects of consumer reports from inaccurate or obsolete information in such reports where used to determine an individual's eligibility for credit, insurance, or employment). It is obviously outside the scope of a book such as this to examine in detail these various statutes administered by the commission. Interested readers should consult recent treatises in the area, such as Kintner, *A Primer on the Law of Deceptive Practices.*

To summarize, then, the commission enforces and administers a series of statutes designed to preserve and promote free and fair competition. The basic provision is Section 5 of the Federal Trade Commission Act, which prohibits "unfair methods of competition" and "unfair or deceptive acts or practices." Under this provision the commission reaches all methods or acts which amount to direct violations of the Sherman Act or Clayton Act. The commission may also proceed against incipient violations of the Sherman Act, without having to wait until trade is actually restrained or a monopoly is effected. In a small class of cases the commission has utilized the broad language of Section 5 to reach methods which, although not literally prohibited by the Clayton Act, still amount to violations of the policy and spirit of that Act. This basic law also enables the commission to proceed against all forms of deceptive advertising, and in this area the commission may function with a view toward consumer protection as well as toward promotion of competition. In addition, Section 5 covers a wide variety of acts and practices which have been characterized as evincing "bad business morals." Finally, the commission administers a group of statutes dealing specifically with the labeling and advertising of certain fabrics and furs.

CHAPTER 15

EXEMPTIONS

THE antitrust laws we have discussed are not all-inclusive. Even before the Sherman Act was passed, various groups began lobbying for exemptions from its proposed provisions. Over the years Congress has enacted various exemptions from the prohibitions of the antitrust laws. Some industries are, for all practical purposes, free from any type of regulation as a result of these exemptions. Others have been exempted from the antitrust laws, merely to be transferred to a different and more rigorous type of supervision by some government regulatory agency. Some of the exemptions came into existence because the persons engaged in the particular industries exempted were not strong enough to compete actively in unrestricted competition. For example, the unorganized laborer could not effectively bargain by himself for a beneficial contract of employment. The lone farmer was incapable of selling his wares for a fair return to organized marketing agents. These individual weaknesses resulted in an early recognition by Congress that labor and agriculture should be exempted from the coverage of the antitrust laws. Other exemptions occurred because various industries needed to be carefully and systematically regulated by either federal or state agencies to insure adequate service to the public. In cases of this nature an exemption from the antitrust laws becomes merely a transfer of regulation from these laws to the specialized control of other agencies or laws. The exemption accorded the transportation industry is an example of exemption for the purpose of other regulation. The regulatory agencies concerned may govern such activities as market entry, mergers, prices, and other areas where concerted action would normally be a violation of one of the antitrust laws.

A problem exists when industries are subject to extensive regulation by federal agencies, yet are not specifically or completely exempted from the coverage of the antitrust laws. In such a case a particular situation or act may be a violation both of the antitrust laws and of the regulations of the administrative agency. When this occurs, a determination on the primacy or exclusiveness of jurisdiction must be made. Normally, when the conduct subjected to antitrust coverage falls within the regulatory statute, and if this statute provides an appropriate remedy, antitrust judicial action will be refused, and the regulatory agency will receive exclusive jurisdiction. If the remedy of the regulatory agency does not adequately solve the problem or compensate those injured, the antitrust action may be merely postponed rather than totally barred; there is merely primary jurisdiction in the agency. If the regulatory statute in question fails to provide for detailed and comprehensive economic regulation of the industry, the courts may be less willing to postpone or bar antitrust action. Therefore, when a particular activity is regulated by an administrative agency, the activity is not safe from antitrust prosecution unless an exemption is specifically spelled out and delineated.

One of the earliest statutory exemptions from the antitrust laws is that accorded to agricultural cooperatives and associations. Prior to the enactment of the Sherman Act in 1890, various farm leaders unsuccessfully sought a specific exemption from the proposed antitrust laws. Between the passage of the Sherman Act and the passage of the Clayton Act (1914), several state courts initiated and successfully prosecuted antitrust charges against agricultural cooperatives. To prevent similar federal prosecutions, Congress enacted a statutory exemption from the antitrust laws for farmers and agricultural cooperatives in Section 6 of the Clayton Act. As it applies to agricultural cooperatives, this section states:

> Nothing contained in the antitrust laws shall be construed to forbid the existence, and operation of labor, agricultural, or horticultural organizations, instituted for the purposes of mutual help, and not having capital stock or conducted for profit, or to forbid or restrain individual members of such organizations from lawfully carrying out legitimate objects thereof; nor shall such organizations or the members thereof, be held or construed to be illegal combinations or conspiracies in restraint of trade, under the antitrust laws.

In 1922 the Capper-Volstead Act broadened the scope of Section 6 by extending the exemption to corporate or noncorporate agricultural associations with or without capital stock. In addition, collective activities relating to processing, preparing for market, handling, and marketing agricultural commodities in interstate and foreign commerce were specifically allowed. The Capper-Volstead Act did not accord complete and unlimited freedom to such associations, however, for it provided that, if the secretary of agriculture had reason to believe that any association was monopolizing or restraining trade to "such an extent that the price of any agricultural product is unduly enhanced by reason thereof," he should initiate a cease and desist proceeding.

Two other Congressional acts further defined the agricultural exemption. Section 5 of the Cooperative Marketing Act of 1926 stated that agricultural associations could "acquire, exchange, interpret, and disseminate past, present, and prospective crop, market, statistical, economic and other similar information by direct exchange between . . . such associations. . . ." Finally, Section 4 of the Robinson-Patman Act stated that a cooperative association was not prevented from returning to its members the whole or any part of the net earnings or surplus resulting from its trading operations in proportion to such members' purchases from or sales to or through the association. Thus, agricultural cooperatives were specifically exempted from the coverage of the antitrust laws, and various concerted practices among them were specifically condoned.

Several court cases have indicated that cooperatives are still subject to some of the antitrust laws in certain situations. The *Borden* case involved a conspiracy to fix prices among several exempt associations and others not exempted, such as major distributors, labor officials, and municipal officials. The Supreme Court reached the conclusion that although agricultural producers may unite in preparing for market and marketing, they cannot combine and conspire in restraint of trade with others not so exempted. In addition, if a cooperative engages in predatory and unlawful acts which are generally considered to be in restraint of trade, it cannot claim immunity. Thus, when a cooperative had engaged in a conspiratorial secondary boycott with other cooperatives and noncooperatives, a federal court concluded that the illegal restraint of trade exceeded the approved methods of achieving the permitted goals of the cooperatives. A similar conclusion was reached in a case involving the Maryland & Virginia Milk Producers Association. The defendants supplied approximately 86 per cent of the milk purchased by milk dealers in the Washington, D.C., metropolitan area. The Supreme Court held that an agricultural association in and of itself can be guilty of monopolizing in violation of Section 2 of the Sherman Act by engaging in predatory acts, such as boycotts, and in attempts to induce and compel dealers to purchase their supply of milk exclusively from the cooperative. In another important case, the Supreme Court was faced with the problem of a conspiracy to monopolize by three separate cooperatives. The court held that because the members of the three cooperatives could have organized one cooperative rather than three, agreements among the three for legitimate purposes were not illegal. The court was quick to emphasize, however, that this case in no way weakened the conclusion reached in the *Borden* case that a cooperative can be guilty of conspring with noncooperatives, or the conclusion in the *Maryland & Virginia* case that an agricultural cooperative can be guilty of monopolizing.

A second important and somewhat controversial exemption from the antitrust laws is that of organized labor. Three interdependent statutory sections define the scope of this exemption. Section 6 of the Clayton Act, as it applies to labor, states that the labor of a human being is not a commodity or article of commerce and then exempts labor organizations not having capital stock in the same manner as it exempted cooperatives. A labor union itself is not a combination or a conspiracy in restraint of trade under the antitrust laws. The second applicable law is Section 20 of the Clayton Act, which, in essence, bars the issuance of federal injunctions prohibiting activities such as strikes, boycotts, or picketing "in any case between employees or between persons employed and persons in employment, involving, or growing out of, a dispute concerning terms or conditions of employment." Several court decisions drastically limited the exemption by strictly construing its application solely to labor disputes directly involving an employer and his present or prospective employees. To broaden this provision, Congress in 1932 enacted the Norris-LaGuardia Act. This Act defined a "labor dispute" as "any controversy concerning terms or conditions of employment . . . regardless of whether or not the disputants stand in the proximate relation of employer and employee." Thus, a labor union's activities, though otherwise in restraint of trade, are exempted from antitrust coverage if they are carried out with relation to a labor dispute, regardless of whether or not the disputants are directly related to each other as employer and employee.

As in the case of an agricultural cooperative, a labor union is not completely exempt from actions under the antitrust laws. Although a union may engage in almost any acts approved by Section 20 of the Clayton Act and Section 4 of the Norris-LaGuardia Act, it may not conspire with an employer or other outsider to boycott other employers whose policies meet with the disapproval of the union. For example, in the *Allen-Bradley* case a union of electrical workers in New York had extracted an agreement from various contractors to purchase equipment solely from local manufacturers who had closed-shop agreements with the local union. In addition, the union had obtained an agreement from several manufacturers to confine their local sales to contractors employing the union's members. The acts of the union in making agreements with employers and manufacturers were held to be violations of the antitrust laws, because the exemption was limited to labor unions and labor disputes.

In addition, the labor exemption does not protect labor unions which seek in some direct manner to fix prices or otherwise control a market. One case involved a union composed of fishing crew members, some of whom owned fishing boats, who sought to coerce certain fish canners to purchase a season's catch of fish at fixed rates per pound. When the canners declined to comply, the union ceased to supply fish and agreed with other fishermen to boycott the canners. A complaint by one of the canners, seeking treble damages under the antitrust laws, was held to state a cause of action. This was not a "labor dispute" and, therefore, not exempted under the Norris-LaGuardia Act.

Similarly, protective wage agreements—whereby the collective bargaining agreement with one employer states that the union will not enter into any contract with any other employer covering wages, hours, or working conditions, on any other basis than those delineated specifically in the agreement—were held, by the Supreme Court, in *Lewis v. Pennington,* to be within antitrust scrutiny. Such "most-favored-nations" clauses tamper with the price structure by prohibiting individual negotiations on wages, which are a significant factor in pricing.

A third important exempted area is that of foreign trade. This was the direct outgrowth of a broad-scale inquiry by the Federal Trade Commission, in 1915 and 1916, into foreign trade conditions. In 1916 the commission presented to Congress an exhaustive report which focused attention on entrenched combinations and cartels in foreign countries with which American exporters were forced to compete. It stated that American producers seeking business abroad met aggressive competition from powerful foreign combinations which were sometimes aided by their governments. According to this report, in order for Americans to enter the markets of the world on equal terms with their organized competitors and their organized customers, small American producers and manufacturers had to be free to unite their efforts. The commission recommended passage of remedial legislation permitting cooperative efforts in export trade by competing American exporters and removing any doubt concerning the antitrust implications of such cooperation. However, it urged that appropriate safeguards be provided against misuse of this power to cooperate. Congress passed the Webb-Pomerene Act in response to this report.

Within certain closely circumscribed bounds, the Act authorizes cooperative activity among American exporters for the purpose of promoting American foreign trade. At the time of their formation export associations are required to file with the commission association papers or articles of incorporation and full descriptions of their organizational structure. Each year thereafter they are required to make a similar report to the commission, bringing up to date their original submittals. The commission on its own initiative may require submission of any additional information pertaining to an association's organization and practices. Failure to supply requested information subjects the association to suit in federal courts.

Under Section 5 of the Act the commission is charged with supervisory authority over export trade associations and with the corollary duty of inquiring into and recommending reform of activities which are outside the Act's permissive area. If an association fails to comply with the commission's recommendations for readjustment of its practices, the commission is empowered to refer the matter to the attorney general for appropriate action.

As in the case of the other exemptions, the Webb-Pomerene Act does not totally exempt export associations from the provisions of the antitrust laws. Under Section 2 such an association is subject to prosecution if it artificially or intentionally enhances or depresses within the United States prices of the type of commodity exported by the association, or if it substantially lessens competition within the United States or otherwise restrains trade therein. The Act also directs the Federal Trade Commission to supervise the operations of export associations and, concurrently with the Department of Justice, to eliminate abusive association conduct. The Federal Trade Commission has ruled that price-fixing agreements by the associations and their foreign competitors are not within the exemptions of the Webb-Pomerene Act. Because both the Federal Trade Commission and the Department of Justice are constantly reviewing the lawfulness of the activities of every export association with a view toward spotlighting antitrust violations, such associations must strive to confine their concerted activities to the areas of foreign trade enumerated in the exemption.

Another exemption of interest to a businessman is that granted to small business concerns. Normally, if a number of small businessmen were to pool their resources and cooperate in research and development, such an arrangement might be held to be a combination or conspiracy in restraint of trade or an attempt to monopolize. To encourage cooperation among small businessmen, the Small Business Acts of 1953 and 1958 included an exemption permitting the formation and operation of small business pools. Under this exemptios the administrator of the Small Business Administration is authorized to consult with the representatives of small business concerns with a view toward assisting and encouraging such firms to undertake joint programs for research and development. These joint programs may include, among other things, the acquisition and construction of laboratories for research, the collection and dissemination of research information to members, patent services, and the organization of corporations designed to exploit patent obtained. To obtain immunity from the antitrust laws, a group contemplating such a combined effort must make application to the administrator of the Small Business Administration. If the administrator feels that the joint program will maintain and strengthen the free enterprise system and the economy of the nation, he may, after consultation with the attorney general and the chairman of the Federal Trade Commission, approve any such agreement between small businesses. This approval may be withdrawn whenever it appears that the joint program is no longer in the best interests of the competitive, free enterprise system. The Act also authorizes the Small Business Administration administrator to consult with representatives of small business concerns with a view toward the organization of groups of corporations for the purpose of obtaining loans to use for raw materials, equipment, and other necessities. This exemption greatly assists small concerns which would normally be handicapped and placed at a competitive disadvantage in the field of research and development.

Other miscellaneous exemptions are accorded various industries for different purposes. During times of war or national emergency Congress may suspend the enforcement of the antitrust laws in regard to particular industries. Most of these acts require that a regulatory agency grant specific immunity to a certain group or class of industries. Thus, the antitrust laws are never completely suspended, because the coverage of the exemption is defined and procedural safeguards are established.

Insurance companies have a partial exemption. The federal antitrust laws are applicable only to insurance organizations not regulated by state laws. This exemption is not complete, for agreements to boycott, coerce, or intimidate, or acts directed toward these ends, even when regulated by the states, are still covered by the Sherman Act.

Under the Fisheries Cooperative Marketing Act persons engaged in the fishing industry are allowed to organize and act together in associations, both corporate or otherwise, in collectively catching, producing, preparing, processing, and marketing their products in either interstate or foreign commerce.

As of this writing, professional baseball enjoys an exemption as a result of case law, rather than statute. An early Supreme Court case based the exemption on the absence of interstate commerce. More recent cases have held all other major professional sports subject to the antitrust laws on the ground that organized sports "affect" interstate commerce even though a ball or a hockey puck or a boxing glove does not cross a state line in any given contest. Despite these holdings recent lower court cases continue to embrace "America's number one pastime" with the shroud of immunity. The logic of these opinions is that Congress certainly has knowledge of the early Supreme Court opinions; because it has done nothing legislatively to change the exemption, it, therefore, implicitly endorses it. In its recent *Flood* case, the Supreme Court called the exemption an aberration, but sustained it any way on the ground that it was an "established aberration."

This chapter has not attempted to explain and define exemptions granted to industries when the primary purpose of the exemption is to transfer control to specialized regulatory agencies. For example, the Interstate Commerce Commission carefully controls rates and other matters in the transportation industry. Air carriers are governed by the Civil Aeronautics Board and the Federal Aviation Agency. In like manner the Federal Communications Commission and the Federal Power Commission regulate their respective industries. In most of these examples primary or exclusive jurisdiction in regard to antitrust matters is vested in the particular regulatory agency. The antitrust laws are applicable only when the administrative remedies are inadequate to cope with the violation or when the acts involved are not subject to the regulatory body.

CHAPTER 16

ENFORCEMENT BY THE DEPARTMENT OF JUSTICE

THE oldest agency of antitrust enforcement is the Antitrust Division of the Department of Justice. This division alone is entitled to enforce the Sherman Act, and, with the Federal Trade Commission, it also enforces the Clayton Act. In an effort to dispel some of the mystery surrounding the operation of the division, we shall discuss in this chapter the means by which the division discovers possible violations of the laws, the methods by which it investigates such possible violations, the standards governing the division's decision to proceed formally in court, the nature of an antitrust proceeding, the nature of decrees entered in antitrust suits, and the informal methods of dealing with the division.

The businessman will first learn that he is suspected of a possible antitrust violation when he is approached, or hears that his customers or competitors have been approached, for information concerning his business or his competitors' businesses by representatives of the division or agents of the Federal Bureau of Investigation. Occasionally, the businessman will not learn of the division's interest until he receives orders to produce certain documents before a grand jury or to the division pursuant to a civil investigative demand (a method of pretrial discovery that will be discussed later in this chapter). In whatever manner he learns of the division's concern, however, he will first want to know what started the division's desire to investigate him and his industry.

With the exception of merger and monopoly cases, antitrust proceedings are usually initiated by the complaint of a competitor or customer to the division. A customer who feels he is being victimized by an industrywide price-fixing conspiracy would be apt to complain to the division. The electrical equipment price-fixing conspiracy came to the division's attention in this manner. Similarly, a competitor who is adversely affected by a boycott might turn to the division for help.

Often, of course, the complaints turn out to be groundless. Initially, therefore, the division makes a preliminary analysis to determine whether a more detailed investigation is warranted. If the complaint itself reveals that the questioned conduct does not violate the antitrust laws, the whole matter can be dropped immediately. For example, if a customer complains that a manufacturer would not deal with him and alleges nothing more, no antitrust violation has taken place, and further investigation would be futile. Another consideration is whether the challenged conduct is in or affects interstate commerce. Broad as the present definition of interstate commerce may be, some conduct will still be outside the reach of the Sherman and Clayton Acts.

The division must decide whether a proceeding would be in the public interest. Because stopping any antitrust violation would appear to benefit the public, this question may seem out of place. But more is involved than the simple truth that all violations should be prevented. Like all government agencies, the division receives only a limited amount of money each year. Necessarily, therefore, only a limited number of investigations and actions can be undertaken. Accordingly, the division must choose cases that will derive the greatest public benefit from the money expended. In short, the division aims to spend its enforcement dollar wisely. Cases will be chosen with a view to reaching situations of the greatest magnitude. The division also seeks to prosecute those cases which will lead to an orderly growth in the scope and content of the laws themselves. By pursuing these joint goals, the division attempts to insure maximum compliance with the antitrust laws.

As a final preliminary step, the division checks with the Federal Trade Commission to see if that agency is interested in the same matter. Naturally, an investigation will not be undertaken or an action begun if the commission is already working on the same case. Double enforcement serves neither the public nor the industry involved.

After these initial considerations have been satisfied, an attorney in the division must decide what further action is required. The nature of the investigation will often depend upon the type of violation involved. Because the measure of proof for a *per se* violation is far less exacting than that for violations calling into play the rule of reason, the scope of such an investigation may be correspondingly limited. For example, if a complaint relates to a large manufacturer's use of tie-in sales in distributing his products, the attorney may only need to ascertain whether or not such tie-ins are used. If they are, a violation exists. On the other hand, if requirements contracts are involved, a far more extensive investigation may be necessary. In such a context the attorney must obtain complete industry data as well as evidence relating to the reasonableness of the contracts.

The scope of the investigation necessary will determine the next step taken by the division attorney. If only limited investigation is required, the attorney may carry it out himself. Where more extensive research is indicated, the services of the Federal Bureau of Investigation will probably be used. The bureau may conduct interviews of potential defendants, their customers, suppliers, and competitors. Additionally, any other people who could have knowledge of the violation or of the industry in which it is alleged to have occurred might be contacted. The bureau might also request the opportunity to examine the documents of anyone interviewed.

Quite possibly, the investigation carried out by the attorney or the bureau will provide enough information to determine either that an action should be instituted or that the matter should be dropped. Whenever either decision is taken, of course, further investigation is halted. If further information is necessary, it may have to be obtained through the use of procedures requiring a potential defendant to produce the data in question. There are several methods of compulsory discovery available to the division. The choice will depend mainly on the initial determination whether to try the case civilly or criminally. We shall have more to say about the considerations underlying this decision later in this chapter. What is important to note here is that the initial determination is only provisional in nature. From the evidence the division possesses at the time compulsory discovery is initiated, a decision may be made to seek a criminal indictment. If the data and testimony obtained by a grand jury investigation reveal that the character of the offense is not sufficiently pernicious to warrant criminal prosecution, the division retains the right to institute civil proceedings instead. Similarly, information obtained through a civil investigative demand may reveal a far more flagrant violation than the division had at first suspected. A criminal action might then be brought.

First, let us consider what the businessman might expect if the division feels that criminal prosecution is warranted. Assuming the attorney general's concurrence in the division's recommendation, grand jury proceedings will probably be instituted. A grand jury is a frightening thing to those who have never experienced such an investigation. Grand jury proceedings are carried on in absolute secrecy, and a potential defendant will know nothing of the probable outcome until an indictment is returned or the grand jury is dismissed.

The businessman will probably first become aware of the threat of criminal prosecution against some or all members of his industry when he receives a subpoena *duces tecum* requiring him to assemble certain documents and transmit them to the grand jury. Typically, subpoenas are extremely broad in their demands for documents. Thus, if a price-fixing conspiracy is suspected, the subpoena might direct submission of all documents relating to prices and pricing of certain products for a period of four or five years. Some subpoenas are even more broadly drawn. The process of assembling the required documents often imposes a tremendous burden on a company. Many personnel will be required to sort through the mountain of paper that is amassed over the years by the normal corporation. Additionally, some means of copying or otherwise noting the documents that are produced must be devised.

Before any document search is instituted, legal counsel should be obtained. The language of subpoenas is often very technical, and legal advice on just what documents must be produced will save a company wasted hours of searching. Further, a company's attorney can often work out ambiguities by contacting the division attorney responsible for the subpoena. For example, the subpoena might call for "all" documents relating to a certain subject. In practical effect this might require a company to produce a literal carload of paper that appears to have no conceivable relevance to any possible subject of investigation. By contacting the division attorney and describing to him the particular documents that appear valueless, a company's lawyer might be able to avoid their submission to the grand jury. This will not only save the time of the company's employees but also minimize the inevitable disruption of the company's business attendant to the delivery of company documents to a grand jury. Finally, a lawyer can examine those documents which the company believes are called for by the subpoena and determine if any unnecessary documents are being produced. Not only will this prevent the submission of irrelevant documents, but it will also serve to familiarize the attorney with the facts concerning any potential liability of the company.

Failure to produce documents requested under a grand jury subpoena is a contempt of court and subjects the violator to severe criminal penalties. Identical penalties await those who destroy documents in order to avoid producing them before the grand jury. In short—and this cannot be overemphasized—documents called for by a grand jury subpoena *must* be produced in good faith.

Often the documents requested by the grand jury will not, after examination, satisfy all the questions that must be answered. Alternatively, new areas of investigation might arise. In either event, a second subpoena may be issued. The whole procedure just described must be undertaken a second time.

After consideration of a company's documents the division attorney might decide to call officers of the company as witnesses before the grand jury. One called as a witness in such circumstances has no right to take his attorney with him into the grand jury room. Furthermore, he may himself be prosecuted criminally under the Sherman Act concerning anything about which he may testify or concerning evidence he may present unless he is specifically granted immunity under the terms of the Crime Control Act of 1970.

Suppose, now, that the Antitrust Division had decided that any potential action will be civil rather than criminal in character. In such a case information will probably be sought by a civil investigative demand.

This method of discovery was inaugurated in 1962. Prior to 1962 the division had no really suitable way to obtain data if voluntary cooperation was not forthcoming from the persons possessing the data. Use of the grand jury process for a case obviously destined to be civil had been held by the Supreme Court to be an abuse of process. The other possibility was to file a skeleton complaint in the district court and then use discovery methods available under the Federal Rules of Civil Procedure to obtain the information necessary to prove the violation. But because it is improper to bring a proceeding to see if a proceeding should be brought, this alternative scarcely satisfied the division's need to obtain information. To answer this need, Congress created the civil investigative demand especially for the Antitrust Division.

This statute permits the attorney general or the assistant attorney general in charge of the Antitrust Division, whenever either has reason to believe that a person under investigation has documents relevant to an investigation being made to determine if the antitrust laws have been violated, to issue and serve upon such a person a civil investigative demand requiring production of the documents for examination. The demand must state the nature of the conduct being investigated and the statute which it is alleged to violate, must describe the documents to be produced with sufficient "definiteness and certainty as to permit such material to be fairly identified," must prescribe a reasonable return date, and must identify the custodian to whom the material should be made available. The demand may not contain requirements that would be held unreasonable in a grand jury subpoena and may not require production of documents that would be exempt from disclosure to a grand jury. Persons receiving demands that are unreasonable may petition the local federal court for an order modifying or setting aside the demand. Finally, failure to comply with the demand subjects a person to severe criminal penalties.

A number of procedural rules are embodied in the statute. Thus, for example, a demand may be issued only before a complaint is filed. Any time after this, of course, the regular discovery rules of the Federal Rules of Civil Procedure are available, thus obviating any need for a civil investigative demand. Also, the statute permits the division only to inspect or copy the documents. This salutary rule prevents the complete disruption of a business through deprivation of vast numbers of important documents for a substantial period of time, or, alternatively, avoids the tremendous cost to the company of having to copy all the required documents. Documents copied by the division are to be kept secret.

Let us now take a brief look at the different ways in which merger and monopolization cases arise. Normally, merger cases do not come to the division's attention by complaint from customers or competitors. Rather, they are discovered simply from reports in trade journals and other periodicals. When a merger is thus spotted, a division attorney makes a cursory investigation in standard reference works of the size of the merging companies and their position in the industry. If legality or illegality is still not clear, then further investigation will be made, using the normal discovery techniques described above.

In monopolization cases the pattern is somewhat different. Because monopoly implies tremendous relative size in an industry, competitor complaints are not normally necessary to excite the division's interest. But actual monopolization is tremendously difficult to prove. Therefore economic surveys must be prepared by division economists, a task that takes a substantial expenditure of funds and a vast amount of time. Although these surveys depend in part on material gleaned from normal antitrust investigations, other sources must also be utilized.

When the division has completed its investigation, a decision must be made on the type of enforcement action, if any, to be used. Of course, if the investigation reveals no violation, then no action will be instituted. If a violation exists, there is the question of whether enforcement should be pursued by civil or criminal means, or both. A number of factors are taken into consideration. Generally speaking, criminal prosecutions are brought only against price-fixing conspiracies and other types of *per se* violations of the Sherman Act. Criminal actions may also be brought where a specific intent to restrain trade or to monopolize can be shown. Similarly, extremely predatory practices may invite criminal attack. Finally, the chances of criminal prosecution are much greater if the defendant has been guilty of similar violations in the past or if the defendant is aware that his conduct has been declared illegal in an action against other persons. If none of these criminal indicators is present, the division is almost certain to institute civil proceedings and forego a grand jury indictment.

Even though a decision is made to prosecute criminally, a civil action might also be brought. A court might find that the conduct is not criminal—even though it may constitute a civil violation—because the exacting criminal standard of proof beyond a reasonable doubt of injury to competition might not be made, whereas injury to competition might be shown by the preponderance of the evidence and thus sustain a finding of a civil violation. A more important justification for filing a companion civil suit, though, is the need to secure injunctive relief against future violations. If the division feels that the imposition of criminal penalities against the defendant is not adequate to deter future misconduct, civil remedies will also be sought.

Let us assume that the division has instituted action against a company for alleged violations of the antitrust laws. What should the officers of that company expect during the preparation for trial and during the trial itself? They should expect to spend a great deal of time educating their attorneys on the facts of the case. And they should expect months or even years of having to deal with the case. To discover what the company and its officers will face, let us follow the normal course of an antitrust action.

The first thing that must be done, of course, is to familiarize the company's counsel with the operations of which the division has complained. If the same attorney who aided the company in the production of documents under a grand jury subpoena or civil investigative demand is used, the task will be easier. The education of the attorney in the relevant facts will be a continuing process, extending over the life of the case. The facts are the raw material out of which the company's counsel will attempt to develop a defense to the action. Only by being completely open and candid with him can a company hope to prevail.

Not all the facts relevant to the action, however, will usually be in the possession of the company attacked. The company's attorney will have to use the discovery devices available to him to obtain from the government and from other persons the data necessary for him to prepare his case and for him to discover the nature of the division's case. This can be a long and costly process, but it is absolutely essential to a proper presentation of a company's case.

The extent to which discovery will be available to a company depends primarily on whether a civil or a criminal case is involved. The Federal Rules of Civil Procedure provide for the liberal use of pretrial discovery. As an example, let us examine the devices a company could use to learn the facts in a suit brought by the division alleging a horizontal merger in violation of Section 7 of the Clayton Act. The major issues in such a case are likely to be the size and nature of the relevant geographic and product markets. To learn this, a company must discover, among other things, the amount of its competitor's sales, the areas in which those sales are made, the nature of the products which compete with the company's product, and the nature and location of the customers for the product. The first discovery device available to the company is the deposition. Officers of competitor companies may be required to appear and give testimony with respect to relevant facts. The deposition may be taken upon oral examination or written interrogatories. In either case the deponent will be required, except as he is protected by certain privileges, to answer all relevant questions. If he cannot answer a question, he may be required to give the name of a person in his company who can. He may also be required to reveal the nature and description of documents which could have a bearing on the case. The use of depositions is tremendously important in preparing a case, because it is both the easiest and most reliable method of developing the facts.

Other tools are available to the civil defendant for obtaining information from the government. For example, written interrogatories may be served on the government to learn relevant facts. Upon a showing of good cause, documents in the possession of the division may be obtained to aid in the company's preparation. Finally, the division may be required to admit facts that are not in dispute, thus relieving the company of the burden of producing evidence on these matters at trial.

In a criminal trial, unfortunately, many of these useful devices are not available to the defendant company. Without going into details, it is sufficient to say that the use of discovery in such circumstances is severely limited. This difficulty would be obviated by the use of the civil devices in a companion civil case. If that alternative is not available, then a company will have to prepare without the aid of liberal discovery.

During the time that the facts of the case are being prepared, the company's counsel and the division's attorneys, with the aid of the court, will be attempting to frame and narrow the issues properly so that a speedy resolution of those issues at trial can be accomplished. Commonly, factual issues which are not in dispute will be admitted by the parties. Procedural matters, such as the date of trial, will be arranged. In short, everything possible will be done to facilitate the handling of the case.

Because of the complexity of the issues in an antitrust case, the actual trial of the matter can be a long and expensive venture. In one famous case the opening statements of the parties took sixty trial days over four calendar months to complete. And this all occurred before any evidence was introduced! Fortunately, not all trials are that complex, but the businessman must expect a reasonably lengthy trial.

If a violation is found, separate hearings are usually held on the relief to be granted to the government. In a criminal case this will relate simply to the amount of the fine and the extent and necessity for jail sentences. In a civil case, however, a hearing can involve such a knotty question as the proper nature of an order of divestiture. The scope of the relief is of tremendous importance to a company, and great care must be exercised to obtain a decree which will prevent antitrust violations but at the same time allow the company a maximum of competitive freedom.

Because of the tremendous cost of an antitrust trial, as well as the business uncertainty attendant to it, many companies prefer to attempt settlement of the case through the division's consent decree program. Obviously, the urge to take advantage of this program increases directly as the probability of proof of violation increases. In addition to the cost savings and the avoidance of business uncertainty, the acceptance of a consent decree has two other major advantages. First and most important, a consent decree cannot be used in a private damage suit to prove that the defendant company has violated the antitrust laws. As we will discover in Chapter 18, Section 5 of the Clayton Act provides that a final judgment in favor of the United States in an antitrust suit shall be *prima facie* evidence of violation of the law in any other antitrust action based on the same facts, *except* if the judgment was entered by consent or before any testimony had been taken. This provision relieves the private claimant of a tremendous burden of proof. Naturally, companies are loath to invite treble-damage suits, and a consent judgment offers one means of avoidance. A second advantage of a consent judgment is that it keeps a company's dirty linen from being aired in court and in the newspapers. Consumers may well become incensed at what appears to be business duplicity. To avoid such public castigation, a company may wish to embrace a consent settlement.

Brief reference should be made here to certain collateral issues that arise in antitrust litigation. Occasionally, parties in an antitrust suit will agree to be bound by the judgment in a companion case. Assume, for example, that General Motors, Ford, and Chrysler are all attacked under the antitrust laws for the use of a particular practice. In such a situation, Ford and Chrysler might agree to be bound by the finding in the General Motors case. This avoids duplicative litigation of identical issues. Another technique is the submission of the case on an agreed statement of facts. The court then has only to decide the legality of a given practice, and the parties are able to avoid the costly and time-consuming process of adducing evidence in court in support of contentions of fact.

A decree, whether entered by consent or after contest, provides a guide by which the defendant company must live. Not surprisingly, problems often rise concerning what the decree really requires a defendant to do or to refrain from doing and concerning the need to modify the terms of the decree. Normally, the terms are relatively easy to understand. Occasionally, however, an ambiguous provision in a decree must be construed by a court to determine the meaning intended. The rule of construction followed is that specific provisions should be read in a way that furthers the general purposes of the decree. The rule of construction does not permit a court to modify a decree silently under the guise of construing its meaning. At times, though, courts have appeared to do just this.

Sometimes conditions have changed so markedly since the decree was entered that a company bound by the decree may desire its modification. Modification is not easily obtained from a court. If the conditions existing at the time of the entry of the decree have not changed sufficiently, modification will not be granted. And not every changed condition will warrant modification. As one court put it: "Change is inevitable, but it is only change that reaches the underlying reasons for the decree that is relevant. Conditions existing at the time of the original entry must be compared with conditions at the time of requested modification, and the significance of the difference measured in the light of those original reasons." In short, "nothing less than a clear showing of grievous wrong evoked by new and unforeseen conditions" will lead a court to relax and modify the provisions of an antitrust decree.

So far we have discussed the problems that the businessman may have with the Antitrust Division. But in other contexts the division can be most helpful to a businessman faced with antitrust problems. The three areas in which the help is most often forthcoming are the receipt of complaints concerning violations by competitors, the release program, and the merger clearance program.

A company experiencing business difficulty because of the antitrust violations of its competitors, customers, or suppliers may wish to file a formal complaint with the division. All that is necessary to accomplish this is to write to the attorney general the facts which the company believes to indicate antitrust violation by another. The division will handle the matter thereafter. One danger in taking advantage of this right of complaint should be mentioned. If the division becomes interested in the industry affected by the violation, it may institute a full-scale investigation of that industry. The investigation may reveal that the complaining company also has been guilty of antitrust violations. In such a situation the division will not hesitate to prosecute. Accordingly, a company should insure that its own house is in order before complaining of the antitrust violations of others.

Before instituting a new and costly business program, a company may submit that program to the division for a release letter. If a granted, this "railroad" release assures a company that it will not be criminally prosecuted for its use of the program. Although the division does reserve the right to file a civil suit alleging the program to be in violation of the antitrust laws, a release letter will not normally be issued if there is any question concerning the legality of the program. If a release is obtained, a company can be relatively sure that no antitrust suits will result from its use of the program thus cleared.

There are a number of limitations and restrictions on the use of the release program. The most important limitation is that the release must be sought only with respect to a method of operation that is purely prospective. If the method is already being used by the company, the division will not consider it. Any request for release must be in writing and must fully disclose all relevant business facts. Further, a company must be willing to furnish any additional facts which the division desires. Failure to make full disclosure will render any release valueless, for the division will retain its right to institute criminal proceedings. Of course, if facts disclosed in the request for release reveal present antitrust violations, the division may begin an action at once. Notwithstanding these risks and limitations, the release program can be of inestimable value to a company contemplating the use of a new business method.

Closely allied to the release program is the division's program relating to advance clearance of mergers. A company proposing to acquire the stock or assets of another company should seriously consider submitting all relevant data to the division for advance clearance of the merger. If cleared, the company will learn that the division *at the present time* does not plan to institute action should the merger be consummated. This does not prevent the division from filing suit at some later time because of unforeseen competitive results of the merger. Nonetheless, this program offers a degree of certainty to a company contemplating a merger and reduces the risk of business disruption through divestiture attendant to a later successful prosecution of the merger.

CHAPTER 17

THE FEDERAL TRADE COMMISSION: PRACTICE AND PROCEDURE

THE Federal Trade Commission was established by Congress in 1914 as an independent regulatory agency. The commission is composed of five commissioners, appointed by the president and confirmed by the Senate for terms of seven years. No more than three commissioners may be members of the same political party. Since 1950 the president has by law designated one of the commissioners to serve as chairman. The chairman has broad authority over commission personnel, including appointments and promotions. The chairman, subject to the policy guidance of his four colleagues, also has broad authority over the use and expenditure of funds and the distribution of business within the commission. Under the direction of the chairman, the executive director is the chief administrative officer, who exercises supervisory authority over the various offices within the commission and over the staff of the commission's correspondence and records. The general counsel is the commission's chief legal expert. His office is responsible for representing the commission in federal courts, preparing legal memoranda, and advising the commission. An economic adviser, an Office of Congressional Relations, and the Office of Public Information report directly to the chairman. There also are an Office of Policy Planning and Evaluation and an Office of Administrative Trial Judges. The latter office provides the FTC's independent administrative judges for the formal proceedings.

Effective July 1, 1970, the work of the commission was divided into two main areas, that of antitrust and restraint of trade matters, under the title of the Bureau of Competition, and a Bureau of Consumer Protection, which is an expanded version of the former Bureau of Deceptive Practices.

The Bureau of Competition, which largely includes the work done by the former Bureau of Restraint of Trade, is headed by a director and seven assistants who supervise the following divisions: Accounting, Compliance, Evaluation, General Litigation, Industry Guidance, Small Business, and Special Projects.

The Bureau of Consumer Protection is subdivided into nine separate areas, each supervised by an assistant director. The divisions are the following: Compliance, Consumer Education, Evaluation, National Advertising, General Litigation, Rules and Guides, Scientific Opinions, Consumer Credit and Special Programs, and Textiles and Furs.

A third operating bureau, the Bureau of Economics, performs the same work as in the past, allocated to three divisions of Economic Evidence, Financial Statistics, and Industry Analysis.

The commission's employees total over 1,200, of which nearly 500 are attorneys and 125 are other professional personnel. The FTC's headquarters is in Washington, D.C., but more than 300 employees are located in eleven field offices throughout the country, in the following places: Atlanta, Boston, Chicago, Cleveland, Kansas City, Los Angeles, New Orleans, New York, San Francisco, Seattle, and the Washington, D.C., area. In addition to their traditional investigative role, these field offices also may handle the trial of some formal cases. They also coordinate local consumer protection work, including participating actively in consumer councils.

Violations of the law are brought to the commission's attention in a variety of ways. Letters are received from consumers, business competitors, suppliers, and customers, sometimes directly, sometimes from other agencies of the government. The procedure for filing a complaint is very informal. All that is necessary is a letter to the commission detailing the facts which are believed to constitute a violation of the law.

The commission possesses extremely broad investigative powers under the Federal Trade Commission Act. This Act provides the commission with the power of access to documentary evidence, the authority to require annual and special reports from any firm, and the power of subpoena. The power to require special reports from corporations has been used to gather information for the Quarterly Financial Report for Manufacturing Corporations, prepared jointly by the Federal Trade Commission and the Securities and Exchange Commission. Extensive use of this special report power has been made in connection with general economic surveys conducted by the commission. Special reports have also been used to gather data in the trial of specific antimonopoly cases, particularly merger cases, as well as to investigate compliance with outstanding cease and desist orders under Section 5 of the Federal Trade Commission Act and Section 11 of the Clayton Act. In recent years the commission has used its special report power to conduct general legal investigations of alleged widespread violations of the antitrust laws and trade regulations throughout an entire industry.

When a possible violation of the law comes to the commission's attention, either through its own investigation or through one of the media previously mentioned, the procedures for enforcement are varied and flexible. The Federal Trade Commission Act provides that if it appears that a formal proceeding would be in the interest of the public, the commission may issue a complaint against the alleged offender and set a hearing date. Such hearings are conducted before trial judges, and the proceedings are similar to those employed in federal courts. The rules of evidence are somewhat relaxed in such hearings, yet they remain subject to due process requirements of fairness. The respondent is given an opportunity to cross-examine witnesses and to present evidence in rebuttal. After the hearings are completed and evidence has been received from the commission's lawyers and the lawyers representing the respondent, the trial judge makes an initial decision. This decision becomes final if not appealed from or modified by the commission within thirty days. If the initial decision is appealed to the full commission for review, or if the commission reviews the matter of its own volition, the commission may modify the order in any way it sees fit. If the decision is against the respondent, the commission may issue an order to "cease and desist." Such an order is like an injunction and remains in effect indefinitely, unless later modified or dismissed for reasons of changes in the circumstances of fact or law. If violated, the respondent may be prosecuted in a district court for civil penalties, which may run as high as $5,000 for each violation, with each day of a continuing violation counting as a separate offense. A cease and desist order does not become final until sixty days after it has been served on the respondent. During this period the respondent may appeal to a court of appeals. Before such courts the commission's findings regarding the facts are conclusive if supported by substantial evidence. Cease and desist orders include a provision that respondents file, within sixty days from the date of the service of the order, a report of compliance setting forth the manner of compliance. Other statutes under the commission's purview, such as the Clayton Act, also provide for this procedure.

The commission seeks to encourage compliance with the requirements of the laws it administers by a number of means other than the formal proceedings just outlined, as informal techniques may be quicker, cheaper, and equally effective. These methods include administrative treatment, trade practice conferences, trade regulation rules, the issuance of guides, advisory opinions, and consent settlement procedures. It is important to note that there is a commission policy of effecting industrywide compliance, whenever possible or practicable, if alleged violations of law are extensive. This policy is a most important one in the agency's current program.

Administrative treatment is the simplest and one of the newest of the informal methods and is used by the commission chiefly in the area of misrepresentation through advertising. Letters of discontinuance or affidavits signed by responsible officials of the offending concern, accompanied by evidence of compliance with the law and assurance that the questioned practices will not be resumed, are accepted in settlement of many smaller infractions. In this connection it is important to note that currently the commission's eleven field offices have authority in proper instances to accept administrative settlements or alleged violations. However, the field office must obtain enough facts to disclose a probable violation and may not accept a settlement tendered by a businessman seeking to avoid further government involvement, without regard to whether or not the facts indicate that a violation has occurred.

Until the change in its rules of practice effective August 1, 1963, the commission did not apply informal voluntary compliance procedures to Robinson-Patman and other antimonopoly violations. With the removal of this restriction, however, commission spokesmen made it clear that such procedures would be sparingly used in such areas of law enforcement and that first violators would be the most likely subjects. The rules state: "In determining whether the public interest will be fully safeguarded through such informal administrative treatment, the Commission will consider (1) the nature and gravity of the alleged violation; (2) the prior record of good faith of the parties involved; and (3) other factors, including, where appropriate, adequate assurance that the practice has been discontinued and will not be resumed."

In 1962 provision was made for issuance of trade regulation rules applicable to unlawful trade practices. These rules are designed to express the judgment of the commission, based on facts of which it has knowledge derived from its past experience, regarding practices clearly violative of the law. Such rules may be sharply limited to particular areas of industries or to particular product or geographic areas, as appropriate. Provision is made for reliance upon these rules in litigated cases if the respondent is given a fair hearing on the legality and propriety of applying a particular rule to a particular case. Although now being subjected to a court test, rules of this nature increasingly are being used by the commission to solve industrywide problems.

For many years the commission has provided procedures for trade practice conferences upon the application of businessmen and their trade associations in a particular industry or upon the commission's own motion. If the commission concludes that such a conference would be useful and proper, notice is given to members of the industry concerned. They and other interested parties appear and freely express their views regarding practices that are prevalent in the industry, practices which perhaps should be eliminated. Such conferences may, where appropriate, voluntarily repudiate widespread illegal practices in a particular industry. Conferences always involve formal trade practice rules with which members of a given industry may signify their willingness to comply. Recently such trade conference procedures have been merged into the industry guides program. One group of such rules prohibits as unfair practices certain activities deemed to violate the laws administered by the commission. Compliance with such rules is not permissive, because they merely express what the law already prohibits. Other rules, which the members of an industry may voluntarily agree to follow, condemn practices which the particular industry deems to be harmful or unethical even though such practices are not illegal. Trade practice rules, upon adoption, often becomes the basis for settlement of investigative matters pending against members of the industry concerned.

In recent years the commission has published a series of guides in an effort to make clear to businessmen those practices which the law prohibits and which should be avoided. These guides are also useful to the consumer in educating him to the dangers of bait advertising, false guarantees, and fictitious bargain prices. Guides, unlike the trade practice rules, may deal with practices common to many industries. Although preparation of guides which are both informative and accurate is not an overnight task, there is no necessity for hearings or conferences concerning them. The guides are not intended to cover gaps in the law by dealing with factual situations that have not yet come before the courts or before the commission in any form. Rather, they set forth in easily understood language the principles already established by the courts and the commission in decided cases. Their purpose is to give the businessman some knowledge of what the law requires of him. Additionally, the guides, by delineating areas of potential trouble, should alert the businessman to consult his lawyer when a problem arises and before a violation of law occurs. The commission has sought the greatest publicity for its guides in an effort to reach as many businessmen as possible. Copies are available without charge upon request to the commission. Two of the guides, those on cigarette advertising and tire advertising, deal with deceptive practices in specific industries. Others—including the *Guides Against Deceptive Pricing*, the *Guides Against Bait Advertising*, and the *Guides Against Deceptive Advertising of Guarantees* —deal with deceptive practices which may arise in the preparation of many types of advertising copy. The reception that these guides have received is a testimony to their educational value. The commission has also issued guides dealing with practices violative of Sections 2(d) and 2(e) of the Clayton Act as amended by the Robinson-Patman Act. Although these guides do not deal with false and misleading advertising, they provide valuable aid to honest advertisers by furnishing guidance in the thorny area of advertising allowances. The Trade Practice Rules and Guides, together with special conferences called by the commission staff from time to time, are all designed to educate businessmen in the requirements of the law and to encourage them to avoid illegal practices.

In this age of increasing corporate complexity it is often extremely difficult for businessmen and their legal counsel to determine accurately the legality of proposed business action. Some assistance may be obtained by seeking an advisory opinion from the commission. Informal advice may be obtained from members of the commission's staff or from its eleven field offices. Although such advice is not binding on the commission in regard to future activity of the requesting party, such advice will normally allow the businessman to proceed with greater certainty.

In connection with the advisory opinion procedure it is important to note the circumstances in which the commission will not give advice:

> (1) where the course of action is already being followed by the requesting party; (2) where the same or substantially the same course of action is under investigation or is the subject of a current proceeding by the Commission against the requesting party; (3) where the same or substantially the same course of action is under investigation or is or has been the subject of a proceeding, order or decree initiated or obtained by another government agency against the requesting party; or (4) where the proposed course of action is such that an informed decision thereon could be made only after extensive investigation, clinical study, testing or collateral inquiry.

Texts or digests of advisory opinions of general interest may be published "subject to statutory restrictions against disclosure of trade secrets and names of customers and to considerations of the confidentiality of facts involved and of meritorious objections made by the requesting party to such publication."

Finally, the commission may employ the consent decree procedure to halt illegal practices. Following notification by the commission of its determination to issue a complaint, a party may indicate to the commission its willingness to have the proceedings disposed of by the entry of an order. The consent decree, by which the objectionable practices may be effectively prohibited, is negotiated with various members of the staff. If an agreement is approved by the commission, the complaint and proposed order will be issued. If the proposed consent settlement is rejected, the complaint is issued and the matter set down for adjudication in regular course.

The commission shares with other agencies the job of enforcing many of the laws for which it is responsible. Many practices at the same time violate laws with whose enforcement the commission is charged and laws for which another agency is responsible. In such a case the practice in question could be attacked by either enforcement agency. Although many have criticized this dual enforcement, the intersection of regulatory activity by two or more government agencies need not cause overlapping of effort, undue harassment of the industries regulated, or constant jurisdictional quarrels. The Federal Trade Commission and other agencies responsible for preventing certain practices have long worked to eliminate all of these possible dangers. Thus, since World War II, working agreements setting forth the primary responsibilities of each agency, the areas of sole jurisdiction, the policies governing duplication of proceedings, and the nature of liaison between the agencies have been concluded with these other agencies.

Exemplary of these working relationships is the one prevailing between the commission and the Antitrust Division of the Department of Justice. This relationship has been characterized by willing interchange of information, avoidance of the duplication of effort, and the careful assignment of cases to the agency whose action will be likely to do the most good. At the same time, in recognition of their mutual and separate responsibilities, each agency has preserved its individual freedom to take independent action whenever it believes it to be necessary. A closer examination of the nature of the relationship now prevailing between the commission and the division will provide a suitable illustration of the practical way in which dual enforcement operates.

The commission and the division are jointly responsible for preventing certain practices both because of Congressional intent and because of the overlapping provisions of three laws. Both agencies are charged with the enforcement of the Clayton Act. Although the division is solely responsible for exacting compliance with the provisions of the Sherman Act, conduct violative of that Act is also an "unfair method of competition" subject to commission action under Section 5 of the Federal Trade Commission Act.

To avoid duplication of enforcement efforts, an elaborate system of notification and negotiation has been worked out. If either agency begins an investigation, the other agency is promptly notified. If the commission schedules a trade practice conference, the division is immediately informed. If the agency notified has any objections, a conference is held to effect a workable compromise. Although each agency retains its right to initiate separate proceedings, in practice their working agreement has wholly prevented wasteful duplication. Similarly, only rarely will either the division or the commission institute action when a private suit has been brought against the same conduct.

Certain ground rules have been established to govern the normal way in which cases are handled. The commission normally enforces the provisions of the Clayton Act, unless the Clayton Act violation is part of a larger pattern of illegality characterized also by Sherman Act violations. The commission also handles virtually all public enforcement of the Robinson-Patman Act. For practices violative of both the Sherman Act and Section 5 of the Federal Trade Commission Act, a number of factors are considered. For example, if criminal proceedings are in order, the division naturally will be the agency of enforcement. Similarly, the magnitude of the violation or its *per se* character may dictate division action. In an area where the commission's economic *expertise* can be profitably put to advantage, however, the division may stand aside. The nature of the relief required may be of importance. If immediate interlocutory relief is desirable, the division will probably handle the case. Finally, that agency which has prior experience and, therefore, familiarity with a particular company or industry will in all likelihood deal with future violations by that company or in that industry, except for *per se* violations of the antitrust laws, such as price fixing.

This working relationship is obviously tailored to avoid duplication of enforcement effort. Prior *expertise* is utilized whenever possible, and other means of increasing the effectiveness of both agencies are readily embraced. The system has been remarkably effective in practice, and this alone is a tribute to the practical bent of those charged with the enforcement of the antitrust laws. Similar working arrangements between the commission and the Food and Drug Administration, the Federal Communications Commission, and the U. S. Postal Service have been equally successful. It would appear, therefore, that there is little to fear from multiple enforcement, and a great deal to be gained.

CHAPTER 18

PRIVATE ENFORCEMENT

IN addition to the enforcement of the antitrust laws by the Department of Justice and the Federal Trade Commission there is always the possibility of action by private parties. Indeed, private action has often been praised as the most effective means of enforcing the antitrust laws, for two reasons. First, it has been thought that violations will be more readily detected by persons who are directly affected by them. Second, private parties often will be able to bring suit with greater ease than the governmental enforcement agencies, which are burdened by budgetary problems. To encourage such private enforcement, Congress has provided that a successful litigant can recover three times the actual damages sustained by his business as a result of the antitrust violation, plus a reasonable attorney's fee. Not surprisingly, this has been a tremendous incentive to private suits, and the importance of such suits has increased markedly with the passing years.

Private actions to enforce federal antitrust laws may be brought only in federal district courts. This requirement precludes an injured company from bringing suit in a state court and even prevents the company from counterclaiming in a state court when sued by the violator on some other cause of action. A defendant in a state court case—for example, breach of contract—can, of course, assert antitrust violations of the plaintiff as affirmative defenses.

Although suit is normally brought directly by the injured company or companies, actions may arise in other ways. In an interesting case, a group of miners, on their own behalf and for those similarly situated, sued two mining companies, alleging, among other things, that they had been damaged by the conspiracy between the companies to fix at an unreasonably low level the price at which the companies would purchase raw ore. By suing both for themselves and for others similarly situated, the miners had brought what is termed a class action. Eventually, the miners recovered. Because a class action was involved, miners who were not parties to the original action could intervene in the proceedings and recover simply by proving that they were members of the class and injured by the violation. The necessity of proving that the defendants had violated the antitrust laws was no longer essential, as this had been accomplished by the original plaintiffs. Additionally, the original action suspended the statute of limitations for those miners later intervening in the proceedings. Obviously, this device, which is so useful to antitrust plaintiffs, can prove disastrous to antitrust defendants.

Another unusual means of private antitrust enforcement is an action by shareholders of the injured company. If the directors of the company arbitrarily refuse to bring suit, the shareholders may then bring what is commonly termed a "derivative suit" in order to recover for the company the damages to which it is entitled. For example, in one case the shareholders were allowed to enforce the company's cause of action even though the directors of the company had voted not to bring action, because it appeared that the directors of the company were under the control of the corporation which had been violating the antitrust laws. In short, shareholders are allowed to enforce a company's rights when those in control of the company unreasonably fail to do so. To be distinguished from such a derivative suit is an action by the shareholders seeking to recover on their own account damages to the value of their stock interest caused by an antitrust violation. The basis for such an action is that the violation has so injured the company that the value of its stock has declined and the shareholders have thereby been directly injured. But such a cause of action has never been allowed, because courts have felt that the likelihood of such an injury was too tenuous to warrant the grant of relief. An additional ground for the denial of relief will be discussed below.

Section 4 of the Clayton Act provides that "any person who shall be injured in his business or property by reason of anything forbidden in the antitrust laws may sue therefore . . . and shall recover threefold the damages by him sustained, and the cost of suit, including a reasonable attorney's fee." The antitrust laws to which reference is made include Sections 1 and 2 of the Sherman Act and Sections 2, 3, 7, and 8 of the Clayton Act. Although the Supreme Court has not yet spoken on the matter, some recent lower court cases have held Section 5 of the Federal Trade Commission Act to be an antitrust statute for these purposes. The nature of the right of private action thus created involves a number of complex problems, the explanation of which will occupy most of the remainder of this chapter.

Only those damages to the *business or property* of the plaintiff caused by antitrust violations can be recompensed under Section 4. The injury to a shareholder resulting from the diminution in value of his stock brings no right to treble recovery, for stock ownership was no part of the shareholder's business or property. Similarly, one cannot recover for an antitrust violation that prevents the establishment of a new business.

Because by definition no business exists until it is started, the violation that prevented a business from opening could not work an injury to the business or property of the claimant. The injury must be to actual assets and not to a mere expectancy of future assets. This distinction serves to explain a case in which recovery was allowed for antitrust violations that had prevented the plaintiff from opening a business. In that case the injured party had contracted to distribute milk to be furnished by the other contracting party. Fearing competition, the existing milk distributors banded together to induce the milk producer to breach the contract. The court allowed recovery on the basis that the contract was part of the plaintiff's business or property, that the violation had rendered it valueless, and that such diminution in value was a recoverable element of damages.

An additional requirement of Section 4 is that there be *injury* to the plaintiff's business or property *caused* by the defendant's antitrust violations. A private litigant has no right to enforce the antitrust laws unless the violation has caused actual injury to his business from the violation. Only the attorney general has an absolute right to exact compliance with the law.

Let us look at examples of injury not caused by antitrust violation. No recovery would be allowed if the injury resulted simply from normal competitive stresses or from mismanagement by the company's officers. So also, if the violation had no effect on the plaintiff, an action would fail. For example, suppose it appeared that a price-fixing conspiracy had not resulted in higher prices. Customers of the conspirators could not then be injured by the conspiracy, no matter how great the antitrust violation. Similarly, if any higher prices charged to customers were passed on by them to their own customers, without thereby losing any sales, no measurable financial injury to the conspirators' customers would have occurred, and, therefore, no recovery would be allowed. The passing-on defense is not without its critics, however. Literally applied, it may allow antitrust violators to go unpunished. In short, there must be economically measurable *injury,* which is a *direct result* of an antitrust violation, before any private action can succeed.

Antitrust violations are often difficult to prove. This is particularly so for the private litigant, often a small businessman who is already a financial victim of an economically stronger antitrust violator and unable to bear the burden of litigating the issue of violation. Recognizing the economic burden, as well as the public interest in encouraging private enforcement, Congress enacted a special provision, Section 5 of the Clayton Act, designed to aid private litigants in carrying this burden of proof. Section 5 provides that a final judgment or decree, resulting from any civil or criminal antitrust action (except damage suits) instituted by the United States, which affirms that the defendant has violated the antitrust laws can be used in other actions as proof of those facts necessarily proved in the government's action. This relieves the private litigant of the task of proving the existence of an antitrust violation; all that he need prove is that the violation caused injury to his business or property. Not surprisingly, the practical result of this provision often is a host of private actions following a successful prosecution by the government for antitrust violations.

There is one major exception to this provision. Section 5 states that this rule will not apply to "consent judgments or decrees entered before any testimony has been taken." This exception is of tremendous practical importance, and it acts as a spur to antitrust defendants to refrain from contesting actions brought by the government in order to avoid a subsequent flood of private litigation should the case be lost. But the provision also works to the government's benefit, for it saves the time and money necessarily lost in an antitrust trial, time and money therefore available for use in other enforcement activities.

One of the more interesting current questions concerning Section 5 arose out of the electrical price-fixing conspiracy. The question is whether or not the exception for consent judgments and decrees entered before any testimony is taken applies also to guilty pleas made in criminal actions. Because a guilty plea removes the burden of proving a violation, the probable answer is that guilty pleas cannot be used under Section 5 as proof of violation in another action. Under the laws of evidence, however, such pleas might be admissible as proof of the violation, quite apart from the provisions of the Clayton Act. Such was the position of a district court judge in a recent decision. The same judge, however, distinguished guilty pleas from *nolo contendere* pleas, the latter not being evidence under Section 5. At the moment the law is not clear on either of these points, but the question will most certainly be resolved within the next few years.

In 1955 Congress enacted a four-year statute of limitations applicable to private antitrust actions. It provides that no antitrust cause of action may be the basis of a suit more than four years after it has accrued. The first question raised, therefore, is when the cause of action accrues. The general rule is that a cause of action accrues when injury to the plaintiff occurs. This does not mean, however, that measurable economic damage must take place just then. Rather, it means that those acts have occurred which injure the plaintiff and which necessarily will result in present or future economic damage.

A slightly more complicated set of rules governs the accrual of a cause of action based on a civil conspiracy. Again, the significant date is the date of injury to the plaintiff, not the date on which the violation takes place. Once an act by the conspirators has injured the plaintiff, a cause of action has arisen, and the statute of limitations starts to run. It continues to run until it bars the suit four years later. The fact that the conspiracy continues in no way affects the running of the statute in regard to those damages caused by any particular act of the conspirators. But a new cause of action arises with each conspiratorial act causing injury. The plaintiff can recover for those damages which resulted from overt acts of the defendant conspirators occurring within four years of the institution of plaintiff's action. For example, suppose that a conspiracy commences in 1955. The conspirators commit injurious acts in furtherance of the conspiracy until 1971. In 1971 an injured person files an action. Absent a showing of fraudulent concealment of the conspiracy, the plaintiff can recover only for injuries inflicted during the four-year period 1967–1971.

A significant exception to the rules governing the statute of limitations is contained in Section 5 of the Clayton Act. It provides that the running of the statute on any private right of action arising under the antitrust laws shall be suspended during the pendency of any civil or criminal government action (except a damage suit) designed to prevent, restrain, or punish violations of the antitrust laws. A private litigant, to take advantage of this provision, must base his cause of action "in whole or in part" on violations alleged by the government action. The suspension of the statute of limitations is not absolute. Rather, the suspension lasts only during the pendency of the government action and for one year thereafter, and any private action must be commenced either within four years after the cause of action accrued or during the period of suspension. For example, suppose that a cause of action accrued in 1958, that the government instituted suit for the same violation in 1960, that this suit was terminated in 1966, and that a private action was commenced in 1968. The private suit would be barred, because it was instituted more than four years after the cause action accrued and not during the period of suspension. This is so even though the statute was suspended for five of the eight years after the accrual of the cause of action.

Another important situation in which the statute of limitations is suspended has assumed importance because of the electrical conspiracy cases. These decisions appear to indicate that the federal antitrust statute of limitations will be suspended during the period in which the antitrust violator has engaged in acts designed to prevent the plaintiff from discovering the existence of a cause of action. This suspension results from a doctrine known as "tolling by fraudulent concealment." In order to take advantage of this doctrine, a plaintiff must show that the defendant affirmatively acted to conceal the facts underlying the cause of action from the plaintiff's view and, therefore, that the plaintiff could not have discovered his cause of action in the exercise of reasonable diligence. The applicability of the doctrine of fraudulent concealment to the antitrust statute of limitations has not been definitely decided. At present, however, it appears likely that the doctrine will be held to apply.

A number of defenses are available in private antitrust actions. Many of these, of course, are equally available in any lawsuit. Three defenses which are interrelated deserve special mention because of their special importance in antitrust litigation. The first of these is the defense of *in pari delicto* (equal fault). In the past, the courts were hesitant to allow treble recovery for damages caused by antitrust violations to plaintiffs who were also guilty of antitrust violations. In part this hesitance was based on the feeling that it would be inequitable to allow one violator to point the finger of guilt at another violator and recover what amounted to punitive damages. This illustrates an important point in private antitrust litigation. Because of the drastic nature of treble relief, courts have required perhaps even a higher degree of proof by private plaintiffs than by the government, feeling that such harsh punishment should be inflicted only after a strong showing of illegality. This attitude strongly influenced the application of the *in pari delicto* defense in the past. Not only was a clear showing of illegality required, but a plaintiff also had to establish itself as a paragon of business virtue before any relief could be obtained.

This puritanical approach to private antitrust enforcement has abated in recent years. The reason is the judicial recognition that an antitrust violator should not elude punishment simply because he has injured a party who might also be engaging in antitrust violations. The injured party may be subject to other enforcement proceedings without adding the additional penalty of the loss of a justified cause of action. Accordingly, the scope of the *in pari delicto* doctrine has shrunk, and it is now applied only when the plaintiff has engaged in the identical violation upon which it bases its cause of action. For example, suppose the plaintiff and defendant have entered into a contract which violates the antitrust laws. The plaintiff will not be allowed to recover damages for its participation in that illegal contract unless it can show that it was coerced by economic threats or economic necessity into entering the contract. In its recent *Perma Life* decision, however, the Supreme Court rejected the *pari delicto* defense even where the parties "actually favored and supported" some of the restrictions. The Court said "they cannot be blamed for seeking to minimize the disadvantages of the agreement once they had been forced to accept its more onerous terms as a condition of doing business."

A closely related defense is that of *volenti non fit injuria* (he who consents to an act is not wronged by it). Assume, for example, that the plaintiff and defendant enter into a dealership arrangement, terminable at will, which violates the antitrust laws. Even if the plaintiff were to overcome the defense of *in pari delicto,* relief might be barred because the plaintiff could have ended the contract at any time. The rationale of the *volenti* doctrine is that it is inequitable to allow a person to observe a contract voluntarily and then recover treble damages for having done so. Indeed, such an allowance would invite companies to incur damages from antitrust violations so that they could enjoy the punitive trebling of those damages.

The final defense, closely related to the other two, is that of mitigation of damages. A party being injured by antitrust violations is under an obligation to avoid as much of the resultant damage as possible. A chain of stores losing money as a result of the illegality of another's conduct would probably not be allowed to recover for additional losses caused by the opening of new stores, because it knew that such further losses were inevitable. Similarly, a person buying equipment he knows he will not be able to use because of antitrust violations by others will not be permitted to recover the cost of that equipment. The duty to minimize the extent of damage deserves strict enforcement in private antitrust litigation. If it is not strictly enforced, a terrible temptation will be created to increase one's damages unjustifiably in order to enjoy an even larger gratuitous recovery because of the trebling provision of Section 4 of the Clayton Act.

A brief word should be said about the proof and measure of damages in private antitrust actions. That a plaintiff is entitled to recover for all damages proximately caused by an antitrust violation has already been noted. But the actual amount of damage suffered must be proved. A court or jury is not entitled to award damages, particularly when they will be trebled, simply by speculating how much the plaintiff *may* have lost or by compromising on what *appears* to be a just award under all the circumstances. Even when proof looks easy, it may not be. For example, suppose that a price-fixing conspiracy or unlawful price discrimination resulted in an additional cost of 10 cents a unit to a customer. On the surface, damages would appear to be 10 cents multiplied by the number of units purchased at this higher price. Many other factors, however, enter into a determination of actual damages. If the customer was able to pass the higher cost on, in whole or in part, to his customers, then he suffered no compensable injury at all, or only a limited injury. On the other hand, such action may have resulted in a loss of customers. This, in turn, created additional compensable damages. Numerous other factors affect the reasonably precise ascertainment of the amount of damages. Suffice it to conclude that proof of damages is probably the biggest hurdle facing a private antitrust litigant.

Section 16 of the Clayton Act allows private litigants to seek injunctive relief against threatened loss or damage by a violation of the antitrust laws. The partial dispensation for private parties to enforce the antitrust laws is hedged about by a number of limitations. First and most important, the antitrust violation in question must actually threaten direct and serious loss or damage to the business or property of the plaintiff. Second, such relief will be limited to enjoining the violation; no attempt will be made to put the plaintiff in a preferred position. Normally, a court will not enjoin conduct which is already proscribed under a government decree. It goes without saying that a private injunction cannot run counter to the provisions of a government antitrust decree.

Courts have been hesitant to grant sweeping injunctive relief at the request of a private litigant, though such relief might be granted to the government. They have felt that such drastic remedies as divestiture of acquired companies, with the business disruption attendant thereto, or mandatory licensing of patents, trademarks, and copyrights should be granted only when it is in the public interest as evidenced by public enforcement. Nonetheless, private injunctive relief is still significant and likely to become more so in coming years.

A special form of injunctive relief—though it does not seem to come under the provisions of Section 16 of the Clayton Act, has recently assumed great significance. The circumstances are very simple: Suppose a customer sues a supplier for treble damages under the antitrust laws. What remedy, if any, does the customer have if the supplier attempts through economic coercion to force the customer to drop the suit by threatening to refuse to sell to him in the future? In two cases two federal courts of appeals reached contrary decisions on whether the customer should be entitled to a court order requiring the supplier to continue to sell to him during the pendency of the antitrust suit. An examination of some of the considerations involved in answering this question will provide a suitable conclusion to our chapter on private enforcement.

It has been antitrust dogma for years that a supplier has an absolute right, in the absence of a conspiracy or a purpose to monopolize, to deal or to refuse to deal with a customer for any reason or for no reason at all. The exercise of this right to select the customers with whom one will deal has been generally considered to be *per se* lawful. Requiring a supplier to continue dealing with a customer when the supplier wishes not to, of course, is simply contrary to this well-established rule. Furthermore, it may require the continuation of a customer relationship when that is particularly difficult because of the antagonistic positions in which the parties find themselves. Put another way, it might be extremely hard for companies that are sworn enemies in the courtroom to generate the mutual trust and confidence outside the courtroom that is necessary to develop and maintain an effective and satisfying supplier–customer relationship.

In the cases that have been decided so far, the defendant has admitted that it stopped dealing solely to induce the plaintiff to drop its antitrust suit. In each instance, courts recognized that this action by the defendant had the effect of thwarting the public's interest in encouraging private suits for enforcement of the antitrust laws. But the courts have diverged in their assessment of the relative importance of this public interest and the private interest in free choice of customers.

If injunctive relief is to be granted, its basis will probably not be Section 16 of the Clayton Act. As we noted, refusal to deal is not normally an antitrust violation, and such a violation is a *sine qua non* to the use of Section 16. Relief may be granted, however, by reference to the inherent powers of a court of equity to enjoin acts interfering with the maintenance of a lawsuit in order to maintain judicial integrity. But that a court has the power to enjoin a refusal to deal does not in itself answer the question of whether that power should be utilized.

Plainly, there is a strong public interest in private antitrust enforcement. Equally plain is the necessary thwarting of that interest by private use of economic coercion. In some industries, such as the drug industry, customers must have certain products. A pharmacist is required to follow the brand designation in a physician's prescription. If he is unable to obtain that brand, his business will end. In such circumstances a refusal to deal for the purpose of private litigation is bound to succeed.

On the other hand, many countervailing factors militate against granting injunctive relief. We have already mentioned the supplier's interest in the right to choose his customers for any reason at all and the difficulty of maintaining a supplier–customer relationship when litigation is pending between the parties. Further, if forced dealing is required during the pendency of an action, this will still permit economic coercion in the form of a threatened refusal to deal after the action's completion. Of course, refusal to deal after the action serves no economic interest of the supplier, but simple vindictiveness might still lead to such a refusal. Permanent forced dealing could be required, with all its compulsory overtones, but even this might create further problems. If such a mandatory injunction were issued, it might prevent a refusal to deal based on sound business reasons. A company should not lose its business freedom in the future simply because of a past wrong.

It is apparent that serious problems are posed by the current efforts to obtain injunctive relief against coercive refusals to deal directed at ending private antitrust enforcement. It would be presumptuous to predict what the final outcome of these battles will be. The very existence of the battles, however, indicates the tremendous importance which is now attached to private enforcement.

CHAPTER 19

STATE ANTITRUST ENFORCEMENT

ONE of the many benefits of the federal system of government is the opportunity for education and experimentation at the local or grass-roots level. The enactment of national legislation has often been presaged by similar legislation at the local level. One readily recalls early state efforts at limiting and regulating hours and conditions of employment. The experiment in prohibition at the national level was preceded by similar legislation in many of the states. This recurrent theme of American history may also be witnessed in the field of antitrust enforcement. Even before the enactment of the Sherman Act in 1890, several of the states had enacted statutory measures against combinations and conspiracies in restraint of trade. Today most of the states have antitrust laws of one sort or another. A few states even have antitrust provisions in their constitutions. Moreover, even in the absence of statutory antitrust authority state courts have called upon underlying common law prohibitions in condemning unreasonable restraints of trade.

Initially, it must be noted that the existence of and the enforcement of such antitrust legislation are two very different things. State efforts at the enforcement of their own antitrust laws are a relatively recent development. For many years vigorous enforcement of antitrust measures was, by reason of default by the states, an almost exclusive domain of the federal government. Such development was not accidental. The antitrust field long occupied a place of fundamental importance in federal policy. With an ever-increasing role and interest in enforcement being assumed by the states, antitrust statutes on the state level are now something more than a subject for academic study.

In enacting antitrust legislation, the states were moved by many of the same considerations which led to federal antitrust legislation. The excesses of trust power in the late nineteenth century produced both federal and state legislation aimed at curbing such abuses. In drafting legislation, the states, like the federal government, could look back upon developments in English and American common law directed against combinations seeking to restrain the freedom of the marketplace. In fact, early antitrust legislation in many of the states—a prime example being New York—was almost a codification of the English common law against commercial restraints. The rule of reason is generally accepted by the states in determining the legality of a business combination. In general, the body of substantive antitrust law as developed in the state courts in applying state statutes has closely paralleled federal antitrust law as developed by the Supreme Court under the Sherman Act.

Two preliminary questions require discussion: Why is state antitrust enforcement necessary in light of the historically persistent enforcement at the federal level? What is the permissible scope of state enforcement in light of this vigorous federal enforcement in the antitrust field?

Under the Constitution and applicable antitrust statutes the federal government regulates commercial activities in and affecting commerce between and among the states. *Intrastate* commerce, however, remains within the domain of the states, even under the federal "flow of commerce" rationale. There is a genuine need for antitrust activity in relation to businesses which are carried on exclusively or even primarily within a state. It does not require a fertile imagination to think of businesses which normally furnish goods and services on a purely local basis. The annual volume of such businesses may run into many thousands and even millions of dollars, and their activities may have vital effects upon the welfare of the entire nation. If necessary industries can be tied up through predatory practices or restrictive agreements, the public will suffer seriously.

In addition to areas of purely intrastate commerce, where the federal government has no power to act, state antitrust activity is often required in areas where the federal government could constitutionally act but has declined to do so. Although the Supreme Court has indicated that Congress meant "to go to the utmost extent of its Constitutional power in restraining trust and monopoly agreements," practical considerations may often prevent federal enforcement. Limited budgets and the lack of sufficient personnel often make it impossible for federal enforcement agencies to police and protect against every antitrust violation. Moreover, the wisdom of such ubiquitous enforcement is somewhat doubtful in light of the primarily domestic nature of many of the problems encountered. In the field of concurrent jurisdiction the state agencies are often better equipped to handle restraints of primarily local effect. In fact, the statute under which the Federal Trade Commission operates prevents the commission from acting in certain areas, even when interstate commerce is affected. The commission operates under the statutory authority "to prevent unfair methods of competition *in commerce* and unfair or deceptive acts or practices *in commerce*." In a key case the Supreme Court made it clear that this grant of authority over commerce did not include authority to prevent sales by unfair methods in intrastate commerce, even though the methods used placed out-of-state competitors at a disadvantage and had an incidental effect on interstate commerce. As the Court noted, a contrary result would have given the commission "pervasive control over myriads of local businesses in matters heretofore traditionally left to local custom or local law."

Another area where state interest in antitrust enforcement is vital is that a treble damage recovery under federal law. Often a state or city is the principal party injured by antitrust violations of federal and state law. If federal law is violated, a state or city or subdivision thereof may sue under federal law to recover treble damages. To insure the effectiveness of such a remedy, the states must have antitrust officials who will work with federal authorities in protecting the interest of the state and its citizens. Often state investigative techniques or resources may prove inadequate. In such instances cooperation with the federal authorities, more experienced in the direction and proof of antitrust violations, can redound only to the benefit of the states.

Unlike many other federal regulatory schemes, the federal antitrust laws do not preclude or pre-empt state antitrust action in areas of concurrent jurisdiction. This was made clear by the 1910 decision in *Standard Oil Company* v. *Tennessee*. In that case the Supreme Court upheld the imposition of criminal sanctions by Tennessee for violations of the state antitrust laws which occurred within the state but in the course of interstate commerce. Speaking for a unanimous Court, Mr. Justice Holmes observed: "The mere fact that [the statute] may happen to remove an interference with commerce . . . does not invalidate it." The Court did not specifically rule that federal law also applied to the case but considered that such a question was not material. "How far Congress could deal with such cases we need not consider but certainly there is nothing in the present state of the law at least that excludes the states from a familiar exercise of their power." The existence of concurrent jurisdiction is also confirmed by the legislative history of the Sherman Act and by many state court decisions on the subject, several of them handed down almost contemporaneously with the passage of the Sherman Act. Indeed, we know from records of the Senate debate that Senator Sherman, author of the 1890 act, clearly contemplated that the federal statute would supplement antitrust enforcement already under way in several of the states. Federal exemptions, however, do pre-empt state enforcement. In its *Milwaukee Braves* decision, the Wisconsin Supreme Court held that no violation of the Wisconsin antitrust law could be made out against professional baseball because of its exemption under federal law. The notable point about this decision is that the historical reason for the federal exemption is the absence of interstate commerce. The antitrust statutes of California, although somewhat more detailed and thorough than the enactments in many states, are illustrative of the approach taken by the states to antitrust enforcements. Recent antitrust activity in that state is new evidence of the renascence of state antitrust enforcement. California's counterpart to the Sherman Act, the Cartwright Act, prohibits all trusts, defined in the Act as combinations of two or more persons to carry out any of a number of purposes, such as the creation of restrictions in commerce, the limitation of production, or the fixing of prices. The California courts have recognized that the framers of the Cartwright Act intended to codify the common law against restraints. Indeed, one court stated: "Cases decided under the Sherman Act and the common law policy against restraint of trade are applicable to problems arising under the Cartwright Act." Such a conclusion follows from the fact that the Sherman Act, as the basic federal prohibition against illegal combinations, is couched in the language of the common law and draws upon the precedents established under that law. The rule of reason is a judicial recognition that the Sherman Act is a partial codification of common law strictures against combinations. Inasmuch as the Clayton Act goes beyond common law prohibitions, it has not been relied upon as persuasive authority in the interpretation of the Cartwright Act. Additional antitrust provisions in California, however, reach much of the conduct that is proscribed by the Clayton Act.

The Cartwright Act is directed against combinations in restraint of trade. Unlike the Sherman Act, the Cartwright Act has no specific prohibitions against monopolies resulting from the action of a single person or corporation. An individual refusal to deal as part of a scheme to monopolize would violate Section 2 of the Sherman Act, but such activity would apparently not transgress the Cartwright Act, which is aimed only at the activity of two or more persons. In roughly half the states, unilateral as distinguished from multilateral action (conspiracy, combination) in restraint of trade is not specifically prohibited by statute. In such states the common law against monopolies as developed in early American cases may be applied against such restraints of commerce. As might be expected, the California courts have condemned price fixing among competitors as violative of the Cartwright Act. In fact, most states by statute specifically prohibit conspiracies to fix prices. Until recently, however, the California approach to resale price maintenance is not as clear as the federal condemnation of such activity. In the past some resale price maintenance programs have survived judicial scrutiny by the California courts. Concerted refusals to deal, on the other hand, have been treated by the California courts and the federal courts in much the same way.

The old adage that an ounce of prevention is worth a pound of cure is not without truth in the field of antitrust. The idea that monopoly should be attacked in its initial stages and that regulation short of criminal proceedings is often a salutary method of operation led to the creation of the Federal Trade Commission in 1914. The state of Wisconsin came to similar conclusions and enacted legislation designed to carry out such concepts. Wisconsin set up an antitrust enforcement body under the state

Department of Agriculture designed to insure that "trade practices and methods of competition shall be *fair*. . . ." Such activity in the field of enforcement has made that state a leader in the antitrust field. New York and Texas are also leading antitrust enforcement states with active and vigorous antitrust programs which can boast significant accomplishments. These programs have demonstrated the importance of antitrust in preserving free competitive enterprise in intrastate activities. The New York attorney general's office, for example, has already uncovered and put a stop to pricing fixing and the allocation of customers and territories in such significant industries as milk distribution, dry cleaning, and private cartage. The cartage cases alone involved more than 300 persons who controlled the private collection of refuse in the New York City area.

Recent years have also witnessed a new cooperation between federal and state antitrust enforcement officials. On the federal level, arrangements between the Department of Justice and the Federal Trade Commission designed to facilitate the exchange of information to avoid duplication of effort have long been in effect. Such an arrangement now exists between the New York attorney general's office and the New York branch office of the Federal Trade Commission. A great deal of antitrust information is exchanged between federal and state officials at bar association meetings, commercial clubs, and meetings sponsored by the federal and state governments. Such activity is a necessary concomitant of the resurgence of state enforcement and substantially contributes to the protection of the free enterprise system and the individual consumer.

CHAPTER 20

THE WONDERFUL WORLD OF ADVERTISING

A Brief History of American Advertising

Will Durant once wrote, "Trade begins in piracy; it culminates in morality." Certain it is that advertising began in piracy, and although a culmination in morality has not yet been reached, there is ground for hope.

The early proponents of *laissez faire* practiced the belief that a seller had a natural right to describe the attractions of his goods in any manner he saw fit. One of the famous early English cases on which most first-year law students cut their teeth involves the sale of a Bezor stone. Apparently, Bezor stones were thought to have curative powers some 400 years ago. The seller told the buyer, "This is a Bezor stone." After the sale had been consummated, the buyer realized that the item he had purchased was not a Bezor stone. He then sued the seller. The court denied him recovery, saying that the buyer had a remedy only if the seller had said, "I *warrant* this stone to be a Bezor stone." The court went on to state that the seller's simple declaration that the stone was a Bezor stone was merely legitimate puffing of the article for sale.

This case represents the apogee of the doctrine of *caveat emptor*. For the next 300 years some protection was afforded to buyers by the steadily enlarging law of warranty, but in the main the buyer was left to develop his own armor against false and misleading claims, and most sellers felt no compunctions about describing their goods in the most wildly extravagant terms. This legal and ethical climate prevailed almost to the birth of the twentieth century. Indeed, as the industrial revolution progressed, conditions grew worse. As education spread, so did the circulation of published material. As the railroad net spread and improved, the means for the widespread distribution of goods were at hand. These two conditions fostered the development of a new technique in marketing. It was now feasible to market a branded consumer product on a nationwide basis. It was now easy to distribute the product from a central location, and the tremendous growth of the publishing media, coinciding with the rapid increase of literacy, meant that it was possible to create widespread public familiarity with a brand name through advertising. Unfortunately, among the first to recognize and exploit the new marketing technique was a horde of quacks. Stewart Holbrook, in his delightful book *The Golden Age of Quackery,* describes some of the popular patent medicines, nostrums, and healing devices and the extravagant claims that were made for them. Let there be no mistake: some of these early patent medicines did have a powerful effect. Mr. Holbrook presents his analysis of one of the most popular of these sovereign remedies, Hostetter's Celebrated Stomach Bitters. At the time of the Civil War, Mr. Holbrook writes, "the Bitters contained modest amounts of cinchona bark, gentian root, orange peel, anise, and a less than modest dose of alcohol. Whether or not the alcoholic content was increased during the war is not clear, but for many years it ran to approximately 47 per cent by volume." This 94-proof compound undoubtedly warmed many a prim and temperate soul. The patent medicine king reigned supreme from the end of the Civil War to the early twentieth century. The magazines, newspapers, posters, and brochures of this period are loaded with announcements of miraculous cures of persons afflicted with every disease known to man. The advertisements are replete with testimonials from Congressmen, admirals, actresses, and, most often, clergymen.

A further example may be found in Ernest Turned's book *The Shocking History of Advertising.* An American magazine published in the 1880's carried an advertisement for one Dr. Scott's Electric Corsets, wherein the "doctor" made extravagant claims for the benefits to be derived from his corset. The corset would "cure" extreme fatness or leanness "in most cases." The product should be tried by women suffering from "any bodily ailment" and by those who wished to "ward off and cure disease." The corset would "bring the magnetic power into constant contact with all the vital organs." The advertisement went on to state that "it is affirmed by professional men that there is hardly a disease that electricity and magnetism will not benefit and cure." As authority, the name of a former surgeon-general of the United States was prominently mentioned.

The "doctor" could make these assertions with impunity in the 1880's. There were no legal sanctions against such advertising. Public education was at a comparatively low level, public taste was a factor not even to be considered, and Dr. Scott was obviously not concerned with building goodwill for his business for the distant future.

It was not long before the manufacturers of other branded consumer products grasped the possibilities of the new marketing technique. Soon soaps, cereals, cough drops, and canned milk all joined in the game of nationwide advertising and distribution.

It was in the field of patent medicines and healing devices that the drive for ethical standards in advertising began. Courageous journalists, medical societies, aroused and public-spirited citizens, and advertising men concerned with the future of advertising all contributed to the exposure and condemnation of the untruthful claims of the quacks. Samuel Hopkins Adams made a monumental contribution through his famed series on patent medicines that appeared in *Collier's* in 1906. Many historians credit the Adams series for tipping the balance in favor of passage of the Pure Food and Drug Act of 1906. That Act was designed as a truth-in-labeling statute of limited application. The principal protection it afforded to consumers was its requirement for the correct description of the contents of a medicinal product on the package.

The year 1911 was for several reasons a signal one in the history of advertising. In that year the first volume of the American Medical Association series entitled *Nostrums and Quackery* appeared. Moreover, it was in 1911 that the advertising industry itself made the first major effort against all forms of deceptive advertising. The Pure Food and Drug Act of 1906 did not meet the need for a general prohibition against deceptive advertising of all products. To fill this need, the movement for a model state statute prohibiting false advertising was launched by *Printers' Ink* in 1911. An attempt was made to have it enacted in every state legislature. The fight was waged by advertising men throughout the nation. As part of the movement to secure clean advertising and appropriate legislation, the Associated Advertising Clubs of the World at their Boston convention in 1911 adopted as a motto "Truth in Advertising" and two years later drew up a "Declaration of Principles" which today guides and controls the policies of all Better Business Bureaus. The Associated Advertising Clubs and later the Better Business Bureaus fought manfully for the passage of the model statute. This epic battle resulted in the passage of false advertising statutes in forty-four states.

The federal government also moved against all forms of false and misleading advertising. Federal action, however, did not take the form of direct prohibition against deceptive advertising, replete with criminal penalties. The federal effort began with the establishment of the Federal Trade Commission in 1914.

Early proponents of the proposal to establish a trade commission were not immediately concerned with deceptive advertising. Rather, their principal interest was the efficient enforcement of the antitrust laws. Some observers felt that the Sherman Antitrust Act of 1890 had been weakened through interpretation, notably by the Supreme Court's decision in *Standard Oil Company* case in 1911. They felt that an administrative agency would be more successful in banishing the specter of monopoly from the American scene. Broad support for the proposal was soon marshaled. In 1912 the platform of each of the three political parties (Republican, Democratic, and Progressive) contained a plank advocating the creation of a trade commission. Once in office, President Wilson vigorously pushed the proposal. In 1914 the Federal Trade Commission

Act was passed. Section 5 of the original FTC Act contained this basic prohibition: "That unfair methods of competition in commerce are hereby declared unlawful."

During the early years of the commission's history some people argued that this basic grant of authority was limited to the enforcement of the antimonopoly policy of the federal government. This view was vigorously challenged. Those who argued for a broad interpretation of the commission's power pointed to the view held by the original sponsors of the Act and their deliberate decision to leave the boundaries of the prohibition undefined. Mr. Justice Brandeis, a vigorous proponent of the idea of a trade commission, explained the basic theory in this manner:

> Instead of undertaking to define what practices should be deemed unfair as had been done in earlier legislation, the act left the determination to the commission. Experience with existing laws had taught that definition, being necessarily rigid, would prove embarrassing, and, if rigorously applied, might involve great hardship. Methods of competition which would be unfair in one industry, under certain circumstances, might, when adopted in another industry, or even in the same industry under different circumstances, be entirely unobjectionable.
>
> Furthermore, an enumeration, however comprehensive, of existing methods of unfair competition must necessarily soon prove incomplete, as with new conditions constantly arising novel unfair methods would be devised and developed. [Dissenting opinion in *Federal Trade Commission* v. *Gratz*].

The commission began to proceed against false and misleading advertising early in its history. One of the first commission orders to reach the courts (1919) involved false advertising. The Supreme Court approved a commission order to cease and desist from false and misleading advertising as early as 1922. It has been estimated that as early as 1925 orders directed against false and misleading advertising constituted 70 per cent of the total number of orders issued annually by the commission.

Until 1931 one important question remained unresolved: whether the commission could prohibit advertising that misled the public even though there was no evidence of competitive injury to truthful advertisers. Of the twenty-nine orders of the commission against false and misleading advertising reviewed by the courts prior to 1931, twenty-two were upheld and seven reversed. In none of the cases in which the order of the commission was upheld was the decision expressly grounded on a finding that honest competitors had been injured by the objectionable advertising. On the other hand, in at least one of the cases reversing the commission, the order was set aside on the express ground that the misrepresentation had no tendency to injure competitors.

This basic question was resolved adversely to the commission by the Supreme Court in the landmark 1931 case of *Federal Trade Commission*

v. *Raladam Company.* The Court held that the commission lacked jurisdiction to proceed against false advertising unless substantial competition, present or potential, was shown to have been injured or clearly threatened with substantial injury by the advertising in question.

This decision dealt a hard blow to the commission's enforcement effort. Agitation soon developed for Congressional action to broaden the commission's power in order that it might protect the consuming public as well as honest competitors. These efforts resulted in the passage of the Wheeler-Lea amendments to the Federal Trade Commission Act in 1938. The basic prohibition of Section 5 now reads as follows, "Unfair methods of competition in commerce, *and unfair or deceptive acts or practices in commerce,* are hereby declared unlawful." [Italics denote words added by amendment.]

The primary purpose of the amendment to Section 5 of the Act was to counteract the *Raladam* decision, but the Wheeler-Lea amendments were not limited to this purpose. The 1938 amendments also added Section 12 to the FTC Act, declaring certain advertisements of foods, drugs, devices, and cosmetics unfair or deceptive acts or practices in commerce within the meaning of Section 5, and armed the commission with additional procedural weapons against the false advertising of these products. In addition to these powers, Congress has since granted the commission specific powers over the false advertising of fur products and textile fiber products. Under Section 5 and Section 12 the commission acts through an administrative adjudicatory proceeding which may result in an order to cease and desist. But Sections 13 and 14 of the Act provide additional means of stopping the dissemination of false advertising of food, drugs, devices, and cosmetics by injunctions and criminal penalties.

Since 1938, then, the Federal Trade Commission has been armed with a variety of potent weapons in its never-ending war against false advertising and other unfair trade practices. Suffice it to say that the nation has come a long way from Dr. Scott and his electric corset. Although the buyer must still beware, the seller now also must beware.

No history, however brief, would be adequate without a glance at the background of that vital institution, the advertising agency. It is generally agreed that the forebear of the agency arose in this country during the 1830's, when individual newspaper employees functioned as advertising solicitors. Morton J. Simon, in his excellent work *The Law for Advertising and Marketing,* describes these individuals as newspaper agents, distinct from advertising agents. In the 1860's there developed the practice of "space wholesaling," whereby the individual agent purchased large amounts of advertising space at a discount. He would resell the space to the advertiser. Gradually, the agent purchased more and more space in a greater number of newspapers, ultimately reaching the stage where he could offer an advertiser space in a large number of papers. The year 1875 saw the emergence of F. Wayland Ayer's famous "open contract," under which he acted as exclusive agent for advertisers in dealing with the publisher. Ayer, incidentally, was one of the founders of N. W. Ayer & Son. In 1893 came the American Newspaper Publishers' Statement. The publishers agreed to pay commissions to recognized agencies and to allow no discounts to direct advertisers. The same policy was adopted by the Curtis Publishing Company in 1901. The announcement by Curtis, of course, brought the *Saturday Evening Post* and the *Ladies' Home Journal* within the ambit of the agency. Thus the policy spread from newspapers to periodicals, resulting in the development of the advertising agency as we know it today.

The Role of Advertising in a Free Economy

Twelve billion dollars of advertising annually is a powerful economic force. This force has played a mighty role in building and sustaining our American system of free competitive enterprise, which has produced the highest standard of living ever achieved by free people in the history of the world.

As our ability to produce goods has increased through mechanization and higher productive efficiency, distribution and consumption have become important problems. All these gains of mass production and advanced technology would go for naught without a means of reaching a market of potential consumers. Customers must be sought and taught, often persuaded, to move up in the living scale. Personal selling is one way. But we are now manufacturing mountains of goods which are of better quality and are produced more economically than ever before. Personal selling must be augmented by mass selling in order to bring these goods to the consumer.

Advertising should and indeed does acquaint the public with new products and new methods—products and methods which in most cases are safer, easier, and cheaper. We can readily see the force of advertising as it applies to our system of free enterprise. It provides the opportunity for new companies and new products to flourish and grow; at the same time, advertising helps the manufacturer with an established name to maintain his position. The result of this process is to increase the over-all freedom of individual consumers to choose among different products.

Mass selling means advertising, which multiplies the personal salesman by millions. Advertising is to distribution and consumption what improved machines are to production. Advertising is the accelerator which puts speed and power into sales. Sales mean more income for more people. In turn, these people desire more goods and services, not only for the basic needs of food, clothing, and shelter, but for the enjoyment of leisure hours, for the opportunities of participating in communal and cultural activities. Without this accelerator, advertising, we could not have the kind of life we enjoy in America today.

A summary definition of the social responsibilities of advertising would, at a minimum, embrace these three elements:

1. To function as an efficient instrument of free and fair competition by focusing public attention on the demonstrable merits of competing products and services.
2. To foster innovation by affording new entrants to the marketplace an efficient means for winning public acceptance.
3. To furnish to consumers the information necessary for intelligent choices.

These responsibilities are affirmatively stated. Viewed negatively, we may state the summary in this way:

1. To avoid perverting free competition by using advertising as an unfair method of competition. Disparagement of worthy competitors or the diversion of sales through deception are obvious examples of foul competition.
2. To avoid the use of deception or the exercise of market power to stifle innovation. Advertising can be used as a tool of monopoly, just as it can be used as an instrument of free competition.
3. To avoid flooding consumers with false and misleading statements which pervert the right of free choice. The economic damage to consumers produced by such practices is vicious; the weakening of public confidence in a free enterprise economy resulting from such practices is a far greater vice.

The functions of advertising must be tuned to an overriding obligation. That obligation, in essence, is to speak the truth. Speaking the truth involves something more than the mere avoidance of the half-truth, and that is the inclusion of the fact that is essential to the formation of an accurate judgment on the qualities of the article or services described. The difficulty comes in the reconciliation of purpose with obligation. There is a constant tension in any form of activity that seeks to win attention from competition, but if we say that attention cannot be won honorably, then we admit that advertising is an improper social activity. It is the firm opinion of the author that there is no need to make such an admission.

Advertising bears a basic responsibility to trusting consumers—consumers who themselves are the beneficiaries of the rising sophistication in American life. As the levels of public education and public taste rise, so must the minimum standards of advertisers rise. The proverbial advertising man who addresses his pleas solely to twenty-year-olds is becoming obsolete, as indeed he should. This individual does a disservice to himself, his product, his industry, and, most important, to the increasingly aware consumer.

Advertising has never been able to sell an inferior product for a prolonged period of time. Too often we give the consumer too little credit for ability to see fraud, deception, and trickery. But the American consumer soon gets wise to chicanery, and fraudulent purveyors of shoddy and shady merchandise have to close up shop and move elsewhere, or else find new tricks and gimmicks. As a matter of fact, even worthy products have had to give up the ghost because for some reason or other the public would not accept them. The consumer has always exercised and is exercising today a censorship over advertising, because falsely advertised products find it harder and harder to make advertising pay off. It seems absolutely certain that the manufacturer of good products, promoted by advertising in good taste, will dominate the advertising scene long after the opportunist has withdrawn his shadily advertised product from the market or has given up business completely.

A further aspect of the over-all role of advertising lies in the inescapable fact that advertising is the showcase of our free enterprise system to all the world. This showcase reveals itself both in the United States and overseas. Our mass media are capable of reaching into the most remote corners of the world; indeed the day has come when an American television commercial may be viewed simultaneously in Europe. Surely, in this perspective every businessman must realize the importance of truthful advertising conducted in good taste. Here in the United States, on display to visiting diplomats, students, and tourists, is the giant showcase of American wares and a full-scale presentation of how they are sold. Let us take a concrete example—that of foreign diplomats stationed in our nation's capital. As soon as they arrive, they get the treatment: "Dear Friend" letters by direct-mail sellers, double-spread ads of sensationally reduced prices, breathless bargains barking out of their TV and radio sets, and the yellow pages of the telephone book offering an infinity of "free" inspections and "guaranteed" services. To these persons, some of them highly influential, Washington offers an illustration of our free enterprise system, not as we preach it but as we practice it. And any instance of business chicanery carries a far greater impact on them than on us. We recognize skullduggery as the handiwork of an individual or, at most, of a corporation; they regard it as a revelation of national degeneracy. Nor is such superficial judgment peculiar to foreigners in America. Just ask an American tourist his opinion of the national character of the country where he paid for a pearl and got a white marble.

We may view advertising and its impact as a small skirmish in what has been described as the "battle for men's minds." In such a context it is certain that the picture of American free enterprise is badly dirtied by offensive and deceptive advertising. Just as certainly, we can and must realize that our picture is strongly bolstered by truthful advertising presented in good taste.

Finally, in analyzing the role of advertising in our economy, we must conclude with a note of caution. All intelligent businessmen realize that advertising has many critics. Much has been said about the sins of advertisers, their agencies, and the media. On the other hand, many good and constructive things have been done by responsible groups in the advertising industry. We shall examine some of these efforts in a later chapter. Of course, the good work being done by some does not justify the shortcomings of others which may not yet have been corrected. But the value of legitimate advertising to our economy is too important to permit the abuses of some to bring the entire industry into general disrepute. Certainly there are some jackals on the fringes of advertising, as in any other industry. Law enforcement agencies such as the Federal Trade Commission were created to root out the weeds, but there is danger in harming the carefully cultivated plants by the misapplication of weed killer. Care must be exercised in combating the evils found in some advertising, lest in the process all advertising be harmed. This would be a catastrophe, not only to advertising, but to our entire economic system.

CHAPTER 21

DECEPTIVE SCHEMES AND HOW THEY OPERATE

ADVERTISERS and advertising agencies should have no doubts about the kind of advertising that can be safely shown on television or pictured in print. The safe territory is a field both wide and fertile. Unfortunately, that is not enough for some advertisers. In their enthusiastic explorations along the brink of illegality, they insist on pushing themselves up to the edge and all too frequently fall in. Some critics desire such a sharp definition of the brink that no amount of ingenuity or skullduggery could obscure it. This would be an excellent idea—but for one major difficulty. It is impossible to chart a precise legal line through the future craftiness of savagely competitive advertisers. This fact was recognized by Congress half a century ago when the Federal Trade Commission was created. Congress recognized the futility of trying to outlaw specific unfair acts and practices, some of which had yet to be devised by the ingenuity of man. Far better to couch the law in broad language and leave it up to the commission to apply the intent of the law to specific acts and practices as they came into being. Such flexibility was only a practical means of coping with future chicanery. Hence, we must begin with the broad language of the statute itself: "unfair methods of competition and . . . unfair or deceptive acts or practices. . . ."

With the passage of years thousands of cases have been decided, and a vital body of case law marks the course of business morality. Like buoys identifying the channel of a river, the commission's actions provide guidance to the business pilot. Ideally, it would be most beneficial if the exact limits could be so marked that even the most daring shortcutter would never run aground, even in untraveled sections of the river. But this is impossible. The intelligent businessman and his counsel are best advised to study the pattern of channel markers and set a safe course.

Despite the difficulty inherent in precise definitions, many of the cases do fall into certain recognizable patterns of deceptive techniques having the same basic scheme, although the practical application may vary. With the warning that no discussion of the subject can ever be an ultimate definition, let us proceed to an examination of the basic categories of deceptive advertising. In this analysis we will occasionally draw from some of the Federal Trade Commission's guides, including the *Guides Against Deceptive Pricing*, the *Guides Against Bait Advertising*, and the *Guides Against Deceptive Advertising of Guarantees.*

Basic Rules of Advertising

We must first list the basic rules which govern all advertising. These rules have evolved through years of practice; they have been stated and restated by the courts and are regularly applied by the commission and its staff in analyzing advertising for unfair or deceptive tendencies.

1. The crucial factor of deceptive advertising is a *tendency* to deceive. There is no requirement that the government prove *actual* deception of a particular consumer.

2. Next is the rule of which any intelligent businessman must be aware —he proceeds at his own peril. In a case of false advertising the government does not have to prove knowledge on the part of the advertiser. As one court has said: "*Whether or not the advertiser knows the representations to be false,* the deception of purchasers and the diversion of trade from competitors is the same." (Italics supplied.)

3. In a similar vein is the rule that the intent of the advertiser is entirely immaterial. An advertiser may have a wholly innocent intent and yet violate the law. The Supreme Court has stated the rule this way: "A *deliberate effort to deceive is not necessary* to make out a case of using unfair methods of competition or unfair or deceptive acts or practices. . . ." (Italics supplied.)

There are four more general rules laying down the standards against which the courts and the commission will examine a particular piece of advertising. They refer to ways of reading or viewing advertisements.

4. Advertisements will be read by the courts and the commission as though through the eyes of the public, at least that portion of the public to whom the advertisement is directed. It is immaterial that an expert reader might be able to decipher an advertisement and determine, for example, that a "6% Plan of Financing" on automobiles really amounted to approximately 11.5 per cent simple annual interest on an unpaid balance. The Supreme Court has held that advertising laws "are made to protect the trusting as well as the suspicious."

5. Then, too, advertisements are "not intended to be carefully dissected with a dictionary at hand, but rather to produce an impression upon the ordinary purchaser."

6. Next, an advertiser cannot present one over-all impression and yet protect himself with reservations of a contrary impression which appear as small and inconspicuous portions of the whole. As the Supreme Court has said: "Advertisements as a whole may be completely misleading al-

though every sentence separately considered is literally true. This may be because things are omitted that should be said, or because advertisements are composed or purposefully printed in such a way as to mislead."

7. Finally, if the meaning of an advertisement is ambiguous, the ad will nonetheless be read by the courts and the commission to effect the purpose of the law. The purpose of the law is the prohibition of advertising which has a tendency and capacity to mislead. In other words, if an advertisement can be read to have two meanings, one of which is false or misleading, then the particular advertisement is illegal.

Deceptive Pricing in "Savings" Advertisements

Deceptive pricing in "savings" advertisements is found in those advertisements which in one way or another represent to the consumer that the purchase of the advertised article may be made at a reduction or saving on a regular established price. When investigation reveals that the advertised regular price is fictitious, then the advertiser is in trouble with the commission. Let us look at some examples.

A retail furniture store advertised by newspaper a sale of various sets of furniture. Each set carried the statement "You Save," followed by a dollar figure. One set of bedroom furniture stated, "You Save $80." It was found that the prices in the ad represented no reduction at all from the ordinary price charged by this retailer. There was no saving at all to the consumer. The same advertisement ran again several months later, but this time one item of furniture had been reduced $10. The advertisement still claimed "You Save $80." The commission found that the consumer this time would save only $10. In these instances the commission examined the invoices of the advertiser in order to determine his ordinary retail price.

Household appliances are a common field for this form of deceptive advertising. A St. Louis retailer advertised by newspaper:

Telephone-Lounge with Swivel Lamp
Reg.
$39.59 $24.88
Refrigerators, Freeezrs, Washers and Dryers at Big Savings!
$219.95 Hotpoint Family-Size Refrigerator $158
$329.95 Hotpoint 12 cu. ft. Refrigerator $219

In fact, each item advertised normally sold for the so-called reduced price, a fact which the advertiser frankly admitted regarding most of his merchandise. The company had never sold any of the items at the higher price stated by the advertisement to be "regular."

A Philadelphia department store advertised the sale of carpeting at $10.89 or $10.95 per square yard. The advertisement stated that this merchandise "regularly" or "usually" sold for $15.95 or $16.95 per square yard. The truth of the matter was that this department store had never sold these particular carpets before and thus had no regular or usual price at all. Clearly, the advertisement was false and misleading. This case goes even a step further and should serve as a warning to the perceptive businessman. The department store sought to defend its advertising on the ground that *other stores* in Philadelphia normally and usually sold that particular carpeting at the prices it had advertised. The company took this case to a federal court of appeals, which ruled in favor of the Federal Trade Commission and against the store. The court held that the prices of other stores did not detract from the deceptive nature of the advertisement. If the department store wanted to indicate that its prices were lower than those of other stores, then it should have said so. The terms *regular* and *usual* refer to the practices of the advertiser, and the public cannot be expected to guess at a different meaning.

Another sore spot is the use of terms such as *list price* or *manufacturer's list price*. The commission has ruled in several cases that, by the comparison of a "list price" against a lower sales figure, the consumer is led to believe that the difference is actually a saving from the usual and customary retail price of the product so advertised. In ruling on the facts in a case involving this question the commission explained:

> It has been and is a recognized business custom for manufacturers and wholesalers to publish or quote "list" or "catalog" prices which are subject to discount to retailers, the difference between the net prices and the list or catalog prices representing the profit to the retailers, with the list or catalog prices being the approximate prices at which the merchandise is expected to be sold at retail. The public is well aware of such long-established custom and relies thereon, and has come to believe that list or catalog prices are approximately the usual and ordinary retail prices, and that any dealings by which any price reduction is obtained below such list or catalog prices represent and are savings from regular retail prices.

An instructive illustration is the case of a manufacturer of power lawn mowers, who would give retailers literature using the phrase *suggested list*. The retailers would then sell to the public, making full use of the manufacturer's literature. Included in this assortment of printed matter would be price sheets and trade paper advertisements placed by the manufacturer himself. To potential new retailer customers the manufacturer would furnish a file of clippings showing local newspaper advertisements placed by his other retailer customers. In each case the material would state a suggested list price and an actual selling price. The trouble was that the mowers had virtually never been sold by anyone at the suggested list price. Some idea of the true price relationship can be gleaned from one mower which bore a suggested list price of $154.95. In point of fact, the retailer could purchase the mower from the advertiser for $47 and would normally resell it to the consumer for $77. Indeed, the consumer price would even drop to $68 when the mower was sold as a closeout item at the end of the season. As a result of all this, the manufacturer was ordered by the commission to cease and desist from using the deceptive literature. This case has another good lesson. The reader has undoubtedly observed that this manufacturer did not deal directly with the public, unlike the furniture store, the appliance store, or the department store. Nevertheless, he was held responsible by the government for deceptive advertising in commerce. The case of the lawn mower manufacturer provides a clear example of the familiar rule that he who puts into the hands of another means by which it is possible to mislead the public is himself guilty of deception.

In short, when the commission has considered such terms as *list price* or *manufacturer's list* or *suggested list*, it has consistently held that such a phrase must mean the "bona fide regular established selling prices of the [products] advertised and offered for sale, as established by the usual and customary sales in the normal course of business." In addition to the expressions used in the examples preceding, the commission's *Guides Against Deceptive Pricing* list other terms which have been held to represent a usual and customary retail price. For example: "formerly," "originally," "reduced," "was____now____," "made to sell for," "our list price," "____% off," "special," and "$50 dress–$35." In the same category are *sold nationally at* and *nationally advertised at.*

Wholesale

On numerous occasions the commission has found that firms representing themselves as wholesalers were actually retailers selling to consumers and doing little or no wholesale selling at all. Such advertising is obviously false and deceiving to the public. As the commission found in one case: "There is a preference on the part of a portion of the purchasing public for dealing with wholesalers . . . due either to the fact that they are obtaining wholesale prices or prices less than the customary and usual retail prices, or to their belief that they are obtaining such prices."

Let us look briefly at one example. A large jewelry firm did a mail-order business utilizing catalogues, circulars, cards, etc., in which appeared the following representations:

> Wholesale Watch and Jewelry Co.
> Direct Jobber of American Watches
> Industrial Jobbers
> Recognized as industrial jobbers. We can sell nationally advertised merchandise at our jobbing prices.

After an investigation and hearing, the commission found that this company was neither a wholesaler nor a jobber and indeed sold strictly to the consuming public. As for the purported wholesale prices, the commission concluded: "The prices of respondent's merchandise are not wholesalers' or jobbers' prices but are retail prices, being approximately the prices at which such merchandise is customarily offered for sale at retail." There was simply no saving or discount to the customer at all. In this case the commission held that the words *wholesale* and *jobbers* were in themselves misleading and deceptive.

A further variant in the "wholesale" scheme is the practice of listing a so-called wholesale price in comparison with a so-called suggested list retail price. This device often runs afoul of the law, either because the "wholesale" prices are not wholesale or because the "list" retail prices are in excess of the customary retail price for the article. Indeed, there have been instances when both statements were deceptive. The commission brought a complaint against a large mail-order house whose catalogues contained such statements as these:

> HOW TO FIND YOUR WHOLESALE COST
> Your Cost is Part of Our Coded Stock Number
> Here is a Typical Price Example
> No. 1014W1285 . . . .$26.95
> Your Cost is $12.85
> Just point off 2 decimal places from the last number on right
>
> All list prices shown are either the suggested or retail prices set by the manufacturer.
>
> Once again we wish to impress on you that we will sell . . . at WHOLESALE PRICES—not merely at discount prices.

In its complaint against this advertising the commission attorneys alleged that in many instances the coded wholesale prices were higher than the actual wholesale prices and, further, that the supposedly suggested or retail prices were most often higher than the actual customary retail prices. Thus, said the commission, someone making a purchase from this catalogue would be deceived in that he would not realize the savings which were claimed. This case illustrates the combination of two deceptive techniques: the use of *wholesale* together with the use of *suggested list* or *retail.* If the commission's complaint should be borne out by evidence and both prices are fictitious, then this company is clearly in serious trouble.

At this point we must sound two more warning notes on the dangers of the improper use of the term *wholesale*. First, many states have specific laws which make it illegal to use the term unless the user is in fact engaged in the represented trade. Moreover, a further possible violation of federal law occurs in this area. If firms representing themselves as wholesalers are actually engaged in the retail trade, they may be in violation of the Robinson-Patman Act. That statute, as we have seen in Chapter 9, prohibits a firm from illegally inducing a discriminatory price allowance, and it is possible that firms who falsely represent themselves as wholesalers may improperly induce a manufacturer to sell to them at wholesale prices rather than at the price customarily charged to retailers.

Factory

Closely related to the deceptive use of the term *wholesale* is the illegal use of the terms *factory, factory-priced,* and the like. For example, one concern calling itself the ___ Clothing Manufacturing Company advertised by means of signs, stationery, labels, and radio announcements. It also utilized pictures of workmen in a factory. The literature and the radio announcements carried some of these representations: "from their own factory direct to you"; "their factory controls the manufacturing cost"; and "factory direct-to-you store." The true facts of the case were that this company did not own, operate, or control any factory. The photographs had actually been taken in plants operated by someone else. The commission found that the merchandise was not sold direct to the consumer and that the price did include a middleman's profit. The prices were not wholesale at all. The "factory showroom" was actually a retail store. All of these advertising practices were false and misleading and were halted by a commission order.

The same fate befell a company which used the terms *Thread Mills* and *Mills* in its name and advertisements. This company was not a manufacturer at all and did not sell at mill prices. Consequently, it also was prohibited from using this sort of deceptive advertising.

Preticketing

Preticketing is a practice whereby a manufacturer or distributor places a price tag on a product so that when the product is sold by the retailer to the consumer, it appears that the preticketed price is the usual and customary retail price of the product. The commission has taken innumerable actions against those who preticketed merchandise in a manner which deceived consumers as to available savings. In one case a distributor of watches preticketed its goods at a price well in excess of the regular and usual retail price of the items. For example, it preticketed at \$33.75, \$47.50, and \$71.50 certain watches that customarily sold at retail for \$17.95, \$19.95, and \$22.95, respectively.

The company tried to defend on the basis that it did not control the prices at which the retailer sold the watches to the public. The company argued that it had no knowledge at the time it shipped the watches whether the price tags would remain affixed thereto at the time of resale, nor did it then know the prices at which the watches would be resold.

Therefore, it was claimed, the company could not be held accountable for the acts of the retailers in selling the watches for prices below those on the attached tags.

All of these arguments were rejected by the hearing examiner, whose decision was affirmed by the commission. The hearing examiner reasoned that it did not matter whether or not the distributor could know beforehand that every watch would be sold with the tag attached and at below-tag prices, because the distributor knew or had reason to believe that in the normal course of events its watches would in fact be resold in such a manner. The fact that a retailer could, if he chose, remove a price tag before resale or possibly resell the watch at the tagged price did not gainsay the fact that the distributor was chargeable with the ordinary "facts of life" concerning what happened to its product. The hearing examiner added that the company could not insulate itself from responsibility for the natural consequences of its actions on the specious theory that its customers were free agents. This case is another application of the familiar rule that the one who puts the deceptive means into circulation is himself liable for the deception—notwithstanding the fact that retailers or any other party may intervene in the normal course of business before the goods actually reach the consumer.

Two-for-One

On the matter of two-for-one the rule is quite simple. As the Guides state: "No statement . . . of an offer to sell two articles for the price of one . . . should be used unless the sales price for the two articles is the advertiser's usual and customary retail price for the single article in the recent, regular course of his business."

Thus, advertising was held illegal when two pints of a certain motor lubricant were advertised for sale at 85 cents on a two-for-one basis when the normal price of the same two pints was 90 cents. Commission reports show that this scheme has been tried several times in the sale of men's suits. In many instances the total two-for-one price was exactly equal to the regular retail price of two suits. In one instance the advertised price was even higher than the regular retail price of the two suits!

A variant of the "two-for-the-price-of-one" scheme is "buy one, and get one free." A case in point involved the Mary Carter Paint Company which had offered, and usually sold, "every second can [of paint] FREE, gallon or quart." The problem was that the usual and customary price for a single can of paint had never been established. A customer paid $6.98 per gallon or $2.98 per quart and either accepted or rejected the additional "free" equivalent quantity. The FTC, in attacking the practice, found that the cost of the second can must necessarily have been included in the price paid by the purchaser; accordingly, the second can was not given free of charge and the scheme was deceptive.

The Fifth Circuit reversed, but the Supreme Court reinstated the commission's decision. According to the Supreme Court, Mary Carter was "marketing twins." In setting the price charged, it must have considered the second can because it never sold a single can for less money. It was a variation of the problem challenged in "two-for-one" deals, that is, the stated price for the unit of two, including the so-called free item, is found to be the price a customer would have to pay if he chose to purchase two under normal conditions. It is then a matter of comparison and simple arithmetic as to whether one item in the unit is "free" in the sense that the purchaser is buying or paying for only one item in the unit.

The same clear standard governs the advertising of "half-price" sales or "1-cent sales" in which the savings are conditioned upon the purchase of other merchandise. The commission requires the conditions of the sale to be "conspicuously disclosed in immediate conjunction with the offer." It is further required that any representation of savings be true when balanced against the advertiser's usual retail prices. Similarly, the price charged for the article which the consumer must buy in order to take advantage of the offer must be the customary and regular retail price of the item. In other words, a company cannot advertise a sale of this nature and then proceed to raise its normal price on the merchandise which the customer must buy.

"Bait-and-Switch" Advertising

"Bait" advertising is an alluring but insincere offer to sell a product or service which the advertiser in truth does not intend or want to sell. Its purpose is to interest the consumer in the advertised product in order to sell something else, usually at a higher price or on a basis more advantageous to the advertiser. The primary aim of a bait advertisement is to obtain leads to persons interested in buying merchandise of the type offered.

At this point we must recognize a distinction between bait advertising and the attribute of salesmanship popularly known as "trading up"; that is, legitimately trading a customer up from the advertised merchandise to higher-priced merchandise. In the trading-up situation the advertiser has a sufficient stock of the advertised item to meet the reasonably anticipated demand. Although he may extol the virtues of the higher-priced goods, he does not disparage the advertised item or choose that moment to make it appear less desirable than he had claimed it to be in his ad. Finally, he is willing to sell the advertised item to those customers who are unimpressed with his salesmanship without forcing them to win two out of three falls.

The Federal Trade Commission has actively prosecuted and exposed a great number of bait schemes. This form of advertising is particularly prevalent in commodities such as used automobiles, combination storm windows, furs, furniture, home appliances, jewelry, pianos, radio and TV sets, sewing machines, upholstery, and vacuum cleaners. As an illustration of illegal bait advertising, let us take a look at a typical commission case in which the respondents advertised a sewing machine, purported to sell for as much as $119.50, for prices as low as $38.88. The advertisements, published an average of three or four times a week in most of the newspapers in Washington, D.C., invited interested parties to call for a home demonstration and to reserve a machine. Usually, when a person called in response to the advertisement, an appointment was made for a salesman to call at the customer's home to demonstrate the machine. The salesman, in almost every instance, brought with him a more expensive machine in addition to the advertised machine.

The testimony of most of the witnesses at the hearing described how the salesman discouraged the sale of the advertised machine by advising the customer not to purchase it, by disparaging its performance, by stating that it did not perform operations—although such operations were among the advertised features of the machine—and by displaying a general attitude of reluctance to sell the machine. This was followed by an inducement to buy the more expensive machine. Most of the witnesses referred to the unusually noisy performance of the advertised machine and mentioned, in some instances, that this had been emphasized by the salesman as an indication that the machine was undesirable. Contrary to the claims made in the advertisement, it was pointed out to the customer that the machine did not sew backward and forward, that it skipped stitches, that the stitch could not be regulated, that it did not sew over pins, that you could not get parts for the machine, that it was a toy, and that it had a long bobbin, which was less desirable than the round bobbin on the more expensive machine the salesman just happened to have with him. After the customer had been sufficiently discouraged by the disparaging remarks of the salesman and noisy performance of the machine, the salesman then tried to sell a more expensive machine.

None of the witnesses had been successful in their efforts to obtain the advertised machine. They were given various excuses and were shunted back and forth between the salesman and persons at the store, all to no avail. In several instances the salesman would not take a deposit, but told the customer to telephone the store or that a driver would get it. The customers who telephoned the store were given some excuse, such as the fact that the advertised machines were "oversold" or that the machines in stock had certain attachments which the customer would have to take at additional cost. Several witnesses who did get the salesman to accept a deposit were later told, upon telephoning the store, that the machines were sold out. Some customers who went directly to the store in response to the advertisement were told that none of the advertised machines were in stock.

With regard to the noisy operation of the machine, the hearing examiner stated:

> There are undeniably a number of instances in the record where customers rejected the *** machine because of its deficiencies in performance, particularly its unusual noise in operation, and where there is no evidence of any overt criticism or disparagement by the salesman. However, this does not necessarily impugn the testimony of those witnesses who claimed that the salesman had discouraged them from purchasing the machine, nor does it necessarily disprove the bait advertising charge. In the first place, the examiner is not convinced that the noisy performance of the *** machine was due entirely to the fact that it had a long bobbin, as contended by respondents. The testimony of so many of the witnesses on both sides concerning the unusually noisy performance of the machine suggests that the demonstrated models had been tampered with in some way so as to accentuate the noise.

From these facts the hearing examiner concluded that the offer was not a bona fide effort to sell the advertised product. The commission agreed with him by adopting his decision and issuing an order against the practice.

The essence of a "bait-and-switch" practice is a scheme to switch the consumer from the advertised product to a product which the baiter actually wants to sell. This can be done blatantly or by subtlety. An experienced shopper would recognize an obvious bait situation where the advertised product is "nailed to the floor" and its qualities are disparaged by the salesman.

Because of increased efforts by government and voluntary groups to combat this evil, the baiter has resorted to a more sophisticated approach. This involves "switch after sale." The ridiculously low-priced vacuum cleaner or sewing machine will be willingly sold to the consumer without any disparagement whatsoever on the part of the salesman. In service the vacuum cleaner will not pick up dust because a cardboard insert has been placed in it. The sewing machine will operate, perhaps with the efficiency of a machine gun, but also with as much noise, because of tampering by the baiter. When the consumer's expected dissatisfaction has ripened, a second call by the salesman is made, at which time Mrs. Housewife is more than delighted to know that she can return the product she purchased. But her relief is tempered when she is told that the first machine can be returned only as a trade-in on a more expensive machine. This is not to say that any attempt to adjust consumer complaints is a bait practice; however, such a technique has often been used as a part of a bait scheme.

The Federal Trade Commission has been very active in the effort to eliminate deceptive bait advertising. In 1959 the commission issued its *Guides Against Bait Advertising*, covering definitions of bait advertising, standards controlling the advertised offer itself, examples of acts which constitute discouragement of purchase of the advertised bait, and rules dealing with the switch after sale. In addition to the guides, the commission has covered the subject of bait advertising in its *Trade Practice Rules* for five specific industries: the musical instrument and accessories industry, the hearing aid industry, the combination storm window and door industry, the metal awning industry, and the rabbit industry.

False and misleading forms of bait advertising have also concerned the state governments. In 1955 the Council of State Governments recommended a model statute to the states for their adoption. At least nineteen states now have specific statutes against the practice. Among these states are California, Connecticut, Georgia, Hawaii, Illinois, Kansas, Maine, Maryland, Massachusetts, Michigan, Minnesota, Missouri, New York, Ohio, Pennsylvania, Rhode Island, Tennessee, West Virginia, and Wisconsin. Virtually all of these statutes make bait advertising a criminal offense. In some of these states the convicted baiter can be fined as much as $1,000 or imprisoned for as long as one year. In addition to criminal provisions, a few states have enacted laws which permit injunctions to be issued against illegal bait and bait-and-switch advertising.

In summary, we shall set forth the basic precept embodied in Guide I of the bait advertising guides: "No advertisement containing an offer to sell a product should be published when the offer is not a bona fide effort to sell the advertised product." By following this clear rule, the reputable businessman can generally avoid trouble with either the state or the federal authorities.

"Free" Goods

For many years advertisements representing "free" goods have posed problems for the commission. Of course, if the particular item really is an unconditional gift, there can be no complaint. The difficulty arises in the great bulk of instances in which the scheme requires the consumer to purchase certain merchandise in order to obtain the free article.

Beginning in 1953, the commission laid down the rules which currently govern the advertising of "free" goods. Prior to that time, generally speaking, it was considered unfair and deceptive to advertise "free" goods conditioned upon the purchase of other items. Now, however, a businessman may advertise "free" goods in conjunction with other purchases *provided* that he fully complies with the commission's requirements.

The first requirement is that "all the conditions, obligations, or other prerequisites [be] clearly and conspicuously set forth at the outset so as to leave no reasonable probability that the terms of the offer will be misunderstood. . . ." For example, it was ruled illegal when a television repair business advertised by newspaper that it furnished "free shop estimates," when in fact the estimates were free only if the set was left for repair. On the other hand, the commission has dismissed complaints if the terms of the offer were set out with sufficient clarity. A corporation which distributed women's hosiery to retailers had issued circulars and mailers which offered, among other things, one box of stockings free if the consumer purchased three additional boxes. In ruling upon this case, the hearing examiner and the commission found that the terms of the offer were adequately informative. Here is how this corporation made things clear in its "free" offer:

> When you mail to us the enclosed subscription form, you will receive [one] *gift box* of three pairs of nylons at once. Beginning one month later, you will receive 1 box of three (3) pairs each month for the next three months, and you will be billed on your regular charge account in the amount of $4.50 for each box of three pairs. If you cancel your subscription before its completion, it will be necessary for us to charge you for the *gift box.*

The second major rule governing the use of "free" offers is that the advertiser may not raise the price of the article to be purchased to absorb the cost of the free item. A large corporation which produced, distributed, and sold electric shavers devised a plan undoubtedly aimed at avoiding the effect of this rule. The plan was thwarted by the commission, however, and the corporation ultimately agreed to the entry of a cease and desist order against certain of its advertisements. This company had launched a nationwide campaign known as the "Lucky Lady Special Offer." Under the terms of this offer the purchaser of a certain model men's shaver would receive "free" a certain model women's shaver. The company advertised on a large scale in newspapers, in magazines, and on radio and television. Virtually all of the advertising stated, "Buy His—Get Hers Free." The way the company got into legal difficulty was not by openly raising the price of the men's shaver, but rather by eliminating all trade-ins on men's shavers presented by the customer who wanted to purchase a new men's shaver and "get hers free." Thus, the normal retail price for the men's shaver in question was $29.50. The company ordinarily allowed a standard $7.50 trade-in on an old men's shaver. In other words, the usual net price of the particular shaver which the customer had to buy in order to get the "free" women's shaver was $22. But during the period of the offer the corporation simply refused to grant a trade-in allowance to any customer who wanted to participate in the "free" offer. Therefore, in effect, the company had violated the rule against raising the price of the item to be purchased in a "free" offer.

The other rules relating to "'free" offers are in the same vein as the rule against raising the price. To this extent, the law of "free" goods offers is settled. Since 1953, however, it has outgrown the rather narrow limits of the rule, principally with respect to the role that pricing plays in these promotional schemes. Subsequent cases suggest that the question has become, "How free is 'free'?" and the answer has been found by examining the ordinary and usual price of the article required to be purchased. The *Guides Against Deceptive Pricing* (see Appendix II), promulgated by the commission in 1958, contain helpful standards for the businessman attempting to keep pace with the law. In the future, however, his efforts may be substantially alleviated by a new set of guidelines. In March 1969 the FTC announced the *Proposed Guide Concerning the Use of the Word "Free" and Similar Representations* which, with the 1953 rule as its core, incorporates relevant provisions of the pricing guides as well as suggestions for the use of practices not covered in the old rule. For example, continuous "free" offers, introductory offers of "free" merchandise, and "combination" offers are defined and the fair limits of their use prescribed. As promulgated on November 16, 1971, the provisions of the guide supersede those contained in the 1953 rule and should contribute substantially to the constructive information and advice so sorely needed by the business community.

If the advertiser adheres to the standards of these rules, he may legally advertise "free" goods conditioned upon the purchase of other merchandise. But care must be taken in compliance; evasive schemes will result only in expense, annoyance, and commercial embarrassment for the businessman. In this area—as, indeed, with all forms of potentially deceptive advertising—the best advice is that of competent legal counsel, whose opinion should be sought early in the game whenever possible doubt may arise concerning advertising plans.

Deception by Nondisclosure

As we have previously seen, the Supreme Court has held that an advertisement may be completely misleading "because things are omitted that should be said. . . ." The problem for the prudent businessman is to determine, with reference to his particular product, just what things should be said. Generally speaking, an advertisement should set forth whatever the purchaser would normally want to know about the nature and use of the product. If certain information could affect the tendency to buy or not to buy, then it is a pretty safe bet that such information should be disclosed in advertising.

The cases in this area are voluminous and cover almost every variety of nondisclosure. For practical reasons, therefore, we shall examine only a few examples in which the commission has prohibited certain advertising or ordered that future advertising disclose critical information.

Obvious instances are those in which the public health or safety might be endangered through continued nondisclosure of facts. To illustrate, in several cases the commission has ordered manufacturers and distributors of certain electrical products to cease advertising without a warning against possible electric shock or instructions for proper use. It has often been required that such information actually be affixed to the item. Disclosure has been compelled of the flammable tendencies of certain dresses, hats, sweaters, furniture polish, automobile polish, and household detergents. Possible dangers from radioactivity caused the commission to order disclosure, warning, and advice with reference to a product designed to eliminate static electricity from phonograph records.

Another familiar type of deceptive nondisclosure is that relating to the foreign origin of a product. The commission has recognized that many American consumers prefer products of American origin and manufacture rather than products of foreign origin. For example, the commission has required disclosure of foreign origin in cases involving imitation pearls, smoking supplies, tops, watchbands, binoculars, various pens and pencils, hats, and tools. A company is not within the law when its markings of foreign origin are virtually illegible or when it obliterates or conceals markings already placed upon the merchandise. Similarly, the commission has not hesitated to require disclosure of the fact that certain parts of foreign origin have been incorporated into an article.

The publishing of "abridged" or "condensed" books has also received federal attention. The commission has always taken the position that when books are in fact abridged or condensed from other works, such information must be disclosed. The disclosure must be prominent; it cannot be "buried" in small type, or at an inconspicuous point, or in a noncontrasting color. Closely related to this problem is the case of the publisher who substitutes titles and issues what appears to be a new book. This conduct is prohibited by the commission unless the facts of the substitution are set forth clearly and conspicuously, generally on the cover and the title page. The same rule applies to the manufacture and distribution of goods which are "rebuilt," "reconditioned," "used," "second-hand," and so forth. In other words, whenever the merchandise is not new—as the consumer would ordinarily expect it to be—then the businessman should say so, and say so plainly and clearly enough for all to see.

A further category of illegal nondisclosure concerns simulated materials; that is, goods which appear to be made of a certain substance but in fact are not. For example, there have been several cases involving watch manufacturers who had treated a base metal used in watch bezels so that it looked like a precious metal, generally gold. In these cases the commission has ordered the manufacturer to disclose the fact of simulation and thereby prevent deception of the consumer.

Finally, the commission, in its *Geritol* opinion, held that affirmative disclosure may be required if the impression given by an advertisement was that the effects of the product were greater than was actually the case. The commercial in question depicted the "transformation of a wan, lackadaisical housewife into a veritable tigress." This was held to be misleading because it gave the impression that "Geritol is a generally effective remedy for tiredness." Because the number of people experiencing tiredness symptoms as a result of deficiency in the ingredients of Geritol was "infinitesimally small," the suggestion in the commercial that tiredness is equatable with iron deficiency anemia and, therefore, curable by

Geritol was false and misleading. Such advertisements, to be legal, would have to disclose affirmatively that Geritol would relieve the symptoms for only a very small portion of those people suffering from tiredness.

Product or Name Simulation

If imitation is the sincerest form of flattery, then, according to the commission's case record, a great number of American firms can feel deeply flattered. Imitation or simulation may be illegal. Certain specific practices are directly prohibited through the law of patents, trademarks, and copyrights. There are a great number of cases which do not fit neatly into any of these areas but which nonetheless involve highly unfair and deceptive practices within the scope of the Federal Trade Commission.

Direct name simulation for an identical product is, one hopes, a thing of the past. Perhaps the very brazen nature of such a scheme is self-defeating in light of the growing sophistication of the American public. However, names are still taken and abused in a variety of deceptive ways. For example, there is the technique of openly adopting the name of a kindred or related product. One corporation manufactured automotive metal specialties, including spark plug cable sets. On the sets, as well as on price lists, cartons, and various advertising matter, appeared the name *Champion.* The company in question, of course, had nothing to do with the Champion Spark Plug Company and had no right to mislead the consumer by creating the impression that its goods were made by Champion. The fact that Champion made spark plugs, whereas the corporation involved made only spark plug cable sets, was immaterial. The tendency to deceive was just as great, and the company was ordered to cease and desist from utilizing the name *Champion.* Another instance of such simulation occurred in the case of a commercial portrait photographer whose salesmen solicited on a door-to-door basis for customers. The salesmen distributed certificates and coupons. The photographer called himself Warner Studios, and his literature, in addition to carrying this name, also proclaimed: "Operating Exclusively with Movie Lighting Equipment" and "New Motion Picture Film Used." The net effect of all this, said the commission, was to cause many purchasers to believe that the photographer was in some way connected with the Warner Brothers motion picture studio in Hollywood.

Indeed, illegal name simulation may occur even when the imitator engages in a wholly different business. An illustration is the case of the manufacturer of pen points who placed the name Waltham on certain of his products. He did this, incidentally, at the request of one particular customer who was marketing pens under that name. This practice was prohibited by the commission on the theory that the public was thereby deceived into believing that the pen points were manufactured by the Waltham Watch Manufacturing Company, a concern which has an excellent reputation for craftsmanship. The manufacturer sought to defend on the ground that he had only followed the instructions of his customer in marking the points "Waltham," but this defense was quickly overruled by a federal court of appeals as "patently without merit." The manufacturer was another victim of the doctrine that he who initiates the process of deception may be held liable.

Illegality does not necessarily depend upon a precise, literal copying of a name. This point has already been illustrated in the case of Warner Studios vis-à-vis Warner Brothers motion picture studios. Another instance involved a manufacturer of fountain pens who placed the inscription *Waterson* on his fountain pen levers, clips, and points. For good measure he also designated certain of the parts as "14 K Waterson." This scheme was a shabby attempt to capitalize on the name built by the L. E. Waterman Company, and so it was determined by the commission, which prohibited this deception. Just for the record, we should also note that the "14K" mountings were actually made of "brass thinly gold plated or coated with gold wash." Attempts to skirt the law of illegal name simulation have even extended to the use of meaningful initials. Certain motion picture cameras were manufactured in Japan, and a representation was made to the effect that the lens had been produced by "C. Z., Jena." This scheme sought to identify the lens as a product of Carl Zeiss of Jena, Germany, a firm of high reputation. The commission issued a cease and desist order against this form of name simulation.

Another tactic is that of broadly and improperly expanding the otherwise legitimate use of a certain name. For example, one corporation was engaged in the mail-order selling and distribution of kitchenware. In particular, it sold a certain cooker-fryer which it purchased from the manufacturer. This cooker-fryer did in fact include within it a certain heat control unit built by the Westinghouse Corporation. But in its initial advertising the firm presented the article in a way that led the public to believe that Westinghouse actually produced the entire unit. Westinghouse brought suit, and a settlement was reached with court approval. Notwithstanding the lawsuit, this company modified its advertising slightly and went right on emphasizing the name *Westinghouse.* Its advertising now carried prominent statements such as, "Equipped with Nationally Famous WESTINGHOUSE Thermostat." At this point the commission entered the picture and, after a hearing, concluded that the firm's advertising had been and still was deceptive, in that prospective purchasers were led to believe that the entire cooker-fryer had been manufactured by Westinghouse. This same scheme was tried by another company, which dealt in cooker-fryers, electric irons, and skillet casseroles.

This time the name improperly emphasized was *General Electric*. Again, the commission halted the advertising. The commission orders in these cases certainly do not prohibit the firm from telling the truth; that is, from advertising that certain named parts are indeed made by Westinghouse or General Electric, as the case may be. What the commission does attempt to eliminate is the kind of advertising which conveys to the public the impression that the entire article is produced by some well-known concern.

There are even some cases in which companies have sought to simulate the actual product of a larger and better-known producer, sometimes with a similar name and sometimes with a different name. For instance, the man who made the Waterson pens also carefully simulated the barrel levers, pocket clips, and points on his pens to make them look very much like Waterman pens. One corporation simulated the general style, title, and appearance of the familiar *Who's Who* biographical publication. This fraud produced over $25,000 from individuals whose biographies had been solicited for the bogus volume and who had willingly ordered copies. Another illustration of actual product simulation is that of a small corporation and certain individuals who dealt in perfume. They went so far as to copy the script, wrapping, packaging, bottle shape, and trade name of a nationally known perfume. Naturally, this grossly unfair and deceptive practice was terminated by the commission.

In 1964 the Supreme Court did an about-face on the question of the legality of product simulation in its *Sears* and *Compco* decisions. In *Sears, Roebuck & Company* v. *Stiffel Company*, the plaintiff in the lower court, Stiffel Company, had secured federal design and mechanical patents on a pole lamp, a device consisting of a vertical tube running from ceiling to floor with lamps affixed. Sears produced a similar pole lamp which the lower court described as a "substantially exact copy" of Stiffel's product. Stiffel brought suit alleging federal patent infringement and also a violation of the Illinois unfair competition law. At trial, the federal patents were invalidated on the ground that they lacked the necessary invention, but plaintiff nonetheless prevailed with the unfair competition claim under state law. The appellate court affirmed, observing that the critical issue was the likelihood of customer confusion as to the source of the products rather than the need to show any palming off of the goods. Noting the near identity of the two products, the court concluded such confusion was inevitable.

The Supreme Court, through Justice Black, reversed the decision with respect to the applicability of the state unfair competition law. Justice Black grounded his decision on the exclusivity of the constitutional authorization allowing Congress to grant exclusive patent rights. The primary purpose of this constitutional directive was the encouragement of invention through the reward of an exclusive monopoly. Because the source of authority for the patent laws is constitutional, as enacted they are the supreme law of the land and pre-empt any state law "that clashes with the objective of the federal patent laws."

On the same day, the Supreme Court handed down the companion decision in *Compco Corp.* v. *Day-Brite Lighting, Inc.* The product feature in that case was a reflector ribbing for fluorescent lighting fixtures commonly used in commercial establishments. Again a design patent had been obtained on the product feature. Compco employed a similar cross-ribbing in its fixtures, and Day-Brite brought a federal infringement suit as well as an unfair competition suit under the Illinois statute. At trial, the design patent was invalidated and relief was granted solely on the basis of unfair competition. Relying on *Sears,* the Supreme Court reversed the determination and further observed:

> A State of course has power to impose liability upon those who, knowing that the public is relying upon an original manufacturer's reputation for quality and integrity, deceive the public by palming off their copies as the original. That an article copied from an unpatented article could be made in some other way, that the design is "non-functional" and not essential to the use of either article, that the configuration of the article copied may have a "secondary meaning" which identifies the maker to the trade, or that there may be "confusion" among purchasers as to which article is which, or as to who is the maker may be relevant evidence in applying a State's law requiring such precautions as labeling; however, neither these facts nor any other can furnish a basis for imposing liability for or prohibiting the actual acts of copying and selling, regardless of the copier's motives.

The full range of these two far-reaching decisions has not yet been accurately measured. Some commentators have speculated that the decisions virtually eliminate common law unfair competition, and others will concur that at least state remedies for product simulation are no longer viable. What is certain about the decisions is that they will dominate all future considerations of nonfederal remedies for unfair competition.

Any discussion of *Sears* and *Compco* would not be complete without an examination of the dual causes of action brought in each case. In both instances, a federal cause of action for patent infringement was coupled with a state cause of action for unfair competition by product simulation. Both plaintiffs alleged that the same facts which would support a cause of action for patent infringement would also support one for product simulation, and neither plaintiff attempted to show any fraudulent activity on the part of the defendant beyond the mere fact of copying. Both of the products involved relied for their popularity on the appealing nature of their design rather than on any trade-mark or trade name association. Thus, in the narrowest reading of these decisions, the Supreme Court was called upon to decide whether a state could afford protection for a product shape that the federal patent laws had thrust into the public domain.

The Court's negative response to this question was grounded solely on the theory of federal pre-emption. Article I, Section 8, clause 8 of the Constitution, which authorizes federal legislation covering patents, is a comprehensive grant of power intended to reach all potential areas of patentable products without respect to state borders or interstate commerce. Because of this sweeping grant of authority, the pre-emption which accompanies the patent and copyright laws must be distinguished from the more typical federal pre-emption which occurs when a statute is enacted pursuant to the commerce or taxing powers of Congress. Under the commerce clause, a specific basis in interstate commerce must first be established before the federal law becomes applicable to a particular transaction. Thus, the federal statute will only pre-empt *conflicting* state enactments, that is, those which have an influence or an effect upon the interstate characteristics of the subject matter. In sharp contrast, the constitutional patent and copyright authority recognizes no state exceptions which would permit local regulation of parents or copyrights. This total exclusivity or complete "occupation" of the field would invalidate not only state laws which limit rights granted under federal statutes, but also state laws which extend rights to the subject matter beyond that offered by the federal statute.

Returning to the specific facts of *Sears* and *Compco*, the subject matter under both the federal and state laws in question was clearly the configuration of the goods, the actual substance of the product itself. In such circumstances, the only state law which would not conflict with the federal enactment would be one which neither expands nor contracts the rights available under the patent laws. Because this would be a type of legislative redundance equally prohibited by federal pre-emption, it would be effectively impossible for a state to pass any law addressed to an area where the federal grant of authority is constitutional in origin and comprehensive in scope. This was the literal holding of *Sears* and *Compco*.

False Disparagement of Competing Products

Representations which falsely disparage competing products are unfair and deceptive and thus can often result in commission cease and desist orders. There should be no difficulty in isolating such illegal advertising; one or two examples will illustrate the point.

A large corporation was engaged in the sale and distribution of stainless steel cookware, a product which is sold in vigorous competition with aluminum cooking utensils. Included in its advertising material and in the sales "pitch" for its salesmen were the following representations about the competing aluminum:

> Governmental reports of the deleterious effects of this material. . . .
> The metal is soft and forms various poisons with the food with which it is in contact.
> There is no objection to the use of this metal for casket purposes or as a mordant in the dye which is used to color the clothing which covers a corpse.
> [Aluminum] . . . is used for tanning hides, wall paper sizing . . . making bricks, sewer pipe, and road building materials.
> Did you ever find maggots in your aluminum pans? Do you know that such pans may be full of the most deadly bacteria known to science?
> Almost daily you read in the press of hundreds being poisoned by eating food cooked in aluminum.

Of course, as the commission determined, there was absolutely no scientific or medical basis for any of these disparaging claims. A cease and desist order was issued, and this was subsequently affirmed by a federal court to which the company appealed.

A familiar technique in disparagement is utilized by the door-to-door salesman who enters the home of a prospective purchaser and proceeds to criticize a competitor's product which he sees in that home. On occasion, the salesman compounds this scheme by representing himself as some sort of independent "expert," "safety man," "inspector," or even an official of some local or federal governmental agency. These tactics are not practiced only by "shoestring" operators who come and go. For example, one large and well-known manufacturer of furnaces found itself in serious difficulty with the commission on this score. Salesmen for this corporation gained entry to the homes of prospects—often upon false representations of identity—and, once in, began the process of disparagement. Persons were told that their furnaces were "no good," that they were not repairable, and that they were dangerous. The salesman employed scare tactics by warning the prospect that continued use of his present furnace would result in "asphyxiation, carbon monoxide poisoning, explosions, fires, or other damage." Through such devices many persons were deceived and misled and thus drawn into the purchase of new furnaces. This company also strongly contested the commission proceeding and carried its case on to a federal court of appeals, which affirmed the opinion of the commission. A state court, in a proceeding involving a similar company and its practices, disenfranchised the company—in effect, a corporate death sentence upon petition of the state attorney general.

There are other varieties of disparagement, all just as illegal. A firm may not falsely represent that a competitor is now out of business. A competitor may not be falsely disparaged by credit slurs or remarks pertaining to its financial condition. A raft of cases lay down the rule that a businessman may not falsely state that a competitor has infringed upon his patent, copyright, or trademark, nor that a competitor is in legal difficulty with the antitrust or trade regulation authorities.

False Representations of Approval

Claims of approval are governed by the same standards of truth that govern any other form of potentially deceptive advertising. Obviously, an advertiser cannot lawfully state that a certain testimonial or endorsement has been given when such is not the case. Similarly, when such a statement of approval has in fact been made, the advertiser is certainly not free to manipulate it as he pleases. He cannot distort the original meaning or garble the endorsement. And, of course, he clearly cannot expand its scope to new areas not covered by the original terms.

Some of these devices are illustrated by a commission case which was ultimately affirmed by the Supreme Court. In this case a publisher of a certain encyclopedia engaged in many deceptive practices, one of which was the improper use of testimonials. According to the producer of the encyclopedia, the work had been approved by certain named individuals: the reference librarian of the University of Notre Dame, a college professor of physiology, a newspaper editor, two prominent physicians, and a leading clubwoman. The truth of the matter was that some of these testimonials had been made for an older encyclopedia, published years earlier than the book in question. This older work was described by the commission as "quite different in form, in material and in purpose" from the encyclopedia purportedly endorsed. The other testimonials were wholly fictitious. The corporation went on using all of these testimonials —the old and the fictitious—for a period in excess of fifteen years. Indeed, the firm used them to endorse two different editions of its books. The testimonial was always precisely the same; only the name of the encyclopedia was changed. This tactic was continued even in the face of stern protests from the individuals who had purportedly given the testimonials. Ultimately, the commission entered an order prohibiting these practices and, as we have observed, the corporation lost its battle and its testimonials in the Supreme Court.

The scheme of expanding an otherwise legitimate endorsement is closely related to the practice of name simulation by improperly broadening the otherwise truthful use of a well-known firm name. Not surprisingly, the same corporation which tried to convey the impression that Westinghouse had produced its cooker-fryer and not just a thermostat also tried to convey the impression that *Good Housekeeping* magazine had endorsed the entire unit and not just a part. This was done by representations such as, "With Famous Fire King Glass Cover as Guaranteed by Good Housekeeping." The commission halted this advertising, along with the Westinghouse gambit.

When a problem of illegal endorsement appears, a company may be liable for the statements of its salesmen even though it has taken pains to avoid any falsity. For example, a certain publisher had a contractual agreement with the Smithsonian Institution of Washington, D.C. Under the terms of the arrangement material would be written by Smithsonian men, and the name *Smithsonian* could be used in a certain limited way. Beyond this, Smithsonian had nothing to do with the commercial aspects of the campaign. Yet several salesmen led the public to believe that the books in question were actually published and sold by Smithsonian, that they themselves (the salesmen) were Smithsonian personnel, and that sales proceeds would go to the Institution. The commission instituted proceedings to eliminate this deception. At the hearing the publisher introduced evidence to show that it had made a bona fide effort to insure that its salesmen would not present a misleading picture. The company argued that it had prepared sales materials, carefully checked sales talks, and promptly discharged violating salesmen. Nevertheless, this defense was overruled by the commission, and the case was affirmed by a federal appellate court. The actions of the salesmen had subjected the employer corporation to the pains and penalties of commission action.

In this connection it should be observed that on scores of occasions the commission has seen fit to institute proceedings against firms which misrepresented some form of United States government approval. The advertiser is warned to exercise extreme caution in this area. Fictitious government endorsement is a serious matter. Just as serious is the practice of expanding or distorting some form of actual government approval. When a firm desires to utilize some form of government endorsement, including that of state and local units, its advertisements had better set forth all the relevant information in an entirely truthful manner. Nothing less is tolerated.

Another troublesome area for many advertisers lies in sweeping claims of approval from "doctors," "medical experts," "scientific experts," and so forth. Let us look at the case of a nationally known toothpaste firm whose advertising campaign was halted by the commission and the courts. The firm made such representations as these:

> Do you know that . . . twice as many dentists personally use __________ Tooth Paste as any other dentifrice preparation.
> Dentists choose __________ for Personal use 2 to 1 over any other dentifrice.
> In a recent nationwide survey, more dentists said they recommended __________ for their patients' daily use than the next two dentifrices combined. . . .
> That is why so many dentists recommend massage with __________.
> So many dentists suggest the helpful stimulation of __________ and massage.

The facts were that out of some 66,000 dentists practicing in the United States at the time, the firm had selected some 10,000 at random and sent them a questionnaire. Only 1,983 were returned. Six hundred and twenty-one dentists did say that they used the product personally. Four leading competitive products were used by 258, 189, 144, and 128 dentists, respectively. As for the dentists' recommendations to patients, 461 of those replying said that they did recommend the advertiser's product. Recommendations of leading competitive products ran 195, 125, 106, and 94, respectively. The commission and the court felt that in light of the whole truth, the advertising was deceptive and misleading. In upholding the commission order, the court said: "We are of the opinion that these sweeping statements were not justified by the answers. . . ."

The facts and result of this case call for a few words on the proper use of scientific tests and surveys. We are, after all, a nation of science worshippers. The visual demonstration of a scientific "fact" in a laboratory setting and the straightforward claim that "independent tests prove" can produce results at the sales counter. The advertiser, the scientists, and the commission all have important responsibilities in insuring that the demonstrations actually demonstrate and that the tests actually prove. The commission has uncovered numerous instances of trickery in testing, but it certainly does not condemn all testing conducted for advertising purposes. In analyzing cases, the commission gives no special weight to the fact that a given test may have been conducted by an "independent" concern; all scientific claims are treated alike, regardless of their source. In examining these cases, the commission asks these questions: Has the experiment been properly designed? Has it been performed correctly? Have a significant number of tests been conducted? Have the test results been recorded accurately? Are the results internally consistent and coherent? Do the test results actually warrant the conclusions drawn? Can the conclusion be expressed in a meaningful, accurate way to consumers who lack scientific training?

If an advertisement based upon test results is challenged by the commission, the professional reputations of all involved will suffer. This will be even true if the concern is not subjected to the restrictions of a cease and desist order. It is both in the public interest and in self-interest for all parties to discharge professional responsibility in this area of "scientific" advertising.

Finally, the intelligent businessman must be wary of the use of misleading advertisements involving "awards" and the like. There are many cases involving commission action against fictitious awards; that is, awards which never existed or were never made. In another type of case the commission has stepped in to halt the advertising of awards which were not presented in good faith. When advertising has implied the existence of awards based on objective competition and such did not really exist, the advertising has been barred. In several cases the commission has endeavored to insure that future advertising of awards be conducted on a thoroughly truthful basis. This is not to suggest that all advertising of awards is deceptive. Quite to the contrary, in the majority of instances the advertiser has received a bona fide award of which he is legitimately proud. In such circumstances, of course, the advertiser may make full representation of his accomplishments.

Guarantees

One of the true sore spots in all of advertising is the deceptive use of guarantees. In 1960 the Federal Trade Commission issued its *Guides Against Deceptive Advertising of Guarantees,* elucidating in plain language the major principles applicable in this area. For any problem of guarantee advertising, the reader or his counsel are encouraged to refer to the Guides. By *guarantee,* incidentally, the commission means not only what is called a guarantee as such, but also warranties or any promise or representation of that nature.

The principal fault in advertising guarantees is the failure to state what the guarantee is. Concerning this an appellate court stated: "Ordinarily the word, guarantee, or warranty, is incomplete unless it is used in connection with other explanatory words. To say a [product] or other subject is guaranteed is meaningless. What is the guarantee? The answer to this question gives meaning to the word, 'guaranteed.'"

The general principle applicable to all advertising of guarantees, as stated in Guide I, is:

> In general, any guarantee in advertising shall *clearly* and *conspicuously* disclose
> (a) *The nature and extent of the guarantee,* and
> (b) *The manner in which the guarantor will perform,* and
> (c) *The identity of the guarantor.*

Although the guides do not define *clearly and conspicuously,* it is certainly doubtful that small print in the left lower corner of the page would suffice.

Guide I requires simply that the advertiser tell the public what the guarantee is. The advertising should answer questions such as: What product or part of a product is being guaranteed? For how long a time? Will the guarantor repair the product, replace part of it, and charge the owner for labor? Will he give him a new product? Who is guaranteeing the product, the manufacturer or the dealer?

Guide II deals with pro rata adjustments of guarantees, the problem which the commission encounters most frequently. For example, many complaints were received pertaining to advertisements of automobile battery guarantees. The complainants alleged that they had been led to believe that a battery was unconditionally guaranteed, but that they had found later that there were hidden conditions not revealed in the advertising. Investigation confirmed the charges. Thus, it was found that when a battery which was guaranteed for three years gave out at the end of the first year, the purchaser was not entitled to a new battery, as he had been led to believe, but merely to a credit on a new battery. Moreover, hidden conditions in the manner of applying the credit sometimes resulted in little or no saving to the consumer in his purchase of a new battery.

Realizing that the use of guarantees was a method of competition among merchandisers of batteries, the commission, to prevent competitive inequities, gave each of the companies making such guarantee claims an opportunity to enter into a stipulation. All but one of the thirty-one companies involved signed stipulations, agreeing to make a clear disclosure of any conditions contained in their guarantees. Formal proceedings were promptly brought against the one holdout company. By these actions a practice which had plagued the industry and the public was quickly corrected with a minimum of expense and without placing any member of the industry at a competitive disadvantage.

Information also was received that similar practices were prevalent in the merchandising of tires. For example, Harry bought a new tire "listed" at $42 for the "special" price of $16.95. He had been attracted to this brand not only because of the special price but also because of the "lifetime" guarantee. Twelve months later Harry had a blowout and returned to the dealer, expecting to get a new tire free. Harry was then informed that *lifetime* did not apply to his life, nor to his car's life, nor even to the life of the tire. It applied to the life of the tread. The dealer's treadometer indicated that 50 per cent of the treadlife had been used, so he "gave" Harry a new tire for $21. Harry paid the $21 without checking the price of tires without a guarantee. If he had, he would have paid $16.95 for the tire which was still on "special." When Harry read his newspaper that night, he saw the "special" price and realized he had been duped. He had really been duped in three ways. The meaning of *lifetime,* the fact that the guarantee was prorated, and, most important of all, the fact that the prorating was based upon a fictitious list price (also an illegal practice) were not revealed.

Other common forms of advertising also run afoul of rules relating to "guarantee" claims. The words *satisfaction or your money back* mean just that, and any advertiser who does not plan to refund the purchaser's money on demand should avoid the use of the phrase. Advertisers have apparently found that *guaranteed for life* is a valuable claim in selling. It has turned out that the "life" referred to is, variously, the life of the purchaser, the life of an automobile, or the life of the tread on a tire. The advertiser should make it plain just whose life he has in mind—the purchaser's, the manufacturer's, the retailer's, or the Federal Trade Commission's. In one case a vendor of sewing machines advertised "a full 10-year guarantee on parts." Actually, replacement parts for the machine were unobtainable. A cease and desist order was entered against the seller.

The commission has recognized that in advertising a guarantee the advertiser may at the same time make statements about the qualities of the product. Thus, it may well be that when a battery is guaranteed for thirty-six months, it is thereby claimed that the battery would normally last for thirty-six months. Likewise, *guaranteed to grow hair or money back* is an out-and-out claim for the product's hair-growing properties; *guaranteed lowest prices in town* is a claim for prices; and *We guarantee you will earn $500 a month* is a statement that employees will earn $500 each month. In all of these cases the advertiser should abide by the rule of truth and be prepared to live up to his guarantee. If he is not so prepared, he should desist from such representations.

Deceptive Television Advertising

The area of television advertising has been an active one for the commission in recent years. Most of the problems have revolved around the standards governing television demonstrations. Television demonstrations frequently use what are termed mock-ups. A mock-up is a visual representation of the product or some other object which is not the product or object itself. Mock-ups are necessary because of the technical requirements of the medium. If real ice cream is used in an advertisement, it will melt under the hot television lights and present to the public a particularly unappetizing spectacle. To avoid this, advertisers use a mock-up that looks like ice cream but which does not melt during the commercial.

Prior to the change of administrations in March of 1961, the Federal Trade Commission took the position that mock-ups were not illegal as such. Illegality only attached if the mock-up materially misrepresented the nature of the advertised product or some competitor's product. Subsequent to 1961 many observers felt that the commission believed that mock-ups were *per se* illegal, and that every visual presentation had to be an absolutely truthful representation.

As an illustration of what appeared to be this later commission view, let us examine the well-publicized case of the "sandpaper" shaving demonstration. The facts are simple and largely undisputed. The advertiser claimed that its shaving cream possessed a "supermoisturizing" power so great that it could be used to shave sandpaper. The difficulty was—as the advertiser and the advertising agency admitted—that the "sandpaper" shown on television was not really sandpaper at all. Instead, it was a "mock-up of loose sand spread on Plexiglass." Further, ordinary sandpaper had to soak for an hour before it could be shaved, whereas the mock-up was shaved immediately. Thus, in fact, the shaving cream did not have the properties which the demonstration indicated it possessed. The commission brought proceedings against both the advertiser and the agency involved, alleging an unfair and deceptive advertisement. Ultimately, a cease and desist order was issued.

On appeal of the case to First Circuit Court of Appeals, the court first noted that the advertisement was in fact false. The product in question was not suitable for shaving sandpaper in the manner advertised. The manufacturer contended that even if the advertisement was untrue, that fact was not material because no one purchased the product to shave sandpaper. The court's retort to this contention is the heart of its decision: "If a misrepresentation is calculated to affect a buyer's judgment it does not make it a fair business practice to say the judgment was capricious." The court then held that the commission had properly ordered the advertiser and its agency to cease and desist from publishing this particular advertisement or any other deceptive advertisement.

The court next considered the scope of the commission's order to cease and desist. That order, in the court's view, went beyond forbidding "demonstrations which represented a product as doing something it could not do, or as appearing to have qualities which it did not possess." The order forbade any demonstration in which the actual substance used in the television studio was not the exact substance it was represented to be. The court rejected this order and held that as long as the visual presentation looked like or correctly depicted the nature of the product advertised, it mattered not that other substances were used to make this accurate visual presentation.

In 1965 the Supreme Court reversed the First Circuit. The question the Supreme Court asked was, "Is it a deceptive practice within Section 5 of the Federal Trade Commission Act to represent falsely that a televised test, experiment, or demonstration provides a viewer with visual proof of a product claim, regardless of whether the product claim is itself true?" The answer was yes. The Court did not deal directly with the problem of dishonest representations (for example, a demonstration which "proves" a nonexistent fact), for all through the long appellate procedure this was conceded to be a Section 5 violation.

The Court quoted with approval from its prior decision in the *Algoma Lumber Co.* case: "The public is entitled to get what it chooses, though the choice be dictated by caprice or by fashion or perhaps by ignorance." According to the Court there is little difference between the use of false testimonials and invented testing agency certificates and the use of a mock-up in a demonstration to show even a true representation.

> In each case the seller has used misrepresentations to break down what he regards to be an annoying or irrational habit of the buying public. . . . In each case the seller reasons that when the habit is broken the buyer will be satisfied with the performance of the product he receives. Yet, a

misrepresentation has been used to break the habit and . . . a misrepresentation for such an end is not permitted.

In answering the advertising industry's dismayed cry that the standards would be too tough to follow, the Court said,

> If, however, it becomes impossible or impractical to show simulated demonstrations on television in a truthful manner, this indicates that television is not a medium that lends itself to this type of commercial, not that the commercial must survive at all costs.

Since this definitive pronouncement on the use of undisclosed mock-ups, the commission and a federal court of appeals have had another chance to review the decision, and have affirmed it, the court saying "that the undisclosed use of mock-ups [is] a deceptive practice even though the test, experiment or demonstration actually prove[s] the product claim." Thus, in *Libby-Owens-Ford Glass Co* v. *FTC*, an automobile glass company was accused of using undisclosed mock-ups unfairly to disparage competing products. By use of different camera angles, more oblique for the competitor's product, and Vaseline smeared on the competitor's glass, the advertiser "successfully" demonstrated the heightened distortion of all brand X glass. The commission, in a decision which was upheld by the United States Sixth Circuit Court of Appeals, concluded that even if by use of these "tricks" the result appeared as truthful, the practice was deceptive because of the undisclosed mock-ups. The result is that if an advertiser is going to ask the public to believe a claim and to test that belief by seeing, then he must be totally truthful and use only the genuine product.

The commission has, of course, acted upon many other deceptive television commercials. One illustrative case involved the familiar "white coat" theme, wherein a man in a white coat, called "Doctor," recommended a certain digestive aid. The "doctor" was, of course, not a physician at all. The order in that case required that the advertiser stop representing "by the use of a white coat or any other object, device or words indicative of the medical profession, that doctors or the medical profession recommend [the product], unless the representation is limited to numbers of doctors not greater than had been ascertained to be the fact." Although no determination was made of the merits of the product, the collateral visual suggestion that the product had been recommended by the medical profession was found to be misleading.

In another case the commission issued a complaint against a cigarette advertiser for a television commercial which represented that a filter demonstration, in which a liquid was poured into a tube containing the material of which the advertised cigarette's filter was made, and then into another tube containing the material of which another cigarette's filter was made, proved that the advertised cigarette's filter absorbed and retained more of the tars and nicotine in cigarette smoke than the filter of other cigarettes. The order of the commission prohibited the use of demonstrations purporting to prove claims which the demonstration does not prove.

The commission has challenged purported demonstrations of other types of products when such visual presentations were not in fact valid. These have included demonstrations of household aluminum foil, the capacity of one toothpaste to remove tobacco stains and of another to form a shield protecting against tooth decay, a demonstration of the danger in actual use of "round-head" razors, a depiction showing what was represented as a comparison between the "moist and creamy" qualities of competing shaving creams, and still another alleged to show the superiority of an aerosol shaving cream over competing brands.

It is hoped that these examples have at least served to alert the reader to the distinct possibility of litigation over deceptive television demonstrations. The moral of these cases is clear: if a demonstration is to be shown or an idea depicted, and such demonstration or idea is material to the sale of the product, then the visual presentation should be absolutely truthful.

Conclusion

We have now examined some, though certainly not all, of the prevalent deceptive advertising schemes. Practical limitations prevent extensive discussion of the problems involved in deceptive descriptions of the contents or elements of certain products. Interested readers should consult Kintner, *A Primer on the Law of Deceptive Practices.* A mass of commission cases have served to delineate the areas of truthful advertising of various specific substances. For example, a manufacturer of combs cannot represent his combs as "rubber" when they are in fact composed of 15 per cent unvulcanized synthetic rubber and 85 per cent plastic. Nor have we discussed the area of misrepresentation of special qualities or functions for a product. Another interesting field of which space precludes analysis is that of false claims of potential earnings in the advertising of certain employment opportunities. Many commission orders have been issued in this category of deceptive advertising. Whatever the subject may be, the best guide is always that of truth coupled with good taste.

Careful compliance with legal requirements need not be inconsistent with good programming or effective advertising. It would be a mistake to conclude from the Federal Trade Commission's vigorous enforcement of the laws against deceptive practices that the commission opposes all good showmanship. A good show is a wonderful thing. A show which cheats and deceives an audience is not. Making a product look good legitimately is a part of old-fashioned American salesmanship, but making trick comparisons or claiming for one's product virtues which it does not have is modern hucksterism, which America does not respect.

Honest advertising does not require that a cosmetic manufacturer use only homely women in its advertisements, nor that a tire manufacturer show its tires only on beat-up, prewar station wagons, but there is an important difference between legitimate dressing up of a product and deceptive painting up of a product. One reasonable test which anyone can use to decide whether his advertising is acceptable is the following: Would I have reason to complain if my competitor used this sort of advertising? If the advertising would falsely disparage your product or lie about the quality of your competitor's product, you do have a right to complain, and so does he, if you do it to him.

If a person is victimized himself or feels victimized by a competitor, what should he do? If the issue involves a product which is clearly sold on a national basis by national advertising, then the Federal Trade Commission is as close as the telephone. In addition to the Washington headquarters, the commission maintains branch offices in Atlanta, Boston, Chicago, Cleveland, Kansas City, Los Angeles, New Orleans, New York, San Francisco, and Seattle. Complaints and inquiries may also be made by mail, of course, and they should set forth full particulars and details about the advertising in question. Too often the commission receives only generalized denunciations of a firm's business methods. For example, one woman wrote to the commission and stated simply that "the store" in North Carolina where she had shopped had sold her a "lousy bargain," and would the commission "look into it." Obviously, this sort of complaint is woefully insufficient. When local matters are involved, the Better Business Bureaus and state authorities should be informed in full detail.

Legitimate complaints should be encouraged. In this way, the few shabby operators on the fringe can be eliminated; as the light of publicity is cast on them and their methods, so the impetus to ethical conduct is all the greater. In the next chapter we shall examine some of the efforts which have been made and which must continue and grow in strength in order to achieve the goal of ethical advertising.

CHAPTER 22

TOWARD ETHICAL ADVERTISING: A PLAN

THE fall of 1959 brought public confidence in advertising to a crisis. First came the astonishing revelations of the "rigged" television quiz shows. Then came the "payola" scandals. The public outcry was deafening, and cynicism was rampant. Such criticism had been heard before, albeit not to the same intense degree. In 1946 an ex-Madison Avenue copywriter named Frederic Wakeman published a novel about the advertising world and thereby touched off a full-blown literary trend. Few would accord the accolade of greatness to *The Hucksters,* but it has the distinction of being a prototype. Folk heroes live in a popular fiction, and as more and more former advertising men produce more and more novels, a new folk hero-rogue has entered the stream of national consciousness, supplanting the Mississippi River pilot, the Indian fighter, the foreign correspondent, and the young, blasé Wall Street bond salesman of the 1920's. The new hero is the bright and earnest young man-about-Madison Avenue, complete with gray flannel suit, attaché case, and the most sincere smile imaginable.

The stereotype plot goes something like this: An intelligent, earnest, idealistic, but naïve young man lands a job in a huge, glittering New York advertising agency. The young man's brilliance wins a few early successes; then his dreams are shattered by a sudden revelation of the harsh immorality of the world of Madison Avenue. The issue is presented: will our young hero, now stripped of his naïveté, pack up his untarnished ideals and go home, or will he surrender them and worship the goddess Success unashamedly? In most of the novels he chooses the latter course and then proceeds to drown himself in a sea of cynicism, alcohol, and sensuality. Our hero is not left to wallow in the Slough of Despond, however. At the final crisis the mask of cynicism is stripped from his eyes, usually with the help of a fatherly colleague or the love of a good woman. He then proceeds to deliver a ringing denunciation of Madison Avenue and all outlying advertising provinces, packs up his rejuvenated ideals and his girl, and flies away to buy a small-town newspaper or write The Great American Novel. Sometimes, if the author is unusually optimistic, the hero is allowed to remain in the world of advertising, achieving success and hanging on to his integrity at the same time.

As a result of all of this, not a few Americans have hastily concluded that advertising is wholly devoid of ethics. On the contrary, it is hereby submitted that advertising is as susceptible to principled performance as any other form of economic activity. Since the shocks of rigging and of payola, remarkable progress has been made in the provision of an ethical framework for advertising. But much yet remains to be done.

In an era when control over advertising is a serious issue, it is particularly necessary to analyze the nature and sources of the necessary controls and restraints. A society can benefit if harmful forms of activity are curbed by beneficent restraints. But a society can be mutilated if inept and unduly harsh restraints proscribe useful activity. At this point let us isolate the sources of restraint necessary to achieve the wholly realizable goal of ethical advertising:

Vigorous Federal Enforcement
Encouragement of Improved State and Local Enforcement
A Sense of Professionalism and Resulting Self-regulation
Media Cooperation
Consumer Education

Vigorous Federal Enforcement

The enactment of legal prohibitions has a practical effect far beyond the mere exposition of an institutionalized ethical standard. The presence of legal mandates and a vigorous and effective program for enforcing those mandates strengthens the hand of the advertiser who is genuinely concerned with adherence to a high moral standard. There cannot be a climate favorable to elimination of deception without the certainty that the irresponsible few will be deterred. One way in which to achieve widespread ethical conduct in the advertising world is to silence those who say, "We have to hit below the belt because everybody else does." If sanctions against that tiny minority that is willfully unscrupulous are swift and sure, then honest advertisers can look to their own efforts without fear of unfair competition.

For some years prior to the disclosures of rigging and payola, the Federal Trade Commission had instituted a policy of monitoring radio and television advertisements. When the crisis arose, swift and effective action was needed. Consequently, the commission's monitoring program was intensified, and the staff was doubled. Attorneys were transferred from other areas of the commission's work to monitoring and investigating radio and television advertising claims. Additional investigators were assigned to the New York City area for the sole purpose of handling cases selected for full investigation. Seven trial attorneys were assigned to assist in the investigation and preparation of these cases for trial. All commercial advertising on network stations was monitored throughout the broadcast day. In December of 1959 the monitoring unit referred 519 advertisements to various other bureaus and divisions within the commission. These offices had requested all advertising dealing with particular products or entire product lines. Examples of the latter included all advertising of cigarettes, reducing devices, cold remedies, furniture, and TV sets and tubes. During November and December of 1959 the monitoring unit examined nearly 41,000 commercials and screened out almost 2,800 television commercials to determine which would require full-scale investigation. As a result, several products were named in commission complaints which set forth allegations of camera trickery or the omission of important facts.

To take just one example, there was the case of the television commercial advertising a certain oleomargarine. In this commercial, drops of moisture were shown on the advertised oleo and on butter as well. A competitive oleo was shown without any such drops. The announcer claimed that the drops were indicative of the flavor and quality of the particular brand of oleo. The Federal Trade Commission disagreed. The commission found that the moisture drops had nothing at all to do with the product, but had actually been applied to the product just for purposes of the television demonstration. Furthermore, the drops were magnified. Finally, they did not determine the flavor and quality of the oleo. A cease and desist order was issued, and both the advertiser and the agency involved agreed to discontinue such deception.

The same vigorous action took place in cleaning up the disgraceful practice of payola. This practice involved a direct money payment from record manufacturers and distributors to disc jockeys and other broadcasting personnel for promoting certain records by playing them with particular frequency. Depending upon the broadcast appeal of a given disc jockey and the popularity of his show, the consideration ranged from sporadic payments of various amounts to weekly or monthly payments on a regular basis from several record manufacturers and distributors. In the Philadelphia, Boston, New York, Cleveland, and Chicago areas, investigation revealed that cash payments ran into thousands of dollars. Sometimes the inducement was other than cold cash. All sorts of arrangements were devised to secure increased program exposure of certain records.

Promptly upon obtaining the facts, the commission acted. Nearly 100 complaints were issued in the fiscal year of 1960. Fifty-seven respondents consented to the orders and agreed to terminate all forms of payola. Some of the consent orders involved large and well-known recording enterprises.

This is the sort of vigorous federal enforcement needed to clean up that minority which persists in deceptive advertising. Such enforcement supplies the answer to those who seek refuge in the justification that "everyone else is doing it." Such enforcement provides the necessary effective deterrent. Public interest demands swift elimination of any poison that creeps into the economic system. Public interest, as we have seen, created the commission, and that interest must be served by strong measures when necessary. In this way federal enforcement helps to clear the path for the great number of businessmen who believe in and practice ethical advertising.

Vigorous federal enforcement, of course, goes well beyond the area of formal complaints and orders. As we have seen in the chapter dealing with commission procedure, there are many techniques which are comparatively informal but which amount to enforcement nonetheless. The commission recognizes a duty to encourage those who would be honest as well as a duty to correct those who would be dishonest. For example, the holding of trade practice conferences and the ultimate adoption of trade practice rules contribute measurably to the goal of ethical advertising. Other conferences are held with a particular local industry, as in the case of the jewelry industry in New York City. During fiscal 1960, personnel of the commission met with over 100 representatives of the retail jewelry industry in New York City to discuss the advertising and sale of jewelry. The commission's guides program has many facets, one of which is to suggest the sanction of federal enforcement. The *Tire Advertising Guide* was issued during fiscal 1959; in its 1960 report the commission indicated that fifty assurances had been received from the tire industry to the effect that certain deceptive practices would terminate. The *Cigarette Advertising Guide* is another excellent example of vigorous federal enforcement short of the iron fist. During fiscal 1960 the administration of that guide resulted, according to the commission's annual report, in the elimination of sixty-two questionable claims involving thirty different brands. Most significantly, through the guides program seven major manufacturers agreed to remove from their advertising all tar and nicotine claims. Another instance of federal activity resulting in voluntary compliance is the case of refrigerator advertising. During fiscal 1961 the commission sent a letter to all members of the refrigerator industry calling attention to various misrepresentations of the storage capacity of particular units. The industry had represented capacity in gross terms, including space occupied by coils, panels, etc. As a result of the commission letter the responsible concerns promptly agreed to eliminate the deception and speak only in terms of net space.

These examples might be multiplied endlessly, but the lesson is always the same. Vigorous federal enforcement plays a vital role in helping to achieve a national standard of truth in advertising. But federal enforcement is just one part of the solution. If state and local authorities are not equally active, if the advertising industry itself does not develop the necessary professional responsibility, if self-regulatory measures do not appear from within, if media cooperation is not secured, and, finally, if consumers are not educated—then the goal of ethical advertising still remains distant.

Encouragement of Improved State and Local Enforcement

When it comes to achieving ethical advertising, there is a familiar tendency—as in all areas of the economy—to refer all problems to the federal government in Washington. The federal role is important, but we must not make the mistake of shifting the entire burden of responsibility. In this regard the development of widespread ethical standards in advertising is no different from any other American goal. State and local authorities have a vital responsibility, and their activity must constitute an integral part of any solution.

Not only is local participation essential to the maintenance of our system of free enterprise, but there are also compelling practical considerations which justify an active program on the part of state and local authorities. First of all, there is a great mass of advertising which is conducted on a purely local basis. As we have seen earlier, the power of the Federal Trade Commission is properly limited by the concept of interstate commerce. Malefactors in the area of purely local advertising may be wholly beyond the reach of federal authority. Yet the annual sales volume of local concerns will often run into many thousands and even millions of dollars. Many local concerns are also engaged in activities which have vital effects upon the welfare of the community. When vigorous enforcement is necessary to weed out a few shoddy practitioners whose scope is purely local, the responsibility rests upon state and local authorities. A second practical reason for encouraging a greater role in local enforcement lies in the concrete problem of a limited budget. There are many cases in which the commission could exercise jurisdiction but chooses not to expend its limited funds and personnel on matters which may more properly be handled by the states themselves.

An extensive catalogue of state laws regulating deceptive advertising is beyond the scope of this book. Let us simply examine some of the general areas of local statutory regulation and some of the problems encountered thereunder.

Beginning in 1911, the *Printer's Ink* model law was adopted in whole or with modifications in most states. Today all but four states (Arkansas, Delaware, Mississippi, and New Mexico) have on their books some form of this statute. The substance of the original model reads as follows:

> Any person, firm, corporation or association, who with intent to sell . . . anything . . . directly or indirectly, to the public . . . or with intent to increase the consumption thereof, or to induce the public . . . to enter into any obligation relating thereto . . . makes, publishes, disseminates, circulates or places before the public, or causes to be placed before the

> public . . . an advertisement of any sort . . . which advertisement contains any assertion, representation or statement of fact which is untrue, deceptive or misleading, shall be guilty of a misdemeanor.

The original statutes were directed primarily at printed advertising. Many states have by now expanded the coverage to include radio and television. Seventeen states have added to the model, by use of the word *knowingly*, a requirement of proof. In these states, in order to sustain conviction, the prosecution must prove that the seller had knowledge that the statement in question was false.

Obviously, there are serious problems under these laws. The difficulty of proof under the statutes requiring prior knowledge tends to thwart prosecutions. Indeed, *Printer's Ink* itself has taken the position that by adding the word *knowingly* many states have weakened the model statute. But proof is only part of the problem. After all, these are not civil but *criminal* laws, and, as such, they embody all the stigma of any criminal law. Local authorities are often wary of attempting to brand the deceptive advertiser as a criminal. In addition, a higher standard of proof, proof beyond a reasonable doubt, is imposed by criminal statutes. Then too, there are practical problems for the state enforcement authorities. In virtually all cases the enforcement of *Printer's Ink* statutes is the responsibility of the county and district attorneys or the state attorneys general. Clearly, these officials must devote substantial portions of their time to the regular course of prosecutions involving the usual felonies and misdemeanors. The amount of time, personnel, and money which they can devote to the elimination of deceptive advertising is severely limited.

Still, the statutes can be and have been used effectively. Two New York cases provide instructive examples of the sort of work which can be done at the local level. A seller of toys in the suburban New York City area advertised by means of signs in his store window. Several signs read, "Toy Discount Super Market, 20% to 40% Off." The practice of the dealer was to establish prices higher than those normally charged by his competitors and then to mark the prices down to a competitive level. Some of his prices, even after the "markdown," were still slightly above those of the normal market. This seller was convicted under the New York version of the *Printer's Ink* statute. The theory of the prosecution was simply that he had conveyed the impression through advertising that his prices were 20 per cent to 40 per cent less than those prevailing in the market, when in fact his prices were either at or above the market level. Another instance is that of the New York City jeweler who advertised in his store window, "1 Ct. Perfect Diamond. Platinum Setting $265." The state investigators determined that a ring so marked actually weighed only three quarters of a carat and had several imperfections. For this advertising the jeweler was convicted.

State efforts to eliminate deceptive advertising have not been limited to the *Printer's Ink* statutes. The states have moved to regulate in many specific areas of advertising—alcoholic beverages, food, drugs, cosmetics, lotteries, securities, flag advertising, outdoor advertising, political advertising, trading stamps and premiums, tax-absorption advertising, and the advertising of obscene matter. As one study observed, the state's hand is generally strongest in that area of the economy where it exercises a licensing power. This factor lies behind state efforts at control of the advertising of alcoholic beverages. Similarly, the licensing power acts as a firm control on the advertising of hairdressers, barbers, real estate dealers, and funeral directors. The same force is felt effectively in advertising by the legal, medical, and dental professions.

Some states have acted specifically to eliminate deceptive pricing in advertising. For example, Michigan, Minnesota, Oklahoma, and Tennessee have specific statutes prohibiting the use of words such as *wholesaler, manufacturer,* or similar designations unless the seller is actually engaged in the represented trade.

Nineteen states have enacted laws against bait-and-switch advertising. Some of the statutes even provide for the use of injunctions to eliminate the practice.

The examples and instances set forth here are only illustrative of the vast network of state legislation aimed at the elimination of misleading and deceptive advertising. For a more extensive listing the reader should refer to the sources listed in the bibliography to Kintner, *A Primer on the Law of Deceptive Practices.* One note of caution: the intelligent businessman faced with a potential legal advertising problem cannot afford to ignore the effect of state law and must consult his legal counsel in regard to possible local liability.

Whatever may be said for the difficulties involved in state and local enforcement, the need for such activity is undisputed. Perhaps we may soon see the advent of administrative agencies organized by the state and operated on a state level. A few states have already taken this step and have thus removed much of the burden from their regular law enforcement officials. As of this writing, eight states have enacted a model state statute directed against unfair methods of competition and false advertising. The significance of this statute is the provision for civil remedies for these practices, thus supplementing the criminal remedies provided in the *Printer's Ink* statutes.

We may see state legislatures and municipal bodies devoting greater attention to the problem of deceptive advertising. A body of civil law, as distinguished from strict criminal sanction, may be developed. It is to be hoped that a greater allocation of funds and personnel at the local level can be achieved.

Ultimately, great progress can be made through state and local enforcement toward reaching the goal of ethical advertising. Increasingly vigorous enforcement at this level will add meaningfully to the effort to eliminate the fringe of persistent and willfully dishonest advertisers. Clearly, there is a competitive inequity in requiring compliance with standards of honesty on the part of merchandisers of products sold in interstate commerce, while local merchants who sell only locally but compete for the same consumer's dollar may continue to use deceptive sales appeals. Vigorous and alert local enforcement can correct this inequity, and the recalcitrant minority can be silenced. Then the great number of honest advertisers will not succumb to the temptation to reply in kind. The resulting atmosphere will lend strength to all those who sincerely desire an effective ethical framework for advertising.

An examination of ethical goals for advertisers cannot end with law enforcement. For we must recognize that law does involve imposition as well as expression. If we are not to abandon the premise that ethical conduct is an individual responsibility, we must not place our sole reliance upon the law. By definition, in a free society responsibility must ultimately be assumed by individuals. Law cannot do much more than express standards and provide a favorable climate for the exercise of individual responsibility. We must turn, then, to the scope and nature of professionalism and self-regulation in the advertising industry.

A Sense of Professionalism and Resulting Self-regulation

At this moment millions of purchasers are making millions of buying decisions. It is fair to surmise that in the great bulk of these transactions the purchaser is buying a reputation. In some instances it will be the reputation of the manufacturer; in others, that of the retailer; in still others, that of an advertising media. But in each instance reputation is an important factor. Therefore, the preservation of a reputation for propriety and decency is a matter of intense self-interest. But such an effort must go even deeper; it should be and is a matter of self-respect. Temptations in the marketplace can be severe, but no businessman with a shred of dignity can for one moment imagine that any material gain is worth the destruction of his own pride, his own code of ethics, and his own sense of vocation. Thus, advertisers must insure that every message bearing their imprint is a truthful message. Every medium must insure that no false voices speak through it. And the creators of advertising must assume a special professional responsibility.

Professional responsibility extends far beyond the mere avoidance of legal penalties and observance of legal boundaries. Professionalism means a willingness to disagree respectfully with one's client; to tell one's client forthrightly that there are severe objections to a proposed course of action; to recommend an unobjectionable program; and, yes, to resign from the service of the client if he persists in violating the ethical precepts of his adviser. If advertising men and women develop this sense of professionalism, and if advertisers absorb the lesson that good will and public reputation slowly and painfully acquired can easily be dissipated by an ill-advised and offensive short-term campaign, public respect for advertising will be assured.

The acceptance of professional responsibility requires courage. It also requires a sense of one's own worth and dignity, and a sense of the importance of one's work. The man who works only for money can have no true dignity. The man who is prepared to sacrifice everything for financial gain can have no pride in his work. If advertising is to become something more than the rat race described in popular novels, then each individual in the industry must demonstrate that he can exercise professional responsibility.

During the years which have elapsed since the rigging and payola scandals and the resulting highwater mark in public cynicism, a host of advertising men and women have come to appreciate the necessity for individual responsibility. It is true that these individual efforts are difficult to measure. Self-imposed restraints by individuals are tested in the privacy of offices; responsible actions induced by these restraints receive no publicity. On the other hand, harmful actions by individuals who recognize no restraints inevitably command public attention. Nevertheless, careful and impartial observers of advertising can detect a perceptible increase in the ranks of those who stand for honest advertising.

The reinvigoration and extension of the self-policing efforts of voluntary groups are more easily measured. In the past few years all segments of the advertising industry have developed self-regulatory, self-policing programs which are the broadest in scope and effectiveness that business has ever known. Let us review some of these voluntary efforts in more detail.

The American Association of Advertising Agencies (A.A.A.A.) represents, as its name implies, the nation's advertising agencies. This organization has performed a key role in the industry's step-up of self-regulation. In April of 1962, A.A.A.A. published its new *Creative Code*, embodying standards of truthfulness and good taste which would govern the production of advertising. The guidelines are set forth in this language by the association:

> Therefore, we, the members of the American Association of Advertising Agencies, in addition to supporting and obeying the laws and legal regulations pertaining to advertising, undertake to extend and broaden the application of high ethical standards. Specifically we will not knowingly produce advertising which contains:
>
> a. False or misleading statements or exaggerations, visual or verbal.
> b. Testimonials which do not reflect the real choice of a competent witness.
> c. Price claims which are misleading.
> d. Comparisons which unfairly disparage a competitive product or service.

e. Claims insufficiently supported, or which distort the true meaning or practicable application of statements made by professional or scientific authority.
f. Statements, suggestions or pictures offensive to public decency.

The code goes on to provide for the expulsion of agencies for "clear and willful violations. . . ."

Further regulation is provided by the Committee for Improvement of Advertising Content, operated jointly by A.A.A.A. and the Association of National Advertisers, Inc. The latter organization (A.N.A.) has for many years maintained an over-all conscientious effort to supply leadership and direction to national advertisers in all their advertising activities. Under the procedure of the joint committee, as described in the January 15, 1963 issue of *Advertising Age*, any agency or advertiser may enter a criticism of a particular advertisement at any time. Indeed, persons in the advertising industry are asked to note objectionable advertising. The individual observing the item preserves a written advertisement or jots down the pertinent details of a radio or television advertisement. Such a report is then forwarded through a local A.A.A.A. or A.N.A. representative to the committee headquarters in New York. The identity of the person initiating the criticism is kept anonymous, and the objection is evaluated by a panel of twenty individuals—ten members from each organization. Each panel member examines the advertisement in question, and a vote is taken. If a majority determine that the advertisement is "seriously objectionable," a report is sent to the responsible advertiser and agency requesting corrective action. After thirty days, *Advertising Age* explains, both the advertiser and agency must come forward with a satisfactory answer. If there is no answer, or if the answer is unsatisfactory, the committee notifies the boards of directors of A.A.A.A. and A.N.A. for "appropriate action, which can mean expulsion from either association."

Of course, this program relies on voluntary self-regulation. But it has helped bring about a large number of improvements, many of them in advertisements which have wide exposure. What is particularly significant is that much of the committee's work involves the critical problem of bad taste. This is an area generally beyond the scope of federal enforcement and which the industry itself must eliminate on a voluntary basis.

In an effort to deal on the local level with complaints regarding truth and taste in advertising, the board of governors of the A.A.A.A. Cleveland Council devised "The Cleveland Plan for Maintaining Public Confidence in Advertising." With the cooperation of the Cleveland Advertising Club and the Cleveland Better Business Bureau, the plan was put into operation in early 1960. This plan is so significant in terms of local self-regulation that some details should be submitted for the record here.

The sponsors of the plan divided objectionable advertising into four categories and provided machinery for dealing with each. The categories are "Local, untruthful," "Local, bad taste," "National, untruthful," and "National, bad taste." The objective of the plan is stated this way: "to eliminate, insofar as possible, all four kinds of objectionable advertising in Cleveland—both metropolitan and suburban areas—newspapers, radio, television, outdoor and direct mail." Depending upon the category, complaints are handled by the local Better Business Bureau, the Cleveland Advertising Panel, the National Better Business Bureau, and the National A.A.A.A. Committee.

One particularly effective aspect of the plan was the way it was put before the public. Cleveland newspapers carried full-page advertisements which boldly asked the reader, "What do *you* think of advertising?" The public was asked to send in specific criticisms of specific advertisements, and form letters were even provided to facilitate the mailing of criticism. The forms called for some details of the offending advertisement, the medium carrying it, the date and time, and a statement of why the individual regarded the advertisement as objectionable.

This plan proved so successful that other A.A.A.A. Councils have used it as a model in organizing programs. Such plans are now in operation in Philadelphia, Pittsburgh, Dayton, Dallas, Denver, Phoenix, San Francisco, Oakland, and many other cities.

Returning now to the Association of National Advertisers: that organization has made a continuing effort to give individual advertisers a sense of their own responsibilities and to point up areas in which these responsibilities are not being met. The A.N.A. has widely disseminated the *Text of Purex Corporation's Advertising Policy* in print and from the speaker's platform. This text is one of the many good examples of the program of a national advertiser that has recognized its individual responsibilities and adopted a definite code of advertising practices. We have already noted the role of the A.N.A. on the Joint Committee for Improvement of Advertising Content. Then too, this association has widely distributed a most valuable booklet compiled by its General Counsel, Gilbert H. Weil, *Legal Rules of the Road to Honest Advertising*.

Credit must also be given to the Advertising Federation of America (A.F.A.). This is the organization which binds together the advertising clubs in nearly all major American cities. These advertising clubs, in most instances, were responsible for the local Better Business Bureau movements. The A.F.A. is thus a grass-roots organization in the fullest sense. Long before the television scandals, representatives of the A.F.A. came to officials of the Federal Trade Commission to offer cooperation in improving advertising and to urge that the government do more toward educating business in the requirements of law. These representatives requested numerous copies of the FTC advertising guides and placed the power and machinery of their organization behind wide distribution of the guides. Then, too, the A.F.A. published and distributed Morton Simon's effective work *The Advertising Truth Book*.

The Better Business Bureau movement from the beginning epitomized voluntary self-regulation and self-discipline at the grass roots. There are now over 120 local bureaus throughout the country, representing approximately 125,000 companies. The present National Better Business Bureau (N.B.B.B.) is the offspring of the former National Vigilance Committee, which was originally organized to police fraudulent advertisers. Today the N.B.B.B. operates in the sphere of national advertising, functioning, as we have seen in the example of the Cleveland Plan, as a sort of clearinghouse for objections to national advertising. The local bureaus, on the other hand, work to clean up deceptive advertising at the local and regional level.

The *New York Times* has described the principal work of the Better Business Bureaus as "quiet investigation and patient persuasion," and this is an accurate picture. The bureaus do a large share of the donkey work of business self-regulation; this quiet, difficult work must be accomplished at the local level. There is now a closer cooperation between the advertising industry and the Better Business Bureaus than ever before. Many advertisers and agencies now consult the bureaus prior to placing advertising. This practice is proceeding at an ever-increasing pace; the number of advertising agencies contacting the N.B.B.B. in New York, for example, has doubled since 1958.

Space precludes more than passing mention of many other effective efforts at industry self-regulation. There are, for example, programs of the Associated Business Publications, the Direct Mail Advertising Association, the National Association of Transportation Advertising, the National Editorial Association, National Business Publications, and the Outdoor Advertising Association of America. Laudable efforts have been made by groups in literally dozens of specific industries, such as automobile dealer groups, the Air Transport Association, the Electronics Industry Association, and so on, all of which have adopted advertising codes. One of the most intelligent and determined programs is that of the American Home Laundry Manufacturers Association. There have been a multitude of self-regulatory programs within individual businesses, including a large number of advertising agencies. Some, like McCann Erickson, have assigned a top executive to screen advertising for truth and taste. The Lennen & Newell agency has employed a scientist who is responsible for insuring that scientific claims and demonstrations developed by the agency are factual and fair.

Many excellent publications serving the advertising industry, such as *Advertising Age*, *Broadcasting*, *Sponsor*, and *Sales Management*, have strongly supported self-regulatory programs in the industry. This has been done both through education on the problems of advertising and encouragement of voluntary solutions by the industry. *Advertising Age*, for instance, carried a series entitled "Advertising We Can Do Without," which featured advertisements forwarded by readers which seemed to cross the lines of truth and good taste. In the series the magazine reproduced the actual ad, thus exposing the advertiser and his defects.

Of all the trade publications, however, one deserves special mention. *Printer's Ink,* founded in 1888, has traditionally played a leading role in the movement for truth in advertising. In its earlier days, as we have seen, this publication led the successful fight for the adoption of a model advertising statute by the states. *Printer's Ink* also strongly supported the development and growth of Better Business Bureaus. In recent years it has launched other programs for truth and taste in advertising. It published a candid series of articles designed to alert advertising to the scope of the problem, to spell out the dangers of laxity, to pinpoint responsibility for action, and to show what action could be taken. These articles prove that *Printer's Ink,* which may be thought of as the editorial conscience of the advertising industry, is very much alive to its self-appointed, historical role.

To conclude this section on self-regulation in advertising, the author must remark that the entire advertising industry is on trial. It has been on trial since late in 1959; it will continue to be on trial for a long time into the future. In large measure the outcome of this trial rests with the advertising industry. If it succumbs to ineffectual handwringing or cynicism or intransigence in the face of the public interest, a bitter outcome is certain. The only way to avert that outcome is to demonstrate responsibility. In whatever way we wish to define the function of the advertising industry, that function must include as an indispensable element the duty to tell the truth in a tasteful manner.

Advertising men and women must find within themselves a belief in their capacities to meet responsibilites and the will to discharge those responsibilites. It was John Stuart Mill who said that "one person with a belief is equal to a force of ninety-nine who have only interests." As we have seen, many in advertising have demonstrated that they have beliefs. But the work cannot stop. The demonstrations must continue and increase in scope and effectiveness. Only in this way can persons in advertising show—as they must—that they are determined to be responsible citizens in a free society.

Media Cooperation

The public and moral responsibility of advertisers and those who serve the industry must in turn be shared by the advertising media—newspapers, magazines, periodicals, radio, and television. The question of whether the Federal Trade Commission should hold media *legally* responsible for deceptive advertising has been a subject of much public comment. This possible extension of legal responsibility is a matter involving serious policy considerations. It is the firm hope of the author that the commission will never find it necessary to name an advertising medium as respondent in a deceptive advertising case. If federal and state authorities engage in the sort of vigorous enforcement which is necessary, and if the whole of the advertising industry, in cooperation with all advertising media, does the proper job of intensive self-regulation, it would seem that this serious legal step need not be taken.

The mere fact that the recent crisis in public confidence had its origin in television does not mean that other media can or should relax. First of all, practical considerations of self-interest dictate against such an answer. Visual deception in a television commercial may have an immediate impact upon public confidence in all television commercials, but the cynicism thus aroused may also result in a skeptical attitude toward printed assertions of advertisers. No medium can afford complacency toward problems of other media.

Nor can advertisers lightly dismiss a decline in public confidence engendered by a scandal in a particular medium. Today many advertisers conduct campaigns in many media simultaneously in order to achieve maximum effect for a promotion. If the product is deceptively described in one medium, then public confidence in the product as well as the medium is adversely affected. The task of maintaining public confidence by insisting upon truthful advertising cannot be shrugged off merely by finding an isolated whipping boy. Anyone concerned with advertising in any of its ramifications has a duty to insist upon truthfulness. Developing a sense of professionalism and a high degree of self-regulation is as much the responsibility of the media as it is of the advertising industry itself. This responsibility must be borne as a vital part of the quest for ethical advertising.

The acid test of media self-regulation probably comes in the actual acceptance or rejection of advertising. It is here that the newspaper industry provides an excellent example. The American Newspaper Publishers Association has encouraged each of its member newspapers to fix their own advertising acceptability standards. Assistance in this task is available to newspaper executives by use of the FTC guides relating to certain types of deceptive advertising. Further help may be had from the various codes and standards adopted by the advertising industry itself. In this regard, *Advertising Age* reports that "virtually every major U.S. daily newspaper" has a guide of some sort delineating acceptable and unacceptable advertising.

That the newspapers have done their part is indicated by a survey of the Publishers Association, which stated that in the year 1958 a total of 219 newspapers rejected $8,909,700 worth of advertising. One year later the number of newspapers rose to 348, but the rejections dropped off to just over $6,000,000. For 1960 the association reported that 755 newspapers rejected $7,645,408 in advertising which failed to meet the high standards of truthfulness and good taste set by the individual papers. It is significant not only that advertising *is* being rejected—and in vast amounts—but also that the volume of rejection has not risen in proportion to the number of papers reporting. There is no evidence of any softening of ethical fiber on the publishers' part. The association had an explanation for this trend, and it is particularly instructive in the context of our examination of the means for achieving ethical advertising. Said the publishers:

> Hundreds of newspapers reported to ANPA that offerings of false and misleading advertisements had slowed to a trickle for two reasons: (1) Consistent adherence to high standards of truthfulness and good taste have convinced the small minority of businessmen who succumb to temptation that it is useless to try to get daily newspapers to publish their copy, and (2) Widespread public discussion of "truth in advertising" campaigns in newspapers and other media have had a beneficial effect everywhere in the public interest.

Thus, the individual publisher can and must police his columns to insure that no false and misleading advertising ever blackens a page of his newspaper. When a newspaper prepares copy for its advertisers, it can insure that the advertisement conforms to all legal and moral standards. In the last analysis, all the conscientious newspaperman need do when confronted by a questionable ad is to consult his own conscience. One need not be a philosopher or a lawyer to recognize truth and taste. Self-regulation may require the rejection of a small number of ads and some immediate monetary loss, but it would seem that such loss will be short-term. Rising standards of acceptability throughout the community and the nation will soon force all advertisers to recognize that any short-term advantage in sales resulting from a deceptive practice may be far outweighed by the long-term damage to the seller's public reputation.

Similar efforts have been made in the magazine field. In 1960 the Magazine Publishers Association organized a copy advisory committee to act in a purely advisory capacity, the individual magazines retaining all rights to accept or reject advertising. When any magazine has a question concerning the acceptability of a certain piece of copy, it may submit the copy to the committee. A collective opinion is then given on the advisability of accepting, requesting a change in, or rejecting the copy submitted. Such an opinion is solely for the guidance of the individual publisher in arriving at his own decision.

According to *Advertising Age,* most leading magazines formulate standards of advertising acceptability. For example, *The New Yorker* magazine made a concerted effort over a period of several years to eliminate superlatives and exaggerations from its advertising pages. As a result, the magazine reported that it had measurably reduced the frequency with which certain expressions appeared. As an illustration, the term *World's Best* reportedly appeared 312 times during the first six months of the year 1956. For the same time period in 1961 the phrase appeared only seventy-nine times. *Advertising Age* reports that during the first four months of 1962 *The New Yorker* rejected some $260,000 in advertising.

The downfall of rigged quiz shows and the revelations of widespread payola practices in broadcasting brought to the surface a public distrust of the broadcast media which was wider than many informed observers had suspected. Television, after all, is a peculiarly intimate medium. It brings simultaneous sight and sound into the living room before an audience of all ages. This intimacy makes television all the more vulnerable to public criticism for possible abuses of its responsibility. The entire broadcasting industry thus owes to the public and to itself a most rigorous and searching variety of self-regulation. The broadcasting industry cannot afford to shrug off public cynicism with the attitude that "it will all blow over." "It" has not blown over and will not blow over.

Fortunately, the great majority of people in broadcasting do not take this light-hearted approach. There is no doubt that the broadcasting industry is now engaged in good faith in a massive effort to clean its house and to maintain public good will and approval of the advertising carried by radio and television. Lest there be any doubt of this self-awakening, let us look at the statement of one expert witness, the president of the National Broadcasting Company. In early 1960, following the rigging and payola scandals, this executive said, "We in broadcasting have undergone severe criticism—*and in part it is legitimate criticism*—for deceitful and dishonest program practices that developed within our very fast growing, extremely potent medium."

The principal source of self-regulation in broadcasting is the Television Code of the National Association of Broadcasters (NAB). The code itself deals with program standards as well as advertising standards. Over 75 per cent of the individual stations, all three television networks, and numerous film producers subscribe to the NAB code. In an effort to check up on observance of the code, the association runs a widespread monitoring program. The standards are enforced by a Code Review Board composed of station representatives. The method of enforcement is largely persuasive, although the sanction of expulsion is always available. Member television stations are permitted to display the "Seal of Good Practice," which it is hoped will become a prestigious symbol to the industry and to viewers. Code offices have been established in Washington, Hollywood, and New York to police the industry more effectively.

As a result of this program, increasing numbers of advertisers, agencies, stations, networks, and film producers are using the Board's facilities for the purpose of obtaining advisory opinions on code compliance before a particular program or commercial has so far advanced in production that change is impossible. Then, too, code members are notified of important decisions made by the Federal Trade Commission and regularly receive other educational material on advertising pitfalls from various self-regulatory sources.

The other self-regulatory arm of broadcasting is the Radio Code of Good Practice, which operates on substantially the same basis as the television code.

The self-regulatory effort to ban illegal and tasteless advertising in broadcasting will not achieve its maximum potential until nearly 100 per cent of the nation's radio and television broadcasters become members of the code operation. Only in this way can an industrywide program of self-policing be effected. Failing such a program, police efforts will undoubtedly come from other and perhaps harsher sources. Any reasonably discerning broadcaster who wets his index finger and turns it toward the winds blowing from Washington must rapidly conclude that increased support of group self-regulation is vital.

Consumer Education

We have already noted the significant rise in the level of sophistication of the American public as a potent factor shaping the climate within which ethical advertising may be achieved. Everyone connected with the process of advertising—advertisers, agencies, and media alike—must reexamine their work in light of a new evaluation of the American audience. That audience grows better educated and more discerning day by day. The proverbial advertiser who, as we have observed previously, addresses his messages to twelve-year-olds continues to do so at his peril. As Virginia Knauer has pointed out: "If mass advertising is collectively aimed at the third grade level of appeal, then that is because the market researchers and their creative counterparts view most of us on that level." A brief backward glance is sufficient to highlight the sharply rising level of taste and sophistication of the American audience.

James Webb Young, a great advertising pioneer, discusses a 1913 advertisement of Postum in a *Saturday Review* article. The ad points out the advantages of Postum over Brazilian coffee, attributing the following ills to coffee:

> Sallow Complexions; Stomach Trouble; Bad Liver; Heart Palpitations; Shattered Nerves; Caffeine, a Drug; Weakness from Drugging.

Mr. Young then quotes a judgment on the changes that forty years of education can bring: "We doubt if the present owners of Postum would OK copy like this today. Even if they did not own Maxwell House." We all realize that the incredible claims of yesterday would not be convincing today.

Every increase in cultural sophistication, every advance in education, every exposure to wider experience places an additional seal of doom on shoddy, tasteless, and irresponsible advertising. Despite the appearance in recent years of some very sophisticated institutional advertising, it still seems that advertisers are sometimes the last to weigh the American audience at its true value. As Walter Weir, himself in the advertising industry, noted: "In the name of competition and profit we engage in many practices considerably more expedient than wise, which bring no long term benefits, which cause confusion and distrust, and which threaten either forceable restraint or eventual ruin." Certain it is that today's consumer is aware, and that he resents being patronized as an unsuspecting boob.

During the crisis in public confidence engendered by the television scandals, the author received hundreds of letters from resentful and disillusioned consumer-viewers. Many letters were referred to the commission's Bureau of Investigation as specific complaints against deceptive advertising. For obvious reasons, it would not be appropriate to quote from such letters in this book. A number of other letters, however, were general in nature, and their tone is a meaningful indication of consumer awareness. A selection follows.

From a lady in Los Angeles:

> I'd like to see a return to the straightforward advertising of quality in merchandise so that we could have some confidence in the reliability of the manufacturer.
>
> Modern merchandising is too lazy to plan and execute good things. They have apparently swallowed their own line, that the American people read, listen to or watch only the lowest, least, lousiest, most unholy, degrading kind of program. . . . The average American is better educated and of better stuff than ever before.

A housewife in Rochester, New York:

> We as a family are tired of gagging over vials of mucous, beakers of stomach acid and tubes of fatty acids during the dinner hour. . . . Much of TV advertising is thoroughly disgusting and shows up most advertising men as cultural nitwits.

Most important for present purposes is the question of what the aware consumer will do about false or objectionable advertising. Some of the letters provide the answer.

A citizen of Richmond, Virginia:

> When we see an offensive or misleading ad, we add it to our list of those products not to be bought under any circumstances. This also includes hucksters who shout their message so that you have to get up and turn down your TV set. Conversely, we reward those whose advertising is straightforward, truthful, and well within the bounds of decency.

From a New Jersey housewife:

> Many people are becoming more and more disgusted by these types of commercials dealing with articles of an intimate and private nature which are not fit for discussion in mixed company. They certainly are not necessary on television and radio.

> As a woman, I deeply resent them and refuse to purchase the advertising brands. I will join the many women who are offended by them and will do my best to influence public opinion.

A Maryland housewife:

> We *can* hear normal voices on television and the commercial assault on our eardrums is not only insulting—it is painful. I, for one, have registered a vow not to buy any products the merits of which are screamed at me!

From Cleveland, Ohio:

> And some products I refuse to buy on account of over-emphasis.

Finally, a letter from a housewife in Red Oak, Iowa:

> I agree wholeheartedly with all you have said about illegal huckstering on TV, and everyone in small towns such as mine feel the same way. Multiply the small towns by the cities and it must be the same all over the United States.
>
> . . . We get the feeling that the sponsors are convinced that the listening public is just a bunch of morons that will swallow anything and sit raptly waiting to absorb more and more of the same.
>
> We . . . have favorite programs that each week are looked forward to with happy expectancy, only to have the time come and be so irritated by the commercial drivel, or the loud raucous music . . . that we end the evening by hating the sponsor and his product, and almost hating the favorite program. . . . We have squirmed in our seats, and covered our ears, and shut our eyes during some of the commercials. And after that, does the sponsor think for one moment that we, the suffering public, would ever even take his product as a gift. I personally have turned against some products that I had no reason to dislike, excepting for the irritation I had suffer over it, just to get to hear a favorite program. . . .

The lesson should be obvious to all those concerned with advertising. Insult the public intelligence long enough and hard enough, deceive and mislead the public often enough, and you will produce an almost devastating alienation. Further, we must not assume that because the public wrath fell upon the broadcasting field, other media are immune. In fact, much of the same objectionable material has also been disseminated through printed media in both local and national advertising campaigns.

We must, therefore, recognize the emergence of a new weapon in the war against trickery in the marketplace—the consumer himself. The public interest is served not only by restraining deception in selling but also by overcoming gullibility in buying. Or, in blunt language, "The gyp seller depends on the sucker buyer and can't exist without him."

Fully aware of the power represented by a knowledgeable public, the

Federal Trade Commission in December of 1959 called its first Conference on Public Deception. The conference was held in Washington with over fifty conferees present, representing consumer and public service organizations from all over the nation. The conference was also fully open to the members of the press.

Topics discussed included food and drug advertising, direct selling practices, fictitious pricing and bait advertising, labeling of wool, fur, and textile products, and the misrepresentation of employment opportunities. In each area formal presentations were made by commission officials and by spokesmen from consumer and service groups. Following the statements the floor was opened for discussion. After the conference the commission kept in contact with the participants in order to report further developments as they occurred.

The consumer movement has continued to mushroom since the first edition of this book. In 1959, Senator Estes Kefauver introduced legislation, which was never passed, to establish a cabinet-level Department of Consumers. In his March 15, 1962, message to Congress, President Kennedy declared that the "Federal Government—by nature the highest spokesman for all the people—has a special obligation to be alert to the consumer's needs and to advance the consumer's interest." As a result of the message, a Consumer Advisory Council was established, consisting of newly appointed assistants for consumer matters from each agency.

The impetus to giving the consumer a federal voice was accelerated by President Johnson. On January 3, 1964, a Committee on Consumer Interests was established. The committee was headed by a Special Assistant for Consumer Affairs. The other members were assistant cabinet secretaries and agency heads whose activities were most concerned with consumer interests. Weaknesses in the program were the fact that the Special Assistant was a part-time position and that there was a lack of money and enforcement powers.

On October 24, 1970, President Nixon by Executive Order 11583 created the Office of Consumer Affairs, abolishing the President's Committee on Consumer Interests. The new office has a budget twice that of the budget of the President's Committee and a staff of about eighty people, most of whom are on loan from other government bodies. Development of consumer legislation, liaison with Congressional committees, codification of state laws, encouragement of voluntary efforts by industry to aid consumers, assisting state and local organizations with consumer problems, consumer education programs, and the processing of consumer complaints (4,000 to 7,000 letters per month) are among the many functions performed by the new office.

In addition to the federal authorities many state officials have contributed to this crucial program of consumer education. Several state attorneys general have recognized the need for coordinated discussion by representatives of law enforcement, media, and consumer groups and have as a result called conferences similar to the federal Conference on Public Deception. Such local conferences have had a strong impact in the effort to clean up deceptive advertising by alerting consumers.

Media, too, deserve credit for the exposure which they have given to various revelations of advertising and marketing trickery. Intelligent press coverage of Federal Trade Commission action, for example, has added immeasurably to the effect of the commission's work. Press coverage of the Conference on Public Deception did much to advance the objective of public education. National magazines such as *Redbook* and *Good Housekeeping* have lent their support by carrying feature articles on deceptive pricing. The award-winning articles of Miriam Ottenberg in the *Washington Star* are a splendid example of the manner in which the press can bring fraudulent schemes to the public's attention and thereby destroy such schemes. The articles dealt with racketeering in used-car sales in the District of Columbia. As a result of this disclosure, significant procedural and administrative reforms were effected, the public was alerted, and many of the shady operators were forced to close up shop.

Finally, many of the self-regulatory groups in industry have themselves added to the impetus of consumer education. The Federal Trade Commission guides on such subjects as bait advertising, guarantees, tire advertising, and deceptive pricing have been reprinted by industry groups and given wide dissemination. In this way hundreds of thousands, if not millions, of consumers are made increasingly aware of a variety of illegal and deceptive tricks in advertising.

In the last analysis, the education of the consumer may truly be the best guard against the use of chicanery in the marketplace. For example, imagine how difficult it would be for fraudulent operators if we could alert every member of the buying public to put up his guard whenever he sees or hears one of the following six "sucker" signals:

"Buy Now or Lose the Chance . . ."
"You Have Been Specially Selected . . ."
"It's Only a Legal Form . . ."
"Just a Few Easy Lessons . . ."
"You Can Save Up To . . ."
"Yours Absolutely Free . . ."

An aware and intelligent consumer capable of exercising discriminating judgment is one of the essentials in the effort to achieve ethical advertising. All intelligent businessmen must recognize—as indeed most have—the importance of alert consumers who are able and willing to bring to bear upon the shoddy trickster the fiercest economic weapon of all—the simple refusal to buy.

Conclusion

We have analyzed the various sources from which support may be drawn in the quest for ethical advertising. Broadly, the means for achieving this societal goal can be grouped as follows:

1. Individual responsibility
2. Voluntary group effort
3. State and local government
4. Federal government

What shall be the relative contribution of these sources?

In a nation that places individual liberty at the highest point on its scale of values, it is obvious that the most desirable resolution of this issue entails a large contribution from the first source and contributions of geometrically descending proportions from the three succeeding sources. If the vast majority of individuals engaged in a given activity recognize the necessity for self-imposed restraints to prevent harm to others, then voluntary group effort is necessary only to reinforce and support the conscientious effort of individuals. If all necessary restraint could be furnished by individual responsibility and voluntary group effort, then no contribution would be necessary from government.

Descending from the ideal to the practical, we often find that a few individuals engaged in activity where restraint is necessary refuse to recognize their responsibilities. If voluntary group effort cannot impose necessary restraints upon these civic failures, then the necessity for governmental action is apparent. Historically, governmental contributions to necessary restraints have often come first from state and local governments, with a contribution from the federal government coming only after demonstration that the combined efforts of individuals, voluntary groups, and local governments have been unable to achieve a satisfactory level of beneficial restraints.

Just as nature abhors a vacuum, so does a civilized society abhor a vacuum in the imposition of needed restraints. It is important to realize that the failure of one source of necessary restraints will result only temporarily in the absence of restraint; the pressure of public opinion will soon force the needed contribution from another source.

Pressures for increased governmental control of advertising have been building in recent years. It is possible that these pressures will result in controls more extensive than really ought to be necessary to insure that advertising's responsibilities will be met. The best defense against such pressures is a demonstration that individuals and groups within the advertising industry can meet their responsibilities on a voluntary basis. The record in this regard is encouraging, but the hard work must continue.

I believe in self-regulation. A free man can and will accept responsibility as well as privilege; free men recognize that freedom means responsibility. Some advertising men have adopted a cynical attitude toward self-regulation. One of these pessimists said, "Talk of self-policing leaves me very cold." Another told a prominent magazine that only the Federal Trade Commission had the power to clean up advertising and that to suggest any other means was to invite futility. This attitude is as dangerous as it is false. Certainly, vigorous enforcement of prohibitions against false advertising by the Federal Trade Commission is a must, but individual integrity is also a must. If industry fails to accept its responsibility for truthful advertising, then we can secure truth only by massive government control. This alternative is appalling, because, at bottom, those businessmen who pass their moral responsibilities on to the government are advocating a police state. It is difficult to believe that effective trade regulation can be brought about only by a Gestapo. Individual integrity is the mortar cementing the foundations of our system of government. If the mortar cracks and crumbles in spots, it can be repaired. But the house will not stand without mortar.

In short, the goal of ethical advertising can be reached. The Federal Trade Commission and state law enforcement officials can provide the sanctions that are an indispensable part of any civilized activity. The men of advertising can, in cooperation with the media, guide their efforts by firm ethical standards, thus providing the largest contribution. Consumers and consumer protection groups, by public education and by vociferous protest against tasteless advertising, can achieve ever-higher levels of good taste. If all of these social entities perform conscientiously and efficiently, then we can provide one more illustration that the complex balance of forces that is the American system can respond to challenge without surrendering individual freedom.

EPILOGUE

THE PROPER ROLE OF GOVERNMENT IN THE ECONOMY

I

THIS nation's antitrust and trade regulation laws are solidly based upon principles that form the very foundations of the American system. Both the American political system and the American economic system are grounded in the belief that the citizenry of a free nation benefit most when the nation's course is charted by the aggregate of many individual decisions rather than by a single decision imposed and enforced by a single power source. Our nation was early committed to the belief that free competition is the only instrument which can, in the long run, produce maximum benefits for all. This same belief constitutes a basic premise of antitrust and trade regulation laws: that the nation's economy is best regulated by the interplay of free market forces.

History demonstrates that free and fair competition can produce unprecedented benefits; on the other hand, an absence of free competition or the presence of unfair competition have the potential to destroy our society. Such a destruction can arise in either of two ways. First, it can occur by the absolute concentration of power in the hands of a few ruthless monopolists. Or the converse might appear: a countermovement toward massive statism, once the dangers of untrammeled competition were revealed.

Fortunately, America has not chosen either of these paths. When the first great strides in economic progress were being consolidated late in the nineteenth century, and when oppressive tendencies in the use of large aggregations of capital were becoming manifest, that peculiarly American invention—antitrust—was devised. The laws did not embody any of the class-oriented proposals of the Continental socialists and communists. Rather, they represented the effort of a people dedicated to capitalism to save capitalism. In the area of business regulation America has surrendered neither to the forces of predatory combination nor to the forces of statism. We have merely developed pragmatic devices to confine the areas of conflict while preserving our system of free competition. Thus, as we observed in the Prologue to this book, the antitrust laws embody a principle of conservatism. They were designed to preserve competition, not to eradicate it. The laws attack those forces which would restrict the right to compete. They afford means for avoiding the concentration of power, whether in private hands, as in monopoly, or in government hands, as in a statist regime.

This is an appropriate place for me to reaffirm my belief in limited government and the viability of a free enterprise economy. I have long believed that "that government is best which governs least." To me, a system of free enterprise implies that the great mass of decisions affecting the interplay of market forces will be made by private citizens. It implies that the government will make decisions only when the defense of the nation or national health and safety require massive, concerted effort. Free enterprise also implies that governmental proscription or regulation of economic activity will be limited, in the main, to the promulgation and enforcement of the ground rules under which fair and vigorous competition may take place and to the penalization of those who become strong through the use of unfair methods. The government fails in its regulatory role if the monopolist or the predator imperil the freedom of the marketplace; it fails just as tragically if an iota of the freedom of individuals is unnecessarily sacrificed in the effort to contain the monopolist or fence in the predator.

During my years with the Federal Trade Commission, including six as general counsel and nearly two as chairman, I did a good deal of thinking about the goals which a government agency, the commission in particular, should pursue. I think that the policies which should guide a government agency or division rest upon three basic concepts of enforcement: (1) the idea of meaningful compliance as an overriding goal; (2) the need for activism; and (3) a proper regard for fundamental fairness.

I choose the term *meaningful compliance* to signify the principal enforcement goal for a number of reasons. First, this term focuses attention, quite properly I think, on industry conditions rather than enforcement techniques. Indeed, to achieve meaningful compliance, an enforcement agency with limited resources must necessarily exercise flexibility in the choice of methods. If the desired end is to be achieved, there must be a judicious adaptation of methods to circumstances as competitive situations change, and there must be a willingness to exploit multiple approaches successively and simultaneously as the situation may require.

A second reason for choosing the term *meaningful compliance* to describe my enforcement goal is that this term is free of the semantic barnacles that encrust the historic terms used to describe enforcement philosophy. Two principal approaches to antitrust enforcement were evolved during the history of the Federal Trade Commission. The first of these was vigorous, all-out enforcement through compulsory procedures. The second was an appeal to industry for self-regulation, supported by a government educational program. In the course of time these two approaches acquired labels. The first approach came to be called hard enforcement, and the second approach, soft enforcement. These positions were thought to be antithetical.

Hard enforcement came to be equated by the public with all-out prosecution engendered by suspicion, if not open hostility, toward business motives and practices. In the minds of some the hard-enforcement position required that any and every suspected violation be met with a formal complaint, without regard to the magnitude of the offense, the relative degree of public interest, the availability and proper allocation of limited funds and skilled manpower, the propriety of informal techniques, or the problems of a given industry. Justly or unjustly, this position came to be equated with a concentration on successful prosecution rather than meaningful compliance. The important thing was to get an order—an ever-increasing number of orders—without much consideration of the effect of the order. The emphasis on new prosecutions was to be maintained even at the expense of inadequate or nonexistent policing of compliance with outstanding orders. This total emphasis on prosecution meant that no advance warnings would be given to the business community, either through general education or by careful explanation of the rationale of formal opinions, lest an advantage be surrendered to an implacable adversary.

The soft-enforcement position in the course of time acquired equally unfortunate connotations. This position was equated with a benign willingness to allow business conduct to go unregulated. The emphasis on business education was not coupled with any overriding emphasis on thoroughgoing compliance when such compliance required resort to compulsory procedure.

It seems to me that both of these historical positions are unsatisfactory. If our goal is to insure the operation of our nation's economy in conformity to the antitrust and trade regulation laws, neither position alone is likely to achieve it. But are the two positions mutually exclusive? I believe not. I am firmly convinced that vigorous enforcement, on the one hand, and meaningful business education in the requirements of the laws, followed by effective self-regulation, on the other hand, are not antithetical. Rather, they are complementary tools for achieving the same goal. Vigorous enforcement alone cannot do the job: the time and resources of the enforcement agency are cruelly limited. A program of business education without additional measures cannot do the job, for honest men are likely to succumb to temptation if dishonest men are not deterred.

I hope that my policy as chairman of the Federal Trade Commission was the combination of a vigorous enforcement program with an intensive program of business education. I felt that the commission should prosecute vigorously and quickly when prosecution was needed, but that it should also encourage self-regulation by honest businessmen at the same time.

The concept of meaningful compliance implies a degree of flexibility in the employment of available techniques and in the timing and emphasis of actions. Because time and resources are limited, and the relative degree of public interest shifts as circumstances change, there must be a careful selection of the areas of greatest impact for any given action. There must be a careful adaptation of technique to situation in order to achieve a state of compliance in the cheapest and quickest way possible. The minimum effort necessary to correct any given situation must be employed in order to cover the broadest total area possible. If a situation will not yield to any of the commission's traditional techniques, then new techniques must be evolved, and, most important, the focus must be firmly fixed on the goal of meaningful compliance, with no method or technique exalted at the expense of that goal.

Passive enforcers can never produce meaningful compliance. Government regulation is a mockery unless the enforcement agency and its personnel actively pursue their statutory mandates. The proper role of government in the economy is that of a referee, not of a player; but this does not mean that the referee should remain supinely idle while one player gouges another and the contest turns into chaos. There must be a vigorous enforcement of the ground rules of competition. A government agency charged with the enforcement of the antitrust and trade regulation laws and the proscription of unfair trade practices must actively use every resource available to it to insure that competition is free and fair.

The third consideration which should guide enforcement activity is a regard for fairness. An administrative agency charged with the enforcement of the antitrust and trade regulation laws must show continuous, careful regard for the procedural requirements which insure fairness in adjudicative proceedings. The Federal Trade Commission's orders are not instruments of punishment. Rather, they are instruments designed to prevent future violations and to insure meaningful compliance. No order issued without regard to procedural due process can create a climate of meaningful compliance. Shady conduct by the government breeds shady conduct by others. In a government of laws, fairness must be an end in itself.

We must try to prevent the unfairness that results when one company is singled out for attention in a whole industry that is rife with violations. With the broad powers entrusted to the commission by Congress, there is no reason why the FTC should not proceed simultaneously on an industrywide front where necessary. Much remains to be done, and must be done, because administration of the antitrust and trade regulation laws can never be made truly effective if this kind of fairness is lacking.

The administrative process has filled and continues to fill a basic need in our democratic society. The Supreme Court has aptly described this development as a "response to the felt need" for a new instrument of government to overcome the inadequacy of some of the traditional modes. Administrative law has sprung not from a sterile theory of government but from the pragmatic demands of a dynamic society. The process has been directed toward fractional parts of our society rather than the whole —to particular industries or particular segments of an industry. The common thread running through this complex of functions, and indeed the impelling rationale of all administrative agencies, has been the need for specialized attention to specialized problems. Modern administrative government demands men of expertness who are able to devote their full energy and talents to administration.

Legislatures and courts are not fully adapted to the intricate and pressing task of administration. Neither legislators nor judges possess the requisite specialized knowledge or, equally important, the time required for the solution of complex problems met daily in the fields of communication, investment, power transmission, labor relations, and transportation, nor in fact do they have the desire to immerse themselves in the complexities of such activities.

Congress, in creating administrative agencies, has written laws expressing broad outlines, leaving to the particular agency the task of filling out the details. In this process of filling in the skeletal framework, the agency has the advantage not only of its *expertise* but also of a high degree of flexibility. Broadly speaking, the courts know one basic remedy—that of disposing of litigated cases by the entry of some form of judgment. An agency, on the other hand, has many alternatives. Take the case of deceptive advertising. Much of the objectionable advertising screened by the Federal Trade Commission does not warrant use of formal corrective procedures, in the sense of complaints, hearings, and cease and desist orders. At one time the situation may call for such treatment; at another for a trade practice conference or for an administrative treatment based upon voluntary revision or abandonment of a challenged practice. Still other practices may be halted by nothing more than a gentle hint from the commission. Only an independent administrative regulatory agency equipped with a number of flexible procedures can adequately tailor an effective and expeditious remedy to changing circumstances.

I do not mean to say that the administrative process is without defects or that it can ever wholly replace courts of law in specialized areas. But I do suggest that it has filled a real need, and in many cases filled that need well. If adequate funds are allotted to regulatory agencies, and if they maintain their determination to improve their operations, then I think we can expect genuine proof of their efficiency.

Much of what I have said in this chapter has been directed toward the administrative process. One obvious reason for this is that almost all of my legal experience in federal government has been with one regulatory agency. But, in addition, I feel strongly that in the field of trade regulation the Federal Trade Commission will play an even more important role in the future. However, I do feel that the enforcement principles I have outlined would be efficacious in governmental bodies other than administrative agencies. And I am optimistic that if all enforcement agencies would actively but fairly attempt to obtain meaningful compliance, this country would successfully avoid the pitfalls of both monopoly and statism.

II

Finally, I will discuss in the context of these concluding thoughts a matter which from time to time has troubled the business community.

It has been suggested that our antitrust laws are being increasingly enforced and applied so as to stifle competition and discourage efficiency, whereas the true purpose of those laws is to preserve competition and stimulate efficiency. Indeed, the thought is that a number of those antitrust laws—including those concerned with mergers, with exclusive dealing, and with price discrimination—are perhaps themselves anticompetitive in effect, because they are based on unsound theoretical and empirical foundations.

The question of whether our antitrust laws are anticompetitive stems inevitably from the fact that these laws are to an extent directed at the *regulation* of competition. For antitrust philosophy, as we have conceived it in this country, is largely based on the premise that, in order to preserve competition in the long run, you have to place certain restraints on it in the short run. This process of saving competition by restricting it is, admittedly, a difficult and delicate operation, and perhaps one that will not succeed. But, personally, I believe that the laws on the books today have put us on the right road in terms of preserving competition over the long haul. I also think—and this is not intended in terms of any particular actions or rulings—that the federal courts, the Antitrust Division, and the Federal Trade Commission are, in large measure, applying and enforcing the antitrust laws for the benefit of competition, rather than to the detriment of it.

I do not think that those defects which may exist in antitrust methods can be attributed either to fatal flaws in the statutes themselves or to any general misenforcement or misapplication of those statutes. The answer may simply be that the problem of the application of the antitrust statutes, and of their underlying policies, has inevitably been so difficult that "bad" law has been created along with "good" law.

In this connection, I would agree with some observers that, from the point of view of workability, consistency, and clarity of policy, the rules *per se,* such as that applicable to price-fixing, have proven to be the models of our antitrust law. Conversely, the source of weakness in our rules relative to conduct involving exclusionary arrangements or mergers has sprung from the fact that these practices cannot be made the subject of a rule *per se;* that is, in certain situations, these practices can be perfectly justifiable business devices. It does not follow from this, however, that the practices which are not objectionable *per se* are in all, or even in most cases, legitimate competitive devices or that they are so unimportant as to be unnecessary to our antitrust scheme.

The Clayton Act, the Robinson-Patman Act, and the Federal Trade Commission Act, in addition to the Sherman Act, each have a firm empirical base in the economic history of this country, as I have pointed out in the text. For example, it is worth recalling that the enactment of Section 3 of the Clayton Act represented the conclusion of the Congress, following extensive hearings and debate, that exclusive dealing arrangements, requirements contracts, and tying agreements were in fact being used by powerful, dominant firms as important and effective weapons for the attainment and consolidation of monoply power. It was found that such practices were commonly being utilized *coercively* and for the purpose of foreclosing competition, rather than for legitimate economic needs.

Similarly, Section 7 of the Clayton Act was enacted because of well-founded fears that too many corporate mergers in our most vital industries ultimately and gradually would put the American economy in the grip of monopolists. Although a number of the specific applications of this provision by the courts and the Federal Trade Commission are certainly open to criticism, it would, I think, be throwing the baby out with the bathwater to conclude that the provision itself is not appropriate, and indeed necessary, for the preservation of competition.

Hard economic facts and the fear of growing economic concentration were also the basis for the adoption of the Robinson-Patman Act in 1936, as I have indicated in this book. Again the intent was to preserve competition for the long-run by saddling it with certain limitations. The primary objective sought by passage of the Robinson-Patman Act was, of course, the neutralization in large measure of the sheer economic power of the retail chain stores to extract substantially lower prices from their suppliers than their single-unit competitors could obtain. There was good reason to fear that, if this economic power were left unrestrained, the smaller competitors in each industry would eventually be driven out of business. The passage of the Act plainly resulted from a value judgment by the Congress that the preservation of independent local retailing was of greater importance than the temporary benefit of lower prices to consumers effected by the power of the chain retailers.

It can fairly be said, moreover, that the Robinson-Patman Act does not force the larger buyer to give up the advantages stemming from his greater efficiency—he can claim a price benefit to the extent that it is in fact cost-justified. The Act simply limits him in the use of his *economic power.* This, I would suggest, is not too high a price to pay to maintain the many economic benefits which our economy derives from industries that are multimember in their composition.

The spirit and design of each of these antitrust laws is really in favor of competition and in favor of efficiency. They are anticompetitive only in the sense that they oppose the unfettered competition which must eventually lead to the destruction of competition. They are antiefficiency only in the sense that they reject the temporary efficiency offered by the firm seeking dominance in favor of the more gradual, but more stable, efficiency offered by a fully competitive system.

I do not believe that, when fairly and effectively administered and applied, the antitrust statutes are anticompetitive in effect. The comparative youth of our antitrust statutes, their ambitious scope, and their undoubted complexity have, unfortunately, produced a number of questionable judicial decisions, as well as some law enforcement of debatable wisdom. I would be less than candid, however, in expressing my views if I did not suggest that another source of the troubles of antitrust may well be the attitude that has prevailed toward the antitrust laws in some portions of the Bar. In their contacts with their business clients and with other lawyers, some members of the antitrust bar have been too disposed to expend their energies to discredit the antitrust laws or their enforcement. They have been too little disposed to accept the philosophy of the antitrust statutes and in turn to help their business clients to understand those laws and to develop meaningful programs fo compliance.

The ever-continuing controversy over the Robinson-Patman Act serves as a case in point. At Bar Association meeting after Bar Association meeting, the alleged anticompetitiveness, the internal inconsistencies, and the tortuous intricacies of the statute have been debated *ad infinitum,* if not *ad nauseum.* It seems to me that some of the debaters are doing their utmost to create the very situation which they deplore. They encourage disrespect for the clear-cut requirements of the law. They confuse the unsophisticated, maintaining them in a state of continued ignorance of the Robinson-Patman Act.

The debate over marginal questions has contributed nothing to the basic need for developing an understanding in the business community of its actual present responsibilities under the law. The sausage maker or distributor for whom the Robinson-Patman Act may be relevant will not profit from a learned polemic over the foolishness of the objectives or the marginal statutory inconsistencies of the statutory provisions. What he needs to understand are simply the basic concepts of discrimination in price and of discriminatory promotional allowance. He needs help both to understand these basic requirements and to conform his everyday business practices so that they comply with the law. The business community to which the Act is addressed should be more actively encouraged to develop an attitude of respect toward the statute, in place of the resistant attitude toward compliance which the controversy over the Act has fostered. This is not to suggest that we should not periodically, or even continuously, re-examine and reconsider the propriety and efficacy of our antitrust legislation. I suggest only that practicing lawyers should not use this process of re-examination as an excuse for obscuring, and even abdicating, their responsibility to explain to the business community the spirit and letter of the laws which are on the books.

Developments in recent years at both the Department of Justice and the Federal Trade Commission which have enlarged the scope for voluntary compliance with the antitrust laws, are, I think, greatly to be welcomed, both because they provide a new flexibility in enforcement and because they emphasize the need for education of the business community as to its responsibilities under the laws. Although these developments are very welcome, and although I am convinced that there is a great need for education of the business community, it must be kept in mind that business education and voluntary compliance are only one side of the antitrust coin. The first duty of government is vigorous enforcement of the law. Any law becomes a mockery, an ineffectual pious expression, unless it is enforced.

A program of business education, without more, cannot do the job, for honest men are likely to succumb to temptation if dishonest men are not deterred. Likewise, voluntary compliance can have little appeal, and thus little value, where it is not supplemented by swift and sure enforcement as regards the "hard" violations. Vigorous enforcement and voluntary compliance will, hopefully, continue to be regarded as complementary tools—both essential to the achievement of the desired goal—rather than as alternative approaches to the administration of the antitrust laws.

If we can achieve a greater understanding of our antitrust laws, impart more respect for them to the business community, and enforce their prohibitions swiftly and consistently, I, for one, believe that they will safeguard competition in our economy.

APPENDIX I

SELECTED BIBLIOGRAPHY

GENERAL WORKS

ABA Antitrust Section Reports, Vols. 1–40.

Brewster, *Antitrust and American Business Abroad* (New York: McGraw-Hill Book Company, 1958).

Fugate, *Foreign Commerce and the Antitrust Laws* (Boston: Little, Brown & Co., 1958).

Hale and Hale, *Market Power: Size and Shape* (Boston: Little, Brown & Co., 1958).

Hoffmann's Antitrust Law and Techniques (San Francisco: Mathew Bender & Co., 1963).

Kaysen and Turner, *Antitrust Policy* (Cambridge, Mass.: Harvard University Press, 1960).

Lamb and Kittelle, *Trade Association Law & Practice* (Boston: Little, Brown & Co., 1956).

Massel, *Competition and Monopoly* (Washington: Brookings Institution, 1962).

Neale, *The Antitrust Laws of the U.S.A.* (London & New York: Cambridge University Press, 1960).

Oppenheim, *Cases on Unfair Trade Practices* (Saint Paul, Minn.: West, 1965).

________, *Federal Antitrust Laws* (Saint Paul, Minn.: West, 1959).

Report of the Attorney General's National Committee to Study the Antitrust Laws (Washington: Government Printing Office, 1955).

Van Cise, *Understanding the Antitrust Laws* (New York: Practicing Law Institute, 1963).

CHAPTER 3: *A Bird's-Eye View of the Antitrust and Trade Regulation Laws*

Baker and Baum, *Section 5 of the Federal Trade Commission Act: A Contemporary Process of Redefinition,* 7 Vill. L. Rev. 517 (1962).

Bork, *Ancillary Restraints and the Sherman Act,* 15 ABA Antitrust Sec. Rep. 211 (1959).

Oppenheim, *Guides to Harmonizing Section 5 of the Federal Trade Commission Act with the Sherman and Clayton Acts,* 59 Mich. L. Rev. 821 (1961).

Whiting, *Criminal Antitrust Liability of Corporate Representatives,* 21 ABA Antitrust Sec. Rep. 327 (1962).

CASES

Asheville Tobacco Board of Trade, Inc. v. *FTC,* 263 F.2d 502 (4th Cir. 1959) (FTC and interstate commerce).

FTC v. *Bunte Bros.,* 312 U.S. 349 (1941) (FTC and interstate commerce).

FTC v. *Cement Institute,* 333 U.S. 683 (1948) (FTC and interstate commerce).

Ford Motor Co. v. *FTC,* 120 F.2d 175 (6th Cir.), *cert. denied,* 314 U.S. 668 (1941) (FTC and interstate commerce).

Holland Furnace Co. v. *FTC,* 269 F.2d 203 (7th Cir. 1959), *cert. denied,* 361 U.S. 932 (1960) (FTC and interstate commerce).

Mandeville Island Farms, Inc. v. *American Crystal Sugar Co.,* 334 U.S. 219 (1948) ("affecting" commerce).

Moore v. *Mead's Fine Bread Co.,* 348 U.S. 115 (1954) ("affecting" commerce).

Nash v. *United States,* 229 U.S. 373 (1913) (Sherman Act as criminal statute).

Northern Pacific Railway v. *United States,* 356 U.S. 1 (1958) (*per se* rules).

Standard Oil Co. v. *United States,* 221 U.S. 1 (1911) ("the rule of reason").

Swift & Co. v. *United States,* 196 U.S. 375 (1905) ("flow of commerce").

United States v. *Addyston Pipe & Steel Co.,* 85 F. 271 (6th Cir. 1898), *affirmed,* 175 U.S. 211 (1899) (ancillarity).

United States v. *Women's Sportswear Manufacturers Association,* 336 U.S. 460 (1949) (flow of and "affecting" commerce).

White Motor Co. v. *United States,* 372 U.S. 253 (1962) (*per se* rules).

CHAPTER 4: *Contracts, Combinations, and Conspiracies*

Attorney General's National Committee, Antitrust Report, 30–42 (1955).

Hale, *Agreements Among Competitors—Incidental and Reasonable Restraints of Trade,* 33 Minn. L. Rev. 331 (1949).

Turner, *The Definition of Agreement Under the Sherman Act: Conscious Parallelism and Refusal to Deal,* 75 Harv. L. Rev. 655 (1962).

CASES

Albrecht v. *Herald Co.,* 1968 Trade Cases ¶ 72,373 (Sup. Ct. 1968) (implied conspiracy).

Dayco Corp. v. *FTC,* 1966 Trade Cases ¶ 71,810 (6th Cir. 1966) (discontinued agreement).

Deesen v. *Professional Golfers' Ass'n of America,* 358 F.2d 165 (9th Cir. 1966) (boycotts—professional golf).

Eastern States Retail Lumber Dealer's Association v. *United States,* 234 U.S. 600 (1914) (agreement shown by circumstances).

FTC v. *Cement Institute,* 333 U.S. 683 (1948) (agreement shown by circumstances).

Interstate Circuit v. *United States,* 306 U.S. 208 (1939) ("conscious parallelism").

Milgram v. *Loew's, Inc.,* 192 F.2d 579 (3d Cir. 1951) ("conscious parallelism").

Theatre Enterprises, Inc. v. *Paramount Film Distributors Corp.,* 346 U.S. 537 (1954) ("conscious parallelism").

Triangle Conduit & Cable Co. v. *FTC,* 168 F.2d 175 (7th Cir. 1948), *affirmed sub. nom., Clayton Mark & Co.* v. *FTC,* 336 U.S. 956 (1949) ("conscious parallelism").

United States v. *Container Corporation of America,* 393 U.S. 33 (1969) (occasional exchange of price information).

CHAPTER 5: *Price Fixing*

Chafee, *Equitable Servitudes on Chattels,* 41 Harv. L. Rev. 945 (1928).

Lamb and Kittelle, *Trade Association Law Practice* (Boston: Little, Brown & Co., 1956).

Levi, The Parke, Davis–Colgate Doctrine: The Ban on Resale Price Maintenance, 1960 *The Supreme Court Review* 258.

Note, *The Per Se Illegality of Price Fixing–Sans Power, Purpose or Effect,* 19 U. Chi. L. Rev. 837 (1952).

Rahl, *Resale Price Maintenance, State Action, and Antitrust Laws: Effect of Schwegmann Bros.* v. *Calvert Distillers Corp.,* 46 Ill. L. Rev. 349 (1951).

Weston, *Fair Trade, Alias "Quality Stabilization": Status, Problems and Prospects,* 22 ABA Antitrust Sec. Rep. 76 (1963).

CASES

American Column & Lumber Co. v. *United States,* 257 U.S. 377 (1921) (trade association activities).

Appalachian Coals, Inc. v. *United States,* 288 U.S. 344 (1933) (joint marketing plan).

Citizens Publishing Co. v. *United States,* 394 U.S. 131 (1968) (pooling of circulation departments).

Dr. Miles Medical Co. v. *John D. Park & Sons,* 220 U.S. 373 (1911) (resale price maintenance).

FTC v. *Beech-Nut Packing Co.,* 257 U.S. 441 (1922) (resale price maintenance).

Hudson Distributors, Inc. v. *Eli Lilly & Co.,* 377 U.S. 386 (1964) (fair trade).

Kiefer-Stewart Co. v. *Joseph E. Seagram & Sons,* 340 U.S. 211 (1951) (fixing maximum price).

Maple Flooring Manufacturer's Association v. *United States,* 268 U.S. 563 (1925) (trade association activities).

Safeway Stores, Inc. v. *FTC,* 366 F.2d 795 (9th Cir. 1966), *cert. denied,* 386 U.S. 932 (1967) (bakeries).

Schwegmann Bros. v. *Calvert Distillers Corp.,* 341 U.S. 384 (1951) (Miller-Tydings Act).

Simpson v. *Union Oil Co.,* 377 U.S. 13 (1964) (agency contracts).

Skaggs Drug Center, Inc. v. *U.S. Time Corp.,* 1966 Trade Cases ¶ 71, 936 (Ariz. 1966) (fair trade).

Sugar Institute v. *United States,* 297 U.S. 553 (1936) (trade association activities).

The House of Seagram, Inc. v. *Assam Drug Co.,* 176 N.W.2d 491 (S.D. Sup. Ct. 1970) (fair trade).

United States v. *Schrader's Son, Inc.*, 252 U. S. 85 (1920) (resale price maintenance).

United States v. *Bausch & Lomb Optical Co.*, 45 F. Supp. 387 (S.D.N.Y. 1942), *affirmed*, 321 U.S. 707 (1944) (resale price maintenance).

United States v. *Colgate & Co.*, 250 U.S. 300 (1919) (individual refusal to deal).

United States v. *McKesson & Robbins, Inc.*, 351 U.S. 305 (1956) (fair trade).

United States v. *Parke, Davis & Co.*, 362 U.S. 29 (1960) (resale price maintenance).

United States v. *Socony-Vacuum Oil Co.*, 310 U.S. 150 (1940) (*per se* illegality).

United States v. *Trenton Potteries Co.*, 273 U.S. 392 (1927) (*per se* illegality).

United States v. *Utah Pharmaceutical Association*, 201 F. Supp. 29 (Utah), *affirmed per curiam*, 371 U.S. 24 (1962) (prescription fee schedules).

CHAPTER 6: *Boycotts and Refusals to Deal*

Coons, *Non-Commercial Purpose as a Sherman Act Defense*, 56 Nw. U.L. Rev. 705 (1962).

Rahl, *Per Se Rules and Boycotts Under the Sherman Act: Some Reflections on the Klor's Case*, 45 Va. L. Rev. 1165 (1959).

Turner, *The Definition of Agreement Under the Sherman Act: Conscious Parallelism and Refusal to Deal*, 75 Harv. L. Rev. 655 (1962).

CASES

Associated Press v. *United States*, 326 U.S. 1 (1945) (membership device).

Eastern States Retail Lumber Dealer's Association v. *United States*, 234 U.S. 600 (1914) (boycott).

Fashion Originators' Guild v. *FTC*, 312 U.S. 457 (1941) (purpose of boycott unimportant).

Klein v. *American Luggage Works, Inc.*, 206 F. Supp. 924 (Del. 1962) (treble-damage recovery against competing retailer when manufacturer refused to sell).

Klors, Inc. v. *Broadway-Hale Stores, Inc.*, 359 U.S. 207 (1959) (public injury not essential).

Silver v. *New York Stock Exchange*, 373 U.S. 341 (1963) (purpose of boycott unimportant).

United States v. *Frankfort Distilleries*, 324 U.S. 293 (1945) (boycott to obtain fair trade).

United States v. *General Motors Corp.*, 384 U.S. 127 (1966) (location clause).

United States v. *New Orleans Insurance Exchange*, 148 F. Supp. 915 (E.D. La.), *affirmed per curiam*, 355 U.S. 22 (1957) (boycott).

CHAPTER 7: *Limitations on the Resale Market*

Jordan, *Exclusive and Restricted Sales Areas Under the Antitrust Laws*, 9 U.C.L.A.L. Rev. 111 (1962).

Note, *Restricted Channels of Distribution Under the Sherman Act*, 75 Harv. L. Rev. 795 (1962).

Rifkind, *Division of Territory Under the Antitrust Laws,* 1953 Antitrust L. Sym. 173.

CASES

Snap-On Tools Corp. v. *FTC,* 321 F.2d 825 (7th Cir. 1963) (territorial and customer restrictions).

Timken Roller Bearing Co. v. *United States,* 341 U.S. 593 (1951) (foreign market division).

United States v. *Addyston Pipe & Steel Co.,* 85 F. 271 (6th Cir. 1898), *affirmed,* 175 U.S. 211 (1899) (market division).

United States v. *Arnold Schwinn & Co.,* 388 U.S. 365 (1967) (vertical territorial market allocations).

United States v. *Imperial Chemical Industries, Ltd.,* 100 F. Supp. 504 (S.D. N.Y. 1951) (foreign market division).

United States v. *Sealy, Inc.,* 388 U.S. 350 (1967) (horizontal territorial market allocations).

United States v. *Topco Associates,* 402 U.S. 905 (1972) (pro-competitive effects).

White Motor Co. v. *United States,* 372 U.S. 253 (1963) (territorial and customer restrictions).

CHAPTER 8: *Exclusive Dealing and Tie-In Arrangements*

Bok, *The Tampa Electric Case and the Problem of Exclusive Dealing Under the Clayton Act,* 1961 The Supreme Court Review 267.

Burrus, *Tying Arrangements and Reciprocity,* 30 Law & Contemp. Probs. 581 (1965).

Helman, *Partial Requirements Contracts Under Section 3 of the Clayton Act,* 55 Nw. U. L. Rev. 288 (1960).

Lockhart and Sacks, *Relevance of Economic Factors in Determining Whether Exclusive Arrangements Violate Section 3 of the Clayton Act,* 65 Harv. L. Rev. 913 (1952).

Turner, *Validity of Tying Arrangements Under the Antitrust Laws,* 72 Harv. L. Rev. 50 (1958).

CASES

Atlantic Refining Co. v. *FTC,* 381 U.S. 357 (1965) (TBA).

Carvell Corp., Trade Reg. Rep. ¶ 17,298 (FTC Dkt. 8574, 1965) (tying).

Fortner Enterprises v. *United States Steel Corp.,* 394 U.S. 495 (1969) (quantitative substantiality in tied market).

FTC v. *Curtis Publishing Co.,* 260 U.S. 568 (1923) (agency defense to Section 3).

FTC v. *Motion Picture Advertising Service Co.,* 344 U.S. 392 (1953) (exclusive dealing).

FTC v. *Texaco, Inc.,* 381 U.S. 379 (1965) (TBA).

FTC v. *Texaco, Inc.,* 393 U.S. 223 (1969) (TBA).

Hershey Chocolate Corp. v. *FTC,* 121 F.2d 968 (3d Cir. 1941) (reverse exclusive dealing).

International Business Machines Corp. v. *United States,* 298 U.S. 131 (1936) (tie-in to patented product).

International Salt Co. v. *United States,* 332 U.S. 392 (1947) (tie-in to patented product).

Northern Pacific Railway v. *United States,* 356 U.S. 1 (1958) (tie-in of land and railroad services).

Pick Manufacturing Co. v. *General Motors Corp.,* 80 F.2d 641 (7th Cir. 1935), *affirmed per curiam,* 299 U.S. 3 (1936) (justified partial exclusive dealing).

Standard Oil Co. v. *United States,* 337 U.S. 293 (1949) (requirements contract).

Tampa Electric Co. v. *Nashville Coal Co.,* 365 U.S. 320 (1961) (requirements contract).

Times-Picayune Publishing Co. v. *United States,* 345 U.S. 594 (1953) (tie-in of morning and afternoon newspaper).

United States v. *Jerrold Electronics Corp.,* 187 F. Supp. 545 (E.D. Pa. 1960), *affirmed per curiam,* 365 U.S. 567 (1961) (permissible tie-in).

United States v. *Loew's Inc.,* 371 U.S. 38 (1962) (tie-in sale).

CHAPTER 9: *The Robinson-Patman Act: The Federal Price Discrimination Law*

Austin, *Price Discrimination* (Philadelphia: American Law Institute, 1959).

Edwards, *The Price Discrimination Law* (Washington: Brookings Institution, 1959).

Kintner, *A Robinson-Patman* Primer (New York: The Macmillan Company, 1970).

Rowe, *Price Discrimination Under the Robinson-Patman Act* (Boston: Little, Brown & Co., 1962).

Sawyer, *Business Aspects of Pricing Under the Robinson-Patman Act* (Boston: Little, Brown & Co., 1963).

Symposium, *The Robinson-Patman Act: Retrospect and Prospect,* 17 ABA Antitrust Sec. Rep. (1960).

Taggart, *Cost Justification* (Ann Arbor: University of Michigan Press, 1959).

CASES

A. E. Staley Manufacturing Co. v. *FTC,* 324 U.S. 746 (1945) (basing point system).

Alhambra Motor Parts v. *FTC,* 309 F.2d 213 (9th Cir. 1962) (buying group discounts).

Amana Refrigeration, Inc. v. *Columbia Broadcasting System,* 295 F.2d 375 (7th Cir. 1961) (commodity requirement).

American Motors Corp. v. *FTC,* 1967 Trade Cases ¶ 72,222 (6th Cir. 1967).

American Motor Specialties Co. v. *FTC,* 278 F.2d (2d Cir.), *cert. denied,* 364 U.S. 884 (1960) (buying groups).

American News Co. v. *FTC,* 300 F.2d 104 (2d Cir.), *cert. denied,* 371 U.S. 824 (1962) (Section 5 of the Federal Trade Commission Act).

Anheuser-Busch, Inc. v. *FTC,* 289 F.2d 835 (7th Cir. 1961) (primary line injury).

Atlanta Trading Corp. v. *FTC,* 258 F.2d 365 (2d Cir. 1958) (sales at same time).

Atlas Building Products Co. v. *Diamond Block & Gravel Co.,* 269 F.2d 950 (10th Cir. 1959), *cert. denied,* 363 U.S. 843 (1960) (primary line injury).

Automatic Canteen Co. v. *FTC,* 346 U.S. 61 (1953) [Section 2(f)].

Baim & Blank, Inc. v. *Philco Corp.,* 148 F. Supp. 541 (E.D.N.Y. 1957) ("single seller" doctrine).

Balian Ice Cream Co. v. *Arden Farms Co.,* 104 F. Supp. 796 (S.D. Cal. 1952), *affirmed,* 231 F.2d 356 (9th Cir. 1955), *cert. denied,* 350 U.S. 991 (1956) (business considerations).

Borden Co., FTC Dkt. 7129 (January 30, 1963) (private brand goods).

Bruce's Juices, Inc. v. *American Can Co.,* 330 U.S. 743 (1947) (discrimination no defense to suit on contract).

Callaway Mills v. *FTC,* 1966 Trade Cases ¶ 71,799 (5th Cir. 1966) (meeting competition defense).

Carpel Frosted Foods, Inc., 48 F.T.C. 581 (1951) [Sections 2(c) and 2(d)].

Central Ice Cream Co. v. *Golden Rod Ice Cream Co.,* 287 F.2d 265 (7th Cir.), *cert. denied,* 368 U.S. 829 (1961) (interstate commerce).

Champion Spark Plug Co., 50 F.T.C. 30 (1953) (competitive injury; indirect purchasers).

Checker Motors Corp. v. *Chrysler Corp.,* 1968 Trade Cases ¶ 72,392 (S.D.N.Y. 1969) (like grade and quality).

Chicago Seating Co. v. *S. Karpen & Bros.,* 177 F.2d 863 (7th Cir. 1949) (refusal to sell).

Corn Products Refining Co. v. *FTC,* 324 U.S. 726 (1945) (basing point system).

Curtiss Candy Co., 44 F.T.C. 237 (1947) [Section 2(f); secondary line injury; Sections 2(d) and 2 (e)].

Dantzler v. *Dictograph Products, Inc.,* 272 F.2d 172 (4th Cir. 1959) [Section 2(e)].

Day's Tailor-D Clothing, Inc., 55 F.T.C. 1584 (1959) [Section 2(e) consent order].

Elizabeth Arden, Inc. v. *FTC,* 156 F.2d 132 (2d Cir. 1946), *cert. denied,* 331 U.S. 806 (1947) [Section 2(e)].

Elizabeth Arden Sales Corp. v. *Gus Blass Co.,* 150 F.2d 988 (8th Cir.), *cert. denied,* 326 U.S. 773 (1945) [Section 2(e)].

Empire Rayon Yarn Co. v. *American Viscose Corp.,* 354 F.2d 182 (2d Cir. 1965) (brokerage).

Enterprise Industries, Inc. v. *Texas Co.,* 240 F.2d 457 (2d Cir.), *cert. denied,* 353 U.S. 965 (1957) (proof of damages).

Exquisite Form Brassiere, Inc. v. *FTC,* 301 F.2d 499 (D.C. Cir. 1961), *cert. denied,* 369 U.S. 888 (1962) [Sections 2(d) and 2(e) and meeting competition].

Exquisite Form Brassiere, Inc. v. *FTC,* (D.C. Cir. 1965) (meeting competition).

FTC v. *Anheuser-Busch, Inc.,* 363 U.S. 536 (1960) (price discrimination means price difference).

FTC v. *Borden Co.,* 383 U.S. 637 (1966) (like grade and quality).

FTC v. *Fred Meyer, Inc.,* 390 U.S. 341 (1968) (redefinition of purchaser).

FTC v. *Henry Broch & Co.,* 363 U.S. 166 (1960) [Section 2(c)].

FTC v. *Morton Salt Co.*, 334 U.S. 37 (1948) (quantity discounts; broadness of order).
FTC v. *Simplicity Pattern Co.*, 360 U.S. 55 (1959) [Section 2(e)].
FTC v. *Standard Oil Co.*, 355 U.S. 396 (1958) (meeting competition defense).
FTC v. *Sun Oil Co.*, 371 U.S. 505 (1963) (meeting competition defense).
Foremost Dairies, Inc. v. *FTC*, 348 F.2d 674 (5th Cir.), *cert. denied*, 382 U.S. 959 (1965) (price differentials).
Forster Manufacturing Co., FTC Dkt. 7207 (March 18, 1963) (meeting competition defense).
Fred Meyer, Inc., FTC Dkt. 7492 (March 29, 1963) [Section 2(d); dual distribution].
Fred Meyer, Inc. v. *FTC*, 359 F.2d 351 (9th Cir. 1966) (changing conditions).
General Foods Corp., 50 F.T.C. 885 (1954) (primary line injury).
General Foods Corp., 52 F.T.C. 798 (1956) [Section 2(e)].
General Shale Products Co. v. *Struck Construction Co.*, 37 F. Supp. 598 (W.D. Ky. 1941), *affirmed*, 132 F.2d 425 (6th Cir. 1942), *cert. denied*, 318 U.S. 780 (1943) (sales to government agencies).
Gerber Products Co. v. *Beech Nut Lifesavers, Inc.*, 160 F. Supp. 916 (S.D.N.Y. 1958) (primary line injury).
Giant Food, Inc. v. *FTC*, 307 F.2d 184 (D.C. Cir. 1962), *cert. denied*, 372 U.S. 910 (1963) (Section 5 of the Federal Trade Commission Act).
Kay Windsor Frocks, Inc., 51 F.T.C. 89 (1954) [Section 2(d)].
Kraft-Phenix Cheese Corp., 25 F.T.C. 537 (1937) (indirect purchaser).
Krug v. *International Telephone & Telegraph Corp.*, 142 F. Supp. 230 (D.N.J. 1956) (teritary line injury).
Lever Bros. Co., 50 F.T.C. 494 (1953) [indirect price discrimination; Section 2(d)].
Liggett & Myers Tobacco Co., 56 F.T.C. 221 (1959) [Section 2(d)].
Ludwig v. American Greetings Corp., 264 F.2d 286 (6th Cir. 1959) (indirect price discrimination).
Moog Industries, Inc. v. *FTC*, 355 U.S. 411 (1955) (order can take effect though other competitor violators untouched).
Moore v. *Mead's Fine Bread Co.*, 348 U.S. 115 (1954) (predatory conduct).
Mid-South Distributors, Inc. v. *FTC*, 287 F.2d 512 (5th Cir.), *cert. denied*, 368 U.S. 838 (1961) [Section 2(f) and buying groups].
Minneapolis-Honeywell Regulator Co. v. *FTC*, 191 F.2d 786 (7th Cir. 1951), *cert. denied*, 344 U.S. 206 (1952) (primary line injury).
Mueller Co. v. *FTC*, 323 F.2d 44 (9th Cir. 1963) (functional discounts).
Nashville Milk Co. v. *Carnation Co.*, 355 U.S. 373 (1958) (Section 3 no ground for private suit).
National Dairy Products Corp. v. *United States*, 384 U.S. 883 (1966) (unreasonably low prices).
Perkins v. *Standard Oil of California*, 393 U.S. 1013 (1969) (fourth linc injury).
P. Lorillard Co. v. *FTC*, 267 F.2d 439 (3d Cir.), *cert. denied*, 361 U.S. 923 (1959) [Section 2(d)].
Purex Corp., 51 F.T.C. 100 (1954) (geographic price discrimination).
Purolator Products, Inc. v. *FTC*, 352 F.2d 874 (7th Cir. 1965) (cost justification).

Rangen, Inc. v. *Sterling Nelson & Sons, Inc.*, 351 F.2d 851 (9th Cir. 1965) (brokerage).

Russellville Canning Co. v. *American Can Co.*, 191 F.2d 38 (8th Cir. 1951) (secondary line injury).

Sano Petroleum Corp. v. *American Oil Co.*, 187 F. Supp. 345 (E.D.N.Y. 1960) (geographical price discrimination).

Secatore's, Inc. v. *Esso Standard Oil Co.*, 171 F. Supp. 665 (D. Mass. 1959) [secondary line injury; Section 2(e)].

Shreveport Macaroni Manufacturing Co. v. *FTC*, 321 F.2d 404 (5th Cir. 1963) (interstate commerce).

Shulton, Inc. v. *FTC*, 305 F.2d 36 (7th Cir. 1962) (meeting competition).

Skinner v. *United States Steel Corp.*, 233 F.2d 762 (5th Cir. 1956) [Section 2(e)].

Southgate Brokerage Co. v. *FTC*, 150 F.2d 607 (4th Cir.), *cert. denied,* 326 U.S. 774 (1945) [Section 2(c)].

Standard Oil Co. v. *FTC*, 340 U.S. 231 (1951) (meeting competition defense).

State Wholesale Grocers v. *Great Atlantic & Pacific Tea Co.*, 258 F.2d 831 (7th Cir. 1958), *cert. denied,* 358 U.S. 947 (1959) [Section 2(d)].

Students Book Co. v. *Washington Law Book Co.*, 232 F.2d 49 (D.C. Cir. 1955), *cert. denied,* 350 U.S. 988 (1956) (consignment).

Sunshine Biscuits, Inc. v. *FTC*, 306 F.2d 48 (7th Cir. 1962) (meeting competition defense).

Sylvania Electric Products, Inc., 51 F.T.C. 282 (1955) (cost justification).

Thomasville Chair Co. v. *FTC*, 306 F.2d 541 (5th Cir. 1962) [cost justification; Section 2(c)].

Thompson Products, Inc., 55 F.T.C. 1252 (1959) (secondary-line injury).

Tri-State Broadcasting Co., Inc. v. *United Press International, Inc.*, 269 F.2d 268 (5th Cir. 1966) (services).

Tri-Valley Packing Association, FTC Dkt. 7225 (May 10, 1962) (meeting competition defense).

Utah Pie Co. v. *Continental Baking Co.*, 386 U.S. 685 (1967) (seller-level injury).

United States v. *Borden Co.*, 370 U.S. 460 (1962) (cost justification).

United States v. *National Dairy Products Corp.*, 372 U.S. 29 (1963) (Section 3).

Chapter 10: *Patents and Antitrust*

Nordhaus and Jurow, *Patent-Antitrust Law* (Chicago: Jural Publishing Co., 1961).

Note, *Patent Abuses and Antitrust: The Per Se Rules,* 64 Harv. L. Rev. 626 (1951).

Note, *Quality Control and the Antitrust Laws in Trademark Licensing,* 72 Yale L.J. 1171 (1963).

Oppenheim, *Patents and Antitrust: Peaceful Coexistence?*, 54 Mich. L. Rev. 199 (1954).

Wood, *Restrictions Normally and Reasonably Within the Patentee's Pecuniary Reward,* 15 ABA Antitrust Sec. Rep. 318 (1959).

CASES

Alden-Rochelle, Inc. v. *ASCAP,* 80 F. Supp. 888 (S.D.N.Y. 1948) (patent holding company).

Cutter Laboratories, Inc. v. *Lyophile-Cryochem Corp.,* 179 F.2d 80 (9th Cir. 1950) (patent pooling).

General Talking Pictures Corp. v. *Western Electric Co.,* 305 U.S. 124 (1938) (field of use provisions).

Hartford-Empire Co. v. *United States,* 323 U.S. 386 (1944) (monopolizing through pooling).

International Business Machines Corp. v. *United States,* 298 U.S. 131 (1936) (patent tie-in sales).

Lear, Inc. v. *Akins,* 395 U.S 653 (1969) (license estoppel).

MacGregor v. *Westinghouse Electric Co.,* 329 U.S. 402 (1947) (licensee may attack patent used to fix prices).

Mercoid Corp. v. *Mid-Continent Investment Co.,* 320 U.S. 661 (1944) (antitrust violation defense to suit for contributory infringement).

Motion Picture Patents Co. v. *Universal Film Manufacturing Co.,* 243 U.S. 502 (1917) (patentee may not dictate materials to be used in patented machine).

Sola Electric Co. v. *Jefferson Electric Co.,* 317 U.S. 173 (1942) (licensee may attack patent used to fix prices).

Standard Oil Co. v. *United States,* 283 U.S. 173 (1931) (unblocking patents).

Timken Roller Bearing Co. v. *United States,* 341 U.S. 593 (1951) (trademarks and antitrust).

United States v. *Besser Manufacturing Co.,* 96 F. Supp. 304 (E.D. Mich. 1951), *affirmed,* 343 U.S. 444 (1952) (attempt to monopolize).

United States v. *General Electric Co.,* 272 U.S. 476 (1926) (fixing price at which licensee may sell).

United States v. *Krasnov,* 143 F. Supp. 184 (E.D. Pa. 1956), *affirmed per curiam,* 355 U.S. 5 (1957) (patent misuse).

United States v. *Line Material Co.,* 333 U.S. 287 (1948) (price fixing by cross-licensing).

United States v. *National Lead Co.,* 63 F. Supp. 513 (S.D.N.Y. 1945), *affirmed,* 332 U.S. 319 (1947) (market division).

United States v. *Singer Manufacturing Co.,* 374 U.S. 174 (1963) (conspiracy by means of cross-licensing agreements to exclude competitor from market).

United States v. *United States Gypsum Co.,* 333 U.S. 364 (1948) (patent price-fixing conspiracy).

Walker Process Equipment, Inc. v. *Food Machinery & Chemical Corp.,* 382 U.S. 172 (1965) (fraud on the Patent Office).

Zenith Radio Corp. v. *Hazeltine Research, Inc.,* 395 U.S. 100 (1969) (patent pools).

CHAPTER 11: *Mergers and Acquisitions*

ABA Antitrust Section, *Merger Case Digest* (1963).

Bock, *Mergers and Markets* (New York: National Industrial Conference Board, 1962).

Bok, *Section 7 of the Clayton Act and the Merging of Law and Economics,* 74 Harv. L. Rev. 226 (1960).

Casson and Burrus, *Federal Regulation of Bank Mergers,* 18 Am. U. L. Rev. 677 (1969).

Comment, *An Updating of the "Failing Company" Doctrine in the Amended Section 7 Setting,* 61 Mich. L. Rev. 566 (1963).

Handler, *Emerging Antitrust Issues: Reciprocity, Diversification and Joint Ventures,* 49 U. Va. L. Rev. 433 (1963).

Handler and Robinson, *A Decade of Administration of the Celler-Kefauver Antimerger Act,* 61 Colum. L. Rev. 629 (1960).

Kessler and Stern, *Competition, Contract and Vertical Integration,* 69 Yale L.J. 1 (1959).

Neal, *The Clayton Act and the Transamerica Case,* 5 Stan. L. Rev. 179 (1953).

Note, *Section 7 of the Clayton Act: A Legislative History,* 52 Colum. L. Rev. 766 (1952).

von Kalinowski, *Section 7 and Competitive Effects,* 48 U. Va. L. Rev. 827 (1962).

CASES

Brown Shoe Co. v. *United States,* 370 U.S. 294 (1962) (horizontal and vertical acquisitions; market definition; competitive effect).

Consolidated Foods Corp., FTC Dkt. 7000 (November 15, 1962) (conglomerate acquisition; reciprocal buying practices).

Ekco Products Co. v. *FTC,* 347 F.2d 745 (7th Cir. 1965) (conglomerates).

Ford Motor Co. v. *United States,* 403 U.S. 903 (1972) (pro-competitive effects).

Foremost Dairies, Inc., FTC Dkt. 6495 (April 30, 1962) (market definition; horizontal and market-extension mergers: industry concentration).

FTC v. *Consolidated Foods Corp.,* 380 U.S. 592 (1965) (reciprocity).

FTC v. *Proctor & Gamble Co.,* 386 U.S. 568 (1967) (product-extension merger)

International Shoe Co. v. *FTC,* 280 U.S. 291 (1930) ("failing-company" doctrine).

LaPeyre v. *FTC,* 366 F.2d 117 (5th Cir. 1966) (discriminatory leases).

Permanente Cement Co., Trade Reg. Rep. ¶ 17,612 (FTC Dkt. 7939, 1966) (cement merger).

Pillsbury Mills, Inc., 57 F.T.C. 1274 (1960) (market definition and competitive effects).

Reynolds Metals Co. v. *FTC,* 309 F.2d 223 (D.C. Cir. 1962) (conglomerate acquisition).

Scott Paper Co., 57 F.T.C. 1415 (1960), *vacated and remanded,* 301 F.2d 579 (3d Cir. 1962) (acquisition of production facilities).

United States v. *Aluminum Company of America,* 382 U.S. 12 (1965) (divestiture).

United States v. *Columbia Pictures Corp.,* 189 F. Supp. 153 (S.D.N.Y. 1960) (acquisition of licensing rights; competitive effects).

United States v. *Continental Can Co.,* 378 U.S. 441 (1964) (horizontal merger).

United States v. *Dean Foods,* 384 U.S. 597 (1966) (FTC preliminary injunctions).

United States v. *E. I. du Pont de Nemours & Co.,* 351 U.S. 377 (1956) (market definition).

United States v. *E. I. du Pont de Nemours & Co.,* 353 U.S. 586 (1957) (vertical effects thirty years after acquisition).

United States v. *El Paso Natural Gas,* 376 U.S. 651 (1964) (market extension).

United States v. *First City Nat'l Bank of Houston,* 386 U.S. 361 (1967) (bank mergers).

United States v. *First Nat'l Bank & Trust Co. of Lexington,* 376 U.S. 665 (bank mergers).

United States v. *General Dynamics Corp.,* 258 F. Supp. 36 (S.D.N.Y. 1966) (reciprocity).

United States v. *Pabst Brewing Co.,* 384 U.S. 546 (1966) (horizontal merger).

United States v. *Pabst Brewing Co.,* 1969 Trade Cases ¶ 72,723 (E.D. Wisc. 1969) (failing company defense).

United States v. *Penn-Olin Chemical Co.,* 378 U.S. 158 (1964) (joint ventures).

United States v. *Penn-Olin Chemical Co.,* 1967 Trade Cases ¶ 72,301 (Sup. Ct. 1967) (joint ventures).

United States v. *Philadelphia Nat'l Bank,* 374 U.S. 321 (1963) (horizontal merger; market definition; competitive effect).

United States v. *Third Nat'l Bank in Nashville,* 390 U.S. 171 (1968) (bank mergers).

United States v. *Von's Grocery,* 384 U.S. 270 (1966) (horizontal mergers).

CHAPTER 12: *Monopolization*

Adelman, *Integration and Antitrust Policy,* 63 Harv. L. Rev. 27 (1949).

Bork, *Vertical Integration and the Sherman Act: The Legal History of an Economic Misconception,* 22 U. Chi. L. Rev. 157 (1954).

Hale and Hale, *Market Power: Size and Shape Under the Sherman Act* (Boston: Little, Brown & Co., 1958).

Kaysen, *United States* v. *United Shoe Machinery Corp.,* Harvard Economic Studies (Cambridge, Mass.: Harvard University Press, 1958).

Kessler and Stern, *Competition, Contract and Vertical Integration,* 69 Yale L.J. 1 (1959).

Massel, *Competition and Monopoly* (Washington: Brookings Institution, 1962).

Turner, *Antitrust Policy and the Cellophane Case,* 70 Harv. L. Rev. 281 (1956).

CASES

American Tobacco Co. v. *United States,* 328 U.S. 781 (1946) (conspiracy to monopolize).

Gamco, Inc. v. *Providence Fruit & Produce Building,* 194 F.2d 484 (1st Cir. 1952) (market definition).

International Boxing Club v. *United States,* 358 U.S. 242 (1959) (market definition).

Kobe, Inc. v. *Dempsey Pump Co.*, 198 F.2d 416 (10th Cir), *cert. denied,* 344 U.S. 837 (1952) (market definition).

Lorain Journal Co. v. *United States,* 342 U.S. 143 (1951) (monopolization).

Northern Securities Co. v. *United States,* 193 U.S. 197 (1904) (monopolization).

Schine Chain Theatres v. *United States,* 334 U.S. 110 (1948) (monopolization).

United States v. *Aluminum Company of America,* 148 F.2d 416 (2d Cir. 1945) (monopolization).

United States v. *Corn Products Refining Co.*, 234 F. 964 (S.D.N.Y. 1916), *appeal dismissed,* 249 U.S. 621 (1919) (market definition).

United States v. *Crescent Amusement Co.*, 323 U.S. 173 (1944) (conspiracy to monopolize).

United States v. *E. I. du Pont de Nemours & Co.*, 351 U.S. 377 (1956) (market definition).

United States v. *General Motors Corp.*, 1965 Trade Cases ¶ 71,624 (E.D. Mich. 1965) (divestiture).

United States v. *Griffith,* 334 U.S. 100 (1948) (monopolization).

United States v. *Grinnell Corp.*, 384 U.S. 563 (1966) (burden of proof).

United States v. *Klearflax Linen Looms,* 63 F. Supp. 32 (D. Minn. 1945) (monopolization).

United States v. *New York Great Atlantic & Pacific Tea Co.*, 173 F.2d 79 (7th Cir. 1949) (monopolization).

United States v. *Paramount Pictures, Inc.*, 334 U.S. 131 (1948) (market definition).

United States v. *Terminal Railroad Association,* 224 U.S. 383 (1912) (conspiracy to monopolize).

United States v. *United Shoe Machinery Co.*, 247 U.S. 32 (1918) (monopolization).

United States v. *United Shoe Machinery Co.*, 110 F. Supp. 295 (D. Mass. 1953), *affirmed per curiam,* 347 U.S. 521 (1954) (monopolization).

United States v. *United States Steel Corp.*, 251 U.S. 417 (1920) (monopolization).

United States v. *Yellow Cab Co.*, 332 U.S. 218 (1947) (market definition; conspiracy to monopolize).

CHAPTER 13: *Interlocking Directorates*

Comment, *Interlocking Directorates: A Study in Desultory Regulation,* 29 Ind. L.J. 429 (1954).

Kramer, *Interlocking Directorships and the Clayton Act after 35 Years,* 59 Yale L.J. 1266 (1950).

CASES

Paramount Pictures Corp. v. *Baldwin Montrose Chemical Co., Inc.*, 1966 Trade Cases ¶ 71,678 (S.D.N.Y. 1966) (*de minimus*).

Schechtman v. *Wolfson,* 141 F. Supp. 453 (S.D.N.Y. 1956), *affirmed,* 244 F.2d 537 (2d Cir. 1957).

United States v. *Sears, Roebuck & Co.*, 111 F. Supp. 614 (S.D.N.Y. 1953).

United States v. *W. T. Grant Co.*, 345 U.S. 629 (1953).

CHAPTER 14: *The FTC Act and Related FTC Statutes*

Baker and Baum, *Section 5 of the Federal Trade Commisison Act: A Contemporary Process of Redefinition,* 7 Vill. L. Rev. 517 (1962).

Oppenheim, *Guides to Harmonizing Section 5 of the Federal Trade Commission Act with the Sherman and Clayton Acts,* 59 Mich. L. Rev. 821 (1961).

CASES

Fashion Originators' Guild v. *FTC,* 312 U.S. 457 (1941) (relationship between Sherman Act and Section 5).

FTC v. *Brown Shoe Co.,* 384 U.S. 316 (1966) (franchise agreement).

FTC v. *Cement Institute,* 333 U.S. 683 (1948) (relationship between Sherman Act and Section 5).

FTC v. *Colgate Palmolive Co.,* 380 U.S. 374 (1965) (expanded scope of Section 5).

FTC v. *Gratz,* 253 U.S. 421 (1920) ("definition" of unfair methods of competition).

FTC v. *Klesner,* 280 U.S. 19 (1929) (public interest).

FTC v. *Motion Picture Advertising Service Co.,* 344 U.S. 392 (1953) ("definition" of unfair methods of competition).

FTC v. *Raladam Co.,* 283 U.S. 643 (1931) (injury to competitors).

FTC v. *R. F. Keppel & Bro., Inc.,* 291 U.S. 304 (1934) ("definition" of unfair methods of competition).

FTC v. *Royal Milling Co.,* 288 U.S. 212 (1933) (public interest).

FTC v. *Sperry and Hutchinson Co.,* 401 U.S. 992 (1972) (reach of Section 5).

The Sperry & Hutchinson Company v. *FTC,* ATTR No. 482 (1970) (expanded scope of Section 5).

Times-Picayune Publishing Co. v. *United States,* 345 U.S. 594 (1953) (relationship between Sherman Act and Section 5).

CHAPTER 15: *Exemptions*

Bernhardt, *Allen-Bradley Doctrine: An Accommodation of Conflicting Policies,* 111 U. Pa. L. Rev. 1094 (1962).

Fulda, *Competition in the Regulated Industries Transportation* (Boston: Little, Brown & Co., 1961).

Hale and Hale, Competition or Control: Application of Antitrust Laws to Regulated Industries, Parts I–VI, 106 U. Pa. L. Rev. 641 (1958), 107 U. Pa. L. Rev. 585 (1959), 108 U. Pa. L. Rev. 775 (1960), 109 U. Pa. L. Rev. 311 (1961), 110 U. Pa. L. Rev. 57 (1961), 111 U. Pa. L. Rev. 46 (1962).

Note, *Antitrust and the Regulated Industries: The Panagra Decision and Its Ramifications,* 38 N.Y.U.L. Rev. 593 (1963).

Symposium, *Antitrust and Regulated and Exempt Industries,* 19 ABA Antitrust Sec. Rep. (1961).

CASES

Allen-Bradley Co. v. *Local No. 3, International Brotherhood of Electrical Workers,* 325 U.S. 797 (1945) (labor).

American Federation of Musicians v. *Carroll,* 1968 Trade Cases ¶ 72,456 (Sup. Ct. 1968) (labor).

Apex Hosiery Co. v. *Leader,* 310 U.S. 469 (1940) (labor).

California v. *FPC,* 369 U.S. 482 (1962) (regulated industry).

Carnation Co. v. *Pacific Westbound Conference,* 383 U.S. 213 (1966) (price fixing).

Denver & Rio Grande Western R. Co. v. *United States,* 1967 Trade Cases ¶ 72,116 (Sup. Ct. 1967) (mergers).

Hawaiian Tuna Packers v. *International Longshoremen's and Warehousemen's Union,* 72 F. Supp. 562 (D. Hawaii 1947) (labor).

Kaplan v. *Lehman Brothers,* 371 F.2d 409 (7th Cir. 1967) (securities regulation).

Maryland & Virginia Milk Producers Association v. *United States,* 362 U.S. 458 (1960) (agricultural cooperative).

Pan American World Airways, Inc. v. *United States,* 371 U.S. 296 (1963) (regulated industry).

Silver v. *New York Stock Exchange,* 373 U.S. 341 (1963) (securities regulation).

Sunkist Growers, Inc. v. *Winckler & Smith Citrus Products Co.,* 370 U.S. 19 (1962) (agricultural cooperative).

United Mineworkers v. *Pennington,* 381 U.S. 657 (1965) (labor).

United States v. *Borden Co.,* 308 U.S. 188 (1939) (agricultural cooperative).

United States v. *Hutcheson,* 312 U.S. 219 (1941) (labor).

United States v. *King,* 250 F. 908 (D. Mass. 1916) (agricultural cooperative).

Chapter 16: *Enforcement by the Department of Justice*

Dabney, *Consent Decrees Without Consent,* 63 Colum. L. Rev. 1053 (1963).

Decker, *The Civil Investigative Demand,* 21 ABA Antitrust Sec. Rep. 370 (1962).

Emmerglick, *Proposals for Balancing All Public Interests in Fashioning Antitrust Remedies,* 21 ABA Antitrust Sec. Rep. 387 (1962).

Kadish, *Some Observations on the Use of Criminal Sanctions in Enforcing Economic Regulations,* 30 U. Chi. L. Rev. 423 (1963).

Loevinger, "The Department of Justice and the Antitrust Laws," in Van Cise, *Understanding the Antitrust Laws* (New York: Practicing Law Institute, 1963).

Note, *Congress Enacts Antitrust Civil Process Act,* 111 U. Pa. L. Rev. 1021 (1963).

CASES

Ford Motor Co. v. *United States,* 335 U.S. 303 (1948) (modification of decrees).

In re Gold Bond Stamp Co., 221 F. Supp. 391 (D. Minn. 1963) (civil investigative demand).

Hughes v. *United States,* 342 U.S. 353 (1952) (modification of decrees).

Sterling Drug, Inc. v. *Ramsey Clark,* 1968 Trade Cases ¶ 72,549 (S.D.N.Y. 1968 (civil investigative demand).

United States v. *Swift & Co.,* 286 U.S. 106 (1932) (modification of decrees).

United States v. *Swift & Co.*, 189 F. Supp. 885 (N.D. Ill. 1960), *affirmed per curiam,* 367 U.S. 909 (1961) (modification of decrees).

Venn v. *United States,* 400 F.2d 207 (5th Cir. 1968) (subpoenas).

CHAPTER 17: *The Federal Trade Commission: Practice and Procedure*

Baker and Baum, *Enforcement, Voluntary Compliance, and the Federal Trade Commission,* 38 Ind. L.J. 322 (1963).

Burrus and Savarese, *Institutional Decision-Making and the Problem of Fairness in FTC Antitrust Enforcement,* 53 Geo. L.J. 656 (1965).

Burrus and Teter, *Antitrust: Rulemaking* v. *Adjudication in the FTC,* 54 Geo. L.J. 1106 (1966).

Dixon, "The Federal Trade Commission and the Antitrust Laws," in Van Cise, *Understanding the Antitrust Laws* (New York: Practicing Law Institute, 1963).

CASES

American Cyanamid Co. v. *FTC,* 1966 Trade Case ¶ 71,807 (6th Cir. 1966) (prejudice and disqualification).

FTC v. *Dean Foods Co.,* 384 U.S. 597 (1966) (preliminary injunctions in merger cases).

FTC v. *Flothill Products, Inc.,* 1967 Trade Cases ¶ 72,287 (Sup. Ct. 1967) (less than majority decisions).

R.H. Macy & Co., Inc., Trade Reg. Rep. ¶ 17,458 (FTC Dkt. 8650, 1966) (Jencks Act).

CHAPTER 18: *Private Enforcement*

Note, *The Admissibility and Scope of Guilty Pleas in Antitrust Treble Damage Action,* 71 Yale L.J. 684 (1962).

Note, *Clayton Act Statute of Limitations and Tolling by Fraudulent Concealment,* 72 Yale L.J. 600 (1963).

Note, *Discouragement of Private Treble Damage Suits Through a Simple Refusal to Deal,* 71 Yale L.J. 1565 (1962).

Note, *The Role of State Law in Federal Antitrust Treble Damage Actions,* 75 Harv. L. Rev. 1395 (1962).

Pollock, *The "Injury" and "Causation" Elements of a Treble Damage Antitrust Action,* 57 Nw. U. L. Rev. 691 (1963).

Symposium, *The Trial of an Antitrust Action,* 18 ABA Antitrust Sec. Rep. (1961).

CASES

Atlantic City Electric Co. v. *General Electric Co.,* 312 F.2d 236 (2d Cir. 1962), *cert. denied,* 373 U.S. 909 (1963) (tolling statute of limitations by fraudulent concealment).

Bergen Drug Co. v. *Parke, Davis & Co.,* 307 F.2d 725 (3d Cir. 1962) (refusal to deal to prevent private action).

Commonwealth Edison Co. v. *Allis-Chalmers Manufacturing Co.,* 1963 Trade Cases ¶ 70,884 (7th Cir. 1953) (guilty pleas as proof of violation).

Hanover Shoe, Inc. v. *United Shoe Machinery Corp.*, 1968 Trade Cases ¶ 72,490 (Sup. Ct. 1968) (passing on defense).

House of Materials, Inc. v. *Simplicity Pattern Co.*, 298 F.2d 867 (2d Cir. 1962) (refusal to deal to prevent private action).

Keogh v. *Chicago & Northwestern Railway*, 260 U.S. 156 (1922) ("injury caused by" violation).

Kiefer-Stewart Co. v. *Joseph E. Seagram & Sons*, 340 U.S. 211 (1951) (*in pari delicto*).

Momand v. *Universal Film Exchange, Inc.*, 43 F. Supp. 996 (D. Mass. 1942) (accrual of cause of action).

New Sanitary Towel Supply, Inc. v. *Consolidated Laundries Corp.*, 211 F. Supp. 276 (S.D.N.Y. 1962) (shareholder's suit).

North Texas Producer's Association v. *Young*, 308 F.2d 235 (5th Cir. 1962), *cert. denied*, 372 U.S. 929 (1963) (injury to "business or property").

Pennsylvania Water & Power Co. v. *Consolidated Gas, Electric Light & Power Co.*, 209 F.2d 131 (4th Cir. 1953), *cert. denied*, 347 U.S. 960 (1954) (*in pari delicto*).

Perma Life Mufflers, Inc. v. *International Parts Corp.*, 1968 Trade Cases ¶ 72,486 (*in pari delicto*).

Polychrome Corp. v. *Minnesota Mining & Mfg. Co.*, 263 F. Supp. 101 (S.D.N.Y. 1966) (*nolo* pleas).

Rogers v. *American Can Co.*, 305 F.2d 297 (3d Cir. 1962) (shareholder's derivative suit).

Simpson v. *Union Oil Co.*, 311 F.2d 764 (9th Cir.), *cert. granted*, 373 U.S. 901 (1963) (*volenti non fit injuria*).

Union Carbide & Carbon Corp. v. *Nisley*, 300 F.2d 561 (10th Cir. 1961) (class action).

2361 State Corp. v. *Sealy, Inc.*, 402 F.2d 370 (7th Cir. 1968) (Statute of Limitations).

CHAPTER 19: *State Antitrust Enforcement*

Burrus, *Investigation and Discovery in State Antitrust Enforcement* (Ann Arbor: Michigan Legal Publications, 1967).

Mosk, State Antitrust Enforcement and Coordination with Federal Enforcement, 21 ABA Antitrust Sec. Rep. 358 (1962).

Note, *The Present Revival and Future Course of State Antitrust Enforcement*, 38 N.Y.U.L. Rev. 575 (1963).

von Kalinowski and Hanson, *California Antitrust Laws: A Comparison with the Federal Antitrust Laws*, 6 U.C.L.A.L. Rev. 533 (1959).

CASES

State of Wisconsin v. *Milwaukee Braves, Inc.*, 1966 Trade Cases ¶ 71,843 (Sup. Ct. Wisc. 1966) (baseball exemption).

CHAPTER 20: *The Wonderful World of Advertising*

Advertising Age, XXXIV (January 15, 1963).

Holbrook, *The Golden Age of Quackery* (New York: Macmillan, 1959).

Note, *Federal Regulation of Deceptive Packaging: The Relevance of Technological Justification*, 72 Yale L.J. 788 (1963).

Note, *Illusion or Deception: The Use of "Props" and "Mock-Ups" in Television Advertising,* 72 Yale L.J. 145 (1962).

Note, *The Regulation of Advertising,* 56 Colum. L. Rev. 1018 (1956).

Simon, *The Law for Advertising and Marketing* (New York: Norton, 1956).

Stein, *Testimonial Advertising and the Federal Trade Commission,* 17 Geo. Wash. L. Rev. 340 (1949).

Turner, *The Shocking History of Advertising* (New York: E. P. Dutton & Co., 1953).

CHAPTER 21: *Deceptive Schemes and How They Operate*

Kintner, *A Primer on the Law of Deceptive Practices* (New York: The Macmillan Company, 1971).

Kintner, *Federal Trade Commission Regulations of Advertising,* 64 Mich. L. Rev. 1269 (1966).

CASES

Compco Corp. v. *Day-Brite Lighting, Inc.,* 376 U.S. 234 (1964) (product simulation).

FTC v. *Colgate Palmolive Co.,* 380 U.S. 374 (1965) (mock-ups).

FTC v. *Mary Carter Paint Co.,* 382 U.S. 46 (1965) (two for one deals).

Libbey-Owens-Ford Glass Co. v. *FTC,* 352 F.2d 415 (6th Cir. 1965) (mock-ups).

Sears, Roebuck & Co. v. *Stiffle Co.,* 376 U.S. 225 (1964) (product simulation).

APPENDIX II

SELECTED FEDERAL TRADE COMMISSION GUIDES

I. GUIDES AGAINST DECEPTIVE PRICING*

(Originally Adopted October 2, 1958; Revised January 8, 1964)

Introduction

These Guides are designed to highlight certain problems in the field of price advertising which experience has demonstrated to be especially troublesome to businessmen who in good faith desire to avoid deception of the consuming public. Since the Guides are not intended to serve as comprehensive or precise statements of law, but rather as practical aids to the honest businessman who seeks to conform his conduct to the requirements of fair and legitimate merchandising, they will be of no assistance to the unscrupulous few whose aim is to walk as close as possible to the line between legal and illegal conduct. They are to be considered as *guides*, and not as fixed rules of "do's" and "don'ts," or detailed statements of the Commission's enforcement policies. The fundamental spirit of the Guides will govern their application.

The basic objective of these Guides is to enable the businesman to advertise his goods honestly, and to avoid offering the consumer nonexistent bargains or bargains that will be misunderstood. Price advertising is particularly effective because of the universal hope of consumers to find bargains. Truthful price advertising, offering real bargains, is a benefit to all. But the advertiser must shun sales gimmicks which lure consumers into a mistaken belief that they are getting more for their money than is the fact.

Guide I. Former Price Comparisons

One of the most commonly used forms of bargain advertising is to offer a reduction from the advertiser's own former price for an article. If the former price is the actual, *bona fide* price at which the article was offered to the public on a regular basis for a reasonably substantial period of time, it provides a legitimate basis for the advertising of a price comparison. Where the former price is genuine, the bargain being advertised is a true one. If, on the other hand, the former price being advertised is not *bona fide* but fictitious—for example, where an artificial, inflated price was established for the purpose of

* Inquiries concerning these Guides and requests for copies should be addressed to the Bureau of Industry Guidance, Federal Trade Commission, Washington, D.C. 20580.

enabling the subsequent offer of a large reduction—the "bargain" being advertised is a false one; the purchaser is not receiving the unusual value he expects. In such a case, the "reduced" price is, in reality, probably just the seller's regular price.

A former price is not necessarily fictitious merely because no sales at the advertised price were made. The advertiser should be especially careful, however, in such a case, that the price is one at which the product was openly and actively offered for sale, for a reasonably substantial period of time, in the recent, regular course of his business, honestly and in good faith—and, of course, not for the purpose of establishing a fictitious higher price on which a deceptive comparison might be based. And the advertiser should scrupulously avoid any implication that a former price is a selling, not an asking price (for example, by use of such language as "Formerly sold at $________"), unless substantial sales at that price were actually made.

The following is an example of a price comparison based on a fictitious former price. John Doe is a retailer of Brand X fountain pens, which cost him $5 each. His usual markup is 50% over cost; that is, his regular retail price is $7.50. In order subsequently to offer an unusual "bargain," Doe begins offering Brand X at $10 per pen. He realizes that he will be able to sell no, or very few, pens at this inflated price. But he doesn't care, for he maintains that price for only a few days. Then he "cut" the price to its usual level—$7.50—and advertises: "Terrific Bargain: X Pens, Were $10, Now Only $7.50!" This is obviously a false claim. The advertised "bargain" is not genuine.

Other illustrations of fictitious price comparisons could be given. An advertiser might use a price at which he never offered the article at all; he might feature a price which was not used in the regular course of business, or which was not used in the recent past but at some remote period in the past, without making disclosure of that fact; he might use a price that was not openly offered to the public, or that was not maintained for a reasonable length of time, but was immediately reduced.

If the former price is set forth in the advertisement, whether accompanied or not by descriptive terminology such as "Regularly," "Usually," "Formerly," etc., the advertiser should make certain that the former price is not a fictitious one. If the former price, or the amount or percentage of reduction, is not stated in the advertisement, as when the ad merely states, "Sale," the advertiser must take care that the amount of reduction is not so insignificant as to be meaningless. It should be sufficiently large that the consumer, if he knew what it was, would believe that a genuine bargain or saving was being offered. An advertiser who claims that an item has been "Reduced to $9.99," when the former price was $10.00, is misleading the consumer, who will understand the claim to mean that a much greater, and not merely nominal, reduction was being offered.

GUIDE II. RETAIL PRICE COMPARISONS; COMPARABLE VALUE COMPARISONS

Another commonly used form of bargain advertising is to offer goods at prices lower than those being charged by others for the same merchandise in the advertiser's trade area (the area in which he does business). This may be done either on a temporary or a permanent basis, but in either case the advertised higher price must be based upon fact, and not be fictitious or misleading. Whenever an advertiser represents that he is selling below the prices being charged in his area for a particular article, he should be reasonably certain that the higher price he advertises does not appreciably exceed the price at which substantial sales of the article are being made in the area—that is, a sufficient number of sales so that a consumer would consider a reduction from the price to represent a genuine bargain or saving. Expressed another way, if a number of the principal retail outlets in the area are regularly selling Brand X fountain pens at $10, it is not dishonest for retailer Doe to advertise: "Brand X Pens, Price Elsewhere $10, Our Price $7.50."

The following example, however, illustrates a misleading use of this advertising technique. Retailer Doe advertises Brand X pens as having a "Retail Value $15.00, My Price $7.50," when the fact is that only a few small suburban outlets in the area charge $15. All of the larger outlets located in and around the main shopping areas charge $7.50, or slightly more or less. The advertisement here would be deceptive, since the price charged by the small suburban outlets would have no real significance to Doe's customers, to whom the advertisement of "Retail Value $15.00" would suggest a prevailing, and not merely an isolated and unrepresentative, price in the area in which they shop.

A closely related form of bargain advertising is to offer a reduction from the prices being charged either by the advertiser or by others in the advertiser's trade area for other merchandise of like grade and quality—in other words, comparable or competing merchandise—to that being advertised. Such advertising can serve a useful and legitimate purpose when it is made clear to the consumer that a comparison is being made with other merchandise and the other merchandise is, in fact, of essentially similar quality and obtainable in the area. The advertiser should, however, be reasonably certain, just as in the case of comparisons involving the same merchandise, that the price advertised as being the price of comparable merchandise does not exceed the price at which such merchandise is being offered by representative retail outlets in the area. For example, retailer Doe advertises Brand X pen as having "Comparable Value $15.00." Unless a reasonable number of the principal outlets in the area are offering Brand Y, an essentially similar pen, for that price, this advertisement would be deceptive.

Guide III. Advertising Retail Prices Which Have Been Established or Suggested by Manufacturers (or Other Non-Retail Distributors)

Many members of the purchasing public believe that a manufacturer's list price, or suggested retail price, is the price at which an article is generally sold. Therefore, if a reduction from this price is advertised, many people will believe that they are being offered a genuine bargain. To the extent that list or suggested retail prices do not in fact correspond to prices at which a substantial number of sales of the article in question are made, the advertisement of a reduction may mislead the consumer.

There are many methods by which manufacturers' suggested retail or list prices are advertised: large scale (often nation-wide) mass-media advertising by the manufacturer himself; pre-ticketing by the manufacturer; direct mail advertising; distribution of promotional material or price lists designed for display to the public. The mechanics used are not of the essence. These Guides are concerned with *any* means employed for placing such prices before the consuming public.

There would be little problem of deception in this area if all products were invariably sold at the retail price set by the manufacturer. However, the widespread failure to observe manufacturers' suggested or list prices, and the advent of retail discounting on a wide scale, have seriously undermined the dependability of list prices as indicators of the exact prices at which articles are in fact generally sold at retail. Changing competitive conditions have created a more acute problem of deception than may have existed previously. Today, only in the rare case are *all* sales of an article at the manufacturer's suggested retail or list price.

But this does not mean that all list prices are fictitious and all offers of reductions from list, therefore, deceptive. Typically, a list price is a price at which articles are sold, if not everywhere, then at least in the principal retail outlets which do not conduct their business on a discount basis. It will not be deemed fictitious if it is the price at which substantial (that is, not isolated or insignificant) sales are made in the advertiser's trade area (the area in which he does business). Conversely, if the list price is significantly in excess of the highest price at which substantial sales in the trade area are made, there is a clear and serious danger of the consumer being misled by an advertised reduction from this price.

This general principle applies whether the advertiser is a national or regional manufacturer (or other non-retail distributor), a mail-order or catalog distributor who deals directly with the consuming public, or a local retailer. But certain differences in the responsibility of these various types of businessmen should be noted. A retailer competing in a local area has at least a general knowledge of the prices being charged in his area. Therefore, before advertising a manufacturer's list price as a basis for comparison with his own lower price, the retailer should ascertain whether the list price is in fact the price regularly charged by principal outlets in his area.

In other words, a retailer who advertises a manufacturer's or distributor's suggested retail price should be careful to avoid creating a false impression that he is offering a reduction from the price at which the product is generally sold in his trade area. If a number of the principal retail outlets in the area are regularly engaged in making sales at the manufacturer's suggested price, that price may be used in advertising by one who is selling at a lower price. If, however, the list price is being followed only by, for example, small suburban stores, house-to-house canvassers, and credit houses, accounting for only an insubstantial volume of sales in the area, advertising of the list price would be deceptive.

On the other hand, a manufacturer or other distributor who does business on a large regional or national scale cannot be required to police or investigate in detail the prevailing prices of his articles throughout so large a trade area. If he advertises or disseminates a list or pre-ticketed price in good faith (i.e., as an honest estimate of the actual retail price) which does not appreciably exceed the highest price at which substantial sales are made in his trade area, he will not be chargeable with having engaged in a deceptive practice. Consider the following example:

Manufacturer Roe, who makes Brand X pens and sells them throughout the United States, advertises his pen in a national magazine as having a "Suggested Retail Price $10," a price determined on the basis of a market survey. In a substantial number of representative communities, the principal retail outlets are selling the product at this price in the regular course of business and in substantial volume. Roe would not be considered to have advertised a fictitious "suggested retail price." If retailer Doe does business in one of these communities, he would not be guilty of a deceptive practice by advertising, "Brand X Pens, Manufacturer's Suggested Retail Price, $10.00, Our Price, $7.50."

It bears repeating that the manufacturer, distributor or retailer must in every case act honestly and in good faith in advertising a list price, and not with the intention of establishing a basis, or creating an instrumentality, for a deceptive comparison in any local or other trade area. For instance, a manufacturer may not affix price tickets containing inflated prices as an accommodation to particular retailers who intend to use such prices as the basis for advertising fictitious price reductions.

Guide IV. Bargain Offers Based Upon the Purchase of Other Merchandise

Frequently, advertisers choose to offer bargains in the form of additional merchandise to be given a customer on the condition that he purchase a particular article at the price usually offered by the advertiser. The forms which such offers may take are numerous and varied, yet all have essentially the same purpose and effect. Representative of the language frequently employed in such offers are "Free," "Buy One—Get One Free," "2-For-1 Sale," "Half Price Sale," "1¢ Sale," "50% Off," etc. Literally, of course, the seller is not offering anything "free" (i.e., an unconditional gift), or ½ free, or for only 1¢, when he makes such an offer, since the purchaser is required to purchase an article in order to receive the "free" or "1¢" item. It is important, therefore, that where such a form of offer is used, care be taken not to mislead the consumer.

Where the seller, in making such an offer, increases his regular price of the article required to be bought, or decreases the quantity and quality of that article, or otherwise attaches strings (other than the basic condition that the article be purchased in order for the purchaser to be entitled to the "free" or "1¢" additional merchandise) to the offer, the consumer may be deceived.

Accordingly, whenever a "free," "2-for-1," "half price sale," "1¢ sale," "50% off" or similar type of offer is made, all the terms and conditions of the offer should be made clear at the outset.

Guide V. Miscellaneous Price Comparisons

The practices covered in the provisions set forth above represent the most frequently employed forms of bargain advertising. However, there are many variations which appear from time to time and which are, in the main, controlled by the same general principles. For example, retailers should not advertise a retail price as a "wholesale" price. They should not represent that they are selling at "factory" prices when they are not selling at the prices paid by those purchasing directly from the manufacturer. They should not offer seconds or imperfect or irregular merchandise at a reduced price without disclosing that the higher comparative price refers to the price of the merchandise if perfect. They should not offer an advance sale under circumstances where they do not in good faith expect to increase the price at a later date, or make a "limited" offer which, in fact, is not limited. In all of these situations, as well as in others too numerous to mention, advertisers should make certain that the bargain offer is genuine and truthful. Doing so will serve their own interest as well as that of the public.

These Guides supersede the Guides Against Deceptive Pricing adopted October 2, 1958.

Adopted: December 20, 1963.

II. GUIDES AGAINST DECEPTIVE ADVERTISING OF GUARANTEES

(Adopted April 26, 1960)

The following Guides have been adopted by the Federal Trade Commission for the use of its staff in evaluation of the advertising of guarantees. They have been released to the public in the interest of education of the businessman and the consumer and to obtain voluntary, simultaneous and prompt cooperation by those whose practices are subject to the jurisdiction of the Federal Trade Commission.

The Guides enumerate the major principles applicable to the advertising of guarantees although they do not purport to be all-inclusive and do not attempt to define the exact border lines between compliance with and violation of the law.

The Federal Trade Commission Decisions, upon which these Guides are based, indicate that the major difficulty with this type of advertising has been the failure to state adequately what the guarantee is. Concerning this, an appellate court stated: "Ordinarily the word, guarantee, or warrantee, is incomplete unless it is used in connection with other explanatory words. To say a . . . [product] or other subject is guaranteed is meaningless. What is the guarantee? The answer to this question gives meaning to the word, 'guaranteed.' "

The Guides have application not only to "guarantees" but also to "warranties," to purported "guarantees" and "warranties," and to any promise or representation in the nature of a "guarantee" or "warranty."

Adversary actions against those who engage in deceptive advertising of guarantees and whose practices are subject to Commission jurisdiction are brought under the Federal Trade Commission Act (15 U.S.C., Secs. 41–58). Section 5 of the Act declares unlawful "unfair methods of competition in commerce and unfair or deceptive acts or practices in commerce."

The Guides

In determining whether terminology and direct or implied representations concerning guarantees, however made, i.e., in advertising or otherwise, in connection with the sale or offering for sale of a product, may be in violation of the Federal Trade Commission Act, the following general principles will be used:

I. GUARANTEES IN GENERAL

In general, any guarantee in advertising shall *clearly* and *conspicuously disclose*—

(a) *The nature and extent of the guarantee.*
This includes disclosure of—
(1) What product or part of the product is guaranteed,
(2) What characteristics or properties of the designated product or part thereof are covered by, or excluded from, the guarantee,
(3) What is the duration of the guarantee,
(4) What, if anything, anyone claiming under the guarantee must do before the guarantor will fulfill his obligation under the guarantee, such as return of the product and payment of service or labor charges;

and

(b) *The manner in which the guarantor will perform.*
This consists primarily of a statement of exactly what the guarantor undertakes to do under the guarantee. Examples of this would be repair, replacement, refund. If the guarantor or the person receiving the guarantee has an option as to what may satisfy the guarantee this should be set out;

and

(c) *The identity of the guarantor.*
The identity of the guarantor should be clearly revealed in all advertising, as well as in any documents evidencing the guarantee. Confusion of purchasers often occurs when it is not clear whether the manufacturer or the retailer is the guarantor.

II. PRORATA ADJUSTMENT OF GUARANTEES

Many guarantees are adjusted by the guarantor on a prorata basis. The advertising of these guarantees should clearly disclose this fact, the basis on which they will be prorated, e.g., the time for which the guaranteed product has been used, and the manner in which the guarantor will perform.

If these guarantees are to be adjusted on the basis of a price other than that paid by the purchaser, this price should be clearly and conspicuously disclosed.*

Example: "A" sells a tire with list price of $48 to "B" for $24, with a 12 months guarantee. After 6 months use the tire proves defective. If "A" adjusts on the basis of the price "B" paid, $24, "B" will only have to pay ½ of $24, or $12, for a new tire. If "A" instead adjusts on the basis of list price, "B" will owe ½ of $48, or $24, for a new tire. The guarantor would be required to disclose here the following: that this was a 12 months guarantee, that a list price of $48 would be used in the adjustment, that there would be an adjustment on the basis of the time that the tire was used, and that he would

* (*Note:* Guarantees which provide for an adjustment based on a fictitious list price should not be used even where adequate disclosure of the price used is made.)

not pay the adjusted amount in cash, but would make an adjustment on a new tire.

III. "Satisfaction or Your Money Back" Representations

"Satisfaction or Your Money Back," "10 Day Free Trial," or similar representations will be construed as a guarantee that the full purchase price will be refunded at the option of the purchaser.

If this guarantee is subject to any conditions or limitations whatsoever, they shall be set forth as provided for in Guide I.

Example: A rose bush is advertised under the representation "Satisfaction or Your Money Back." The guarantor requires return of the product within one year of purchase date before he will make refund. These limitations, i.e., "return" and "time" shall be clearly and conspicuously disclosed in the ad.

IV. Lifetime Guarantees

If the words "Life," "Lifetime," or the like, are used in advertising to show the duration of a guarantee, and they relate to any life other than that of the purchaser or original user, the life referred to shall be clearly and conspicuously disclosed.

Example: "A" advertised that his carburetor was guaranteed for life, whereas his guarantee ran for the life of the car in which the carburetor was originally installed. The advertisement is ambiguous and deceptive and should be modified to disclose the "life" referred to.

V. Savings Guarantees*

Advertisements frequently contain representations of guarantees that assure prospective purchasers that savings may be realized in the purchase of the advertiser's products.

Some typical advertisements of this type are "Guaranteed to save you 50%," "Guaranteed never to be undersold," "Guaranteed lowest price in town."

These advertisements should include a clear and conspicuous disclosure of what the guarantor will do if the savings are not realized, together with any time or other limitations that he may impose.

Example: "Guaranteed lowest price in town" might be accompanied by the following disclosure:

"If within 30 days from the date that you buy a sewing machine from me, you purchase the identical machine in town for less and present a receipt therefor to me, I will refund your money."

VI. Guarantees Under Which the Guarantor Does Not or Cannot Perform

A seller or manufacturer should not advertise or represent that a product is guaranteed when he cannot or does not promptly and scrupulously fulfill his obligations under the guarantee.

A specific example of refusal to perform obligations under the guarantee is

* (*Note:* The above guarantees may constitute affirmative representations of fact and, in this respect, are governed by Guide VII.)

use of "Satisfaction or your money back" when the guarantor cannot or does not intend promptly to make full refund upon request.

VII. Guarantee As a Misrepresentation

Guarantees are often employed in such a manner as to constitute representations of material facts. If such is the case, the guarantor not only undertakes to perform under the terms of the guarantee, but also assumes responsibility under the law for the truth of the representations made.

Example 1: "Guaranteed for 36 months" applied to a battery is a representation that the battery can normally be expected to last for 36 months and should not be used in connection with a battery which can normally be expected to last for only 18 months.

Example 2: "Guaranteed to grow hair or money back" is a representation that the product will grow hair and should not be used when in fact such product is incapable of growing hair.

Example 3: "Guaranteed lowest prices in town" is a representation that the advertiser's prices are lower than the prices charged by all others for the same products in the same town and should not be used when such is not the fact.

Example 4: "We guarantee you will earn $500 a month" is a representation that prospective employees will earn a minimum of $500 each month and should not be used unless such is the fact.

III. GUIDES FOR ADVERTISING ALLOWANCES AND OTHER MERCHANDISING PAYMENTS AND SERVICES

(Adopted May 29, 1969; Amended August 4, 1972)

These Guides are designed to highlight legal problems that may be encountered by businessmen who want to utilize promotional or advertising allowances and similar merchandising payments or services to stimulate the sale of their products. The Guides are not intended to serve as a comprehensive statement of the law or as a legal treatise, but are instead intended to serve as a practical manual—in the form of basic rules of thumb, specific examples, and carefully considered suggestions—for the honest businessman who wants to conform his conduct to the requirements of the law without giving up the benefits that can be derived from this form of promotional activity. The Guides are designed to furnish guidance and assistance for the businessman seeking to comply with the law and to avoid even inadvertent violations.

Simply stated, what the law requires, in essence, is that those who grant promotional and advertising allowances treat their customers fairly and without discrimination, and not use such allowances to disguise discriminatory price discounts. In interpreting and enforcing the law, the Commission will recognize the practicalities of business while preventing the kind of discriminatory practices at which the law was aimed. Realistic and reasonable enforcement of the law will enable the Commission to enlist the aid of businessmen in eliminating undesirable practices and abuses without interfering with legitimate promotional and merchandising activities.

What the Guides are meant to do. These Guides can be of great value to businessmen who want to avoid violating the laws against giving or receiving improper promotional allowances, including advertising or special services, for promoting products. The Guides will make possible a better understanding of the obligations of sellers and their customers in joint promotional activities.

The Commission's responsibility is to obtain compliance with these laws. It has a duty to move against violators.[1] However, as an administrative agency, the Commission believes the more knowledge businessmen have with respect to the laws enforced by the Commission, the greater the likelihood that voluntary compliance with the laws will be obtained.

For the Commission to perform its responsibilities properly, and for business to avoid violation of the law, it is necessary that every effort be made to furnish individual businessmen a better understanding of these laws. It will help businessmen—and the Commission's law enforcement efforts—if they have a good general knowledge of what they can and cannot do in the field of promotional allowances and services.

What the Guides are not meant to do. It should be made clear too that the Guides are not meant to do several things:

(1) They are not meant to cover every situation. Decided cases dealing with unusual situations are not covered.
(2) They are not a substitute for sound legal advice.
(3) They are not intended to be a legal treatise. They should be read as a nontechnical explanation of what the law means.
(4) They do not make it mandatory (nor does the law itself) that sellers provide promotional allowances, services or facilities to any customer. They only come into play when the seller determines to employ such promotional practices.
(5) The omission in these final guides of any portion which appeared in a previous version should not be construed as necessarily reflecting any change in policy by the Commission.

What the law covers generally. The Robinson-Patman Act is an amendment to the Clayton Act. It is directed at preventing competitive inequalities that come from certain types of discrimination by sellers in interstate commerce. Section 2(d) and (e) of the Act deal with discriminations in the field of promotional payments and services made available to customers who buy for resale. Where the seller pays the buyer to perform the service, Section 2(d) applies. Where the seller furnishes the service itself to the buyer, Section 2(e) applies. Both sections require a seller to treat competing customers on proportionally equal terms in connection with the resale of the seller's products of like grade and quality.

Other law involved. In several places, the Guides are concerned with laws other than Sections 2(d) and (e):

1 The Commission has issued many orders to cease and desist which include proscriptions under Section 2(d) and/or 2(e) of the amended Clayton Act that antedate the Supreme Court's decision in the matter of *Federal Trade Commission* v. *Fred Meyer, Inc.*, et al., 390 U.S. 341 (1968). In this regard, it should be noted that future obligations of those companies and individuals under those orders shall be measured against said decision, as supplemented by these Guides.

(1) A seller who pays a customer for services that are not rendered, or who overpays for services which have been rendered, may thereby violate Section 2(a) of the Clayton Act, as amended. (See Guide 11.)
(2) A customer who receives discriminatory or other improper payments, services, or facilities may thereby violate Section 2(f) of the Clayton Act, as amended by the Robinson-Patman Act, or Section 5 of the Federal Trade Commission Act. (See Guides 11 and 14.)
(3) A third party who helps a customer claim reimbursement greater than that to which he is entitled under a seller's program (by furnishing the customer with a false invoice or other statement, for instance), may thereby violate Section 5 of the Federal Trade Commission Act. (See Guide 15.)
(4) A third party who devises and/or administers a promotional assistance program on behalf of one or more sellers may violate Section 5 of the Federal Trade Commission Act if the use, administration, or operation of the program results in violation of law. (See Guide 13).
(5) The examples are not intended to be all-inclusive. The Guides do not purport to set forth all the legal rules governing a seller's promotional practices or other vertical arrangements, but are directed primarily to the seller's obligation in making promotional offers to notify, and offer proportionally equal terms to, his competing customers. Related practices, not directly involving notification or proportionalization, are not necessarily covered by these Guides.

Guide 1. When Does the Law Apply?

Sections 2(d) and (e) apply to a seller of products in interstate commerce, if he either directly or through an intermediary (a) pays for services or facilities furnished by a customer in connection with the distribution of his products [Section 2(d)], or (b) furnishes such services or facilities to a customer [Section 2(e)] who competes with any other customer in the resale of the seller's products of like grade and quality.

Guide 2. Who Is a Seller?

"Seller" includes anyone (manufacturer, wholesaler, distributor, etc.) who sells products for resale, with or without further processing. Selling candy to a retailer is a sale for resale without processing. Selling corn syrup to a candy manufacturer is an example of a sale for resale with processing.

Guide 3. Who Is a Customer?

A "customer" is someone who buys for resale directly from the seller, the seller's agent or broker; and, in addition, a "customer" is any buyer of the seller's product for resale who purchases from or through a wholesaler or other intermediate reseller. In these Guides, the word "customer" which is used in Section 2(d) of the Act includes "purchaser" which is used in Section 2(e). (*Note:* In determining whether a seller has fulfilled his obligations toward his customers, the Commission will recognize that there may be some exceptions to this general definition of "customer." For example, the purchaser of distress merchandise would not be considered a "customer" simply on the basis of such purchase. Similarly, a retailer who purchases solely from other retailers, or one who makes only sporadic purchases, or one who does not regularly sell the seller's product or who is a type of retail outlet not usually selling such products (e.g., a hardware store stocking a few isolated food items) will not be considered a "customer" of the seller unless the seller has been put on notice that such retailer is selling his product.)

"Competing customers" are all businesses that compete in the resale of the seller's products of like grade and quality at the same functional level of distribution regardless of whether they purchase direct from the supplier or through some intermediary.

Example 1: A manufacturer sells to some retailers directly and to others through wholesalers. Retailer "X" purchases the manufacturer's product from a wholesaler and resells some of it to retailer "Y." Retailer "X" is a customer of the manufacturer. Retailer "Y" is not a customer unless the fact that he purchases the manufacturer's product is known to the manufacturer.

Example 2: A manufacturer sells directly to some independent retailers, sells to the headquarters of chains and of retailer-owned cooperatives, and also sells to wholesalers. The direct buying independent retailers, the headquarters of chains and of retailer-owned cooperatives, and the wholesaler's independent retailer customers are customers of the manufacturer. Individual retail outlets which are part of the chains or members of the retailer-owned cooperatives are not customers of the manufacturer.

Guide 4. What Is Interstate Commerce?

This term has not been precisely defined in the statute. In general if there is any part of a business which is not wholly within one State (for example, sales or deliveries of products, their subsequent distribution or purchase, or delivery of supplies or raw materials), the business may be subject to the Robinson-Patman Act. Sales in the District of Columbia are also covered by the Act.

Guide 5. What Are Services or Facilities?

These terms have not been exactly defined by the statute or in decisions. The following are merely examples—the Act covers many other services and facilities.

(a) The following are some of the services or facilities covered by the Act where the seller pays the buyer for furnishing them:

Any kind of advertising, including cooperative advertising,
Handbills,
Window and floor displays,
Demonstrators and demonstrations.

(b) Here are some examples of services or facilities covered by the Act when the seller furnishes them to a customer:

Any kind of advertising,
Catalogs,
Demonstrators,
Display and storage cabinets,
Display materials,
Special packaging, or package sizes,

Accepting returns for credit,
Prizes or merchandise for conducting promotional contests.

(*Note:* In these Guides, the term "services" is used to encompass both "services and facilities.")

GUIDE 6. NEED FOR A PLAN.

If a seller makes payment or furnishes services that come under Section 2(d) or (e) of the Clayton Act, as amended, he should do it under a plan that meets several requirements. In addition, if there are many competing customers to be considered, or if the plan is at all complex, the seller would be well advised to put his plan in writing. Briefly, the requirements are:

(a) The payments or services under the plan should be available on proportionally equal terms to all competing customers. (See Guide 7.)
(b) The seller should take action designed to inform all of his competing customers of the existence of and essential features of the promotion plan in ample time for them to take full advantage of it. (See Guide 8.)
(c) If the basic plan is not functionally available to (i.e., suitable for and usable by) some customers competing in the resale of the seller's products of like grade and quality with those being furnished payments or services, alternatives that are functionally available should be offered to such customers. (See Guide 9.)
(d) In informing customers of the details of a plan, the seller should provide them sufficient information to give a clear understanding of the exact terms of the offer, including all alternatives, and the conditions upon which payment will be made or services furnished. (See Guide 10.)
(e) The seller should take reasonable precautions to see that the services are actually performed and that he is not overpaying for them. (See Guide 11.)

GUIDE 7. PROPORTIONALLY EQUAL TERMS.

The payment or services under the plan should be made available to all competing customers on proportionally equal terms. This means that payments or services should be proportionalized on some basis that is fair to all customers who compete in the resale of the seller's products. No single way to proportionalize is prescribed by law. Any method that treats competing customers on proportionally equal terms may be used. Generally, this can best be done by basing the payments made or the services furnished on the dollar volume or on the quantity of goods purchased during a specified period. Other methods which are fair to all competing customers are also acceptable.

Example 1: A seller may properly offer to pay a specified part (say 50%) of the cost of local advertising up to an amount equal to a set percentage (such as 5%) of the dollar volume of purchases during a specified time.

Example 2: A seller may properly place in reserve for each customer a specified amount of money for each unit purchased, and use it to reimburse those customers for the actual cost of their advertising of the seller's product.

Example 3: A seller should not select one or a few customers to receive special allowances (e.g., 5% of purchases) to promote his product, while making allowances available on some lesser basis (e.g., 2% of purchases) to customers who compete with them.

Example 4: A seller's plan should not provide an allowance on a basis that has rates graduated with the amount of goods purchased, as, for instance, 1 percent of the first $1,000 purchases per month, 2 percent of second $1,000 per month, and 3 percent of all over that.

Example 5: A seller should not identify or feature one or a few customers in his own advertising without making the same service available on proportionally equal terms to customers competing with the identified customer or customers.

Example 6: A seller who makes his employees available or arranges with a third party to furnish personnel for purposes of performing work for a customer should make the same offer available on proportionally equal terms to all other competing customers. In addition the seller should offer usable and suitable alternatives of equivalent measurable cost to those competing customers to whom such services are not usable and suitable.

Example 7: A seller should not offer to pay a straight line rate for advertising if such payment results in a discrimination between competing customers; e.g., the offer of $1.00 per line for advertising in a newspaper that charges competing customers different amounts for the same advertising space.

(The straight line rate for advertising is an acceptable method for allocation of advertising funds, if the seller offers an alternative to retailers that pay more than the lowest newspaper rate which enables small retailers to obtain the same percent of the cost of advertising as large retailers. Example: A manufacturer's straight line rate of payment of $1.00 per line is based on 50% of the newspaper's lowest contract rate of $2.00 per line. The manufacturer should offer to pay 50% of the newspaper advertising cost of the smaller retailers who established by invoice or otherwise that they paid more than the lowest contract rate of $2.00 per line for advertising.)

Example 8: A seller should not refuse to participate in the cost of ads that feature prices other than the seller's suggested prices. (See Guide 9.)

Guide 8. Seller's Duty to Inform.

The seller should take reasonable action, in good faith, to inform all his competing customers of the availability of his promotional program. Such notification should include all the relevant details of the offer in time to enable customers to make an informed judgment whether to participate. In the alternative, such notification should include a summary of the essential features and a specific source to contact for further details on a specific promotion. Where such one-step notification is impracticable, the seller may, in lieu thereof, maintain a continuing program of first notifying all competing customers of the types of promotions offered by the seller and a specific source for the customer to contact in order to receive full and timely notice of all relevant details of the supplier's promotions. Such notice should also inform all competing customers that the seller offers advertising allowances and/or other promotional assistance that are usable in a practical business sense by all retailers regardless of size. When a customer indicates his desire to be put on the notification list, the seller should keep that customer advised of all promotions available in his area as long as the customer so desires. The seller can make the required notification by any means he chooses, but if he wants to be able to show later that he gave notice to a certain customer, he is in a better position to do so if it was given in writing.

If more direct methods of notification are impracticable, a seller may employ one or more of the following methods, the sufficiency of which will depend upon the nature of the industry and the complexity of his own distribution system. Different sellers may find that different notification methods are most effective for them.

(1) The seller may enter into contracts with his wholesalers, distributors or other third parties which conform to the requirements of Guide 13.

(2) The seller may place appropriate announcements on product containers or inside thereof with conspicuous notice of such enclosure on the outside. Where this notification procedure is utilized, however, the seller should take whatever steps are necessary to help insure that the notice will come to the attention of the customer's managerial personnel.

(3) The seller may publish notice of the availability and essential features of a promotional plan in a publication of general distribution in the trade.

(*Note:* Whatever procedure is used to give notice to the customer it should prove to be effective in practice. In many instances where customers of wholesalers or other intermediaries are involved and it is necessary to coordinate buying for a promotion such as a one-time buy promotion, a minimum lead time for notification may be 60 days or more.)

Example 1: A seller has a plan for the retail promotion of his products in Philadelphia. Some of his retailing customers purchase directly, and he offers the plan to them. Some other Philadelphia retailers purchase his products through wholesalers. The seller may use the wholesalers to reach the retailing customers who buy through them, either by having the wholesalers notify those retailers in accordance with Guide 13, or by using the wholesalers' customer lists for direct notification by the seller.

Example 2: A seller has a plan for the retail promotion of his products in Kansas City. Some of his retailing customers purchase directly and he offers the plan to them. Others purchase his products through wholesalers. The seller may satisfy his notification obligations to them by undertaking, in good faith, one or more of the following measures:

A. Placing on a shipping container or a product package that can reasonably be expected to come to the attention of the managerial personnel of all retailing customers handling the promoted product in time to enable them to participate in the program a conspicuous notice of the availability and essential features of his proposal, identifying a specific source for further particulars and details. In lieu of identifying a source for further particulars, brochures describing the details of the offer may be included in the shipping containers. If it is impractical to include the essential features of the proposed on or in the shipping container, the seller may substitute in the notice, as stated above, a summary of the types of promotions offered (e.g., allowances for advertising in newspapers, hand bills, or envelope stuffers; allowances for radio or television advertising; short term display allowances, etc.) and a statement that such promotions are usable in a practical business sense by all retailers regardless of size. In order to insure that such notices will come to the attention of the appropriate personnel it may well be necessary for the seller to supplement notices on shipping containers, especially during the initial stages of such a procedure, with additional notices, such as trade journal publications, invoice notices, envelope stuffers for use by wholesalers, etc.

B. If a promotional plan simply consists of providing retailers with display materials, including the materials within the product container.

C. Advising customers from accurate and reasonably complete mailing lists. If the product may be sold lawfully only under Government license (alcoholic beverages, etc.), informing all license holders would be sufficient.

D. Placing an announcement of the availability and essential features of promotional programs, and identifying a specific source for further particulars and details, at reasonable intervals in publications which have general and widespread distribution in the trade, and which are recognized in the trade as means by which sellers announce the availability of such programs.

Example 3: The seller has a wholesaler-oriented plan whereby he pays wholesalers to advertise the seller's product in the wholesaler's order books, or in the wholesaler's price lists directed to retailers purchasing from the wholesalers. He should notify all competing wholesalers of the availability of this plan, but the seller is not required to notify retailing customers.

Example 4: A seller who sells on a direct basis to some retailers in an area, and to other retailers in the area through wholesalers, has a plan for the promotion of his products at the retail level. If the seller directly notifies not only all competing direct purchasing retailers, but also all competing retailers purchasing through the wholesalers, as to the availability, terms and conditions of the plan, the seller is not required to notify his wholesalers.

Example 5: A seller regularly promotes his products at the retail level, and during the year he has various special promotional offers. His competing customers include large direct-purchasing retailing customers and smaller customers who purchase through wholesalers. Many of the promotions he offers can best be used by his smaller customers if the funds to which the smaller customers are entitled are pooled and used by the wholesalers in their behalf (newspaper advertisements, for example). The seller may encourage, but not coerce, the retailer purchasing through a wholesaler to designate a wholesaler as his agent for receiving notice of, collecting, and using promotional allowances for him. If a wholesaler or other intermediary by written agreement with a retailer is actually authorized to collect promotional payments from suppliers, the seller may assume that notice of, and payment under, a promotional plan to such wholesaler or intermediary constitutes notice and payment to the retailer. (A seller should not rely on a written agreement authorizing an intermediary to receive notice of and/or payment under a promotional plan for a retailer, if the seller knows, or should know, that the retailer was coerced into signing the agreement. In addition, a seller should assume that an intermediary is not authorized to receive notice of and/or payment under a promotional plan for a retailer unless there is a written authorization signed by such retailer.)

A seller who follows any procedure reasonably designed to inform all his competing customers of his promotional programs, including any of the procedures illustrated under Example 2 above, will be considered by the Commission to have fulfilled his "good faith" obligation under this Guide if he accompanies such procedure with the following supplementary measures: At regular intervals (of at least every 90 days) during the year, a seller who conducts promotional programs takes affirmative steps to verify the effectiveness of his notification procedure by making spot checks designed to reach a representative cross section of his indirect-buying customers. Whenever such spot checks indicate that the notification procedure is deficient, in that some customers who purchase through wholesalers or other intermediaries are not receiving actual notice of the promotion, the seller takes immediate steps to expand or to supplement his notification procedure in a manner reasonably designed to eliminate the repetition or continuation of any such deficiency in the future.

GUIDE 9. AVAILABILITY TO ALL COMPETING CUSTOMERS.

The plan should be such that all types of competing customers may participate. It should not be tailored to favor or discriminate against a particular customer or class of customers, but should in its terms be usable in a practical business sense by all competing customers. This may require offering all such customers more than one way to participate in the plan or offering alternative terms and conditions to customers for whom the basic plan is not usable and suitable. The seller should not either expressly, or by the way the plan operates, eliminate some competing customers, although he may offer alternative plans designed for different customer classes. If he offers alternative plans, all of the plans offered should provide the same proportionate equality and the seller should inform competing customers of the various alternative plans.

With respect to promotional plans offered to retailers, the seller should insure that his plans or alternatives do not bar any competing retailer customers from participation whether they purchase directly from him or through a wholesaler or other intermediary.

When a seller, in good faith, offers a basic plan, including alternatives, which is reasonably fair and nondiscriminatory, and refrains from taking any steps which would prevent any customer, or class of customers, from participating in his program, he shall be deemed to have satisfied his obligation to make his plan "functionally available" to all customers, and the failure of any customer or customers to participate in the program shall not be deemed to place the seller in violation of the Act.

Example 1: A manufacturer offers a plan of short term store displays[2] of varying sizes, including some which are suitable for each of his competing customers and at the same time are small enough so that each customer may make use of the promotion in a practical business sense. The plan also calls for uniform, reasonable certification of performance by the retailer. Because they are reluctant to process a reasonable amount of paper work, some small retailers do not participate. This fact is not deemed to place a manufacturer in violation of Guide 9 and he is under no obligation to provide additional alternatives.

Example 2: A manufacturer offers a plan for cooperative advertising on radio, TV, or in newspapers of general circulation.[3] Because the purchases of some of his customers are too small this offer is not

[2] Allowances that have little or no relationship to cost or approximate cost of the service provided by the retailer may be considered to be in violation of Section 2(d) or subject to the prohibitions of Section 2(a) of the amended Clayton Act, such as an allowance of $1 per case of goods purchased if the retailer furnishes a display or provides specific shelf space, or a promotional allowance of 10% of purchases during a specific period of time if the retailer places an ad of at least 3 column inches in a newspaper. In addition, a customer that induces such allowances may be proceeded against under Section 5 of the Federal Trade Commission Act. Also, the purchase of display or shelf space, whether directly or by means of so-called allowances, may be considered an "unfair method of competition" in violation of Section 5 of the Federal Trade Commission Act.

[3] In order to avoid the tailoring of promotional programs that discriminate against particular customers or class of customers, the seller in offering to pay allowances for newspaper advertising should offer to pay the same percent of the cost of newspaper advertising for all competing customers in a newspaper of the customer's choice, or at least in those newspapers that meet the requirements for second class mail privileges. Examples of promotional plans that may discriminate against small retailers are: (1) a plan that offers to pay 75% of the cost of advertising in daily newspapers, which are the regular advertising media of the seller's large or chain store customers, and only 50% of the cost of advertising in other newspapers that may be used by small retail customers; and (2) a plan that pays allowances for advertising in daily newspapers which are the regular advertising media of the seller's large or chain store customers, but does not pay allowances for advertising in semiweekly, weekly, or other newspapers that may be desirable by small retail customers, who are offered, as an alternative to advertising in daily newspapers, services such as envelope stuffers, handbills, window banners, etc. (See Guide 7.)

"functionally available" to them. The manufacturer should offer them alternative(s) on proportionally equal terms that are usable by them and suitable for their business.

Example 3: The seller's plan provides for furnishing demonstrators to large department store customers. He should provide usable and suitable alternatives on proportionally equal terms to those competing customers who cannot use demonstrators. The alternatives may be usable and suitable services furnished by the seller, or payments by the seller to customers for their advertising or promotion of the seller's product.

Guide 10. Need to Understand Terms.

In informing customers of the details of a plan, the seller should provide them sufficient information to give a clear understanding of the exact terms of the offer, including all alternatives, and the conditions upon which payment will be made or services furnished.

Guide 11. Checking Customer's Use of Payments.

The seller should take reasonable precautions to see that services he is paying for are furnished and also that he is not overpaying for them. Moreover, the customer should expend the allowance solely for the purpose for which it was given. If the seller knows or should know that what he pays or furnishes is not being properly used by some customers, the improper payments or services should be discontinued.

A seller, who, in good faith, takes reasonable and prudent measures to verify the performance of his competing customers will be deemed to have satisfied his obligations under the Act. Also, a seller, who, in good faith, concludes a promotional agreement with wholesalers or other intermediaries and who otherwise conforms to the standards of Guide 13 shall be deemed to have satisfied this obligation. If a seller has taken such steps, the fact that a particular customer has retained an allowance in excess of the cost or approximate cost, if the actual cost is not known, of services performed by him shall not alone be deemed to place a seller in violation of the Act. (When customers may have different but closely related cost in furnishing services that are difficult to determine, such as the cost for distributing coupons from a bulletin board or using a window banner, the seller may furnish to each customer the same payment if it has a reasonable relationship to the cost of providing the service or is not grossly in excess thereof.)

Example: A manufacturer gives "functionally available" promotional allowances for cooperative advertising which require placing advertisements in whatever medium the customer normally utilizes—e.g., radio, newspapers, magazines, handbills, etc. The manufacturer requires that each customer's request for payment be signed and attest that the required performance was rendered. Further, whenever evidence of the advertising—such as a tear sheet or a copy of the invoice from the radio station—is readily available to the customer, the manufacturer requires that such evidence accompany the request for payment. In cases in which such verification is not readily available, the manufacturer spot checks in a manner designed to reach a representative cross section of participating retailer customers to ascertain proof of performance. The manufacturer has satisfied his obligations of verification under the Act.

GUIDE 12. COMPETING CUSTOMERS.

The seller is required to provide in his plan only for those customers who compete with each other in the resale of the seller's products of like grade and quality. Therefore, a seller should make available to all competing wholesalers, any plan providing promotional payments or services to wholesalers, and similarly, should make available to all competing retailers any plan providing promotional payments or services to retailers. With these requirements met, a seller can limit the area of his promotion. However, this Guide is not intended to deal with the question of a seller's liability for use of an area promotion where the effect may be to injure the seller's competition.

Example 1: Manufacturer A, located in Wisconsin and distributes shoes nationally, sells shoes to three retailers who compete with each other and sell only in the Roanoke, Virginia, area. He has no other customers selling in Roanoke or its vicinity. If he offers his promotion to one Roanoke customer, he should include all three, but he can limit it to them. The trade area selected should be a natural one and not drawn arbitrarily so as to exclude competing retailers.

Example 2: A national seller has direct-buying retailing customers reselling exclusively within the Baltimore City trade area, and other customers within that area purchasing through wholesalers. The seller may lawfully engage in a promotional campaign confined to the Baltimore area, provided he affords all of his retailing customers within the area the opportunity to participate, including those who purchase through wholesalers.

Example 3: A seller manufacturers and sells men's suits and sport jackets (of one quality level) to retail stores nationally. He may restrict allowances to Philadelphia area retailers for their promotion of sport jackets during a particular season. He should not restrict allowances in the Philadelphia area for the promotion of certain styles of sport jackets unless all retailers of his sport jackets in the area are offered the opportunity to purchase the promoted styles and participate in the promotion.

(*Note:* The seller should be careful here not to discriminate against customers located on the fringes but outside the area selected for the special promotion, since they may be actually competing with those participating.)

GUIDE 13. WHOLESALER OR THIRD PARTY PERFORMANCE OF SELLER'S OBLIGATIONS

(a) A seller may, in good faith, enter into written agreements with intermediaries, such as wholesalers, distributors or other third parties, including promoters of tripartite promotional plans, which provide that such intermediaries will perform all or part of the seller's obligations under these Guides.

However, the interposition of intermediaries between the seller and his customers does not relieve the seller of his ultimate responsibility of compliance with the law. The seller, in order to demonstrate his good faith effort to discharge his obligations under these Guides, should include in any such agreement provisions that the intermediary will:

(1) Give notice to the seller's customers in conformity with the standards set forth in Guide 8;

(2) Check customer performance in conformity with the standards set forth in Guide 11;

(3) Implement the plan in a manner which will insure its functional availability to the seller's customers in conformity with the standards set forth in Guide 9. (This must be done whether the plan is one devised by the seller himself or by the intermediary for use by the seller's customers);

(4) Provide certification in writing and at reasonable intervals that the seller's customers have been and are being treated in conformity with the agreement.

(b) A seller who negotiates such agreements with his wholesalers, distributors or third party promoters will be considered by the Commission to have justified his "good faith" obligations under this Guide if he accompanies such agreements with the following supplementary measures: At regular intervals (of at least every 90 days) during the year, the seller takes affirmative steps to verify that his customers are receiving the proportionally equal treatment to which they are entitled by making spot checks designed to reach a representative cross section of his customers. Whenever such spot checks indicate that the agreements are not being implemented in such a way that his customers are receiving such proportionally equal treatment, the seller takes immediate steps to expand or to supplement such agreements in a manner reasonably designed to eliminate the repetition or continuation of any such discriminations in the future.

Example 1: A seller should not buy advertising time from a radio station and have the station furnish free radio time only to certain favored customers of the seller.

Example 2: A seller should not participate in a tripartite promotional plan providing for in-store promotion of his products unless all his competing customers are given an opportunity to participate in the intermediary's basic plan and, in the event some cannot use the basic plan, a suitable and usable alternative is made available on proportionally equal terms. A seller may demonstrate his good faith effort to discharge his obligations, in the event the intermediary operates a nondiscriminatory program in a discriminatory manner, by establishing that he has an agreement with the intermediary as described above and has fulfilled his duty to conduct periodic checks of the intermediary's performance.

Example 3: A seller should not participate in a tripartite plan involving many sellers if the customers to whom the plan is offered are required to purchase the products of other participating sellers before they are eligible to receive the benefits of the promotional programs. The customer of any one seller should not be required to purchase or promote other sellers' products as a condition to receiving promotional payments or services from the seller, even though a tripartite program is involved.

(c) Intermediaries administering promotional assistance programs on behalf of a seller may violate Section 5 of the Federal Trade Commission Act if they have agreed to perform the seller's obligations under the law with respect to a program which they have represented to be usable and suitable for all the seller's competing customers if it should later develop that the program was not offered to all or, if offered, was not usable or suitable, or was otherwise administered in a discriminatory manner.

Example: Promoter A devises a program for in-store advertising of grocery products on shopping carts. No alternative means of participation are provided. Seller B enters into a contract with A for participation in the program. In fact, some of Seller B's competing customers do not have shopping carts. Assuming that Seller B is in violation of Section 2(d) of the Clayton Act, as amended, Promoter A may be in violation of Section 5 of the Federal Trade Commission Act for his participation in the program which resulted in B's violation.

GUIDE 14. CUSTOMER'S LIABILITY.

Sections 2(d) and (e) apply to sellers and not to customers. However, a customer who knows, or should know, that he is receiving payments or services which are not available on proportionally equal terms to his competitors engaged in the resale of the same seller's products, may be proceeded against by the Commission under Section 5 of the Federal Trade Commission Act, which prohibits unfair methods of competition. Also, retailers that make unauthorized deductions from purchase invoices for alleged advertising or other promotional allowances may be proceeded against under Section 5 of the FTC Act and/or, under some circumstances, Section 2(f) of the amended Clayton Act.

Example 1: A customer should not induce or receive advertising allowances for special promotion of the seller's products in connection with the customer's anniversary sale or new store opening, unless he has taken such affirmative steps as would satisfy a reasonable and prudent businessman that such allowances are affirmatively offered and otherwise made available by such seller on proportionally equal terms to all of its other customers competing with the customer in the distribution of the seller's products and that usable and suitable alternatives are offered them if the basic offer is not suitable for and usable by them.

Example 2: A customer should not induce or receive seller contributions to the cost of his institutional advertising, unless he has taken such affirmative steps as would satisfy a reasonable and prudent businessman that such allowances are affirmatively offered and otherwise made available by such seller on proportionally equal terms to all of its other customers competing with the customer in the distribution of the seller's products and that usable and suitable alternatives are offered them if the basic offer is not suitable for and usable by them.

Example 3: A customer, an experienced buyer, is offered an allowance of 25 percent of his purchase volume by a seller for cooperative advertising to be paid for 100 percent by the seller. The customer knows, or should know, that most cooperative advertising programs in the industry allow payments of from 3 to 7 percent of purchases, and require 50-50 sharing by the seller and the customer. He would be on notice to inquire of the seller and to take such other affirmative steps as would satisfy a reasonable and prudent businessman that such allowances are affirmatively offered and otherwise made available by such seller on proportionally equal terms to all of its other customers competing with the customer in the distribution of the seller's products.

Example 4: A customer should not receive from a seller or intermediary services such as those performed in connection with a store opening, remodeling or special sales promotion, etc., unless he has taken such affirmative steps as would satisfy a reasonable and prudent businessman that such services are affirmatively offered and otherwise made available by such seller on proportionally equal terms to all of its other customers competing with the customer in the distribution of the seller's products and that usable and suitable alternatives are offered them if the basic offer is not suitable for and usable by them.

Example 5: Frequently the employees of sellers or third parties such as brokers perform in-store services for their grocery retailer customers such as stocking of shelves, building of displays and checking or rotating inventory, etc. A customer operating a retail grocery business should not induce or receive such services when the customer knows or should know that such services are not available on proportionally equal terms to all of the other customers of the seller competing with him in the distribution of the seller's products.

Example 6: Where a customer has entered into a contract, understanding, or arrangement for the purchase of advertising with a newspaper or other advertising media which provides for a deferred rebate or other reduction in the price thereof, he should advise any seller from whom he claims reimbursement for such advertising that the claimed rate of reimbursement is subject to a deferred rebate or other reduction in price. In the event that any rebate or adjustment in the price is received, the customer should refund to the seller the amount of any excess payment or allowance.

Example 7: A customer should not induce or receive an allowance in excess of that offered in the seller's advertising plan by billing the seller at "vendor rates" or for any other amount in excess of that authorized in the seller's promotional program.

GUIDE 15. THIRD PARTY LIABILITY FOR DOUBLE BILLING.

An advertising medium (newspaper, broadcast station, printer of catalogs, etc.) which (1) publishes a rate schedule containing fictitious rates or rates which are not reasonably expected to be applicable to a representative number of advertisers, or (2) furnishes a customer or his representative with an invoice that does not reflect the customer's actual net advertising cost, or that does not clearly state the discounts, rebates, earned rebates, etc., to which the invoice amount may be subject, or to which the invoiced party may be entitled, may violate Section 5 of the Federal Trade Commission Act if the customer uses such deceptive schedule or invoice for a claim for an advertising allowance, payment or credit greater than that to which he is entitled under the terms of the supplier's promotional program.

Example 1: Newspaper A has a "national" rate of $1.50 per inch and a "local" rate of $1.00 per inch. Retailer B places an advertisement with Newspaper A for a product sold to him by Supplier C, from whom he is later to seek reimbursement under Supplier C's cooperative advertising plan. Newspaper A should not furnish two bills to Retailer B, one at the "national" rate of $1.50 per inch, the other at the "local" rate of $1.00 per inch actually charged Retailer B.

Example 2: Newspaper A has various published rates. Retailer B is a large advertiser who in the past has earned the lowest rate. Newspaper A should not submit monthly invoices to Retailer B at a high rate agreed to by the parties unless the invoice discloses that Retailer B may receive a rebate, and a statement as to the amount or approximate amount of the rebate, if known, and if not known, the amount of rebate Retailer B could reasonably anticipate.

Example 3: Radio Station A has a flat rate of $10 for 30-second spot announcements, subject to volume discounts ranging up to fifty percent. Retailer B buys enough spots to qualify for the fifty percent discount. Radio Station A should not furnish Retailer B with an invoice that does not show either the $5 net cost to Retailer B or the fifty percent discount to which the $10 amount is subject.

Example 4: Advertising Agent A purchases a large volume of newspaper advertising space at a low, unpublished negotiated rate. Agent A subsequently sells such space to various retailers at a rate lower than each could purchase the space from the newspaper. Agent A should not furnish the retailers invoices showing a rate charge higher than that actually paid him by the retailers.

GUIDE 16. MEETING COMPETITION.

A seller charged with discrimination in violation of Section 2(d) or Section 2(e) may defend his actions by showing that the payments were made or the services were furnished in good faith to meet equally high payments made by a competing seller to the particular customer, or to meet equivalent services furnished by a competing seller to the particular customer. This defense, however, is subject to important limitations. For instance, it is insufficient to defend a charge of violating either Section 2(d) or 2(e) solely on the basis that competition in a particular industry is very keen, requiring that special allowances be given to some customers if a seller is "to be competitive."

GUIDE 17. COST JUSTIFICATION.

It is no defense to a charge of unlawful discrimination in the payment of an allowance or the furnishing of a service for a seller to show that such payment, service, or facility could be justified through savings in the cost of manufacture, sale or delivery.

IV. SUGGESTIONS BY EARL W. KINTNER FOR COMPLIANCE WITH THE BROKERAGE PROVISIONS OF THE ROBINSON-PATMAN ACT (SECTION 2(c) OF THE AMENDED CLAYTON ACT), MADE TO THE NATIONAL FOOD BROKERS ASSOCIATION, DECEMBER 10, 1960

1. As a general rule, a seller may not pay brokerage or other compensation to the buyer in connection with the sale of goods in interstate commerce.*

This is true whether the payment is made directly or indirectly or whether it is made in the form of a payment or in the form of a reduction on price in lieu of the payment. The law is also violated by the buyer in receiving the payment or discount.

2. *The seller may not pay directly to the buyer brokerage or other compensation in connection with a sale.*

There have been two principal situations in which direct payments have been questioned.

(a) When a broker or other sales representative or intermediary purchases goods for his own account rather than acting as an agent for the seller in the sale of the goods, he is clearly the buyer and the seller may not pay a commission to him on these purchases. If the broker also in other transactions is making sales for the seller as a broker, the seller may pay commissions on such other sales.

(b) In some cases, payments alleged to have been made for services performed by the buyer have been declared unlawful payments of brokerage because the services, such as warehousing or reselling, were of a kind that the buyer would ordinarily perform for himself. These holdings do not preclude the use of legitimate cooperative merchandising plans.

3. *The seller may not pay brokerage or other commissions in connection*

* This applies to the payment of brokerage or other compensation by the buyer to the seller in connection with the sale. This situation is seldom encountered, and, in the interests of brevity and clarity, the discussion is limited to payments or reductions made by the seller.

Questions relating to payments by the buyer may be resolved by substituting "buyer" for "seller" and "seller" for "buyer" in these suggestions.

with the sale of goods to an intermediary who represents or is controlled by the buyer.

The problem here has been whether the intermediary represents or is controlled by the buyer. Several examples where the intermediary has been held to represent or be controlled by the buyer follow.

(a) The broker as a partnership whose partners owned virtually all of the stock of the buyer corporation. Brokerage fees were not paid over to the buyer corporation but were distributed to the partners as individuals. Nevertheless, it was held that the seller's payments of brokerage to the brokerage partnership were illegal.

(b) A broker acted as the agent for several buyers although he received no fees from them in connection with purchases made for them. Nevertheless, he could not lawfully receive a commission from the sellers on these purchases.

(c) A broker under contract with buyers supplied them with market information and purchases for them for a small monthly fee. He placed orders with sellers for goods and obtained brokerage fees from the seller which were credited to the buyers' account. The seller was prohibited from paying the fees.

(d) In a situation similar to the last one, all of the buyers advertised a common trade-mark. The broker obtained fees from the seller for advertising the trade-mark and passed the fees on to the buyers. Here again, the seller could not lawfully make the payments.

(e) All of the stock of a brokerage concern was owned by the buyers. All of the fees obtained by the brokerage concern were required to pay its expenses. The seller was prohibited from paying fees because the brokerage concern represented the buyers.

(f) A broker represented both the buyer and the seller and divided its charges equally between the two so that in effect the buyer and seller each paid half of the brokerage fee. The payments by each were prohibited because they were payments to a representative of the other party to the transaction.

4. A *seller's broker may not pay all or part of the brokerage to the buyer either directly or through a reduction in price by the seller.*

This point was settled in a case where the buyer demanded a lower price than the seller was willing to accept.

A seller's broker was charging a 5% commission for handling the seller's product; in order to make a sale of significant quantities of the product to a particular buyer who would not pay the seller's going price, the seller agreed to lower the price if the broker would lower the commission; the broker agreed and a series of sales to the particular buyer were made on this basis.

It was held that the broker violated the law.

5. *A seller may not reduce his price on the grounds that he has not paid brokerage or other commission on the sale.*

Generally, the fact that the reduction in price was based on a savings in sales commission has been proved by the fact that the price was reduced by the amount ot the commission, but the rule would apply also where the price was reduced by only part of the commission or reduced more than the amount of the commission if this were actual basis of the reduction. But a seller is not required to use brokers at all or to pay any given percentage as a brokerage fee.

6. *Is cost justification a defense?*

No. It is no defense to violation of 2(c) for a seller to show that a reduction in price in lieu of brokerage or the payment of brokerage to the buyer could be justified through savings in cost of manufacture, sale or delivery.

7. *Is meeting competition in good faith a defense?*

No. A seller charged with a violation of Section 2(c) may not defend his actions by showing that the alleged reduction in price in lieu of brokerage or the payment of brokerage to the buyer was made in good faith to meet an equivalent reduction or payment made by a competitor.

8. *Can a broker or other representative of either the buyer or seller be held for violating this law?*

Yes. The buyer's or seller's broker or other intermediary in the sale of goods who receives or passes on the brokerage fee or other commission from one party to the sale to the other violated the law in so doing.

For example: B, acting as the seller's broker, passes on part of his brokerage fee to the purchaser. B violates the law. The buyer in receiving brokerage and the seller in paying a brokerage fee to the buyer also violate the law.

APPENDIX III

SUMMARIES AND TEXTS OF THE PRINCIPAL ANTITRUST STATUTES

SHERMAN ACT[1]

(As amended by Public No. 314, 75th Congress, August 17, 1937)

An Act to protect trade and commerce against unlawful restraints and monopolies.

Be it enacted by the Senate and House of Representatives of the United States of America in Congress assembled, that

Sec. 1. Every contract, combination in the form of trust or otherwise, or conspiracy, in restraint of trade or commerce among the several States, or with foreign nations, is hereby declared to be illegal: *Provided,* That nothing herein contained shall render illegal, contracts or agreements prescribing minimum prices for the resale of a commodity which bears, or the label or container of which bears, the trade mark, brand, or name of the producer or distributor of such commodity and which is in free and open competition with commodities of the same general class produced or distributed by others, when contracts or agreements of that description are lawful as applied to intrastate transactions, under any statute, law, or public policy now or hereafter in effect in any State, Territory, or the District of Columbia in which such resale is to be made, or to which the commodity is to be transported for such resale, and the making of such contracts or agreements shall not be an unfair method of competition under section 5, as amended and supplemented, of the act entitled "An Act to create a Federal Trade Commission, to define its powers and duties, and for other purposes," approved September 26, 1914: *Provided further,* That the preceding proviso shall not make lawful any contract or agreement, providing for the establishment or maintenance of minimum resale prices on any commodity herein involved, between manufacturers, or between producers, or between wholesalers, or between brokers, or between factors, or between retailers,

[1] Sections 1, 2 and 3 of this Act were amended to increase criminal penalties from $5,000 to $50,000 by Public Law 135, 84th Cong., H.R. 3659, approved July 7, 1955.

or between persons, firms, or corporations in competition with each other. Every person who shall make any contract or engage in any combination or conspiracy hereby declared to be illegal shall be deemed guilty of a misdemeanor, and, on conviction thereof, shall be punished by fine not exceeding fifty thousand dollars, or by imprisonment not exceeding one year, or by both said punishments, in the discretion of the court.

Sec. 2. Every person who shall monopolize, or attempt to monopolize, or combine or conspire with any other person or persons, to monopolize any part of the trade or commerce among the several States, or with foreign nations, shall be deemed guilty of a misdemeanor, and, on conviction thereof, shall be punished by fine not exceeding fifty thousand dollars, or by imprisonment not exceeding one year, or by both said punishments, in the discretion of the court.

Sec. 3. Every contract, combination in form of trust or otherwise, or conspiracy, in restraint of trade or commerce in any Territory of the United States or of the District of Columbia, or in restraint of trade or commerce between any such Territory and another, or between any such Territory or Territories and any State or States or the District of Columbia, or with foreign nations, or between the District of Columbia and any State or States or foreign nations, is hereby declared illegal. Every person who shall make any such contract or engage in any such combination or conspiracy shall be deemed guilty of a misdemeanor, and, on conviction thereof, shall be punished by fine not exceeding fifty thousand dollars, or by imprisonment not exceeding one year, or by both said punishments, in the discretion of the court.

Sec. 4. The several district courts of the United States are hereby invested with jurisdiction to prevent and restrain violations of this act; and it shall be the duty of the several United States attorneys, in their respective districts, under the direction of the Attorney General, to institute proceedings in equity to prevent and restrain such violations. Such proceedings may be by way of petition setting forth the case and praying that such violation shall be enjoined or otherwise prohibited. When the parties complained of shall have been duly notified of such petition the court shall proceed, as soon as may be, to the hearing and determination of the case; and pending such petition and before final decree, the court may at any time make such temporary restraining order or prohibition as shall be deemed just in the premises.

Sec. 5. Whenever it shall appear to the court before which any proceeding under section four of this act may be pending, that the ends of justice require that other parties should be brought before the court, the court may cause them to be summoned, whether they reside in the district in which the court is held or not; and subpoenas to that end may be served in any district by the marshal thereof.

Sec. 6. Any property owned under any contract or by any combination, or pursuant to any conspiracy (and being the subject thereof) mentioned in section one of this act, and being in the course of transportation from one State to another, or to a foreign country, shall be forfeited to the United States, and may be seized and condemned by like proceedings as those provided by law for the forfeiture, seizure, and condemnation of property imported into the United States contrary to law.

Sec. 7. The word "person," or "persons," wherever used in this act shall be deemed to include corporations and associations existing under or authorized by the laws of either the United States, the laws of any of the Territories, the laws of any State, or the laws of any foreign country.

Approved July 2, 1890.

Amended August 17, 1937.

FEDERAL TRADE COMMISSION ACT

[Public No. 203–63d Congress, as amended by Public–No. 447–75th Congress, as amended by Public–No. 459–81st Congress, as amended by Public–No. 542–82d Congress, as amended by Public–No. 85-791–85th Congress, as amended by Public–No. 85-909–85th Congress][1]

[H. R. 15613, S. 1077, H. R. 2023, H. R. 5767, H. R. 6788 and H. R. 9020]

An Act to create a Federal Trade Commission, to define its powers and duties, and for other purposes.

Be it enacted by the Senate and House of Representatives of the United States of America in Congress assembled, That a commission is hereby created and established, to be known as the Federal Trade Commission (hereinafter referred to as the commission), which shall be composed of five commissioners, who shall be appointed by the President, by and with the advice and consent of the Senate. Not more than three of the commissioners appointed shall be members of the same political party. The first commissioners appointed shall continue in office for terms of three, four, five, six, and seven years, respectively, from September 26, 1914, the term of each to be designated by the President, but their successors shall be appointed for terms of seven years, except that any person chosen to fill a vacancy shall be appointed only for the unexpired term of the commissioner whom he shall succeed: *Provided, however,* That upon the expiration of his term of office a Commissioner shall continue to serve until his successor shall have been appointed and shall have qualified. The President shall choose a chairman from the commission's membership.[2] No commissioner shall engage in any other business, vocation, or employment. Any commissioner may be removed by the President for inefficiency, neglect of duty, or malfeasance in office. A vacancy in the commission shall not

[1] The Act is published as also amended by Public No. 706, 75th Congress, and by Public No. 542, 82d Congress (see footnote 7), and as further amended, as above noted, by Public No. 459, 81st Congress, Ch. 61, 2d Session, H. R. 2023 (An Act to regulate oleomargarine, etc.), approved March 16, 1950, and effective July 1, 1950 (see footnotes 9, 12, and 13).

[2] Under the provisions of Section 3 of Reorganization Plan No. 8 of 1950, effective May 24, 1950 (as published in the Federal Register for May 25, 1950, at page 3175) the functions of the Commission with respect to choosing a chairman from among the membership of the Commission was transferred to the President. Under said plan, prepared by the President and transmitted to the Senate and House on March 13, 1950, pursuant to the provisions of the Reorganization Act of 1949, approved June 20, 1949, there were also transferred to the Chairman of the Commission, subject to certain limitations, "the executive and administrative functions of the Commission, including functions of the Commission with respect to (1) the appointment and supervision of personnel employed under the Commission, (2) the distribution of business among such personnel and among administrative units of the Commission, and (3) the use and expenditure of funds."

impair the right of the remaining commissioners to exercise all the powers of the commission.

The commission shall have an official seal, which shall be judicially noticed.

Sec. 2. The commission shall appoint a secretary, who shall receive a salary, payable in the same manner as the salaries of the judges of the courts of the United States, and it shall have authority to employ and fix the compensation of such attorneys, special experts, examiners, clerks and other employees as it may from time to time find necessary for the proper performance of its duties and as may be from time to time appropriated for by Congress.

With the exception of the secretary, a clerk to each commissioner, the attorneys, and such special experts and examiners as the commission may from time to time find necessary for the conduct of its work, all employees of the commission shall be a part of the classified civil service, and shall enter the service under such rules and regulations as may be prescribed by the commission and by the Civil Service Commission.

All of the expenses of the commission, including all necessary expenses for transportation incurred by the commissioners or by their employees under their orders, in making any investigation, or upon official business in any other places than in the city of Washington, shall be allowed and paid on the presentation of itemized vouchers therefor approved by the commission.

Until otherwise provided by law, the commission may rent suitable offices for its use.

The Auditor for the State and Other Departments shall receive and examine all accounts of expenditures of the commission.[3]

Sec. 3. The principal office of the commission shall be in the city of Washington, but it may meet and exercise all its powers at any other place. The Commission may, by one or more of its members, or by such examiners as it may designate, prosecute any inquiry necessary to its duties in any part of the United States.

Sec. 4. The words defined in this section shall have the following meaning when found in sections 41-46 and 47-58 of this title, to wit:

"Commerce" means commerce among the several States or with foreign nations, or in any Territory of the United States or in the District of Columbia, or between any such Territory and another, or between any such Territory and any State or foreign nation, or between the District of Columbia and any State or Territory or foreign nation.

"Corporation" shall be deemed to include any company, trust, so-called Massachusetts trust, or association, incorporated or unincorporated, which is organized to carry on business for its own profit or that of its members, and has shares of capital or capital stock or certificates of interest, and any company, trust, so-called Massachusetts trust, or association, incorporated or unincorporated, without shares of capital or capital stock or certificates of interest, except partnerships, which is organized to carry on business for its own profit or that of its members.

"Documentary evidence" includes all documents, papers, correspondence, books of account, and financial and corporate records.

"Acts to regulate commerce" means the Act entitled "An Act to regulate

[3] Auditing of accounts was made a duty of the General Accounting Office by the Act of June 10, 1921, 42 Stat. 24.

commerce," approved February 14, 1887, and all Acts amendatory thereof and supplementary thereto and the Communications Act of 1934 and all Acts amendatory thereof and supplementary thereto.

"Antitrust Acts," means the Act entitled "An Act to protect trade and commerce against unlawful restraints and monopolies," approved July 2, 1890; also sections 73 and 77 of an Act entitled "An Act to reduce taxation, to provide revenue for the Government, and for other purposes," approved August 27, 1894; also the Act entitled "An Act to amend sections 73 and 76 of the Act of August 27, 1894, entitled 'An Act to reduce taxation, to provide revenue for the Government, and for other purposes,'" approved February 12, 1913; and also the Act entitled "An Act to supplement existing laws against unlawful restraints and monopolies, and for other purposes," approved October 15, 1914.

Sec. 5. (a) (1) Unfair methods of competition in commerce, and unfair or deceptive acts or practices in commerce are declared unlawful.

(2) Nothing contained in this section or in any of the Antitrust Acts shall render unlawful any contracts or agreements prescribing minimum or stipulated prices, or requiring a vendee to enter into contracts or agreements prescribing minimum or stipulated prices, for the resale of a commodity which bears, or the label or container of which bears, the trade-mark, brand, or name of the producer or distributor of such commodity and which is in free and open competition with commodities of the same general class produced or distributed by others, when contracts or agreements of that description are lawful as applied to intrastate transactions under any statute, law, or public policy now or hereafter in effect in any State, Territory, or the District of Columbia in which such resale it to be made, or to which the commodity is to be transported for such resale.

(3) Nothing contained in this section or in any of the Antitrust Acts shall render unlawful the exercise or the enforcement of any right or right of action created by any statute, law, or public policy now or hereafter in effect in any State, Territory, or the District of Columbia, which in substance provides that willfully and knowingly advertising, offering for sale, or selling any commodity at less than the price or prices prescribed in such contracts or agreements whether the person so advertising, offering for sale, or selling is or is not a party to such a contract or agreement, is unfair competition and is actionable at the suit of any person damaged thereby.

(4) Neither the making of contracts or agreements as described in paragraph (2) of this subsection, nor the exercise or enforcement of any right or right of action as described in paragraph (3) of this subsection shall constitute an unlawful burden or restraint upon, or interference with, commerce.

(5) Nothing contained in paragraph (2) of this subsection shall make lawful contracts or agreements providing for the establishment or maintenance of minimum or stipulated resale prices on any commodity referred to in paragraph (2) of this subsection, between manufacturers, or between producers, or between wholesalers, or between brokers, or between factors, or between retailers, or between persons, firms, or corporations in competition with each other.

(6) The Commission is empowered and directed to prevent persons, partnerships, or corporations, except banks, common carriers subject to the Acts to regulate commerce, air carriers and foreign air carriers subject to the

Federal Aviation Act of 1958, and persons, partnerships, or corporations insofar as they are subject to the Packers and Stockyards Act, 1921, as amended, except as provided in section 406 (b) of said Act, from using unfair methods of competition in commerce and unfair or deceptive acts or practices in commerce.[4]

[4] Public No. 542, 82d Cong., Ch. 745, 2d Session, H.R. 5767, approved July 14, 1952 (the McGuire Act, 15 U.S.C. 45, 66 Stat. 631), amended Sec. 5(a) of this Act, by inserting in lieu thereof Sec. 5(a) (1) through (6).

Therefore, by subsection (f) of Section 1107, of the "Civil Aeronautics Act of 1938," approved June 23, 1938, Public No. 706, 75th Congress, Ch. 601, 3d Sess., S. 3845, 52 Stat. 1028, the language of former Sec. 5(a) was amended by inserting immediately following the words "to regulate commerce," the words "air carriers and foreign air carriers subject to the Civil Aeronautics Act of 1938," as above set out in Sec. 5(a) (6).

Public No. 85–909, 85th Cong., H.R. 9020, approved September 2, 1958, amended the Packers and Stockyards Act, 1921, as amended (7 U.S.C. 226, 227 and 72 Stat. 1749, 1750) by striking out subsection (b) of Section 406 and inserting in lieu thereof the following:

"(b) The Federal Trade Commission shall have power and jurisdiction over any matter involving meat, meat food products, livestock products in unmanufactured form of poultry products, which by this Act is made subject to the power or jurisdiction of the Secretary, as follows:

"(1) When the Secretary in the exercise of his duties of the Commission that it make investigations and reports in any case.

"(2) In any investigation of, or proceeding for the prevention of, an alleged violation of any act administered by the Commission, arising out of acts or transactions involving meat, meat products, livestock products in unmanufactured form, or poultry products, if the Commission determines that effective exercise of its power or jurisdiction with respect to retail sales of any such commodities is or will be impaired by the absence of power or jurisdiction over all acts or transactions involving such commodities in such investigation or proceeding. In order to avoid unnecessary duplication of effort by the Government and burdens upon the industry, the Commissioner shall notify the Secretary of such determination, the reasons therefor, and the acts or transactions involved, and shall not exercise power or jurisdiction with regard to acts or transactions (other than retail sales) involving such commodities if the Secretary within ten days from the date of receipt of the notice notifies the Commission that there is pending in his Department an investigation of, or proceeding for the prevention of, an alleged violation of this Act involving the same subject matter.

"(3) Over all transactions in commerce in margarine or oleomargarine and over retail sales of meat, meat food products, livestock products in unmanufactured form, and poultry products.

"(c) The Federal Trade Commission shall have no power or jurisdiction over any matter which by this Act is made subject to the jurisdiction of the Secretary, except as provided in subsection (b) of this section."

* * * * * *

The same Public Law also amended Subsection 6 of section 5(a) of the Federal Trade Commission Act (15 U.S.C. 45(a) (6) and 38 Stat. 719) by substituting "persons, partnerships, or corporations insofar as they are subject to the Packers and Stockyards Act, 1921, as amended, except as provided in section 406(b) of said Act" for "persons, partnerships, or corporations subject to the Packers and Stockyards Act, 1921, except as provided in section 406(b) of said Act."

(b) Whenever the Commission shall have reason to believe that any such person, partnership, or corporation has been or is using any unfair method of competition or unfair or deceptive act or practice in commerce, and if it shall appear to the Commission that a proceeding by it in respect thereof would be to the interest of the public, it shall issue and serve upon such person, partnership, or corporation a complaint stating its charges in that respect and containing a notice of a hearing upon a day and at a place therein fixed at least thirty days after the service of said complaint. The person, partnership, or corporation so complained of shall have the right to appear at the place and time so fixed and show cause why an order should not be entered by the Commission requiring such person, partnership, or corporation to cease and desist from the violation of the law so charged in said complaint. Any person, partnership, or corporation may make application, and upon good cause shown may be allowed by the Commission to intervene and appear in said proceeding by counsel or in person. The testimony in any such proceeding shall be reduced to writing and filed in the office of the Commission. If upon such hearing the Commission shall be of the opinion that the method of competition or the act or practice in question is prohibited by sections 41 to 46 and 47 to 58 of this title, it shall make a report in writing in which it shall state its findings as to the facts and shall issue and cause to be served on such person, partnership, or corporation an order requiring such person, partnership, or corporation to cease and desist from using such method of competition or such act or practice. Until the expiration of the time allowed for filing a petition for review, if no such petition has been duly filed within such time, or, if a petition for review has been filed within such time then until the record in the proceedings has been filed in a court of appeals of the United States, as hereinafter provided, the Commission may at any time, upon such notice and in such manner as it shall deem proper, modify or set aside, in whole or in part, any report or any order made or issued by it under this section.[5] After the expiration of the time allowed for filing a petition for review, if no such petition has been duly filed within such time, the Commission may at any time, after notice and opportunity for hearing, reopen and alter, modify, or set aside, in whole or in part, any report, or order made or issued by it under this section, whenever in the opinion of the Commission conditions of fact or of law have so changed as to require such action or if the public interest shall so require: *Provided, however,* That the said person, partnership, or corporation may, within sixty days after service upon him or it of said report or order entered after such a reopening, obtain a review thereof in the appropriate court of appeals of the United States, in the manner provided in subsection (c) of this section.

(c) Any person, partnership, or corporation required by an order of the Commission to cease and desist from using any method of competition or act or practice may obtain a review of such order in the court of appeals of the United States, within any circuit where the method of competition or the act or practice in question was used or where such person, partnership, or corporation resides or carries on business, by filing in the court, within sixty

[5] This sentence was amended by Public Law 85–791, 85th Cong., H.R. 6788, approved August 28, 1958, 72 Stat. 942.

days[6] from the date of the service of such order, a written petition praying that the order of the Commission be set aside. A copy of such petition shall be forthwith transmitted by the clerk of the court to the Commission, and thereupon the Commission shall file in the court the record in the proceeding, as provided in section 2112 of Title 28. Upon such filing of the petition the court shall have jurisdiction of the proceeding and of the question determined therein concurrently with the Commission until the filing of the record and shall have power to make and enter a decree affirming, modifying, or setting aside the order of the Commission, and enforcing the same to the extent that such order is affirmed and to issue such writs as are ancillary to its jurisdiction or are necessary in its judgment to prevent injury to the public or to competitors pendente lite.[7] The findings of the Commission as to the facts, if supported by evidence, shall be conclusive. To the extent that the order of the Commission is affirmed, the court shall thereupon issue its own order commanding obedience to the terms of such order of the Commission. If either party shall apply to the court for leave to adduce additional evidence, and shall show to the satisfaction of the court that such additional evidence is material and that there were reasonable grounds for the failure to adduce such evidence in the proceeding before the Commission, the court may order such additional evidence to be taken before the Commission and to be adduced upon the hearing in such manner and upon such terms and conditions as to the court may seem proper. The Commission may modify its findings as to the facts, or make new findings, by reason of the additional evidence so taken, and it shall file such modified or new findings, which, if supported by evidence, shall be conclusive, and its recommendation, if any, for the modification or setting aside of its original order, with the return of such additional evidence. The judgment and decree of the court shall be final, except that the same shall be subject to review by the Supreme Court upon certiorari, as provided in section 347 of Title 28.

(d) Upon the filing of the record with it the jurisdiction of the court of appeals of the United States to affirm, enforce, modify, or set aside orders of the Commission shall be exclusive.[8]

(e) Such proceedings in the court of appeals shall be given precedence over other cases pending therein, and shall be in every way expedited. No order of the Commission or judgment of court to enforce the same shall in anywise relieve or absolve any person, partnership, or corporation from any liability under the Antitrust Acts.

(f) Complaints, orders, and other processes of the Commission under this section may be served by anyone duly authorized by the Commission, either (a) by delivering a copy thereof to the person to be served, or to a member of the partnership to be served, or the president, secretary, or other executive officer or a director of the corporation to be served; or (b) by leaving a copy

[6] Section 5(a) of the amending Act of 1938 provides:

Sec. 5. (a) In case of an order by the Federal Trade Commission to cease and desist, served on or before the date of the enactment of this Act, the sixty-day period referred to in sections 5(c) of the Federal Trade Commission Act, as amended by this Act, shall begin on the date of the enactment of this Act.

[7] The above two sentences were also amended by Public Law 85–791.

[8] The above section was also amended by Public Law 85–791.

thereof at the residence or principal office or place of business of such person, partnership, or corporation; or (c) by mailing a copy thereof by registered mail or by certified mail addressed to such person, partnership, or corporation at his or its residence or principal office or place of business. The verified return by the person so serving said complaint, order, or other process setting forth the manner of said service shall be proof of the same, and the return post office receipt for said complaint, order, or other process mailed by registered mail or by certified mail as aforesaid shall be proof of the service of the same.

(g) An order of the Commission to cease and desist shall become final—

(1) Upon the expiration of the time allowed for filing a petition for review, if no such petition has been duly filed within such time; but the Commission may thereafter modify or set aside its order to the extent provided in the last sentence of subsection (b); or

(2) Upon the expiration of the time allowed for filing a petition for certiorari, if the order of the Commission has been affirmed, or the petition for review dismissed by the court of appeals, and no petition for certiorari has been duly filed; or

(3) Upon the denial of a petition for certiorari, if the order of the Commission has been affirmed or the petition for review dismissed by the court of appeals; or

(4) Upon the expiration of thirty days from the date of issuance of the mandate of the Supreme Court, if such Court directs that the order of the Commission be affirmed or the petition for review dismissed.

(h) If the Supreme Court directs that the order of the Commission be modified or set aside, the order of the Commission rendered in accordance with the mandate of the Supreme Court shall become final upon the expiration of thirty days from the time it was rendered, unless within such thirty days either party has instituted proceedings to have such order corrected to accord with the mandate, in which event the order of the Commission shall become final when so corrected.

(i) If the order of the Commission is modified or set aside by the court of appeals, and if (1) the time allowed for filing a petition for certiorari has expired and no such petition has been duly filed, or (2) the petition for certiorari has been denied, or (3) the decision of the court has been affirmed by the Supreme Court, then the order of the Commission rendered in accordance with the mandate of the court of appeals shall become final on the expiration of thirty days from the time such order of the Commission was rendered, unless within such thirty days either party has instituted proceedings to have such order corrected so that it will accord with the mandate, in which event the order of the Commission shall become final when so corrected.

(j) If the Supreme Court orders a rehearing; or if the case is remanded by the court of appeals to the Commission for a rehearing, and if (1) the time allowed for filing a petition for certiorari has expired, and no such petition has been duly filed, or (2) the petition for certiorari has been denied, or (3) the decision of the court has been affirmed by the Supreme Court, then the order of the Commission rendered upon such rehearing shall become final in the same manner as though no prior order of the Commission had been rendered.

(k) As used in this section the term "mandate," in case a mandate has been recalled prior to the expiration of thirty days from the date of issuance thereof, means the final mandate.

(l) Any person, partnership, or corporation who violates an order of the Commission to cease and desist after it has become final, and while such order is in effect, shall forfeit and pay to the United States a civil penalty of not more than $5,000 for each violation, which shall accrue to the United States and may be recovered in a civil action brought by the United States. Each separate violation of such an order shall be a separate offense, except that in the case of a violation through continuing failure or neglect to obey a final order of the Commission each day of continuance of such failure or neglect shall be deemed a separate offense.[9]

Sec. 6. The commission shall also have power[10]—

(a) To gather and compile information concerning, and to investigate from time to time the organization, business, conduct, practices, and management of any corporation engaged in commerce, excepting banks and common carriers subject to the Act to regulate commerce, and its relation to other corporations and to individuals, associations, and partnerships.

(b) To require, by general or special orders, corporations engaged in commerce, excepting banks and common carriers subject to the Act to regulate commerce, or any class of them, or any of them, respectively, to file with the commission in such form as the commission may prescribe annual or special, or both annual and special, reports or answers in writing to specific questions, furnishing to the commission such information as it may require as to the organization, business, conduct, practices, management, and relation to other corporations, partnerships, and individuals of the respective corporations filing such reports or answers in writing. Such reports and answers shall be made under oath, or otherwise, as the commission may prescribe, and shall be filed with the commission within such reasonable period as the commission may prescribe, unless additional time be granted in any case by the commission.

(c) Whenever a final decree has been entered against any defendant corporation in any suit brought by the United States to prevent and restrain any violation of the antitrust Acts, to make investigation, upon its own initiative, of the manner in which the decree has been or is being carried out, and upon the application of the Attorney General it shall be its duty to make such investigation. It shall transmit to the Attorney General a report embodying its findings and recommendations as a result of any such investigation, and the report shall be made public in the discretion of the commission.

(d) Upon the direction of the President or either House of Congress to

[9] Foregoing sentence added by subsection (c) of Sec. 4, Public No. 459, 81st Congress. (See footnote 1.)

[10] Public No. 78, 73d Cong., approved June 16, 1933, making appropriations for the fiscal year ending June 30, 1934, for the "Executive Office and sundry independent bureaus, boards, commissions," etc., made the appropriation for the Commission contingent upon the provision (48 Stat. 291; 15 U.S.C.A., Sec. 46a) that "hereafter no new investigations shall be initiated by the Commission as the result of a legislative resolution, except the same be a concurrent resolution of the two Houses of Congress."

investigate and report the facts relating to any alleged violations of the antitrust Acts by any corporation.

(e) Upon the application of the Attorney General to investigate and make recommendations for the readjustment of the business of any corporation alleged to be violating the antitrust Acts in order that the corporation may thereafter maintain its organization, management, and conduct of business in accordance with law.

(f) To make public from time to time such portions of the information obtained by it hereunder, except trade secrets and names of customers, as it shall deem expedient in the public interest; and to make annual and special reports to the Congress and to submit therewith recommendations for additional legislation; and to provide for the publication of its reports and decisions in such form and manner as may be best adapted for public information and use.

(g) From time to time to classify corporations and to make rules and regulations for the purpose of carrying out the provisions of sections 41 to 46 and 47 to 58 of this title.

(h) To investigate, from time to time, trade conditions in and with foreign countries where associations, combinations, or practices of manufacturers, merchants, or traders, or other conditions, may affect the foreign trade of the United States, and to report to Congress thereon, with such recommendations as it deems advisable.

Sec. 7. In any suit in equity brought by or under the direction of the Attorney General as provided in the antitrust Acts, the court may, upon the conclusion of the testimony therein, if it shall be then of opinion that the complainant is entitled to relief, refer said suit to the commission, as a master in chancery, to ascertain and report an appropriate form of decree therein. The commission shall proceed upon such notice to the parties and under such rules of procedure as the court may prescribe, and upon the coming in of such report such exceptions may be filed and such proceedings had in relation thereto as upon the report of a master in other equity causes, but the court may adopt or reject such report, in whole or in part, and enter such decree as the nature of the case may in its judgment require.

Sec. 8. The several departments and bureaus of the Government when directed by the President shall furnish the commission, upon its request, all records, papers, and information in their possession relating to any corporation subject to any of the provisions of sections 41 to 46 and 47 to 58 of this title, and shall detail from time to time such officials and employees to the commission as he may direct.

Sec. 9. For the purposes of sections 41 to 46 and 47 to 58 of this title the commission, or its duly authorized agent or agents, shall at all reasonable times have access to, for the purpose of examination, and the right to copy any documentary evidence of any corporation being investigated or proceeded against; and the commission shall have power to require by subpoena the attendance and testimony of witnesses and the production of all such documentary evidence relating to any matter under investigation. Any member of the commission may sign subpoenas, and members and examiners of the commission may administer oaths and affirmations, examine witnesses, and receive evidence.

Such attendance of witnesses, and the production of such documentary evidence, may be required from any place in the United States, at any designated place of hearing. And in case of disobedience to a subpoena the commission may invoke the aid of any court of the United States in requiring the attendance and testimony of witnesses and the production of documentary evidence.

Any of the district courts of the United States within the jurisdiction of which such inquiry is carried on may, in case of contumacy or refusal to obey a subpoena issued to any corporation or other person, issue an order requiring such corporation or other person to appear before the commission, or to produce documentary evidence if so ordered, or to give evidence touching the matter in question; and any failure to obey such order of the court may be punished by such court as a contempt thereof.

Upon the application of the Attorney General of the United States, at the request of the commission, the district courts of the United States shall have jurisdiction to issue writs of mandamus commanding any person or corporation to comply with the provisions of sections 41 to 46 and 47 to 58 of this title or any order of the commission made in pursuance thereof.

The commission may order testimony to be taken by deposition in any proceeding or investigation pending under said sections at any stage of such proceeding or investigation. Such depositions may be taken before any person designated by the commission and having power to administer oaths. Such testimony shall be reduced to writing by the person taking the deposition, or under his direction, and shall then be subscribed by the deponent. Any person may be compelled to appear and depose and to produce documentary evidence in the same manner as witnesses may be compelled to appear and testify and produce documentary evidence before the commission as hereinbefore provided.

Witnesses summoned before the commission shall be paid the same fees and mileage that are paid witnesses in the courts of the United States, and witnesses whose depositions are taken, and the persons taking the same shall severally be entitled to the same fees as are paid for like services in the courts of the United States.

Sec. 10. Any person who shall neglect or refuse to attend and testify, or to answer any lawful inquiry, or to produce documentary evidence, if in his power to do so, in obedience to the subpoena or lawful requirement of the commission, shall be guilty of an offense and upon conviction thereof by a court of competent jurisdiction shall be punished by a fine of not less than $1,000 nor more than $5,000, or by imprisonment for not more than one year, or by both such fine and imprisonment.

Any person who shall willfully make, or cause to be made, any false entry or statement of fact in any report required to be made under sections 41 to 46 and 47 to 58 of this title, or who shall willfully make, or cause to be made, any false entry in any account, record, or memorandum kept by any corporation subject to this Act, or who shall willfully neglect or fail to make, or cause to be made, full, true, and correct entries in such accounts, records, or memoranda of all facts and transactions appertaining to the business of such corporation, or who shall willfully remove out of the jurisdiction of the United States, or willfully mutilate, alter, or by any other means falsify any documentary evidence of such corporation, or who shall willfully refuse to submit to the commission or to any of its authorized agents, for the purpose of inspection and taking copies, any documentary evidence of such corporation in his possession or within his control, shall be deemed guilty of an offense against the United States, and shall be subject, upon conviction in any court of the United States of competent jurisdiction, to a fine of not less than $1,000 nor more than $5,000 or to imprisonment for a term of not more than three years, or to both such fine and imprisonment.

If any corporation required by sections 41 to 46 and 47 to 58 of this title to file any annual or special report shall fail so to do within the time fixed by the commission for filing the same, and such failure shall continue for thirty days after notice of such default, the corporation shall forfeit to the United States the sum of $100 for each and every day of the continuance of such failure, which forfeiture shall be payable into the Treasury of the United States, and shall be recoverable in a civil suit in the name of the United States brought in the district where the corporation has its principal office or in any district in which it shall do business. It shall be the duty of the various United States attorneys, under the direction of the Attorney General of the United States, to prosecute for the recovery of forfeitures. The costs and expenses of such prosecution shall be paid out of the appropriation for the expenses of the courts of the United States.

Any officer or employee of the commission who shall make public any information obtained by the commission without its authority, unless directed by a court, shall be deemed guilty of a misdemeanor, and, upon conviction thereof, shall be punished by a fine not exceeding $5,000, or by imprisonment not exceeding one year, or by fine and imprisonment, in the discretion of the court.

Sec. 11. Nothing contained in sections 41 to 46 and 47 to 58 of this title shall be construed to prevent or interfere with the enforcement of the provisions of the antitrust Acts or the Acts to regulate commerce, nor shall anything contained in the Act be construed to alter, modify, or repeal the said antitrust Acts or the Acts to regulate commerce or any part or parts thereof.

Sec. 12. (a) It shall be unlawful for any person, partnership, or corporation to disseminate, or cause to be disseminated, any false advertisement—

(1) By United States mails, or in commerce by any means, for the purpose of inducing, or which is likely to induce, directly or indirectly the purchase of food, drugs, devices or cosmetics; or

(2) By any means, for the purpose of inducing, or which is likely to induce, directly or indirectly, the purchase in commerce of food, drugs, devices, or cosmetics.

(b) The dissemination or the causing to be disseminated of any false advertisement within the provisions of subsection (a) of this section shall be an unfair or deceptive act or practice in commerce within the meaning of section 45 of this title.

Sec. 13. (a) Whenever the Commission has reason to believe—

(1) that any person, partnership, or corporation is engaged in, or is about to engage in, the dissemination or the causing of the dissemination of any advertisement in violation of section 52 of this title, and

(2) that the enjoining thereof pending the issuance of a complaint by the Commission under section 45 of this title, and until such complaint is dismissed by the Commission or set aside by the court on review,

or the order of the Commission to cease and desist made thereon has become final within the meaning of section 45 of this title, would be to the interest of the public,

the Commission by any of its attorneys designated by it for such purpose may bring suit in a district court of the United States or in the United States court of any Territory, to enjoin the dissemination or the causing of the dissemination of such advertisement. Upon proper showing a temporary injunction or restraining order shall be granted without bond. Any such suit shall be brought in the district in which such person, partnership, or corporation resides or transacts business.

(b) Whenever it appears to the satisfaction of the court in the case of a newspaper, magazine, periodical, or other publication, published at regular intervals—

(1) that restraining the dissemination of a false advertisement in any particular issue of such publication would delay the delivery of such issues after the regular time therefor, and
(2) that such delay would be due to the method by which the manufacture and distribution of such publication is customarily conducted by the publisher in accordance with sound business practice, and not to any method or device adopted for the evasion of this section or to prevent or delay the issuance of an injunction or restraining order with respect to such false advertisement or any other advertisement,

the court shall exclude such issue from the operation of the restraining order or injunction.

Sec. 14. (a) Any person, partnership, or corporation who violates any provision of section 52(a) of this title shall, if the use of the commodity advertised may be injurious to health because of results from such use under the conditions prescribed in the advertisement thereof, or under such conditions as are customary or usual, or if such violation is with intent to defraud or mislead, be guilty of a misdemeanor, and upon conviction shall be punished by a fine of not more than $5,000 or by imprisonment for not more than six months, or by both such fine or imprisonment, except that if the conviction is for a violation committed after a first conviction of such person, partnership, or corporation, for any violation of such section, punishment shall be by a fine of not more than $10,000 or by imprisonment for not more than one year, or by both such fine and imprisonment: *Provided,* That for the purposes of this section meats and meat food products duly inspected, marked, and labeled in accordance with rules and regulations issued under the Meat Inspection Act shall be conclusively presumed not injurious to health at the time the same leave official "establishments."[11]

(b) No publisher, radio-broadcast licensee, or agency or medium for the dissemination of advertising, except the manufacturer, packer, distributor, or seller of the commodity to which the false advertisement relates, shall be liable

[11] Section 5(b) of the amending Act of 1938 provides:

Sec. 5. (b) Section 14 of the Federal Trade Commission Act, added to such Act by section 4 of this Act, shall take effect on the expiration of sixty days after the date of the enactment of this Act.

under this section by reason of the dissemination by him of false advertisement, unless he has refused, on the request of the Commission, to furnish the Commission the name and post-office address of the manufacturer, packer, distributor, or advertising agency, residing in the United States, who caused him to disseminate such advertisement. No advertising agency shall be liable under this section by reason of the causing by it of the dissemination of any false advertisement, unless it has refused, on the request of the Commission, to furnish the Commission the name and post-office address of the manufacturer, packer, distributor, or seller, residing in the United States, who caused it to cause the dissemination of such advertisement.

Sec. 15. For the purposes of sections 52 to 54 of this title—

(a) (1) The term "false advertisement" means an advertisement, other than labeling, which is misleading in a material respect; and in determining whether any advertisement is misleading, there shall be taken into account (among other things) not only representations made or suggested by statement, word, design, device, sound, or any combination thereof, but also the extent to which the advertisement fails to reveal facts material in the light of such representations or material with respect to consequences which may result from the use of the commodity to which the advertisement relates under the conditions prescribed in said advertisement, or under such conditions as are customary or usual. No advertisement of a drug shall be deemed to be false if it is disseminated only to members of the medical profession, contains no false representation of a material fact, and includes, or is accompanied in each instance by truthful disclosure of, the formula showing quantitatively each ingredient of such drug.

(2) In the case of oleomargarine or margarine an advertisement shall be deemed misleading in a material respect if in such advertisement representations are made or suggested by statement, word, grade designation, design, device, symbol, sound, or any combination thereof, that such oleomargarine or margarine is a dairy product, except that nothing contained herein shall prevent a truthful, accurate, and full statement in any such advertisement of all the ingredients contained in such oleomargarine or margarine.[12]

(b) The term "food" means (1) articles used for food or drink for man or other animals, (2) chewing gum, and (3) articles used by components of any such article.

(c) The term "drug" means (1) articles recognized in the official United States Pharmacopoeia, official Homoeopathic Pharmacopoeia of the United States, or official National Formulary, or any supplement to any of them; and (2) articles intended for use in the diagnosis, cure, mitigation, treatment, or prevention of disease in man or other animals; and (3) articles (other than food) intended to affect the structure or any function of the body of man or other animals; and (4) articles intended for use as a component of any article specified in clause (1), (2), or (3); but does not include devices or their components, parts, or accessories.

(d) The term "device" (except when used in subsection (a) of this section)

[12] Subsection (a) of Sec. 4 of Public No. 459, 81st Congress (see footnote 1), amended sec. 15 of this Act by inserting "(1)" after the letter "(a)" in subsection (a) above, and by adding at the end of such subsection new paragraph (2), above set out.

means instruments, apparatus, and contrivances, including their parts and accessories, intended (1) for use in the diagnosis, cure, mitigation, treatment, or prevention of disease in man or other animals; or (2) to affect the structure or any function of the body of man or other animals.

(e) The term "cosmetic" means (1) articles to be rubbed, poured, sprinkled, or sprayed on, introduced into, or otherwise applied to the human body or any part thereof intended for cleansing, beautifying, promoting attractiveness, or altering the appearance, and (2) articles intended for use as a component of any such article; except that such term shall not include soap.

(f) For the purposes of this section and section 34F of Title 21, the term "oleomargarine" or "margarine" includes—

(1) all substances, mixtures, and compounds known as oleomargarine or margarine;

(2) all substances, mixtures, and compounds which have a consistence similar to that of butter and which contain any edible oils or fats other than milk fat if made in imitation or semblance of butter.[13]

Sec. 16. Whenever the Federal Trade Commission has reason to believe that any person, partnership, or corporation is liable to a penalty under section 54 of this title or under subsection (*L*) of section 45 of this title, it shall certify the facts to the Attorney General, whose duty it shall be to cause appropriate proceedings to be brought for the enforcement of the provisions of such section or subsection.

Sec. 17. If any provision of sections 41 to 46 and 47 to 58 of this title, or the application thereof to any person, partnership, corporation, or circumstance, is held invalid, the remainder of the said sections, and the application of such provision to any other person, partnership, corporation, or circumstance, shall not be affected thereby.

Sec. 18. Sections 41 to 46 and 47 to 58 of this title may be cited as the "Federal Trade Commission Act."

Original approved September 26, 1914.

Amended and approved March 21, 1938.[14]

[13] Subsection (b) of Sec. 4 of Public No. 459, 81st Congress (see footnote 1) further amended sec. 15 of this Act, by adding at the end thereof the new subsection (f) as above set out.

[14] See footnote 1.

CLAYTON ACT (INCLUDING THE ROBINSON-PATMAN AMENDMENT)

Public—No. 212—63rd Congress, As Amended by Public—No. 692—74th Congress,[1] Public—No. 899—81st Congress and Public Law 86-107, 86th Congress
H. R. 15657

An Act to supplement existing laws against unlawful restraints and monopolies, and for other purposes

Be it enacted by the Senate and House of Representatives of the United States of America in Congress assembled, "antitrust laws," as used herein, includes the Act entitled "An Act to protect trade and commerce against unlawful restraints and monopolies," approved July second, eighteen hundred and ninety; sections seventy-three to seventy-seven, inclusive, of an Act entitled "An Act to reduce taxation, to provide revenue for the Government, and for other purposes," of August twenty-seventh, eighteen hundred and ninety-four; and Act entitled "An Act to amend sections seventy-three and seventy-six of the Act of August twenty-seventh, eighteen hundred and ninety-four, entitled 'An Act to reduce taxation, to provide revenue for the Government, and for other purposes,' " approved February twelfth, nineteen hundred and thirteen; and also this Act.

"Commerce," as used herein, means trade or commerce among the several States and with foreign nations, or between the District of Columbia or any Territory of the United States and any State, Territory or foreign nation, or between any insular possessions or other places under the jurisdiction of the United States, or between any such possession or place and any State or Territory of the United States or the District of Columbia or any foreign nation, or within the District of Columbia or any Territory or any insular possession or other place under the jurisdiction of the United States: *Provided,* That nothing in this Act contained shall apply to the Philippine Islands.

The word "person" or "persons" wherever used in this Act shall be deemed to include corporations and associations existing under or authorized by the laws of either the United States, the laws of any of the Territories, the laws of any State, or the laws of any foreign country.

Sec. 2. (a) That it shall be unlawful for any person engaged in commerce, in the course of such commerce, either directly or indirectly, to discriminate in price between different purchasers of commodities of like grade and quality, where either or any of the purchases involved in such discrimination are in commerce, where such commodities are sold for use, consumption, or resale within the United States or any Territory thereof or the District of Columbia

[1] The Robinson-Patman Act (see footnote 2). See also footnote 5 and footnote 10, with respect to the repeal of Section 9, Section 17 in part, Sections 18 and 19, and Sections 21–25, inclusive, by two acts of June 25, 1948, namely, C. 645 (62 Stat. 683) and C. 646 (62 Stat. 896); and footnotes 4 and 6 concerning the amendment of Sections 7 and 11 by act of December 29, 1950, C. 1184 (64 Stat. 1125).

or any insular possession or other place under the jurisdiction of the United States, and where the effect of such discrimination may be substantially to lessen competition or tend to create a monopoly in any line of commerce, or to injure, destroy, or prevent competition with any person who either grants or knowingly receives the benefit of such discrimination, or with customers of either of them: *Provided,* That nothing herein contained shall prevent differentials which make only due allowances for differences in the cost of manufacture, sale, or delivery resulting from the differing methods or quantities in which such commodities are to such purchasers sold or delivered: *Provided, however,* That the Federal Trade Commission may, after due investigation and hearing to all interested parties, fix and establish quantity limits, and revise the same as it finds necessary, as to particular commodities or classes of commodities, where it finds that available purchasers in greater quantities are so few as to render differentials on account thereof unjustly discriminatory or promotive of monopoly in any line of commerce; and the foregoing shall then not be construed to permit differentials based on differences in quantities greater than those so fixed and established: *And provided further,* That nothing herein contained shall prevent persons engaged in selling goods, wares, or merchandise in commerce from selecting their own customers in bona fide transactions and not in restraint of trade: *And provided further,* That nothing herein contained shall prevent price changes from time to time where in response to changing conditions affecting the market for or the marketability of the goods concerned, such as but not limited to actual or imminent deterioration of perishable goods, obsolescence of seasonal goods, distress sales under court process, or sales in good faith in discontinuance of business in the goods concerned.[2]

(b) Upon proof being made, at any hearing on a complaint under this section, that there has been discrimination in price or services or facilities furnished, the burden of rebutting the prima facie case thus made by showing justification shall be upon the person charged with a violation of this section, and unless justification shall be affirmatively shown, the Commission is authorized to issue an order terminating the discrimination: *Provided, however,* That nothing herein contained shall prevent a seller rebutting the prima facie case thus made by showing that his lower price or the furnishing of services or facilities to any purchaser or purchasers was made in good faith to meet an equally low price of a competitor, or the services or facilities furnished by a competitor.

(c) That it shall be unlawful for any person engaged in commerce, in the course of such commerce, to pay or grant, or to receive or accept, anything of

[2] This section of the Clayton Act contains the provisions of the Robinson-Patman Anti-Discrimination Act, approved June 19, 1936, amending Section 2 of the original Clayton Act, approved October 15, 1914.

Section 4 of said Act provides that nothing therein "shall prevent a cooperative association from returning to its members, producers or consumers the whole, or any part of, the neat earnings or surplus resulting from its trading operations, in proportion to their purchases or sales from, to, or through the association.

Public No. 550, 75th Congress, approved May 26, 1938, to amend the said Robinson-Patman Act, further provides that nothing therein "shall apply to purchases of their supplies for their own use by schools, colleges, universities, public libraries, churches, hospitals, and charitable institutions not operated for profit."

value as a commission, brokerage, or other compensation, or any allowance or discount in lieu thereof, except for services rendered in connection with the sale or purchase of goods, wares, or merchandise, either to the other party to such transaction or to an agent, representative, or other intermediary therein where such intermediary is acting in fact for or in behalf, or is subject to the direct or indirect control, of any party to such transaction other than the person by whom such compensation is so granted or paid.

(d) That it shall be unlawful for any person engaged in commerce to pay or contract for the payment of anything of value to or for the benefit of a customer of such person in the course of such commerce as compensation or in consideration for any services or facilities furnished by or through such customer in connection with the processing, handling, sale, or offering for sale of any products or commodities manufactured, sold, or offered for sale by such person, unless such payment or consideration is available on proportionally equal terms to all other customers competing in the distribution of such products or commodities.

(e) That it shall be unlawful for any person to discriminate in favor of one purchaser against another purchaser or purchasers of a commodity bought for resale, with or without processing, by contracting to furnish or furnishing, or by contributing to the furnishing of, any services or facilities connected with the processing, handling, sale, or offering for sale of such commodity so purchased upon terms not accorded to all purchases on proportionally equal terms.

(f) That it shall be unlawful for any person engaged in commerce, in the course of such commerce, knowingly to induce or receive a discrimination in price which is prohibited by this section.

Sec. 3. That it shall be unlawful for any person engaged in commerce, in the course of such commerce, to lease or make a sale or contract for sale of goods, wares, merchandise, machinery, supplies or other commodities, whether patented or unpatented, for use, consumption or resale within the United States or any Territory thereof or the District of Columbia or any insular possession or other place under the jurisdiction of the United States, or fix a price charged therefor, or discount from, or rebate upon, such price, on the condition, agreement, or understanding that the lessee or purchaser thereof shall not use or deal in the goods, wares, merchandise, machinery, supplies, or other commodities of a competitor or competitors of the lessor or seller, where the effect of such lease, sale, or contract for sale or such condition, agreement or understanding may be to substantially lessen competition or tend to create a monopoly in any line of commerce.

Sec. 4. That any person who shall be injured in his business or property by reason of anything forbidden in the antitrust laws may sue therefor in any district court of the United States in the district in which the defendant resides or is found or has an agent, without respect to the amount of controversy, and shall recover threefold the damages by him sustained, and the cost of suit, including a reasonable attorney's fee.

Sec. 4A. Whenever the United States is hereafter injured in its business or property by reason of anything forbidden in the antitrust laws it may sue therefor in the United States district court for the district in which the defendant resides or is found or has an agent, without respect to the amount in controversy, and shall recover actual damages by it sustained and the cost of suit.[3]

Sec. 4B. Any action to enforce any cause of action under Section 4 or 4A shall be forever barred unless commenced within four years after the cause of action accrued. No cause of action barred under existing law on the effective date of this Act shall be revived by this Act.

Sec. 5. (a) A final judgment or decree heretofore or hereafter rendered in any civil or criminal proceeding brought by or on behalf of the United States under the antitrust laws to the effect that a defendant has violated said laws shall be prima facie evidence against such defendant in any action or proceeding brought by any other party against such defendant under said laws or by the United States under section 15a of this title, as to all matters respecting which said judgment or decree would be an estoppel as between the parties thereto: *Provided,* That this section shall not apply to consent judgments or decrees entered before any testimony has been taken or to judgments or decrees entered in actions under section 15a of this title.

(b) Whenever any civil or criminal proceeding is instituted by the United States to prevent, restrain, or punish violations of any of the antitrust laws, but not including an action under section 15a of this title, the running of the statute of limitations in respect of every private right of action arising under said laws and based in whole or in part on any matter complained of in said proceeding shall be suspended during the pendency thereof and for one year thereafter: *Provided, however,* That whenever the running of the statute of limitations in respect of a cause of action arising under section 15 of this title is suspended hereunder, any action to enforce such cause of action shall be forever barred unless commenced either within the period of suspension or within four years after the cause of action accrued.

Sec. 6. That the labor of a human being is not a commodity or article of commerce. Nothing contained in the antitrust laws shall be construed to forbid the existence and operation of labor, agricultural, or horticultural organizations, instituted for the purposes of mutual help, and not having capital stock or conducted for profit, or to forbid or restrain individual members of such organizations from lawfully carrying out the legitimate objects thereof; nor shall such organizations, or the members thereof, be held or construed to be illegal combinations or conspiracies in restraint of trade, under the antitrust laws.

Sec. 7. That no corporation engaged in commerce shall acquire, directly or indirectly, the whole or any part of the stock or other share capital and no corporation subject to the jurisdiction of the Federal Trade Commission shall acquire the whole or any part of the assets of another corporation engaged also in commerce, where in any line of commerce in any section of the country, the effect of such acquisition may be substantially to lessen competition, or to tend to create a monopoly.

No corporation shall acquire, directly or indirectly, the whole or any part of the stock or other share capital and no corporation subject to the jurisdiction of the Federal Trade Commission shall acquire the whole or any part of the assets of one or more corporations engaged in commerce, where in any line of commerce in any section of the country, the effect of such acquisition, of such

[3] Sec. 4A, 4B, 5(a) and 5(b) were added by Pub. Law 137, approved July 7, 1955, 69 Stat. 282, 283.

stocks or assets, or of the use of such stock by the voting or granting of proxies or otherwise, may be substantially to lessen competition, or to tend to create a monopoly.

This section shall not apply to corporations purchasing such stock solely for investment and not using the same by voting or otherwise to bring about, or in attempting to bring about, the substantial lessening of competition. Nor shall anything contained in this section prevent a corporation engaged in commerce from causing the formation of subsidiary corporations for the actual carrying on of their immediate lawful business, or the natural and legitimate branches or extensions thereof, or from owning and holding all or a part of the stock of such subsidiary corporations, when the effect of such formation is not to substantially lessen competition.

Nor shall anything herein contained be construed to prohibit any common carrier subject to the laws to regulate commerce from aiding in the construction of branches or short lines so located as to become feeders to the main line of the company so aiding in such construction or from acquiring or owning all or any part of the stock of such branch lines, nor to prevent any such common carrier from acquiring and owning all or any part of the stock of a branch or short line constructed by an independent company where there is no substantial competition between the company owning the branch line so constructed and the company owning the main line acquiring the property or an interest therein, nor to prevent such common carrier from extending any of its lines through the medium of the acquisition of stock or otherwise of any other common carrier where there is no substantial competition between the company extending its lines and the company whose stock, property, or an interest therein is so acquired.

Nothing contained in this section shall be held to affect or impair any right heretofore legally acquired: *Provided,* That nothing in this section shall be held or construed to authorize or make lawful anything heretofore prohibited or made illegal by the antitrust laws, nor to exempt any person from the penal provisions thereof or the civil remedies therein provided.

Nothing contained in this section shall apply to transactions duly consummated pursuant to authority given by the Civil Aeronautics Board, Federal Communications Commission, Federal Power Commission, Interstate Commerce Commission, the Securities and Exchange Commission in the exercise of its jurisdiction under section 79J of this title, the United States Maritime Commission, or the Secretary of Agriculture under any statutory provision vesting such power in such Commission, Secretary, or Board.[4]

Sec. 8. No private banker or director, officer, or employee of any member bank of the Federal Reserve System or any branch thereof shall be at the same time a director, officer, or employee of any other bank, banking association, savings bank, or trust company organized under the National Bank Act or organized under the laws of any State or of the District of Columbia, or any branch thereof, except that the Board of Governors of the Federal Reserve System may by regulation permit such service as a director, officer, or employee of not more than one other such institution or branch thereof; but the fore-

[4] This section, and also section 11, which amend the respective sections of the Clayton Act, were enacted by Act of Dec. 29, 1950 (P.L., 899; 64 Stat. 1125; 15 U.S.C. 18).

going prohibition shall not apply in the case of any one or more of the following or any branch thereof:

(1) A bank, banking association, savings bank, or trust company, more than 90 per centum of the stock of which is owned directly or indirectly by the United States or by a corporation of which the United States directly or indirectly owns more than 90 per centum of the stock.

(2) A bank, banking association, savings bank, or trust company which has been placed formally in liquidation or which is in the hands of a receiver, conservator, or other official exercising similar functions.

(3) A corporation, principally engaged in international or foreign banking or banking in a dependency or insular possession of the United States which has entered into an agreement with the Board of Governors of the Federal Reserve System pursuant to section 601 to 604A of Title 12.

(4) A bank, banking association, savings bank, or trust company, more than 50 per centum of the common stock of which is owned directly or indirectly by persons who own directly or indirectly more than 50 per centum of the common stock of such member bank.

(5) A bank, banking association, savings bank, or trust company not located and having no branch in the same city, town, or village as that in which such member bank or any branch thereof is located, or in any city, town, or village contiguous or adjacent thereto.

(6) A bank, banking association, savings bank, or trust company not engaged in a class or classes of business in which such member bank is engaged.

(7) A mutual savings bank having no capital stock.

Until February 1, 1939, nothing in this section shall prohibit any director, officer, or employee of any member bank of the Federal Reserve System, or any branch thereof, who is lawfully serving at the same time as a private banker or as a director, officer, or employee of any other bank, banking association, savings bank, or trust company, or any branch thereof, on the date of enactment of the Banking Act of 1935, from continuing such service.

The Board of Governors of the Federal Reserve System is authorized and directed to enforce compliance with this section, and to prescribe such rules and regulations as it deems necessary for that purpose.

No person at the same time shall be a director in any two or more corporations, any one of which has capital, surplus, and undivided profits aggregating more than $1,000,000, engaged in whole or in part in commerce, other than banks, banking associations, trust companies, and common carriers subject to the Act to regulate commerce, approved February fourth, eighteen hundred and eighty-seven, if such corporations are or shall have been theretofore, by virtue of their business and location of operation, competitors, so that the elimination of competition by agreement between them would constitute a violation of any of the provisions of any of the antitrust laws. The eligibility of a director under the foregoing provision shall be determined by the aggregate amount of the capital, surplus, and undivided profits, exclusive of dividends declared but not paid to stockholders, at the end of the fiscal year of said corporation next preceding the election of directors, and when a director has been elected in accordance with the provisions of this Act it shall be lawful for him to continue as such for one year thereafter.

When any person elected or chosen as a director or officer or selected as an employee of any bank or other corporation subject to the provisions of this Act is eligible at the time of his election or selection to act for such bank or other corporation in such capacity his eligibility to act in such capacity shall not be affected and he shall not become or be deemed amenable to any of the provisions hereof by reason of any change in the affairs of such bank or other corporation from whatsoever cause, whether specifically excepted by any of the provisions hereof or not, until the expiration of one year from the date of his election or employment.

Sec. 9. Every president, director, officer or manager of any firm, association or corporation engaged in commerce as a common carrier, who embezzles, steals, abstracts or willfully misapplies, or willfully permits to be misapplied, any of the moneys, funds, credits, securities, property, or assets of such firm, association, or corporation, arising or accruing from, or used in, such commerce, in whole or in part, or willfully and knowingly converts the same to his own use or to the use of another, shall be deemed guilty of a felony and upon conviction shall be fined not less than $500 or confined in the penitentiary not less than one year nor more than ten years, or both, in the discretion of the court.

Prosecutions hereunder may be in the district court of the United States for the district wherein the offense may have been committed.

That nothing in this section shall be held to take away or impair the jurisdiction of the courts of the several States under the laws thereof; and a judgement of conviction or acquittal on the merits under the laws of any State shall be a bar to any prosecution hereunder for the same act or acts.[5]

Sec. 10. No common carrier engaged in commerce shall have any dealings in securities, supplies, or other articles of commerce, or shall make or have any contracts for construction or maintenance of any kind, to the amount of more than $50,000, in the aggregate, in any one year, with another corporation, firm, partnership, or association when the said common carrier shall have upon its board of directors or as its president, manager, or as its purchasing or selling officer, or agent in the particular transaction, any person who is at the same time a director, manager, or purchasing or selling officer of, or who has any substantial interest in, such other corporation, firm, partnership, or association, unless and except such purchases shall be made from, or such dealings shall be with, the bidder whose bid is the most favorable to such common carrier, to be ascertained by competitive bidding under regulations to be prescribed by rule or otherwise by the Interstate Commerce Commission. No bid shall be received unless the name and address of the bidder or the names and addresses of the officers, directors, and general managers thereof, if the bidder be a corporation, or of the members, if it be a partnership or firm, be given with the bid.

Any person who shall, directly or indirectly, do or attempt to do anything to prevent anyone from bidding, or shall do any act to prevent free and fair competition among the bidders or those desiring to bid, shall be punished as prescribed in this section in the case of an officer or director.

Every such common carrier having any such transactions or making any such purchases shall, within thirty days after making the same, file with the Inter-

[5] Repealed by Act of June 25, 1948, c 645 (62 Stat. 683), which revised, codified and enacted into "positive law" Title 18 of the Code (Crimes and Criminal Procedure). Said act reenacted said matter as to substance, as 18 U.S.C., Sec. 660 (62 Stat. 730).

state Commerce Commission a full and detailed statement of the transaction showing the manner of the competitive bidding, who were the bidders, and the names and addresses of the directors and officers of the corporations and the members of the firm or partnership bidding; and whenever the said commission shall, after investigation or hearing, have reason to believe that the law has been violated in and about the said purchases or transactions, it shall transmit all papers and documents and its own views or findings regarding the transaction to the Attorney General.

If any common carrier shall violate this section, it shall be fined not exceeding $25,000; and every such director, agent, manager, or officer thereof who shall have knowingly voted for or directed the act constituting such violation, or who shall have aided or abetted in such violation, shall be deemed guilty of a misdemeanor and shall be fined not exceeding $5,000 or confined in jail not exceeding one year, or both, in the discretion of the court.

Sec. 11. (a) That authority to enforce compliance with sections 13, 14, 18, and 19 of this title by the persons respectively subject thereto is vested in the Interstate Commerce Commission where applicable to common carriers subject to the Interstate Commerce Act, as amended; in the Federal Communications Commission where applicable to common carriers engaged in wire or radio communication or radio transmission of energy; in the Civil Aeronautics Board where applicable to air carriers and foreign air carriers subject to the Civil Aeronautics Act of 1938; in the Federal Reserve Board where applicable to banks, banking associations, and trust companies; and in the Federal Trade Commission where applicable to all other character of commerce to be exercised as follows:[6]

(b) Whenever the Commission or Board vested with jurisdiction thereof shall have reason to believe that any person is violating or has violated any of the provisions of sections 13, 14, 18 and 19 of this title, it shall issue and serve upon such person and the Attorney General a complaint stating its charges in that respect, and containing a notice of hearing upon a day and at a place therein fixed at least thirty days after the service of said complaint. The person so complained of shall have the right to appear at the place and time so fixed and show cause why an order should not be entered by the Commission or Board requiring such person to cease and desist from the violation of the law so charged in said complaint. The Attorney General shall have the right to intervene and appear in said proceeding and any person may make application, and upon good cause shown may be allowed by the Commission or Board, to intervene and appear in said proceeding by counsel or in person. The testimony in any such proceeding shall be reduced to writing and filed in the office of the Commission or Board. If upon such hearing the Commission or Board, as the case may be, shall be of the opinion that any of the provisions of said sections have been or are being violated, it shall make a report in writing, in which it shall state its findings as to the facts, and shall issue and cause to be served on such person an order requiring such person to cease and desist from such violations, and divest itself of the stock, or other share capital, or assets, held or rid itself of the directors chosen contrary to the provisions of sections 18 and

[6] This section, and also section 7, which amend the respective sections of the Clayton Act, were enacted by Act of Dec. 29, 1950. (P.L. 899; 64 Stat. 1125; 15 U.S.C. 21.)

19 of this title, if any there be, in the manner and within the time fixed by said order. Until the expiration of the time allowed for filing a petition for review, if no such petition has been duly filed within such time, or, if a petition for review has been filed within such time then until the record in the proceeding has been filed in a court of appeals of the United States, as hereinafter provided, the Commission or Board may at any time, upon such notice and in such manner as it shall deem proper, modify or set aside, in whole or in part, any report or any order made or issued by it under this section. After the expiration of the time allowed for filing a petition for review, if no such petition has been duly filed within such time, the Commission or Board may at any time, after notice and opportunity for hearing, reopen and alter, modify, or set aside, in whole or in part, any report or order made or issued by it under this section, whenever in the opinion of the Commission or Board conditions of fact or of law have so changed as to require such action or if the public interest shall so require: *Provided,* however, That the said person may, within sixty days after service upon him or it of said report or order entered after such a reopening, obtain a review thereof in the appropriate court of appeals of the United States, in the manner provided in subsection (c) of this section.[7]

(c) Any person required by such order of the commission or board to cease and desist from any such violation may obtain a review of such order in the court of appeals of the United States for any circuit within which such violation occurred or within which such person resides or carries on business, by filing in the court, within sixty days after the date of the service of such order, a written petition praying that the order of the commission or board be set aside. A copy of such petition shall be forthwith transmitted by the clerk of the court to the commission or board, and thereupon the commission or board shall file in the court the record in the proceeding, as provided in section 2112 of Title 28. Upon such filing of the petition the court shall have jurisdiction of the proceeding and of the question determined therein concurrently with the commission or board until the filing of the record, and shall have power to make and enter a decree affirming, modifying, or setting aside the order of the commission or board, and enforcing the same to the extent that such order is affirmed, and to issue such writs as are ancillary to its jurisdiction or are necessary in its judgment to prevent injury to the public or to competitors pendent lite. The findings of the commission or board as to the facts, if supported by substantial evidence, shall be conclusive. To the extent that the order of the commission or board is affirmed, the court shall issue its own order commanding obedience to the terms of such order of the commission or board. If either party shall

[7] Parts of paragraphs two, three, four and five of this section were amended by Public Law 85–791, 85th Cong., H.R. 6788, approved August 28, 1958, 72 Stat. 943.

The first and second paragraphs of this section were redesignated as subsections (a) and (b), the last sentence of subsection (b) was amended, and the third, fourth, fifth, sixth and seventh paragraphs were amended by Public Law 86–107, 86th Cong., S. 726, approved July 23, 1959, 73 Stat. 243–246.

The amendments so made do not apply to any proceeding initiated before the date of enactment of that Act under the third or fourth paragraph of section 11. Each such proceeding continues to be governed by the provisions of such section as they existed on the day preceding the date of enactment of Public Law 86–107.

apply to the court for leave to adduce additional evidence, and shall show to the satisfaction of the court that such additional evidence is material and that there were reasonable grounds for the failure to adduce such evidence in the proceeding before the commission or board, the court may order such additional evidence to be taken before the commission or board, and to be adduced upon the hearing in such manner and upon such terms and conditions as to the court may seem proper. The commission or board may modify its findings as to the facts, or make new findings, by reason of the additional evidence so taken, and shall file such modified or new findings, which, if supported by substantial evidence, shall be conclusive, and its recommendation, if any, for the modification or setting aside of its original order, with the return of such additional evidence. The judgment and decree of the court shall be final, except that the same shall be subject to review by the Supreme Court upon certiorari, as provided in section 1254 of Title 28.

(d) Upon the filing of the record with it the jurisdiction of the court of appeals to affirm, enforce, modify, or set aside orders of the commission or board shall be exclusive.

(e) Such proceedings in the court of appeals shall be given precedence over other cases pending therein, and shall be in every way expedited. No order of the commission or board or judgment of the court to enforce the same shall in anywise relieve or absolve any person from any liability under the antitrust laws.

(f) Complaints, orders, and other processes of the commission or board under this section may be served by anyone duly authorized by the commission or board, either (1) by delivering a copy thereof to the person to be served, or to a member of the partnership to be served, or to the president, secretary, or other executive officer or a director of the corporation to be served; or (2) by leaving a copy thereof at the residence or the principal office or place of business of such person; or (3) by mailing by registered or certified mail a copy thereof addressed to such person at his or its residence or principal office or place of business. The verified return by the person so serving said complaint, order, or other process setting forth the manner of said service shall be proof of the same, and the return post office receipt for said complaint, order, or other process mailed by registered or certified mail as aforesaid shall be proof of the service of the same.

(g) Any order issued under subsection (b) of this section shall become final—

(1) upon the expiration of the time allowed for filing a petition for review, if no such petition has been duly filed within such time; but the commission or board may thereafter modify or set aside its order to the extent provided in the last sentence of subsection (b) of this section; or

(2) upon the expiration of the time allowed for filing a petition for certiorari, if the order of the commission or board has been affirmed, or the petition for review has been dismissed by the court of appeals, and no petition for certiorari has been duly filed; or

(3) upon the denial of a petition for certiorari, if the order of the commission or board has been affirmed or the petition for review has been dismissed by the court of appeals; or

(4) upon the expiration of thirty days from the date of issuance of the mandate of the Supreme Court, if such Court directs that the order of the commission or board be affirmed or the petition for review be dismissed.

(h) If the Supreme Court directs that the order of the commission or board be modified or set aside, the order of the commission or board rendered in accordance with the mandate of the Supreme Court shall become final upon the expiration of thirty days from the time it was rendered, unless within such thirty days either party has instituted proceedings to have such order corrected to accord with the mandate, in which event the order of the commission or board shall become final when so corrected.

(i) If the order of the commission or board is modified or set aside by the court of appeals, and if (1) the time allowed for filing a petition for certiorari has expired and no such petition has been duly filed, or (2) the petition for certiorari has been denied, or (3) the decision of the court has been affirmed by the Supreme Court, then the order of the commission or board rendered in accordance with the mandate of the court of appeals shall become final on the expiration of thirty days from the time such order of the commission or board was rendered, unless within such thirty days either party has instituted proceedings to have such order corrected so that it will accord with the mandate, in which event the order of the commission or board shall become final when so corrected.

(j) If the Supreme Court orders a rehearing; or if the case is remanded by the court of appeals to the commission or board for a rehearing, and if (1) the time allowed for filing a petition for certiorari has expired, and no such petition has been duly filed, or (2) the petition for certiorari has been denied, or (3) the decision of the court has been affirmed by the Supreme Court, then the order of the commission or board rendered upon such rehearing shall become final in the same manner as though no prior order of the commission or board had been rendered.

(k) As used in this section the term "mandate," in case a mandate has been recalled prior to the expiration of thirty days from the date of issuance thereof, means the final mandate.

(l) Any person who violates any order issued by the commission or board under subsection (b) of this section after such order has become final, and while such order is in effect, shall forfeit and pay to the United States a civil penalty of not more than $5,000 for each violation, which shall accrue to the United States and may be recovered in a civil action brought by the United States. Each separate violation of any such order shall be a separate offense, except that in the case of a violation through continuing failure or neglect to obey a final order of the commission or board each day of continuance of such failure or neglect shall be deemed a separate offense.

Sec. 12. That any suit, action, or proceeding under the antitrust laws against a corporation may be brought not only in the judicial district whereof it is an inhabitant, but also in any district wherein it may be found or transacts business; and all process in such cases may be served in the district of which it is an inhabitant, or wherever it may be found.

Sec. 13. That in any suit, action, or proceeding brought by or on behalf of the United States subpoenas for witnesses who are required to attend a court of the United States in any judicial district in any case, civil or criminal, arising under the antitrust laws may run into any other district: *Provided,* That in civil cases no writ of subpoena shall issue for witnesses living out of the district in which the court is held at a greater distance than one hundred miles from the place of holding the same without the permission of the trial court being first had upon proper application and cause shown.

Sec. 14. That whenever a corporation shall violate any of the penal provisions of the antitrust laws, such violation shall be deemed to be also that of the individual directors, officers, or agents of such corporation who shall have authorized, ordered, or done any of the acts constituting in whole or in part such violation, and such violation shall be deemed a misdemeanor, and upon conviction therefor of any such director, officer, or agent he shall be punished by a fine or not exceeding $5,000 or by imprisonment for not exceeding one year, or by both, in the discretion of the court.

Sec. 15. That the several district courts of the United States are invested with jurisdiction to prevent and restrain violations of this Act, and it shall be the duty of the several United States attorneys, in their respective districts, under the direction of the Attorney General, to institute proceedings in equity to prevent and restrain such violations. Such proceedings may be by way of petition setting forth the case and praying that such violation shall be enjoined or otherwise prohibited. When the parties complained of shall have been duly notified of such petition, the court shall proceed, as soon as may be, to the hearing and determination of the case; and pending such petition, and before final decree, the court may at any time make such temporary restraining order or prohibition as shall be deemed just in the premises. Whenever it shall appear to the court before which any such proceeding may be pending that the ends of justice require that other parties should be brought before the court, the court may cause them to be summoned whether they reside in the district in which the court is held or not, and subpoenas to that end may be served in any district by the marshal thereof.

Sec. 16. That any person, firm, corporation, or association shall be entitled to sue for and have injunctive relief, in any court of the United States having jurisdiction over the parties, against threatened loss or damage by a violation of the antitrust laws, including sections 13, 14, 18, and 19 of this title, when and under the same conditions and principles as injunctive relief against threatened conduct that will cause loss or damage is granted by courts of equity, under the rules governing such proceedings, and upon the execution of proper bond against damages for an injunction improvidently granted and a showing that the danger of irreparable loss or damage is immediate, a preliminary injunction may issue: *Provided,* That nothing herein contained shall be construed to entitle any person, firm, corporation, or association, except the United States, to bring suit in equity for injunctive relief against any common carrier subject to the provisions of the Act to regulate commerce, approved February fourth, eighteen hundred and eighty-seven, in respect of any matter subject to the regulation, supervision, or other jurisdiction of the Interstate Commerce Commission.

Sec. 17. That no preliminary injunction shall be issued without notice to the opposite party.[8]

[8] See second paragraph of footnote 11.

No temporary restraining order shall be granted without notice to the opposite party unless it shall clearly appear from specific facts shown by affidavit or by the verified bill that immediate and irreparable injury, loss, or damage will result to the applicant before notice can be served and a hearing had thereon. Every such temporary restraining order shall be endorsed with the date and hour of issuance, shall be forthwith filed in the clerk's office and entered of record, shall define the injury and state why it is irreparable and why the order was granted without notice, and shall by its terms expire within such time after entry, not to exceed ten days, as the court or judge may fix, unless within the time so fixed the order is extended for a like period for good cause shown, and the reasons for such extensions shall be entered of record. In case a temporary restraining order shall be granted without notice in the contingency specified, the matter of the issuance of a preliminary injunction shall be set down for a hearing at the earliest possible time and shall take precedence of all matters except older matters of the same character; and when the same comes up for hearing the party obtaining the temporary restraining order shall proceed with the application for a preliminary injunction, and if he does not do so the court shall dissolve the temporary restraining order. Upon two days' notice to the party obtaining such temporary restraining order the opposite party may appear and move the dissolution or modification of the order, and in that event the court or judge shall proceed to hear and determine the motion as expeditiously as the ends of justice may require.

Section two hundred and sixty-three of an Act entitled "An Act to codify, revise, and amend the laws relating to the judiciary," approved March third, nineteen hundred and eleven, is hereby repealed.

Nothing in this section contained shall be deemed to alter, repeal, or amend section two hundred and sixty-six of an Act entitled "An Act to codify, revise, and amend the laws relating to the judiciary," approved March third, nineteen hundred and eleven.

Sec. 18. That, except as otherwise provided in section 26 of this title, no restraining order or interlocutory order of injunction shall issue, except upon the giving of security by the applicant in such sum as the court or judge may deem proper, conditioned upon the payment of such costs and damages as may be incurred or suffered by any party who may be found to have been wrongfully enjoined or restrained thereby.[9]

Sec. 19. That every order of injunction or restraining order shall set forth the reasons for the issuance of the same, shall be specific in terms, and shall describe in reasonable detail, and not by reference to the bill of complaint or other document, the act or acts sought to be restrained, and shall be binding only upon the parties to the suit, their officers, agents, servants, employees and attorneys, or those in active concert or participating with them, and who shall, by personal service or otherwise, have received actual notice of the same.

Sec. 20. That no restraining order or injunction shall be granted by any court of the United States, or a judge or the judges thereof, in any case between an employer and employees, or between employers and employees, or between employees, or between persons employed and persons seeking employment,

[9] See second paragraph of footnote 11.

involving, or growing out of, a dispute concerning terms or conditions of employment, unless necessary to prevent irreparable injury to property, or to a property right of the party making the application, for which injury there is no adequate remedy at law, and such property or property right must be described with particularity in the applicaiton which must be in writing and sworn to by the applicant or by his agent or attorney.

And no such restraining order or injunction shall prohibit any person or persons, whether singly or in concert, from terminating any relation of employment, or from ceasing to perform any work or labor, or from recommending, advising, or persuading others by peaceful means so to do; or from attending at any place where any such person or persons may lawfully be, for the purpose of peacefully obtaining or communicating information, or from peacefully persuading any person to work or to abstain from working; or from ceasing to patronize or to employ any party to such dispute, or from recommending, advising, or persuading others by peaceful and lawful means so to do; or from paying or giving to, or withholding from, any persons engaged in such dispute, any strike benefits or other moneys or things of value; or from peaceably assembling in a lawful manner, and for lawful purposes; or from doing any act or thing which might lawfully be done in the absence of such dispute by any party thereto; nor shall any of the acts specified in this paragraph be considered or held to be violations of any law of the United States.

Sec. 21. That any person who shall willfully disobey any lawful writ, process, order, rule, decree, or command of any district court of the United States or any court of the District of Columbia by doing any act or thing therein, or thereby forbidden to be done by him, if the act or thing so done by him be of such character as to constitute also a criminal offense under any statute of the United States, or under the laws of any State in which the act was committed, shall be proceeded against for his said contempt hereinafter provided.[10]

Sec. 22. That whenever it shall be made to appear to any district court or judge thereof, or to any judge therein sitting, by the return of a proper officer or lawful process, or upon the affidavit of some credible person, or by information field by any district attorney, that there is reasonable ground to believe that any person has been guilty of such contempt, the court or judge thereof, or any judge therein sitting, may issue a rule requiring the said person so charged to show cause upon a day certain why he should not be punished therefor, which rule, together with a copy of the affidavit or information, shall be served upon the person charged, with sufficient promptness to enable him to prepare for and make return to the order at the time fixed therein. If upon or by such return, in the judgment of the court, the alleged contempt be not sufficiently purged, a trial shall be directed at a time and place fixed by the court: *Provided, however,* That if the accused, being a natural person, fail or refuse to make return to the rule to show cause, an attachment may issue against his person to compel an answer, and in case of his continued failure or refusal, or if for any reason it be impracticable to dispose of the matter on the return day, he may be required to give reasonable bail for his attendance at the trial and his submission to the final judgment of the court. Where the

[10] See footnote 11.

accused is a body corporate, an attachment for the sequestration of its property may be issued upon like refusal or failure to answer.

In all cases within the purview of this Act such trial may be by the court, or, upon demand of the accused, by a jury; in which latter event the court may impanel a jury from the jurors then in attendance, or the court or the judge thereof in chambers may cause a sufficient number of jurors to be selected and summoned, as provided by law, to attend at the time and place of trial, at which time a jury shall be selected and impaneled as upon trial for misdemeanor; and such trial shall conform, as near as may be, to the practice in criminal cases prosecuted by indictment or upon information.

If the accused be found guilty, judgment shall be entered accordingly, prescribing the punishment, either by fine or imprisonment, or both, in the discretion of the court. Such fine shall be paid to the United States or to the complainant or other party injured by the act constituting the contempt, or may, where more than one is so damaged, be divided or apportioned among them as the court may direct, but in no case shall the fine to be paid to the United States exceed, in case the accused is a natural person, the sum of $1,000, nor shall such imprisonment exceed the term of six months: *Provided,* That in any case the court or a judge thereof may, for good cause shown, by affidavit or proof taken in open court or before such judge and filed with the papers in the case, dispense with the rule to show cause, and may issue an attachment for the arrest of the person charged with contempt; in which event such person, when arrested, shall be brought before such court or a judge thereof without unnecessary delay and shall be admitted to bail in a reasonable penalty for his appearance to answer to the charge or for trial for the contempt; and thereafter the proceedings shall be the same as provided herein in case the rule had issued in the first instance.[10]

Sec. 23. That the evidence taken upon the trial of any persons so accused may be preserved by bill of exceptions, and any judgment of conviction may be reviewed upon writ of error in all respects as now provided by law in criminal cases, and may be affirmed, reversed, or modified as justice may require. Upon the granting of such writ of error, execution of judgment shall be stayed, and the accused, if thereby sentenced to imprisonment, shall be admitted to bail in such reasonable sum as may be required by the court, or by any justice or any judge of any district court of the United States or any court of the District of Columbia.[11]

Sec. 24. That nothing herein contained shall be construed to relate to contempts committed in the presence of the court, or so near thereto as to

[11] Sections 21 to 25, inclusive, were repealed by Act of June 25, 1948, c. 645 (62 Stat. 683), which revised, codified and enacted into "positive law," Title 18 of the Code (Crimes and Criminal Procedure). Said act reenacted said matter, excluding Section 23, as to substance, as 18 U.S.C., Section 402 (as amended by Public Law 72, May 21, 1949, 81st Congress), 18 U.S.C., Section 3285 and 18 U.S.C., Section 3691. Section 23 was omitted as no longer required in view of the civil and criminal rules promulgated by the Supreme Court.

The Act of June 25, 1948, c. 646 (62 Stat. 896), which revised, codified and enacted into law, Title 28 of the Code (Judicial Code and Judiciary), repealed the first, second, and fourth pars. of Sec. 17, and repealed Secs. 18 and 19, in view of Rule 65, Federal Rules of Civil Procedure, which covers the substance of the matter involved.

obstruct the administration of justice, nor to contempts committed in disobedience of any lawful writ, process, order, rule, decree, or command entered in any suit or action brought or prosecuted in the name of, or on behalf of, the United States, but the same, and all the other cases of contempt not specifically embraced within section twenty-one of this Act, may be punished in conformity to the usages at law and in equity now prevailing.

Sec. 25. That no proceeding for contempt shall be instituted against any person unless begun within one year from the date of the act complained of; nor shall any such proceeding be a bar to any criminal prosecution for the same act or acts; but nothing herein contained shall affect any proceedings in contempt pending at the time of the passage of this Act.

Sec. 26. If any clause, sentence, paragraph, or part of this Act shall, for any reason, be adjudged by any court of competent jurisdiction to be invalid, such judgment shall not affect, impair, or invalidate the remainder thereof, but shall be confined in its operation to the clause, sentence, paragraph, or part thereof directly involved in the controversy in which such judgment shall have been rendered.

Approved, October 15, 1914.

INDEX

A.A.A.A. (American Association of Advertising Agencies), Code of 212–14
Acres of Diamonds, 5
Adams, Samuel Hopkins, 166
Advertising
  allowances for
    under FTC Act, 77
    under Robinson-Patman Act, 76–81
  conditions in sales of space, 49, 63, 168–169
  deceptive, 173–203
    bait advertising, 146, 181–84
    basic rules, 174–75
    early efforts against, 166
    "factory," 179
    false disparagement of competing products, 192–94, 220
    false representations of approval, 193–97
    of food, drugs, and cosmetics, 121, 168
    "free," 184–86
    FTC action against, 166–69
    FTC guides against, 254–78
    interstate commerce and, 23
    in labeling, 121–23, 167
    and licensing power, 210
    list of cases, 253
    misuse of research, 195–96
    by nondisclosure, 186–88
    preticketing, 179–80
    product or name simulation, 187–92
    "savings," 175–77, 180–81
Advertising [*cont.*]
    television advertising, 199–202, 205–208, 219–20
    under Wheeler-Lea amendments, 117–18, 121, 168
    "wholesale," 177–79
    see also Deceptive acts
  ethical, 204–26
    consumer education, 220–24
    federal enforcement, 205–208
    media cooperation, 216–20
    professionalism and self-regulation, 211–16
    state and local enforcement, 208–11
  history of, 164–69
    advertising agencies, 168–69
  role of, in free economy, 169–72
Advertising Age, 213, 215, 217, 218
A.F.A. (Advertising Federation of America), 214
Agencies, 49–50
Agricultural exemptions from antitrust laws, 125–27
Albrecht v. *Herald Co.* (1968), 237
  and illegal combination, 28
Allen-Bradley Co. v. *Local No.* 3, *International Brotherhood of Electrical Workers* (1945), 127, 249
American Home Laundry Manufacturers Association, 215
A.N.A. (Association of National Advertisers, Inc.), 213–14
Ancillarity in *U.S.* v. *Addyston Pipe & Steel Co.,* 16–17
ANPA (American Newspaper Publishers Association), 217–18

Antitrust Division (Department of Justice), 24
advance clearance of mergers by, 140–41
cooperation with FTC by, 132, 148–49
criminal enforcement by, 133–41
decrees of, 138–39, 152–53
foreign trade and, 128–29
and identical-bid information, 35–36
procedure in cases, 131–41
release program of, 140–41
small business and, 129
Appalachian Coals, Inc. v. *U.S.* (1933), 31, 238
Associated Press v. *U.S.* (1945), 239
bottleneck boycotts in, 40–41
Associations, *see* Professional associations; Trade associations
Attorney General, *see* Antitrust Division
Attorney General's National Committee to Study the Antitrust Laws (1955), 29, 64

Bait advertising, 146, 181–84
Banking institutions
historical development of, 3–4
interlocking directorships in, 108, 111–12, 113
Baseball, exemption of, 130
Better Business Bureau, 166, 214–16
Black, Hugo L.
on *per se* violations, 20–21
on patents, 190–91
Blackout rule, and horizontal market, 21
Block booking in *U.S.* v. *Loew's, Inc.*, 57
Bottleneck boycotts in *Associated Press* v. *U.S.*, 40–41
Boycotts (group), 37–41
bottleneck, 40–41
distinguished from refusals to deal, 37-38
by exempted organizations, 126
illegal combinations and, in *Eastern States Retail Lumber Dealer's Association* v. *U.S.*, 26, 39
as *per se* violations, 20–21, 37, 41
in *Silver* v. *New York Stock Exchange*, 41
and resale price maintenance, 37–39
in *U.S.* v. *Colgate & Co.*, 33–35
Boycotts [*cont.*]
as reverse exclusive dealing (*Hershey* case), 58
See also Refusals to deal
Brand names
as fair trade exception, 34–35
under Robinson-Patman Act, 64–65
simulation of, 187–92
Brandeis, Louis, 13
on jurisdiction of FTC, 167
Bribery, 118
payola, 120, 205–6
Brokerage payments, under Robinson-Patman Act, 76–77
Kintner's suggestions on, 278–80
Brown Shoe Company v. *U.S.* (1962), 246
product market definition in, 94
Burger, Warren, on cooperatives, 46
Buying practices
conglomerate mergers and, 97
See also Boycotts; Exclusive dealing; Refusal to deal; Robinson-Patman Act; Tie-in arrangements

California, antitrust statutes of, 161–62
Capitalism
legal safeguards for, 2, 227–28
rise of, in America, 1–6
See also Free competition
Capper-Volstead Act, 125
Cartwright Act, 162
Caveat emptor, 164
Cease and desist orders of FTC, 144
Cellophane case (1956), relevant market in, 102–104
Chain grocery stores, and Robinson-Patman Act, 59
Civil Aeronautics Board, 130
Civil suits, *see* Antitrust Division, procedure in cases; Private enforcement
Civil War, development of capital in, 4–5
Clark, Tom, on exclusive dealing, 52
Class actions, 150–51
Clayton Act, 21–22, 297–312
compared with Sherman Act, 21–22
enacted, 13
enforcement of, 23–25
see also Antitrust Division; FTC; Private enforcement
FTC Act and, 23–24, 115, 123

Clayton Act [*cont.*]
  Sect. 2, 22, 297–99
    amended, *see* Robinson-Patman Act
  Sect. 3, 48, 233, 299
    see also Exclusive dealing; Tie-in arrangements
  Sect. 4, 151–52, 299–300
    see also Private enforcement
  Sect. 5, 152–54, 300
    see also Private enforcement
  Sect. 6, exemptions from antitrust laws in, 125, 126–27, 300
  Sect. 7, 233, 300–301
    see also Mergers
  Sect. 8, 301–303
    see also Interlocking directorates
  Sect. 11, 143, 304–307
  Sect. 16, 156–58, 308
  Sect. 20, 127, 309–10
  text of, 297–312
Cleveland Plan, 213–14
Colgate doctrine, 34
Collier's (magazine), 166
Colonies, American, rise of capitalism in, 1–6
Combinations, *see* Contracts, combinations, and conspiracies
Commodities, as defined in Robinson-Patman Act, 64
Common carriers, and interlocking-directorates prohibition, 110
Common law
  restraint of trade in, 16–17
  Sherman and Cartwright Acts as based on, 162
  trusts in, 8
Compco Corp. v. *Day-Brite Lighting, Inc.* (1964), 253
  and product simulation, 190–92
Competition, *see* Free competition; Unfair methods of competition
Complaints
  to Antitrust Division, 131–32, 140
  to FTC, 143, 203
Conglomerate mergers
  defined, 91
  product markets in, 93
  tests of legality for, 97
Conscious parallelism, 27–28
Consent decrees
  in court cases, 138–39, 153
  of FTC, 147
Consignment, and Sect. 3 of Clayton Act, 49
Conspiracies, *see* Contracts, combinations, and conspiracies
Consumer Affairs, Office of, 223
Consumers, protection for, 220–24
  See also Advertising, deceptive; Deceptive acts
Contract, freedom of, 2
Contracts, combinations, and conspiracies, 26–29
  list of cases on, 237–38
  for monopolization, 108–109
Cooperative Marketing Act of 1926, 125–26
Cooperatives, and antitrust laws, 125–26
Corporations
  rise of, 5–6, 8–9
  subsidiary, 29
    in foreign trade, 43
    interlocking directorates and, 112
    in price discrimination, 63–64
  and suits by stockholders, 151, 152
  See also Interlocking directorates; Mergers
Cost justification defense, and Robinson-Patman Act, 72–74
Court procedure
  defects of, in antitrust administration, 230–32
  See also Antitrust Division, procedure in cases; Criminal enforcement; FTC appeals of rulings of; Private enforcement
Criminal enforcement
  of Flammable Fabrics Act, 122
  of food and drug provisions of FTC Act, 121
  and guilty pleas, 153
  jail sentences in, 31
  of labeling acts, 121
  and price fixing, 31
  procedure of Antitrust Division, 133–38
  release program and, 140–41
  of Robinson-Patman Act, 61–62, 81
  of Sherman Act, 19–21, 24, 100
"Customer," defined, 64, 71, 264–65
Customer restrictions, 43–44
  in *White Motor Co.* v. *U.S.*, 44–46

Damages, private, *see* Private enforcement

Deceptive acts, 115–23
false guarantees, 197–99
in Flammable Fabrice Act, 122
FTC guides against, 259–62
false packaging, 120
in filling orders, 120
lotteries as, 119–20
under Wheeler-Lea amendments (1938), 25, 117–18
See also Advertising, deceptive; Unfair methods of competition
Decrees, 138–39
consent, 138–39
of FTC, 147
Derivative suits, 151
Directorates, interlocking, *see* Interlocking directorates
Discovery rules of Federal Rules of Civil Procedure, 135, 136–37
Distribution pricing policy, and Robinson-Patman Act, 72–74
Division of markets
between parents and subsidiaries, 29
as *per se* violations, 20–21
Documents, production of
in civil cases, 134–36
in criminal cases, 133–35
Dr. Miles Medical Co. v. *John D. Park & Sons* (1911), 238
resale price maintenance in, 33
Dr. Scott's Electric Corset, 165
Drug advertising, 121, 168
patent medicines, 165
Durant, Will, 164

Eastern States Retail Lumber Dealer's Association v. *U.S.* (1914), 236, 237, 239
concerted refusal to deal in, 39
illegal combinations in, 26
Employment contracts, 118
Endorsements, false, 194–97
Enforcement of antitrust laws, 24–25
basic concepts of, 228–30
defects of court procedure, 230–31
"hard" and "soft" compared, 229
See also Antitrust Division; FTC; Private enforcement
Enticing employees, 118
Espionage, 118
"Established aberration," 130
European Economic Community, conscious parallelism in, 27
Exclusive dealing, 47–59
list of cases on, 240–41
reciprocal dealing as, 55
under Sect. 1 of Sherman Act, 49, 58
under Sect. 3 of Clayton Act, 48–55, 58
effect of, 50
exclusions from, 49–50
interlocking directorates and, 111
justified cases of, 53–55
in *Tampa Electric Co.* v. *Nashville Coal Co.*, 51–52
Exclusive franchises, *see* Exclusive dealing; Franchises
Exemptions from antitrust laws, 124–30
agricultural organizations, 125–26
baseball, 130
export associations, 128–29
foreign trade, 128–29
labor organizations, 126–27
list of cases on, 249–50
regulatory agencies and, 124–25, 130
small business concerns, 129
Export associations, as exempted organizations, 128–29

"Factory" in advertisements, 179
Fair trade
boycott to enforce, 40
fair trade exception, 34–35
Fashion Originator's Guild v. *FTC* (1941), 239
and boycotts, 39–40
Federal Aviation Agency, 130
Federal Communications Commission, 130, 149
Federal contracts
exempt from Robinson-Patman Act, 75
as "national accounts," 44
Federal Power Commission, 130
Federal Reserve System, interlocking directorates and, 113
Federal Steel Company, 9
Federal Trade Commission, *see* FTC
Field-of-use limitation, in patent licenses, 86
Fisheries Cooperative Marketing Act, 130
Flammable Fabrics Act, 122

Flood case, and exemption of baseball, 130
Flow of commerce
  intrastate commerce and, 160
  in *Swift & Co.* v. *U.S.*, 18–19
Food advertising, 121, 168
Ford Motor Co. v. *FTC* (1941), 22–23, 237
  and failing-company defense, 99
Foreign trade, *see* International markets
Fortas, Abraham, on group boycotts, 38
Fortner Enterprises v. *U.S. Steel Corp.* (1969), 240
  and product markets, 56
Franchises
  exclusive, defined, 43
  full-line forcing and, 58
  in *U.S.* v. *General Motors Corp.*, 38
  See also Exclusive dealing
Frankfurter, Felix, on Robinson-Patman Act, 61
"Free," in advertising, 184–86
Free competition
  advertising and, 169–72
  defined, in *Maple Flooring Manufacturer's Association* v. *U.S.*, 32
  government's role in, 227–35
  lessening of, in Sherman and Clayton acts, 22, 50
  rise of, in America, 1–6
  in vertical agreements, 43–44
  See also Unfair methods of competition
FTC, 24, 142–49
  advisory opinions of, 146–47
  appeals of rulings of, 24–25, 144
  board interpretation of power of, 166–67
  complaints to, 143, 202–203
  composition of, 142–43
  Conference on Public Deception, 223
  cooperative with Antitrust Division, 132, 148–49
  Flammable Fabrics Act enforced by, 122
  foreign trade and, 128–29
  guides of, 146, 200–207, 254–78
  and identical-bird information, 38
  investigative powers of, 143
  labeling acts enforced by, 121
  power over interstate commerce of, 22–23, 160–61
  procedure of, 24–25, 143–45, 235
FTC [*cont.*]
  small business and, 129
  state cooperation with, 162–63
  See also Enforcement of antitrust laws; FTC Act; *specific topics*
FTC Act
  enacted, 13, 166–67
  Sect. 5, 22–23
    cease and desist orders under, 143
    list of cases on, 249
    Robinson-Patman Act and, 116
    Sherman and Clayton Acts and, 23, 24, 116, 123
    see also Advertising, deceptive; Deceptive acts; Unfair methods of competition
  text of, 283–96
  Wheeler-Lea amendments to (1938), 24, 117–18, 168
    in food, drug, and cosmetic advertising, 121
FTC v. *Cement Institute* (1948), 237
  conscious adherence in, 27
FTC v. *Fred Meyer, Inc.* (1968), 242
  and indirect purchasers, 64, 71
FTC v. *Henry Broch & Co.* (1960), 242
  unlawful brokerage payments in, 76–77
FTC v. *Mary Carter Paint Co.* (1965), 253
  and advertising, 180–81
FTC v. *R. F. Keppel & Bro., Inc.* (1934), 249
  lottery scheme in, 119–20
FTC v. *Raladam Co.* (1931), 167–68 249
FTC v. *Sperry and Hutchinson Co.* (1972), 249
  and restraint of trade, 116–117
Full-line forcing, 58
Fur Products Labeling Act, 121, 122

Gasoline Cracking case (1931), on patent interchange agreements, 87
Gentlemen's agreements, 28
Geographical markets
  in exclusive dealing, 50–52, 54
    in *Tampa Electric Co.* v. *Nashville Coal Co.*, 51–52, 54
  horizontal restrictions on, 42–44

Geographical markets [*cont.*]
in *U.S.* v. *Addyston Pipe & Steel Co.*, 42
in *U.S.* v. *Sealy, Inc.*, 44
in *U.S.* v. *Topco Associates*, 46
in mergers, 92, 94–95
in monopolization, 101–102
patent licenses for, 86
under Robinson-Patman Act, 77–78
vertical restrictions on, 43
in *U.S.* v. *Arnold Schwinn & Co.*, 45–46
in *White Motor Co.* v. *U.S.*, 43–45
Geritol case, and misleading advertising, 187–88
Gibbons v. *Ogden*, 3
Government regulation of business, 227–35
basic concepts of antitrust enforcement, 228
historical development of, 8–14
Granger movement, 9
Interstate Commerce Act, 10
Grand juries, proceedings before, 133–34
Grange movement, 9
Grant-back arrangements, 83
and the *Transparent Wrap* decision, 83
Group boycotts, *see* Boycotts
Guarantees, false, 197–99
in Flammable Fabrics Act, 122
FTC guides against, 259–62
Guides of FTC, 146, 207, 254–80

Hand, Learned, on Alcoa's intent to monopolize, 107
"Hard enforcement," 229
Harrison, Benjamin, 10
Hershey Chocolate Corp. v. *FTC* (1941), 240
reverse exclusive dealing in, 58
Holbrook, Stewart, *The Golden Age of Quackery*, 165
Holding companies, development of, 8–9
Holmes, Oliver Wendell
on concurrent jurisdiction of states, 161
on Sherman Act, 20
Horizontal agreements, 42–44
in *U.S.* v. *Addyston Pipe & Steel Co.*, 42
Horizontal mergers
Horizontal mergers [*cont.*]
defined, 90
product markets in, 93
tests of legality for, 95, 96

Identical bids, 35–36
In pari delicto, 155
Indirect purchasers, under Robinson-Patman Act, 63–64
and *FTC* v. *Fred Meyer, Inc.*, 64
and *Perkins* v. *Standard Oil Co.*, 70–71
Individuals, and Sherman Act, 26, 28
Industrial Revolution, 2
Injunctive relief, in private enforcement, 156–58
Insurance companies, partial exemption of, 130
Interference settlement agreements, 83
Interlocking directorates
list of cases on, 248
private enforcement and, 149
under Sect. 8 of Clayton Act, 110–13
under Sherman Act, 110, 113–14
International Boxing Club v. *U.S.* (1959), 247
relevant market in, 103–104
International Business Machines Corp. v. *U.S.* (1936), 240
tie-in sales in, 57
International markets
combinations and, 29
exclusive dealing and tie-in sales in, 63
as exempted areas, 128–29
horizontal geographical agreements and, 43
price discrimination in, 63
Interstate Circuit v. *U.S.* (1939), 237
conscious adherence in, 26–27
Interstate commerce
activity affecting, 18–19
development of concept of, 17–19
flow-of-commerce concept and, 18–19, 160
FTC and, 22–23, 160–61
interlocking directorships and, 110–12
mergers and, 91–92
in Robinson-Patman Act, 62–63
state regulation and, 9, 161–62
tie-in sales and, 48–49
unfair methods of competition and, 22–23

Interstate Commerce Act, 10
Interstate Commerce Commission, 10, 130
Intrastate commerce
FTC and, 22, 23, 160–61
state antitrust laws and, 159–63
concurrent federal-state jurisdiction, 161–162
tie-in sales and, 48–49

Johnson, Lyndon B., 223
Joint marketing, in *Appalachian Coals, Inc.* v. *U.S.*, 31
Justice, Department of, *see* Antitrust Division

Kennedy, John F., 35–36, 223
Kiefer-Stewart Co. v. *Joseph E. Seagram & Sons* (1951), 238
on maximum resale prices, 36
Kintner, Earl W., *A Primer on the Law of Deceptive Practices*, 123

Labeling acts
FTC enforcement of, 121–22, 168
Pure Food and Drug Act of 1906, 166
Labor organizations (unions)
"antitrust" outlook of, 10
exempted from antitrust laws, 126–27
Land, sales in, 49
Lawsuits, groundless, 118–19
Lennen & Newell, 215
Lewis v. *Pennington*, 127–28
Libby-Owens-Ford Glass Co. v. *FTC* (1965), 253
and mock-up advertising, 201
"Lifting" products, 119
Local-government contracts
exempt from Robinson-Patman Act, 75
as "national accounts," 44
Lorain Journal Co. v. *U.S.* (1951), 248
on monopoly power, 106
Lottery schemes, 119–20

McCann Erickson, 215
McGuire Act, fair trade exception to, 34
Maple Flooring Manufacturer's Association v. *U.S.* (1925), 238
trade association activities in, 32

Market-extension mergers
defined, 90
tests of legality for, 97–98
Market research, misuse of, 195–96
Markets
agreements to divide
between parents and subsidiaries, 29
as *per se* violations, 20–21
geographical, *see* Geographical markets
international, *see* International markets
joint, in *Appalachian Coals, Inc.* v. *U.S.*, 31
in merger cases, *see* Mergers
product, *see* Product markets
Markets, relevant, *see* Relevant markets in monopolization
Maryland & Virginia Milk Producers Association v. *U.S.* (1960), 250
on monopolizing by agricultural association, 126
Maximum prices in *Kiefer-Stewart Co.* v. *Joseph E. Seagram & Sons*, 36
Meaningful compliance, 228–30
Medical profession, in *U.S.* v. *American Medical Association*, 33
Medicines, patent, 165
Membership device, in *Associated Press* v. *U.S.*, 40–41
Mercantilism, 1
Merchandise, *see* Product markets; Products
Merchandising allowances and services
under FTC Act, 77
FTC guides on, 146, 262–78
under Robinson-Patman Act, 62, 77–81
Mercoid Corp. v. *Mid-Continent Investment Co.* (1944), 245
on patent misuse, 88
Mergers, 90–100
and Antitrust Division, 136, 140–41
conglomerate
defined, 91
product markets in, 93
test of legality for, 97
horizontal
defined, 90
product markets in, 93
tests of legality for, 95, 96
list of cases on, 246–47

Mergers [*cont.*]
market-extension
defined, 90
test of legality for, 97–98
product-extension, 91, 98
remedies against, 99–100
in *Ford Motor Co.* v. *U.S.*, 99
under Sect. 5 of FTC Act, 99
under Sect. 7 of Clayton Act, 22, 91–100
defenses to, 98–99
determination of product and geographic markets, 92–95
and private enforcement, 150–58
under Sherman Act, 99–100
vertical
"backward" and "forward," 91, 96–97
defined, 91
product markets in, 93
tests of legality for, 96–97, 107–108
Mill, John Stuart, 216
Miller-Tydings Act, fair trade exception to, 34–35
Modification of decrees, 139
Monopolization
defined, 101, 109
See also Sherman Act, Sect. 2
Monopoly
defined, 101–102
history of
formation of trusts and holding companies, 8–9
passage of laws, 9–13
railroad pools, 7
tax legislation of 1862, 6
patents as, 82–83
See also Clayton Act; Sherman Act; *specific topics*
Munn v. *Illinois,* 9

Name simulation, 188–90
"National accounts" in *White Motor Co.* v. *U.S.*, 43–45
National Association of Broadcasters (NAB), Code of, 219
National emergencies, antitrust laws in times of, 129–30
National Food Brokers Association, Kintner's suggestions to, 278–80
National Football League, and blackout rule, 21
National Recovery Administration Act, 60
New York City, FTC and jewelry industry in, 207
New York State
antitrust enforcement in, 163
ethical advertising enforcement in, 209
New York Stock Exchange case (1963), 41, 239
New Yorker, The (magazine), 218
Newspapers
self-regulation by, 217–18
See also Advertising
Nixon, Richard, 223
Nonconsent judgments, as evidence of antitrust violations, 25, 138–39, 152–53
Nondisclosure, in deceptive advertising, 186–88
Nonsigner provisions in state fair-trade laws, 34–35
Norris–La Guardia Act, labor exemptions under, 127
North, Simeon, 3
Northern Pacific Railway Co. v. *U.S.* (1958), 237
on *per se* violations, 20–21
Northern Securities Co. v. *U.S.* (1904), 12, 248
on intent to monopolize, 106–107
Nostrums and Quackery, 166

Orders, filling of, deceptive practices in, 120

Packaging, deceptive, 190
"Passing off goods," 119
Patent medicines, 165–66
Patents, 82–89
as exemptions to *laissez faire,* 3
in foreign trade, 43
interchange of rights to (patent pools), 87–89
licenses, 83–85
assignments and nonexclusive licenses, 84
grant-back arrangements, 83
limitations in, 86
price fixing and, 85, 88
procedures for issuing, 82–83
tie-in arrangements and, 85–86

Patents [*cont.*]
list of cases on, 245
misuse of, 88–89
nonuse of, 84
Patents
and product simulation, 190–92
Payola, 118, 120, 205–6
Per se violations of antitrust laws, 20–21
geographical divisions and, 42–46
group boycotts as, 21, 37–41
price fixing as, 20, 21, 30–34
and "special industry facts," 21, 41, 45
subsidiary corporations and, 29
tie-in sales as, 21, 56–59
Perkins v. *Standard Oil Co. of California* (1969), 243
and price favoritism, 70–71
Pool system of railroads, 7–8, 10
Populist Party, 11
Preticketing, 179–80
Price discrimination
in *Perkins* v. *Standard Oil,* 70–71
See also Robinson-Patman Act
Price fixing, 28, 30–36
complaints on, 131–32
and criminal convictions, 30
by export associations, 129–30
flow-of-commerce concept and, 18–19
identical bids in, 35–36
by labor unions, 127–28
list of cases on, 238–39
in patent licensing, 85, 88
as *per se* violation, 20, 21
resale price maintenance, 33–35
in *U.S.* v. *Addyston Pipe & Co.*, 30
in *U.S.* v. *Trenton Potteries Corp.*, 30–31
price stabilization as, 31
rule of reason in, 16–17
in state law, 162, 163
statistical reporting of prices, 28, 31–33
Pricing, deceptive
FTC guides against, 254–59
preticketing, 179–80
in "savings" advertisements, 175–77
Printer's Ink, 166, 208–10, 216
Private enforcement, 25, 150–58
class actions, 150–51
and consent decrees, 138–39, 153
and guilty pleas, 153
defense in, 154–56
Private enforcement [*cont.*]
in federal court only, 150
injunctive relief in, 156–58
list of cases on, 251–52
and nonconsent judgments as evidence of violations, 25, 138–39, 152–53
proof of damages in, 156
statute of limitations on, 25, 151, 153–54
and treble damages, 25, 39, 150
Product markets
in exclusive dealing, 51, 54
in *Tampa Electric Co.* v. *Nashville Coal Co.*, 51–52
in mergers, 92–94
defined, in *Brown Shoe Co.* v. *U.S.*, 94
in monopolization, 102–104
in tie-in sales, 56
Product-extension mergers, 91, 98
Products
deceptive practices in filling orders, 120
false disparagement of, 192–94, 220
"passing off" and "lifting" of, 119
simulation of, 187–92
Professional associations, price fixing by, 33
in *U.S.* v. *Utah Pharmaceutical Association,* 33
Profit pass-over, 44
Promotional allowances
under FTC Act, 77
FTC guides on, 146, 262–78
under Robinson-Patman Act, 77–81
Pure Food and Drug Act of 1906, 12, 166
Purex Corporation, 214–15
"Push money," 118

Quarterly Financial Report for Manufacturing Corporations, 143

Radio, *see* Television and radio
Railroads, 3
government regulation of, 9–10
pool system of, 7–8
Reason, *see* Rule of reason
Reciprocal dealing, 55
Refusal to deal, 37–41
in California law, 162
concerted, *see* Boycotts
distinguished from group boycott, 37–38

Refusal to deal [*cont.*]
- and individuals, 37, 39
- list of cases on, 239
- and resale price maintenance, *see* Resale price maintenance
- Robinson-Patman Act, and, 63

Regulatory agencies and exemptions from antitrust laws, 124–25, 130

Relevant markets in monopolization, 102–104
- and *U.S.* v. *Grinnell Corp.*, 105
- and *U.S.* v. *U.S. Steel Corp.*, 105

Requirements contracts, 58
- justification of, 54–55
- in *Tampa Electric Co.* v. *Nashville Coal Co.*, 51–52

Resale market, limitations on, 42–46
- in *U.S.* v. *Addyston Pipe & Steel Co.*, 42–43
- in *White Motor Co.* v. *U.S.*, 44–45

Resale price maintenance, 33–35
- in California law, 162
- in *Dr. Miles Medical Co.* v. *John D. Park & Sons*, 33
- fair trade exception, 34–35
- maximum prices, 36
- refusals to deal and, 37–39
  - *U.S.* v. *Colgate & Co.*, 33–34

Research and development, by small business concerns, 129

Restraint of trade
- by exempted associations, 125
- interpretation of, 15–17
- monopolization and, 104, 106
- in state laws, 162–63
- *See also* Rule of reason; Sherman Act, Sect. 1

Retailers, *see* Resale market; Resale price maintenance; Wholesalers

Robinson-Patman Act, 60–81
- enacted, 13
- FTC Act and, 116
- FTC enforcement of, 24
- historical background of, 60, 233
- list of cases under, 241–44
- need for, 233–35
- price discrimination defined, 65
- primary objects of, 61
- Sect. 2(a), 61, 62–75
  - defenses to, 72–75
  - foreign commerce, 63
  - indirect purchaser, 63–64
  - and subsidiary corporations, 63

Robinson-Patman Act [*cont.*]
- Sect. 2(b) (competitive pricing), 61
- Sect. 2(c) (unlawful brokerage payments), 61, 76–77
  - Kintner's suggestions on compliance with, 278–80
- Sect. 2(d) and (e) (merchandising allowances and services), 61, 77–81
  - FTC guides on, 146, 262–78
- Sect. 2(f) (prohibitions against buyer), 62, 75–76
- Sect. 3, 62, 81
- Sect. 4, 126
- text of, 283–99
- voluntary compliance procedures and, 145

Roosevelt, Theodore, 11–12

Rule of construction in decrees, 139

Rule of reason
- and Clayton Act, 12–13
- in exclusive-dealing cases, 52–53
- in patent-pool case, 88
- and *per se* violations 20–21
- and reciprocal dealing, 55
- in *Standard Oil Co.* v. *U.S.*, 17–18
- in *U.S.* v. *Addyston Pipe & Steel Co.*, 16

"Savings" advertisements, 175–77

Sears, Roebuck & Co. v. *Stiffel Co.* (1964), 253
- and product simulation, 190–92

Securities and Exchange Commission, 143

Services
- under Robinson-Patman Act, 77–81
- sales of, 49

Sherman, John, 11, 161

Sherman Act, 15–21
- attempts and conspiracies under, 108–109
- common law and, 162
- compared to Clayton Act, 21–22
- criminal provisions of, 19–20
  - constitutionality attacked, 20
  - enforcement of, 24–25
  - in mergers, 99–100
  - *see also* Antitrust Division; Criminal enforcement; Private enforcement
- FTC Act and, 22–24, 115–16, 121
- history of, 11–13
- interlocking directorates under, 110, 113–14
- *per se* violations of, 20–21

private enforcement and, 151
and restraint of trade, 104, 105
Sect. 1., 15, 27–29
tie-in sales and, 47–49
see also Contracts, combinations, and conspiracies; Price fixing; Restraint of trade; Tie-in arrangements
Sect. 2, 15–16, 28, 101–109
Antitrust Division's investigations, 136
criminal penalties under, 100, 101
and exempted organizations, 125–26
intent to monopolize, 106–108
list of cases under, 247–48
and percentage of market, 101–102
and relevant market, determination of, 102–104
in *Standard Oil Co.* v. *U.S.*, 17–18
Supreme Court on, 17–18
text of, 281–83
Silver v. *New York Stock Exchange* (1963), 239
on group boycotts, 41
Simon, Morton J.
The Advertising Truth Book, 214
The Law for Advertising and Marketing, 168
Slater, Samuel, 3
Small business concerns, as exempt from antitrust laws, 129
Smith, Adam, 1
"Soft enforcement" of antitrust laws, 229
"Special industry facts," 21, 41, 45
Standard Oil Co. v. *Tennessee* (1910), on state antitrust enforcement, 161
Standard Oil Co. v. *U.S.* (1911), 166, 237
rule of reason in, 17–18
Standard Oil of New Jersey, 9, 12, 17–18
Standard Oil of Ohio, 8
State contracts
as exempt from Robinson-Patman Act, 75
as "national accounts," 44
State laws
antitrust enforcement, 159–63
list of cases, 252
early policy, 8–11
fair trade exception, 34–35
false advertising statutes, 166, 208–11
interstate commerce and, 9, 160
and product simulation, 190–92
Statute of limitations on private antitrust actions, 153–54
suspended for class actions, 151
suspended for government action, 25, 154
and tolling by fraudulent concealment, 154
Stockholders, suits by, 151
Style piracy, 39–40
Subpoenas
by FTC, 143
by grand juries, 133–34
Subsidiary corporations, *see* Corporations, subsidiary
Swift & Co. v. *U.S.* (1905), 237
flow of commerce in, 18
Sylvania Electric Products, Inc. case (1955), 244
cost justification defense in, 73

Taft, William Howard
and antitrust proceedings, 12
in *U.S.* v. *Addyston Pipe & Steel Co.*, 16–17, 30
Tampa Electric Co. v. *Nashville Coal Co.* (1961), 241
exclusive dealing in, 51–52
Tariffs, 3, 5
Tax policies, and monopoly, 6
Television and radio
and conditions in sales of time, 49, 64
false advertising on, 199–202
federal enforcement, 205–208
licensing old movies for, 92
self-regulation by, 219–20
Textile Fiber Products Identification Act, 121–22
Therapeutic advertising, 121, 168
Tie-in arrangements (tie-in sales), 47–59
defined, 47, 55
full-line forcing, 58
interlocking directorates and, 111
list of cases on, 240–41
patent licenses and, 85–86
as *per se* violations, 21, 57
rule of reason and, 53
Timken Roller Bearing Co. v. *U.S.* (1951), 245
on trademarks, 89
Tolling by fraudulent concealment, 154
Trade associations
agricultural, 125–26

Trade associations [*cont.*]
collection of prices by, 31–33
in *Maple Flooring Manufacturer's Association* v. *U.S.*, 32
export, as exempted associations, 128–29
Trade secrets, stealing of, 118
Trademarks
and fair trade exemption, 34
international division of markets and, 42–43
under Robinson-Patman Act, 64–65
simulation of, 188–92
as vehicles for antitrust violations, 89
Transparent-Wrap case, and grant-backs, 83
Treble damages, 25, 39, 150
Turner, Ernest, *The Shocking History of Advertising*, 165

Unfair methods of competition (under sect. 5, FTC), 48, 115–120
bribery and payola, 118, 120, 205–206
defined, 23, 115
discriminatory grants of allowances and services, 75, 77–81
enticing employees, 118
espionage, 118
exclusive dealing as, 49, 58–59
lawsuits, groundless, 118–19
list of cases on, 249
mergers as, 99
"passing off" and "lifting" goods, 119
See also Advertising, deceptive; FTC Act, Sect. 5
Unions, *see* Labor organizations
U.S. v. *Addyston Pipe & Steel Co.* (1898, 1899), 237, 240
geographical restrictions in, 42–43
price fixing in, 30
rule of reason in, 16
U.S. v. *Aluminum Co. of America* (1945), 248
intent to monopolize in, 107
relevant market in, 102, 103
U.S. v. *American Medical Association*, 33
U.S. v. *Arnold Schwinn & Co.* (1967), 240
and vertical arrangements, 45–46
U.S. v. *Besser Manufacturing Co.* (1951, 1952), 245
on patent rights and monopoly, 84
U.S. v. *Borden Company* (1939), 250
on conspiracy by agricultural cooperatives, 126
U.S. v. *Colgate & Co.* (1919), 239
refusal to deal in, 33–34
U.S. v. *Container Corp. of America* (1969), 238
and price exchange, 28
U.S. v. *General Electric Co.* (1926), 245
on terms to patent licenses, 85
U.S. v. *General Motors Corp.* (1966), 239
and group boycott, 38
U.S. v. *Grinnell Corp.* (1966), 248
and relevant market, 105
U.S. v. *Krasnov* (1956, 1957), 245
on patent misuse, 88
U.S. v. *Line Material Co.* (1948), 245
on cross-licensing, 85, 87–88
U.S. v. *Loew's, Inc.* (1962), 241
tie-in sales in, 57
U.S. v. *McKesson & Robins, Inc.* (1956), 35, 239
U.S. v. *National Dairy Products Corp.* (1963), 81, 244
U.S. v. *Paramount Pictures, Inc.* (1948), 248
relevant market in, 102–3
U.S. v. *Sealy, Inc.* (1967), 240
and horizontal arrangements, 44
U.S. v. *Sears, Roebuck & Co.* (1940), 248
on interlocking directorates, 112
U.S. v. *Socony-Vacuum Oil Co.* (1940), 239
price fixing in, 31
U.S. v. *Topco Associates* (1972), 240
and horizontal restrictions, 46
U.S. v. *Trenton Potteries Co.* (1927), 239
price fixing in, 30–31
U.S. v. *United Shoe Machinery Co.* (1918), 248
monopoly in, 105
U.S. v. *U.S. Steel Corp.* (1920), 248
and relevant market, 105
U.S. v. *Utah Pharmaceutical Association* (1962), 239
prescription fee schedules in, 33

Vertical agreements, 43–46
in *White Motor Co.* v. *U.S.*, 44–45

Vertical mergers
"backward" and "forward," 91, 96–97
defined, 91
product markets in, 93
tests of legality for, 96–97, 107–108
Volenti non fit injuria, 155

Wage agreements, 127–28
War, antitrust laws in time of, 129–30
Webb-Pomerene Act, 128–29
Weil, Gilbert H., *Legal Rules of the Road to Honest Advertising*, 214
Wheeler-Lea amendments to FTC Act (1938), 24, 117–18, 168
in food, drug, and cosmetic advertising, 121
White Motor Co. v. *U.S.* (1963), 240
vertical restrictions in, 44–45
Whitney, Eli, 3
"Wholesale" in advertisements, 176–79
Wholesalers
black lists of, in *Eastern States Retail Lumber Dealer's Association* v. *U.S.*, 26, 39
and fair trade exception, 35
retail price maintenance and, 33, 37–38
See also Resale markets; Robinson-Patman Act
Wilson, Woodrow, 13, 166
Wisconsin, antitrust enforcement in, 162–63
Wool Products Labeling Act of 1941, 121–22

Young, James Webb, 220